AND THE REVS KEEP RISING

DEDICATION

With love and thanks to my wife Wendy and daughter Georgia, whose idea this book was. To my mother Wanda who encouraged me, always, and in memory of Reg who filled our house with books and newspapers and loved good writing.

© Mel Nichols 2013

All rights reserved. No part of this publication may be reproduced, stored in a retrieval system or transmitted, in any form or by any means, electronic, mechanical, photocopying, recording or otherwise, without prior permission in writing from the publisher.

First published in March 2013

A catalogue record for this book is available from the British Library

ISBN 978 0 85733 270 7

Library of Congress control card no 2012948699

Published by Haynes Publishing,
Sparkford, Yeovil, Somerset BA22 7JJ, UK
Tel: 01963 442030 Fax: 01963 440001
Int. tel: +44 1963 442030 Int. fax: +44 1963 440001
E-mail: sales@haynes.co.uk
Website: www.haynes.co.uk

Haynes North America Inc.,
861 Lawrence Drive, Newbury Park,
California 91320, USA

Printed and bound in the USA by Odcombe Press LP,
1299 Bridgestone Parkway, La Vergne, TN 37086

While every effort is taken to ensure the accuracy of the information given in this book, no liability can be accepted by the author or publishers for any loss, damage or injury caused by errors in, or omissions from, the information given.

AND THE REVS KEEP RISING
GREAT DRIVES IN FAST CARS

MEL NICHOLS

HAYNES PUBLISHING

CONTENTS

Acknowledgements	8
Foreword by Steve Cropley	9
Introduction	11

'Remember disbelief 120mph average. I apologise.'   23
Holden Monaro GTS 350 (1970)

HO down The Hume   25
Ford Falcon GT-HO Phase III (1971)

Fast Yank accepts a Sicilian challenge   32
Corvette Stingray (1973)

Monaco to Modena. Fast   36
Lamborghini Countach LP400 #1120001 (1973)

'Mr Ferrari is waiting to see you'   47
A day at Maranello (1973)

Turning on to the Turbo   64
Porsche 911 Turbo (1974)

Taking a Batmobile home to Munich   71
BMW 3.0 CSL (1975)

Big wind, blowing hard   78
Maserati Bora (1975)

A Welsh odyssey   88
Lamborghini Urraco 3000 (1975)

'Signor, you go more slow, eh?'   95
Ferrari 308 GTB (1976)

Singing in the rain   102
Maserati Merak SS (1976)

900 miles in 11 hours: a grand tourer at work 107
Lamborghini Espada (1976)

In the clearing stands a Boxer 109
Ferrari BB 512 (1977)

Convoy! Flat out across Europe 116
Lamborghini Countach, Urraco & Silhouette (1977)

A Porsche to make the Turbo tremble 128
Porsche 911 Kremer (1977)

Road America and the Silver Trashcan 145
Mercedes-Benz 450SEL 6.9 (1977)

From Blackpool with bite 168
TVR Taimar Turbo (1977)

Day of the D-type 176
Jaguar XKD 516 (1977)

…and the revs keep rising 187
Lamborghini Countach S (1978)

Sad sweet song of the last Silhouette 195
Lamborghini Silhouette (1978)

Six days on the road with Enzo's greatest hit 207
Ferrari 250 GTO (1979)

Life in supercar city 220
Among the Modenese (1979)

A rather gentlemanly (fast) carriage 230
Aston Martin Volante (1979)

The car that time can't tame 235
Ferrari 365 GTB/4 Daytona (1980)

Sideways with security in Porsche's masterful driving tool 244
Porsche 928S (1980)

Motoring, not driving 251
Rolls-Royce Corniche Convertible (1980)

Standing tall in Stuttgart 256
Porsche 924 Carrera GT (1980)

Manners maketh the Maserati 263
Maserati Khamsin (1981)

Strike Force Vector: dream or nightmare? 268
Vector W2 (1981)

Rest and be thankful 279
Lotus Turbo Esprit (1981)

Rome for dinner? No problem 295
Maserati Quattroporte (1981)

Chasing the Monte in the Alpes-Maritimes 301
Audi quattro (1982)

Quest for perfection 309
Ferrari 400i (1983)

Take it to the limit? 317
Audi Sport quattro (1985)

Summer's coming. Time to go driving 326
Alfa Romeo 2000 GT Veloce (1986)

Riding shotgun with Hannu Mikkola 330
Audi Sport quattro S1 (1986)

Learning to love the 911 336
Porsche 911 Carrera (1986)

A gathering of horses 340
Ferrari BB 512 & 365 GTC/4 (1986)

Bold, regal, elegant, graceful – and rapid 343
Bentley 'R' Type Continental (1987)

As different as they come 346
Citroën SM (1987)

German groom, Italian bride, talented offspring 349
BMW M1 (1987)

197mph in the original hypercar 357
Porsche 959 (1987)

Young man's fancy 364
1960 MGA 1600 (1987)

West, with a fine saloon 367
Jaguar XJ6 (1988)

'Nothing but sheer performance' 370
Ferrari F40 (1988)

Stuff of legends 377
Jaguar C-type (1993)

1000 miles in Italy in a Mille Miglia sweetie 382
Fiat 1100 S MM (1993)

'Okay mate, that's probably enough.' 387
McLaren F1 (1994)

Dancing with The Temptress 396
Ferrari 275 GTB/4 (1997)

Conversations with a boxer 403
Porsche Boxster S (2001)

Sources 407

Photo credits 409

Index 411

ACKNOWLEDGEMENTS

Warren Brewer, a caring and insightful teacher, started all this when he told me in 1963 to be a journalist. Jack Cherry, editor of the *The Advocate* in Tasmania, had faith too and gave me a job. Cyril Pollard, the kindest and most encouraging of chief sub-editors, got me going.

David E. Davis, Jr. was far more than an inspiration. He became a generous friend. Every Australian motoring journalist owes Bill Tuckey a debt. Douglas Blain reinvented motoring magazines. He and Ian Fraser hired me at *CAR* and gave me the freedom to do the best job I could. Frase provided unwavering encouragement whenever things got tough.

Peter Robinson, venerable sage, has been the best of colleagues, advisors, supporters and road companions. Steve Cropley, always going forward, an eternal inspiration.

Art directors taught me most about making magazines: Peter Laws, Wendy Harrop, Adam Stinson, James Baker, Paul Harpin.

Lindsay Masters and Simon Tindall took me to Haymarket. Simon Taylor supported me always and pushed me higher. So did Eric Verdon-Roe.

Tony Baker, Richard Cooke, Colin Curwood, Richard Davies, Ian Dawson, Dougie Firth, Mervyn Franklyn, Martyn Goddard, Uwe Kuessner, John Mason, Stan Papior, John Perkins, Phil Sayer, Alex von Koettlitz – thank you for the photographs, as ever. Kevin Wood, Kathy Ager at LAT; Chris Gable, Nathan Ponchard, thank you, too.

Bob Wallace cared deeply and always went out of his way at Lamborghini. Franco Gozzi opened up never to be forgotten experiences at Ferrari. How generously Nick Mason lent his precious cars – D-type, Daytona, 250 GTO and Stratos.

Simon Entwistle at Lewis Silkin – copyright advice greatly valued.

Phil McNamara at *CAR* and Patrick Fuller at Haymarket – support and permissions much appreciated.

Mark Hughes at Haynes guided this book and made it happen. Always a gentleman. Lee Parsons and Sophie Blackman, thank you too.

Peter Smith boarded that Alitalia flight with me in 1973 and has been a steadfast friend ever since.

FOREWORD
BY STEVE CROPLEY

ALL MY ADULT LIFE I have moved in Mel Nichols' orbit. Even before I met him in Sydney in 1973, I knew the sound of his voice perfectly well. As a dedicated follower of his stuff in *Wheels* and *Sports Car World* I'll never forget how oddly reassuring it felt to meet a bloke you hadn't met before, yet knew already.

What had dominated our relationship to that point was Nichols' unique journalistic style. He had – and has – this powerful instinct for knowing how to speak directly to the reader in a way the vast majority of his predecessors never achieved. Not only did they never achieve it, they never even saw the need for it. Soon after we started to work together the running joke was that for Nichols the genesis of these abilities – including a facility for writing headlines and coverlines that stopped the traffic in newsagents – developed on Rupert Murdoch's payroll at Sydney's lively afternoon tabloid, the *Daily Mirror*, where Nichols was a young reporter.

The truth is, however, that it all came from within. Nichols has delighted all his life in recording and explaining the minutiae of feelings, forces, characters, impressions and situations. He has also frequently displayed the brass neck it takes to ask for difficult journalistic facilities, followed by the determination to turn them into great stories. Put this together with a love of cars and an empathy with those who feel the same and you soon see where this unique collection of writings has sprung from.

When Nichols brought his talents to the UK having been encouraged to do so by wise colleagues like Peter Robinson and Bill Tuckey, he soon pitched up at *CAR*, an odd mixture of a magazine with English traditions for classy journalism run by Australians whose distance from the establishment encouraged them to speak uncomfortable truths about a failing British motor industry – and everything else important – while the rest of the UK motoring press thought itself part of the defence mechanism.

CAR was admired, but when Nichols arrived it wasn't doing well. He changed all that with great journalism, stirring his newspaper reporter's directness, a new strain of give-no-quarter comparison tests, scoop stories unheard of at the time and his speciality, inspirational flagship stories about driving supercars, into a delicious mixture no-one had tasted before. Soon he also had the help of the talented and highly original graphic designer Wendy Harrop, nowadays Nichols' other half, to carry the message onto compelling covers. Sales turned sharply up. Readers delighted in 'discovering' *CAR*. The growth became exponential. Even the magazine's most obtuse rivals could not fail to notice that good journalism attracted readers and advertisers.

I'd been hired in Sydney in February 1973 to take over the job Nichols was leaving to come to the UK and seek his fortune. The urge must have been catching: I later followed him to *Car* and *Autocar*, so I have had the opportunity of watching his progress and influence at close quarters over 40 years.

Life has changed on today's motoring magazines. The indulgent, extended feature in which we both delighted is less common (though no less appreciated by many readers) as we concentrate on writing shorter and quicker, chase a denser flow of news and feed the thriving websites that will govern our future. Yet in all this we stick like glue to the principles Mel Nichols demonstrated so eloquently in the magazines from which the stories here are plucked: that great journalism, produced according to the purest principles of pleasing readers, happens to be a pretty good driver of commercial success, too. It ought not to have been a revolutionary idea, but it was.

INTRODUCTION

I WAS 15 WHEN the Ferrari 250 GTO began its crushing assault on the racetracks. A friend had a picture of one on his bedroom wall. Menacing nose, sinuous bonnet, fastback cabin; shaped to be *fast*. I used to go to his house often just to look at it. Living in a backwater in far away Tasmania, as we did, neither of us expected ever to see the real thing. We could but dream.

But I hadn't reckoned on journalism and fortune. Eleven years later, I had met Enzo Ferrari and driven many of his cars. Within a few more years, I had not only seen a 1962 250 GTO, the Ferrari often hailed as the greatest of them all – I'd had one to myself for a week.

Yet the fulfilment of my dream was nothing compared with that of the GTO's owner, Nick Mason. At Goodwood in 1964 he'd seen a GTO sweep to victory, looked often at the pictures he snapped, and vowed that somehow, one day, he'd own a 250 GTO. At college, with Roger Waters, Rick Wright and Syd Barrett he formed a band called Pink Floyd. Success meant that he could keep and restore the Aston Martin Ulster he'd bought as his first car. Phenomenal success meant other Astons, then a Ferrari Daytona, a D-type Jaguar and, after *The Dark Side of The Moon*, the 250 GTO.

This all but priceless car, one of only 36, came with almost equally precious licence plates: *250GTO*. But Nick noticed they were masking older plates. He unscrewed them and was stunned. There, underneath, was the registration number of the car he'd photographed. He had bought the very GTO he'd seen at Goodwood 13 years earlier.

By then, I was in England, editing *CAR* magazine. I met Nick at a Ferrari driving day at Goodwood. As casually as I could I asked if I could drive his GTO. Incredibly, he said: 'Sure. Bring it back in a week'. Talk about right place, right time.

Three paths merged to take me there: cars, writing and magazines. I loved cars; and I'd been lucky enough to become a journalist. Mum

AND THE REVS KEEP RISING

reckons that at three or four I could name any car that went past. By 13 I was a devoted reader of car magazines. The few shillings I made after school at the local cattle yards went into our local newsagent's till. When I couldn't afford to buy, kindly Mrs Saunders didn't mind if I stood at her newsracks reading the magazines.

Over time, after trying out every motoring magazine she stocked, I settled on a monthly diet of *Wheels, Sports Car World* and *Car and Driver*. Australian car enthusiasts were blessed to have *Wheels*, launched in Sydney in 1953. It was vibrant, progressive, straight-talking and well-written. Its performance car-focused sister, *Sports Car World*, was outstanding by any standard, too. There was a reason. Its editor was a young Tasmanian called Douglas Blain whose writing was fluid and chatty. He would soon become both the defining influence behind *CAR* magazine in the UK and, as my future colleague Steve Cropley would note, 'the father of modern motoring journalism.' Doug's style drew me into *Sports Car World* and, later of course, *CAR* magazine.

Wheels went into a golden period in 1963 under a wildly energetic editor called Bill Tuckey. Bill's writing was fast-paced, passionate, witty and above all evocative. A Ferrari 275 GTB/4, he said, had 'a gearstick made for the gesticulating right hand of a red-blooded Italian'. And if you've stood in the stillness by a lonely road in the Australian Outback at dusk you'll know what Bill meant when he talked about hearing 'the mad, strange song in the overhead wires'. He criticised bad cars ferociously. He lambasted a Holden for having 'savage power but drum brakes the size of boot polish tins'. He condemned car makers for fitting tyres that were 'dynamite if a seagull peed on the road'. Bill's influence was profound.

British car magazines were rare in our shops. But we had a good range of American magazines. I found *Car and Driver* irresistible. The *Detroit Free Press* called its editor, David E. Davis, Jr., 'Hemingway on wheels'. I loved the way he wrote and the stylish, freewheeling magazine he produced. Elmore Leonard, the gripping crime writer, had been his mentor in a Detroit advertising agency before David went to *C/D*. 'Elmore helped me turn my inherited knack for storytelling into a useful writing skill,' David said. Some skill.

David's doctrine at *Car and Driver* was Terse Eloquence. He gave

INTRODUCTION

us beautifully crafted stories and captivating columns. I devoured the gentle, beautiful cameos woven by Warren Weith. Outspoken, often outrageous Brock Yates. Elegant Charles Fox. Lyrical raconteur Jean Shepherd. *Car and Driver* fed the desires of enthusiasts like me (PJ O'Rourke was another) who were hungry for inspiring writing about cars, not just the nuts and bolts.

Through my teens, these magazines – linked across the Pacific by their efforts to bring literary sensibilities to motoring journalism, and then joined by *CAR* in the UK once émigré Douglas Blain got hold of it – taught me, I'd realise later, the lessons that would shape my career. They taught me about cars and driving. Through them I saw that vivid writing wasn't just for novels like Hemingway's or Steinbeck's, and that New Journalism didn't just belong in magazines such as *Esquire* and *Rolling Stone*. It belonged in enthusiasts' magazines too.

I didn't notice how much it was all rubbing off on me. I'll be forever grateful that a high school teacher called Warren Brewer did. I was 16 when he was going over a history essay with me. 'Look at this,' he said. 'You can write. You *have* to be a journalist.' Prompted by that, and in another stroke of luck, I got a cadetship at our local northwest Tasmania newspaper, *The Advocate*. Demanding but kind reporters and editors taught me how to write snappy, accurate stories and edit copy. At 20 I hopped to the big-city *Daily Mirror* then the *Sunday Mirror* in Sydney. The editor of the *Sunday Mirror* knew I read car magazines and made me the motoring editor. What a break. I was now being paid to write about cars.

But in 1970, at 23, I realised my heart was in magazines. I wanted to write for car enthusiasts who shared my passion. I went to *Wheels* as deputy editor. I was now liberated by the intimate, creative magazine format to start pushing boundaries. The editorship of *Sports Car World,* across the office, came up. I grabbed it with both hands.

Remembering how I'd been drawn in by Blain and Tuckey, Davis, Yates and Weith, it seemed to me that one thing mattered above all else. *I had to put readers in the driver's seat.* I was lucky to be driving amazing cars; I had to share what I was seeing, hearing, feeling, and experiencing. I used my eyes and mind as a sort of movie camera to record what was happening. It was like having a second persona:

AND THE REVS KEEP RISING

one doing the driving, the other analysing and recording; a kind of out-of-body experience.

And what fun it was! Driving every new performance car, charged with finding out what they could and couldn't do, given licence to push to the limits, and drive for miles. A thousand miles, Sydney to Adelaide, sometimes. Was there ever a better job? Perfect timing too. I'd become a motoring journalist in the era of the great Australian muscle cars. Ford versus Holden and Chrysler with big V8s and inline-sixes packing well over 300bhp and a match for pretty much anything on Earth. *HO down The Hume* on page 25 of this book gives an idea of what we enjoyed. Back in the office, trying to write each story better than the last, brought its own, extra adrenaline. So did making the magazine, merging the words, photographs and working with inventive designers to create an enticing package of pages for enthusiasts to enjoy each month, just as I had.

Early in 1973 I started thinking about going to Europe. Something serendipitous happened. By mail, I'd been in touch with Bob Wallace, Lamborghini's exalted test driver. He stopped in Sydney on his way back to Italy after a visit home to New Zealand. We had a drink. I should plan, he said, to be in Italy by May and head straight to Sicily for the Targa Florio. It was going to be the last 'proper' Targa; the last as a round of the World Sportscar Championship. Even the lap record holder, Helmut Marko, had called the 44-mile, 34-minute-a-lap thrash through the mountains and villages insane. Bob hoped to be driving down in the prototype Countach. Maybe I could get a ride with him or one of the others from Lamborghini. Offers like that you don't refuse.

So my pal Peter Smith and I had a target date, sorted out our affairs, bade our farewells not knowing when or if we'd return to Australia, jumped onto an Alitalia flight to Rome and went swiftly on to Palermo. Bob had telegrammed to say he was flat out with the Countach's development programme and wouldn't make it. Instead, Fiat so very obligingly had a 124 Sport Coupé waiting on the tarmac for us. Our bags were carried from the aircraft to the Fiat, a guard opened a gate and we drove straight out into Palermo's pell-mell evening traffic. A tale from that exhilarating week is in this book – *Fast Yank accepts a Sicilian challenge.*

INTRODUCTION

In a long, long day's drive, the Fiat took us north to Modena. We set up base in the old Palace Hotel where the test drivers and people from the car companies drank, began the first of our visits to Ferrari, Lamborghini and Maserati then pulled out for Monte Carlo. We got there two days before the Monaco Grand Prix. So did Bob Wallace, with the Countach. I was in for an exciting trip back to Modena. *Monaco to Modena. Fast.*

Wondrous days in Supercar City followed. Driving Lamborghinis and De Tomasos. Heading off into the hills with the test drivers. Going in to meet Enzo Ferrari. I'd sent him copies of *Sports Car World* whenever I'd run Ferrari articles. Always got a thank you letter signed in the sacred purple ink. Before I left Sydney I'd written and asked if I could come and see him, borrow a car, tour the factory, look at the racing department. Of course, he said, perhaps curious to see these boys from Down Under. Peter and I had a magical day at Maranello and when we left that night I had a tale to tell – *'Mr Ferrari is waiting to see you'.*

In London a few weeks later Ian Fraser, editor of *CAR* magazine, bought my stories. My relationship with the world's most innovative car magazine began. Fraser, from Melbourne, was *CAR*'s second Australian editor. A year later, I would become its third. Douglas Blain had started it off. At 23, not long off the ship from Sydney, he'd landed the assistant editor's job on the ponderously named *Small Car and Mini Owner incorporating Sporting Driver* when it launched in September 1962. The first editor, George Bishop, was fired. Another came and went. Blain, full of colonial bravado, talent and huge ambition, stepped up. He trimmed the name back to *Small Car* then, in 1965, to *CAR*.

Blain started a revolution in motoring journalism. Trained in a newspaper and already a fine writer with a warm confiding style, Douglas had literary aims. He saw magazines as a branch of literature and *CAR* as his platform. Steve Cropley, who succeeded me at *CAR*, is now editor-in-chief of *Autocar* and widely regarded as the doyen of motoring journalists in the UK, says: 'I think of Doug Blain as the father of modern motoring journalism because he was the first to talk to readers in the way they wanted. He was the first to get the tone of voice right.

Blain's *CAR* made waves because the stalwart British magazines,

AND THE REVS KEEP RISING

typified by *The Autocar* (launched in 1895) and *The Motor* (1903), read more like engineering journals. Stories were stiff, mechanical, uncrafted, mealy-mouthed. The writers appeared to see themselves as part of the motor industry, not the publishing industry. They rarely criticised anybody about anything. It was hard to work out what they really thought of cars. You had to read between the lines. David E. Davis, Jr. was one who noticed *CAR*'s impact. In *Car and Driver* February 1968 he said: 'Doug Blain has made something fresh and lively grow in the petrified forest of British automotive journalism.'

It wasn't just wit, vivacious writing and pungent verdicts that made *CAR* stand out in the '60s, '70s and '80s. Blain had understood that good magazines were about striking photography and creative design, too. It was unusual then, but *CAR* had always had an art director – good ones – planning its photography and laying it out. Its influence soon ran far beyond motoring. It was part of the new wave of graphically exciting magazines like *Nova, Town* and *Queen*.

So, late 1974, 27 years old, I was editor of *CAR* magazine. Big shoes to fill. Blain and Fraser as mentors, not just for writing and magazine making. They'd recognised that journalists wanting to please readers with tales about the fastest, most exotic cars should go often to Modena, the old industrial town in central northern Italy. Maserati and De Tomaso were in Modena itself; Ferrari and Lamborghini a few kilometres either side. While other British magazines rarely went there, and waited stoically for importers to offer a test car, *CAR* became the home of the supercar. Erudite contributor Leonard Setright had coined the very term to describe the Lamborghini Miura. Driving regularly to Modena – and Stuttgart, then increasingly Munich – was a pleasing tradition to maintain.

The Modenese carmakers were welcoming, especially once they saw that we'd take time to get good photographs and produce polished articles. But any trip was going to be a bit of a trial. You'd write, for example, to Maserati saying that you were going to be in Modena in two month's time and could you come and see the new car, drive it if possible, talk to the CEO and engineers; chew the fat. Then you'd send a couple of telegrams of confirmation and a week or so before the agreed date phone to double check. Yes, all good,

INTRODUCTION

they'd say; see you then. You'd rock up at the appointed time and, almost word-for-word, get the same reaction. Oh, why didn't you tell us you were coming? If only we'd known, we could have had a car ready. *Or:* Well yes, we did have the car you wanted but a customer begged to buy it; or it had been crashed on a demonstration drive; or the transmission was out awaiting parts.

Franco Gozzi at Ferrari was wont to laugh cheekily and say, with a twinkle in his eye, didn't you know he was a terrible liar and couldn't be trusted – but let's go and have lunch anyway. And guess what? After an impeccably stylish lunch at the Cavallino or, best, Ristorante Fini in Modena, a Boxer or a 308 or a 400 GT or an F40 would magically appear. We'd be given the keys and told to come back when we'd had enough. Or the engineer we wanted to talk to had escaped his meetings or returned from Rome and was at our disposal.

That's how it was, and if you went with the flow you'd get what you wanted, often more. Some visitors didn't understand. In autumn 1987 I got word that the F40 would make its first appearance at Ferrari's 40th anniversary celebration at Imola. After a string of phone calls, Ferrari agreed that I could have a trot in the F40 beforehand or jump in for the 50-mile run from Maranello to Imola. Come on Friday morning they said. At nine, I was in the visitors' room near the gatehouse with photographer John Mason waiting out the usual delay. A journalist and photographer from a German car magazine came in. They'd had the same promise. They got the standard platitudes and shrugs. The journalist was outraged. 'What do you *mean*, the car isn't ready?' he demanded. He protested for a while, assumed there really was no F40 – and left. John and I waited quietly. Usual, pleasant lunch interlude at the Cavallino across the road. At 7pm, the F40 was still out running tests. No problem, I said; I'll come back at eight tomorrow. Sure enough, by mid-morning Saturday the F40 was ship-shape. At Ferrari's adjacent test track, Fiorano, I hopped in with Gianfranco Fantuzzi – was there ever a finer name for a Ferrari test driver? – for a stanza of searing laps, then hit the road and blasted down the *autostrada* to Imola. All par for the course.

AND THE REVS KEEP RISING

Any swift car wearing factory 'Prova' plates was unlikely to be bothered by the police. If you were stopped you soon found – *'Signor, you go more slow, eh?'* – that the policemen just wanted to have a look at the car. You could see their pride.

Sometimes the cars were faster than we were expecting. In 1988 Bob Wallace, talking to Pete Lyons for his excellent tome *The Complete Book of Lamborghini,* admitted that Lamborghini occasionally slipped more potent engines into cars lent to journalists. He hinted that for the Miura there was the standard engine, then a trick V12, then a super-trick V12 with an extra 30 or 40bhp. 'The same thing went on at Ferrari,' Wallace told Pete. 'The same thing went on everywhere, so we were no different.' Did that include the Countach S? Hmm.

Lamborghini, often financially parlous – see *Sad sweet song of the last Silhouette* – went to the ultimate level in making cars available. Rather than putting their cars for the UK on transporters, ever-cheery sales director Ubaldo Sgarzi, or Roger Phillips, the UK concessionaire, were liable to suggest you drive a Countach, Espada, Urraco or Silhouette back to England for them. It was a happy situation that led to two of my best ever drives, *900 miles in 11 hours: a grand tourer at work,* and *Convoy! Flat out across Europe,* perhaps my best-known story. It was a gift, of course: three Lamborghinis, in convoy, through France, early on a Sunday, before there were speed limits. I have special affection for that story. It was a stupendous, unrepeatable experience; an intense few days never to be forgotten. Jeremy Clarkson says *Convoy!* influenced him profoundly.

'*CAR* was undoubtedly the one that made me interested in writing about cars the way I do now,' he told me in a conversation in 2010. 'I don't want to blow smoke up your arse unduly but it was *CAR* that really changed the way it could be done. I was particularly influenced by the story about driving the three Lamborghinis back from Italy. I remember thinking that it was a great, very well written story and how much I'd like to write like that. I still think it's the best-ever drive story. Now I'm trying to do stuff like that, only on television.' Jeremy reckons he learned two key things from *CAR*: that you could write entertainingly about cars; and that you could be witty, even rude. They were lessons he learned par excellence.

INTRODUCTION

In the fervent atmosphere sparked by Blain, writers and photographers bounced off each other and strove to be better, just as they did at *Car and Driver* and *Wheels*. Writing stories well took dedication and effort. On top of the lengthy job of making the magazine, it often meant banging away at the typewriter all night, flinging away countless paragraphs, always trying to bring to life on the page the experience on the road.

It became obvious, and inordinately rewarding, that our efforts were appreciated. Readers sent touching letters. Don Mallet from Yonkers, New York, was kind enough to write: 'Your pieces on various Ferraris, Lamborghinis and Lotuses have been true works of beauty. They describe so well what makes these cars magical.'

In 2011, Londoner Jonathan Elstein emailed: 'Back in the 1970s my father used to bring home *CAR* every month and your articles were always the first ones I read. They must have made a big impression because I have recently bought a Lamborghini Silhouette, inspired to a considerable extent by the *Sad Sweet Song…* feature in August 1977, which is still on the bedroom wall in my parents' house!' I joined Jonathan for a day's driving in his beautifully sorted Silhouette. Its performance seems less stand-out now of course but on meandering Wiltshire roads I was soon reminded of its chassis' charm and the beguiling spread of power from that sonorous V8.

CAR's influence kept spreading. Other magazines tried harder. Life got tougher for journalists primarily in the game to tear about in road test cars without bothering much about writing. Younger, better journalists who'd grown up on *CAR* arrived. Standards rose everywhere.

There was a golden '250 GTO moment' for me in 1976. David E. Davis, Jr. rejoined *Car and Driver* as editor and publisher. He wrote in an editorial that in the 10 years he'd been away he'd been reading *CAR* religiously. David – the self-dubbed 'simple kid from Pulaski County, Kentucky' – didn't know that the editor of the British magazine he admired was a kid from Tasmania whom he'd inspired 14 years earlier. I phoned and thanked him. What happened next is the stuff of dreams. David invited me to cross the United States with him and his wife Jeannie in a Mercedes-Benz 450SEL 6.9. It was a priceless introduction to America – *Road America and the Silver*

AND THE REVS KEEP RISING

Trashcan. Ten years later David started *Automobile* Magazine. I was a columnist. Wrote some features too – *German groom, Italian bride, talented offspring* among them.

Our work inspired people in other ways. Richard Parry-Jones, a teenager in Wales, was motivated by *CAR* to be an automotive engineer. He became Chief Technical Officer of Ford, heading 30,000 engineers, scientists and designers worldwide. We owe the Mondeo and Focus's excellence to him. Martin Smith, famous for drawing the Audi quattro and now executive design director of Ford of Europe, says our stories and photography made him want to be a car designer. Other designers and engineers tell similar stories.

Twenty-nine of the 50 stories in this book appeared in *CAR*, mostly while I was its editor. Many were also in magazines abroad, such as *Car and Driver, Motor Trend, Sports Car Graphic, Wheels, Sports Car World* and *Car Graphic* in Japan. Later stories were in *Automobile;* and *Autocar* and *Classic & Sports Car,* where for the last 22 years of my full-time career until 2009 I was, with great joy, editorial director.

By the early '80s *Autocar* and *Motor*, both published by a complacent company that didn't want them to compete, were foundering, blitzed by *CAR* on one side and *What Car?* on the other. Haymarket Magazines' astute managing director Simon Taylor (who'd launched *What Car?*) and colleague Eric Verdon-Roe – both passionate, knowledgeable car enthusiasts and magazine publishers – knew the value of the world's oldest car magazine. In 1984 they bought *Autocar* in a blinding deal and with vision, commitment and investment promptly began to turn it around. *Motor* had improved but soon lost the battle and was bought by Haymarket, too, then subsumed into *Autocar*. I had the happy task of restoring *Autocar*'s original authority and building the vibrant journalism it needed to succeed in the late '80s and onwards. Not long after, my masterful erstwhile colleague Steve Cropley, who succeeded me at *Wheels, Sports Car World* and *CAR*, joined *Autocar* too. Motoring journalists don't come any better. And latter-day *Autocar* is an ongoing triumph of nous and quality.

Most of the stories here are about fast cars. Two aren't. *Young man's fancy,* about my MGA, and *Summer's coming. Time to go driving,* about my Alfa Romeo GTV 2000, are here because those cars meant

INTRODUCTION

so much to me. The MGA, I realised later, was kind and kept me out of trouble. The Alfa had sensuous qualities that transcended its level of performance, good though that was in the '60s and early '70s for a car of its type and capacity.

Looking back over all these stories from today's perspective, it's fascinating to see how the cars have changed. There are all the obvious developments: safety, build quality, reliability, equipment. But the increase in power, performance and especially fuel economy is gobsmacking. In 1970, 200bhp was potent. Nought to 60mph in less than eight seconds was *fast*. The Lamborghini Miura did it in 6.7sec and hit 0–100 in 15.1sec. *Autocar*'s road testers called that 'enormous'. The Ferrari Daytona, with 5.4sec and 12.6sec, was The Boss. The Ferrari Boxer shaved a bit off that, and the Countach was in similar territory.

Porsche's 959 and Ferrari's F40 raised the bar in the late '80s. It was eight-ish seconds for *0–100mph* now, not 0–60. The 200mph era was here. 'Stupendous' was the right word. So what would we call the McLaren F1's performance a few years later? 'Artillery shell' said *Autocar*, whose timing gear spewed out 0–60 in a staggering 3.2sec and 0–100 in 6.3sec. Could any car ever be faster, we mused. The Bugatti Veyron arrived. Now, as we stare at 2.6sec to 60 and just *5.0sec* to 100, we wonder again.

Forty years on, everyday hot hatches – take a bow, Ford Focus 2.0ST – accelerate faster than a Miura. A standard Porsche 911 Carrera gives you 100mph in 10.4sec. Almost countless Mercedes, BMW, Audi and Jaguar saloons – even estates – are giant killers. We thought, in the '70s, as mid-engined supercars became the norm, that the Daytona – *The car that time can't tame* – was the last front-engined Ferrari Berlinetta. The 550 Maranello in 1996 dashed that lie. In 2013, the front-engined Ferrari F12 – the fastest Ferrari yet – buries it deep. The F12's 730bhp is more than double the Daytona's power. It accelerates almost twice as fast. That speaks volumes about car engineers' ability – and Maranello's in particular – to keep moving on.

What does stepping up to performance in that realm feel like?

A McLaren MP4-12C is a good indicator. On the one hand you have this truly shattering acceleration. And yet, on the other, it unfolds within a broad envelope of civility that's awesome in itself. That's

AND THE REVS KEEP RISING

not to say the best supercars of the past didn't have a fair balance of virtues. They often did. In general, Lamborghinis had surprisingly good rides. Ferrari V12s, flat 12s and V8s were about tractability as well as top-end power. Porsches, lots of liveability. Now, when a high-striving company like McLaren lays down a brief for a more rounded, new-order 600bhp car, technology, materials and accumulated experience make it possible. Equanimity – that's the MP4-12C's triumph. It's calm, composed, approachable, easy. You can trickle in town traffic or roll along with the masses on a motorway where the transmission has slipped into seventh at less than 1000rpm. You'll be impressed by how compliant the ride stays, always, with a flatness that decries the quite remarkable cornering speeds when you fly down a good road. And when you get a chance to open up the 3.8-litre twin turbo V8 and let it whip to 8500 in one gear after another, it's not so much the pressure in your back that dominates your senses – it's the extraordinary, exponential rate the scenery is coming at you. Fast, faster, ever faster. It is, as *Autocar* said without exaggeration, ferociously, apocalyptically quick. Yet for all its sense-shredding, rocket-like speed the MP4-12C remains easy to drive, too. In the end, it's this blend of monumental performance and everyday ease that's locked into your mind. And that's where we are now.

The F12 and whatever Ferrari creates beyond the 458 Italia, the P1 coming from McLaren, Astons reaching for new heights, Porsches pushing ever onwards, Lamborghinis laying down challenges, Jaguars, BMWs, Mercs, Audis, Corvettes, Nissan GT-Rs, Nobles, Paganis – it's not going to stop, and it's going to keep getting better. The supercar world – well, the hypercar world, now – is in a better place than ever; far better than we could have imagined a few decades ago.

Going back over the cars and stories for this book was a joyous journey; a feast of precious memories, some journeys made alone, many with jovial colleagues and most with inventive, adaptable photographers whose eyes were extraordinary, whose commitment to taking masterly photographs was total, and who were perfect company.

These stories, I hope, convey the excitement and rewards of driving great cars. That's what I was trying to do when I wrote them, anyway.

'REMEMBER DISBELIEF 120MPH AVERAGE. I APOLOGISE.'

HOLDEN MONARO GTS 350
1970

THREE HUNDRED AND FIFTY miles northwest of Sydney, New South Wales, there's a town called Nyngan. Next place up the road is Bourke, gateway to the Outback. When Australians refer to somewhere remote they say 'Back o' Bourke'.

The country is red, dry, open, and flat. Roads are arrow-straight. In the 125 miles from Nyngan to Bourke there are just three bends: a long curve out of town, a bit of a squiggle about halfway, and a kink four miles from Bourke. It's fine territory for fast cars.

In the winter of 1970, a mate and I were heading for the dirt roads Back o' Bourke to go hunting. We were in the right car – a new HG series Holden Monaro GTS 350, the latest and fastest version of the General Motors coupé that had won Australia's famous race, the Hardie Ferodo 500 at Bathurst, for the previous two years.

It was a big two-door four-seater with a vast boot and a whopping 35-gallon fuel tank. Just as well: it fed a ravenous four-barrel carburettor on the high-compression 5.7-litre Chevrolet V8 that General Motors-Holden imported from the US. It pumped out 300bhp at 4800rpm and a lusty 380lb/ft of torque at 3200rpm, working through a heavy-duty four-speed gearbox. You soon learned that the meatiness of the thick, short gear lever was a good clue to the car's character.

There were no worries about the toughness of the Monaro's suspension for racing or Outback jaunts like ours. Rugged double

AND THE REVS KEEP RISING

arms with coil springs and an anti-roll bar at the front; live axle (with a limited slip diff), radius rods and hefty four-leaf springs at the rear. Recirculating ball steering and disc brakes up front but still drums at the rear.

The race-bred GTS 350 was fast. It'd give you 55, 79, 99 and 130mph in the gears; 0–60mph in 7.0sec, 0–100 in 16, and 14.8sec for the standing quarter mile. Among contemporaries, only Ford's Falcon GT-HO – another of the great Australian muscle cars of the early '70s – could shade it (just).

Around Sydney the Monaro's heavy controls and concrete ride felt truck-like, although the V8's torque meant you could move off in second gear then drop straight into top, which cut the clutch-and-shift work down. But out on the road, above 60mph, everything clicked and it entered another realm. It meant business.

So, with the first 350 miles behind us, we were clearing Nyngan and looking at that straight road – with no speed limit – spearing across the plains to Bourke. As the town faded, and without a car in sight, I flattened the Monaro through the gears and ran her out until she was sitting on a nice steady 120mph. She was calm and stable in my hands, and I knew there was more in hand.

I pushed the accelerator to the floor and held it there until the Monaro would go no faster. The speedo nudged 133mph – a true 130mph – and stayed there. And stayed there. We gobbled the miles and in precisely one hour we were in Bourke.

'Bullshit!' said Peter Robinson, who was editing *Wheels* magazine where I was deputy editor, when I relayed the story.

A few months later, after Peter had averaged similar speeds in another GTS 350 across the wide, flat Hay Plain in southern NSW, he stopped at a post office and sent me this telegram: 'Remember disbelief 120mph average. I apologise. Robinson'.

The piece he wrote in *Wheels* ended: 'Have no doubts, in the right conditions a Holden Monaro 350 can make many of Europe's so called grand tourers eat its exhaust pollution.'

HO DOWN THE HUME
FORD FALCON GT-HO PHASE III
1971

PAINFULLY, AS IDEALS GIVE way to reality, young journalists learn that certain stories are too hot for publication. Some can never be told; others only years later. This is one of those stories.

It began in the car park of the Ford Motor Company's factory just north of Melbourne, Australia, one afternoon in the middle of 1971. A car was waiting there for me in the feeble wintry sun. A four-door Falcon – one of the first GT-HO Phase IIIs to come off the production lines, so new its existence was still a secret to all but a handful of people outside Ford. And of those people, here was I about to be handed the keys to the fastest, most awesome car Australia had ever produced.

Through good organisation or coincidence – I forget which – I'd arrived to pick up the Phase III in a 5.0-litre V8 Bolwell Nagari, a low, sleek, light and potent Australian coupé. I'd rushed down in it from Sydney, putting most of the 360 miles of the New South Wales section of the Hume Highway behind me in the morning, and accounting for the final couple of hundred through Victoria in the afternoon. Even so, I'd been running late, worried that I wouldn't make it to the factory before the Ford people went home for the weekend, taking the keys of the HO with them. But it was okay because the mechanics were still working on the car even as I called from a roadside phone box to beg them to wait.

And then I was there, pulling in alongside the thing, unwinding myself from the Bolwell and climbing expectantly, half afraid, into the Ford. I can recall not a word Ford's PR man was saying through the open window as the key slid into the ignition. I can remember only the anticipation. And then the trembling of the car and the flick of the Shaker air scoop jutting up through the bonnet as the 5.8-litre (351CID) V8 churned to the starter and shook in its mounts. It fired, and filled the car park with a thunderclap of exhaust as intimidating, it seemed to me, as the snorting of a charging rhinoceros. Then came the popping and sizzling and gulping as I prodded the throttle and the 780cfm four-barrel Holley carburettor dumped too much fuel into the unready combustion chambers. Give it a little while.

I used the time to adjust the mirrors, fine-tune the seating position and tug the belt a snitch tighter until it nailed me to the seat. And then I dared to move the car away, feeling a little tremble in my left leg as it fought against that big brute of a clutch for the first time. The steering seemed light, lighter than in a normal Falcon GT, and it made the job of swinging out of the car park easy, in the wake of the gently burbling Bolwell, and into the peak hour traffic.

My photographer friend, Uwe Kuessner, in the Bolwell, trod on it and the fibreglass car became a yellow streak, charging past the tamer traffic on the wide highway. *Blast him!* Had he forgotten I was following? So I, too, trod hard on my throttle pedal. And braced myself. Without yet completing my arc out through the median strip into the traffic, the car hiccupped... shuddered. Then – *bloody hell!* – it exploded into action. The nose hurled itself forward and upwards like a leaping tiger. The back tyres wailed and the tail snapped 'way out. The GT-HO speared sideways through the rest of the gap in the central reservation. The opposite lock was on, intuitively. No time to think about niceties like steering feel now.

It flicked straight again as it lined up in the outside lane of the road towards Melbourne. The engine's snarling had reached fever pitch. I grabbed second just as the V8 hit its electric rev-cut-out. It died momentarily, then picked up again and simply pelted me forward once more. My senses raced, trying to adjust to the speed. Maximum revs again. But so soon! Third, and I charged forward once more. And then it was hard on the brakes, getting a slight twitch because I was up to 90mph in those scant few seconds and about to run over the top of the Bolwell. We both slowed, both aware of just how much performance we had on hand, and how cautious we needed to be because we were so much faster than the cars around us. So we tiptoed into downtown Melbourne.

That early, blood-stirring blast did me a lot of good. It showed me that the Phase Three was eminently easy to drive, much more so than either of its predecessors, and especially considering just how much power lay just a throttle push away. It was so smooth low down, so docile for a thumping great V8 with an 11:1 compression ratio. Ford listed its punch at 300bhp. More like 380 reckoned those in the know. It was happy to trundle down to 1500rpm – 34mph – in top gear, to idle steadily at 1000rpm instead of something approaching 2000rpm in the GT-HO Phase II. I found I was easing up to 2000rpm, changing up into the next gear and finally dropping into fourth at around 35mph. And so I came, very quickly, to feel quite at ease in the HO. Ready to drive it...

Next morning – Saturday – Uwe and I headed for the open country west of Melbourne to take pictures of the Bolwell and the Ford. I lounged in the warmth of the Falcon while he got on with photographing the Bolwell. When it was time to start shooting some action pictures with the GT-HO, the only open bend we could find wasn't all that tight. I did one run and found that 90mph was too slow to make the car move. It just sat there, hugging the road. Again: this time flat in third at 104mph. Again no understeer, no oversteer; just a little body roll and the nose lifting jauntily. I went to 110mph in fourth on the next run and it was still just as uneventful, but I didn't want to go faster because I wasn't yet entirely sure where the limits lay, even though I was getting a pretty good idea. So I switched to running performance figures instead, on a stretch of marked-out road we often used, ticking off the gear maximums at the 6150rpm redline at 49mph, 73 and 104. There wasn't enough room to run flat in top; that would have to wait. Then there was the acceleration. Experimentation showed that the clutch had to come out at 2700rpm, nothing more and nothing less. If I dropped it at 2500rpm the engine died a little against the grip of the wheels. If I popped it at 3000rpm there was wheel spin for around 200 metres, again wasting time. So 2700rpm it was. At that, 0–100mph came up in 15.2sec on the stopwatches. It was all so easy. It began to rain,

AND THE REVS KEEP RISING

and we headed back to Melbourne and crossed town to return the Bolwell to its makers. After a week of spirited driving it was a sad parting. But what the hell – we still had the GT-HO, didn't we?

Indeed we did – and unbeknown to us at that moment, we were soon to subject it to one of the most exhilarating tests it would undergo on the road; to use it for what's reckoned to be one of the most remarkable journeys ever run in Australia. To thunder it flat out in a drive etched forever on the memories of the two of us who did it.

But, for the moment, we found ourselves tooling quietly through the cold Melbourne drizzle. Saturday night. No plans. Nothing we really wanted to do. Then something made one of us suggest going to Albury, just on 200 miles north on the Victoria–NSW border where we had friends. So we gunned the HO around, hit the main road out of town and headed north into the night. It was 7.30pm.

The rain grew heavier and the night nastier. There wasn't much traffic, and most of that was going the other way. I don't recall much until we were past the little Hume Highway town of Seymour, but I expect we'd been alone with our thoughts and the murmur of the radio, soloist to the steady background swish of the wipers, the hissing of the tyres and the downbeat throb of the V8. I only remember the ease of driving the car; how much at home I felt in it now a real idea of its capabilities was forming clearly in my mind. How comfortably it carried us, its lights hacking through the night. And then came the fast, open bends you strike after Seymour. I can remember the way the car seemed to think itself through them, undeterred by the rain, travelling at ever-increasing speeds and showing me how strongly it could grip and how finely it was balanced.

The next thing I recall – and how clearly I can see it in my mind's eye – is one particular bend on that deserted, sodden road. A bend that's just a simple kink at 70 or even 80mph, but a curve requiring careful choice of line and steering and power at much more, especially in the wet. I flicked a glance at the speedo as we came into it now in the HO. I scarcely believed it: 125mph. But there we were, rock-steady, the car just slicing on through, set up by the merest throttle lift then kept on line with gentle pressure on

FORD FALCON GT-HO PHASE III

the pedal once more, and the tiniest nudge of pressure on the big wheel. Everything about it was so clean, so beautifully and clinically balanced, like walking on a razor's edge and feeling the elation of not slipping off. It was so perfect it was almost nothing.

We continued on holding 125mph for what seemed like dozens of miles, and the only reason we didn't go faster was that at precisely 126mph the windscreen wipers began to lift off. Then we were in Albury, purring gently through the glistening streets after a run that contained nary a sideways twitch, never a sliver of understeer, not a zizz of wheel spin. It was exactly 10pm. We had covered the distance faster than either of us would have imagined possible in ideal conditions, let alone amid the elements' atrocities of that night. Yet it was also the tamest, most uneventful trip either of us had had from Melbourne to the State border. We'd entered the inner sanctum of the GT-HO's world.

We were going to be taken even deeper into that world the next day. Our arrangement with Ford was to hand the Phase III back, at the factory near Melbourne, at 11am on the Sunday morning and then get a lift all the way back to Sydney with a Ford employee who was driving the 560 miles from city to city that day. But we slept late, and at 8.30am we were 200 miles away from our rendezvous. We threw on our clothes and rushed out to the Falcon. She fired up easily, shattering the chilly silence of the town and we found a petrol station and stood back while almost a full 36 gallons sloshed into the huge tank. While the attendant counted the money I worked out our consumption so far. It had been precisely 8mpg.

We checked the tyre pressures, wiped the windows clean, and at two minutes past nine we left for Melbourne. The morning was as perfect as the night before had been foul. We went full out through the gears as we cleared the last speed limit of the border town, with the HO now warm and ready, and thundered straight past a couple of cars and a semi. The car's nose was thrusting forward and upwards with the power once more, and again we were enjoying the feeling of being pressed back into our seats as the beast was given its head. At last it was free of any and all restrictions. There was only open road ahead.

AND THE REVS KEEP RISING

Again we chewed up the miles and spat them out. In remarkably short time we were on the long straights of the Hume Highway as it speared down through northern Victoria, and with the speedo steady on 125mph I squeezed still farther on the accelerator as the ribbon of road ran unwaveringly into the distance.

The shaker heaved in the bonnet, the car sort of shrugged and the nose lifted even further from the road. It might have been a tiger kicked awake; the noise alone said that. The speedo needle went determinedly around the dial, and soon it was showing 145mph – a true 141mph.

But *whoa!* The engine started missing. For Pete's sake – the rev-limiter! We'd run right up to it. In top gear. A full 6150rpm (the tachometer actually said 6700rpm; it was over-reading). And if I kept my foot hard down that hefty V8 just kept thumping away against the cut-out, straining for more. So once Uwe had climbed into the back seat and shot some pictures over my shoulder, to prove it really was happening, I lifted off a fraction to back it off from the limiter at a neat 140mph. For minutes, for mile after mile, we stayed like that. The car was like a locomotive, never deviating from its path. The messages about its steadiness came back through the wheel and the seats as unmistakably as pinpricks. I remember how I felt. Relaxed, but razor-sharp, peering ahead a mile and more; my eyes, my brain, my nervous system forcibly lifted to a new edge to deal with the speed. You feel so competent... so potent. Your mind seems to magnify everything, to pick up an extraordinary amount of information and to digest it amazingly quickly. It's called concentration, and it's delicious.

Road conditions and sparse traffic allowed us to keep the GT-HO close to its maximum speed for many miles more. But nearing Melbourne we came back closer to 100 most of the time, using the tremendous top end acceleration to maintain a fantastically high average and to overtake in a quick rush of power and safety, since our exposure time was so brief and our controllability so vast. We toyed briefly with the stopwatches again, finding out to our amazement that 100 to 120mph took a paltry 6.8 seconds and 120 to 140mph just 8.9 seconds. *That* is top-end performance, with all

FORD FALCON GT-HO PHASE III

the excitement and advantages it entails, and unrivalled in a car with four doors and five seats.

Stunned by the Phase III's ability, amazed by such an extraordinarily rapid but effortless trip, we pulled into Ford at Broadmeadows. It was one minute to eleven. Nearly 200 miles in two hours. Neither of us spoke. We just shared the moment, feeling a special sort of elation; aware that we'd shared something remarkable.

We lifted our gear from the GT-HO's boot, locked it up and walked away. In the backseat of the tamer Falcon GT taking us back to Sydney I thought of how I'd write the story, not yet realising I wouldn't be allowed to tell it all. Back in the office at *Wheels* Magazine, it became clear that, in a climate where tabloid newspapers were ranting about the dangers of cars like the Phase III getting into the hands of youths, and politicians feeling they had to *Do Something*, we couldn't let on how fast we'd gone on the open road.

So the road test we published in *Wheels* October 1971 was rather matter of fact. Peter Robinson, *Wheels'* editor, and I lost a raging battle with the magazine's management to use Uwe's now-famous picture of the GT-HO's speedo indicating 145mph. The art department was ordered to retouch the picture to make the speedo read 104mph and we explained it with a caption saying the car was flat in third gear. But Sunday newspapers still fastened onto the performance figures we printed and kicked up a fuss. Other journalists demanded Ford lend them a GT-HO for test, too. Political pressure mounted and, while it was too late to kill the Phase III, an embattled Ford never put its successor, the Phase IV, into production.

Few people knew just how great the GT-HO Phase III's capabilities *really* were. I'm glad I was one.

I finally told this story in Sports Car World *October 1975, four years after the adventure on the Hume Highway, when Peter Robinson, then also editing* Sports Car World, *asked me to put it all down. Uwe's original unaltered photograph, appeared with it – published in all its glory at last. Since then, it's been reproduced – legally and bootlegged – countless times and is undoubtedly the most famous motoring picture ever taken in Australia. In 2011* Wheels *made it into a limited-edition poster, signed by Uwe and me.*

FAST YANK ACCEPTS A SICILIAN CHALLENGE

CORVETTE STINGRAY
1973

IN THE SPRING OF 1973, Sicily was the place to be. The word was out: after this Targa Florio, there'd be no more. The last great road race, with its 44-mile laps weaving in and out of the mountains, was going to die.

I flew in from Australia, a young man leaving his homeland for the first time. Sicily was staggering. Forbidding walled towns teetering on mountaintops. A tranquil coast giving way to a harsh interior. Enthusiastically friendly people. The image of the Mafia omnipresent.

As the race drew near, motorsport fans trooped in. Many drove from as far away as the United Kingdom. I'd first heard from Bob Wallace, Lamborghini's test driver, how good that long dash down through Italy could be. He often belted down in his latest prototype. Not this year though. The Countach had other commitments.

Among the pilgrims in 1973 was a young American. His name was Pete Lyons. He was travelling Europe reporting the Grand Prix season for *Autosport* magazine. And he was doing it with panache: to travel from circuit to circuit, he'd imported a 1973 Chevrolet Corvette Stingray.

I was leaning over the balcony of my hotel room in a village near Palermo when the 'Vette burbled into the square. Even among the extraordinary array of cars that had been pouring in all week, the Stingray stood out. Its size, shape, and presence were incongruous against the small and delicate European cars and the old dusty walls.

Next day I was out around the circuit, in the Ferrari team's camp

CORVETTE STINGRAY

chatting with drivers Jacky Ickx and Brian Redman, when Pete and the Stingray drew up. Redman was lounging on the bonnet of the team's Dino 246 GT hack. Always the joker, he popped off a few gibes about the Corvette. Pete fired back. The banter typified the conviviality of the Targa, but the point was, Peter Lyons had made a grand entrance courtesy of the Chevrolet.

In that vibrant atmosphere – drivers, mechanics, writers, photographers and race fans drawn together in the Sicilian sun to celebrate the world's best expression of the motor racing spirit – we were soon friends. I asked Pete about the Corvette. How was it on the demanding roads of a place like Sicily?

'Take it,' Pete said. 'Do a circuit and see what you think.' By now I had a fair idea of the challenge presented by the Targa's Piccolo Madonie circuit. I'd driven it a couple of times in the pleasing 124 Sport coupé Fiat had kindly loaned me. More tellingly, I'd been part of the way around with Brian Redman in that much thrashed factory Dino.

It was a lesson as well as a thrill. Just as a hard-driving Redman, who'd won the 1970 Targa with Jo Siffert in a Porsche 908, was pronouncing that he'd at last remembered which way the turns went, we darted into what he reckoned was a fast right hander. It tightened back on itself, hard. 'Oh, Christ,' shouted Brian, arms flailing as he flung the Dino around in a lurid slide. 'This bloody circuit!' In the big 'Vette, on what was still a 'normal' road with two-way traffic, I knew I wouldn't have much scope for getting it wrong.

Before shipping the car, Lyons had removed the detox gear from the 5.7-litre/350CID V8, fitted a Holley carburettor, and tweaked the tune to achieve close to 300bhp rather than the Stateside 250. It drove through a four-speed manual gearbox and a 3.55:1 differential. After the brisk but modest acceleration of the Fiat's 1.8-litre twin-cam four, the thrust from the Corvette's free-revving V8 was sheer, lusty excitement.

Heading from the town of Cerda toward the first of the bendy sections, I revelled in its potency. The 6000rpm redline would come up fast, calling rapidly for the next change with the short-throw shift. It worked with an equally efficient and surprisingly light clutch. The throttle, too, was impressively precise. On the straights, the Stingray soon galloped to its 120mph top speed and felt stable enough, although the steering grew a little woolly beyond 110. In the bends, though, it provided the right sort of directness, and it wasn't as heavy as I'd expected. Indeed, with a pleasingly light and sensitive braking system, the Corvette soon revealed a surprising 'fingers, toes, and seat of the pants' character.

As the Piccolo Madonie's devilish bends began to come thick and fast, I found that it would turn in sweetly and accurately, with – if I was somewhere close to the right line – only a mild touch of understeer. If the understeer grew too strong, it was just a matter of easing off a little, feeling the grip and neutrality come back, and then poking on some more power. Give it a lot from the V8 and the tail would duly thrust out into controllable oversteer.

It didn't take long to learn that the Corvette could cope admirably with the Targa course, singing along smoothly and quickly as I tried to drive fast but without falling foul of one of those treacherous bends. The only problems came with mid-bend bumps, which shook the nose off-line and made the tail hop free. The solution was to read the road carefully and slow down, take care to have room to run wide, or be ready to catch the tail with opposite lock.

Mostly, though, the Corvette ran satisfyingly hard and took me around the 44 miles and back to Pete Lyons without a nasty moment. It had been a fabulous drive around a monumental circuit in a car with exhilarating performance and pretty good behaviour. I was impressed.

Pete Lyons remained that way, too. I phoned him in California a few years later. 'After the Targa,' he said, 'I drove it 18 hours straight through to northern Italy. It was fantastic. I just wanted to keep on going. The truth is, I had intended to sell the Corvette for a good profit soon after getting it to Europe. I'd always considered myself more of a Lotus sort of person: I liked light and nimble cars. But the 'Vette showed no really bad manners and I fell in love with it."

Pete ended up keeping the Stingray for four years. At European speeds, it gave about 12mpg, and there was the occasional worry about repairs, like the time he bent a valve when running flat out around the old Reims road circuit and had to hitchhike to England and wheedle a new cylinder head from a drag-car builder.

'It was kind of like driving a Lamborghini back and forth across the United States,' he said. 'But, God, it was worth it. I will always cherish that time in Europe with the Corvette as one of the high points of my life.'

MONACO TO MODENA. FAST
LAMBORGHINI COUNTACH
LP400 #1120001
1973

EVEN THOUGH THE CAR was parked just 30 feet away in Casino Square, we couldn't catch more than an occasional glimpse of its red paint: the crowd packed around it so tightly.

We were sitting just above it, on the steps of Monte Carlo's Hotel de Paris, chatting quietly in the Friday afternoon sun. Occasionally Bob Wallace, Lamborghini's chief development engineer, would halt his conversation, half-rise, and try to peer through the heads to check that the car was okay; that someone wasn't crushing the alloy bodywork.

I tried hard to see it too. To study it and dwell on the fact that soon I would be riding more than 250 miles in it, the first person outside Lamborghini to make a long trip in it, and get to know just what the Countach is like. Word was that Lamborghini was aiming for a top speed beyond 190mph and that it would be the world's fastest road car.

I tried to be nonchalant as Wallace and I sat there talking with the famous Casino forming a background across the teeming square where everything but the Countach was being ignored. But sometimes it was all I could do to stop bounding down the steps and telling those gaping people that at 8 o'clock on Monday morning I was going to be inside this fascinating car when Bob fired it up to go home to Modena.

It was happening because I was in the right place at the right time. Earlier in the week, at the end of a day visiting the factory, Lamborghini had promised me a run in the Countach. But each and time I drove out from Modena to Sant'Agata Bolognese, or

LAMBORGHINI COUNTACH LP400 #1120001

telephoned, the Countach was in bits. The people from the design office were going over it; a part was out for modification; some new components were being machined.

And by the time, late in the week, that I had to leave for Monaco for the Grand Prix I'd come no closer than admiring its breathtaking shape through the door of the experimental workshop. I left with only a hope that Bob might find time to take it to Monte Carlo to show it off to the wealthy during the Grand Prix weekend. He didn't want to. Four days out of his test schedule were too much. I knew he meant it. I'd dined with him three evenings in Modena. He would come in to Modena from Sant'Agata, tired, never before 8pm, after a day on the road that often began at 4.30am.

He wasn't having big problems with the Countach's development and wasn't behind schedule. There was just so much to do. Lamborghini was determined this car would push the Miura's legacy onwards and get the edge on its new mid-engined Ferrari opponent, the 365 GT4 BB.

So Wallace reckoned he wouldn't be going to Monaco, and neither would he nor the rest of the development crew be having summer holidays. But, on the Thursday night as I strolled through Casino Square, I saw it. It was parked outside the Hotel de Paris, still tick-ticking from its fast run from Modena. Wallace had made it after all! I found him at the Automobile Club, and asked gingerly if he'd come alone. Yes. Would it, then, be possible to ride back to Modena with him after the Grand Prix? Yes.

At five to eight on Monday morning I pull into Casino Square. The only people about are spanner-wielding workmen dismantling the Armco from the Grand Prix. My pal Pete parks our Fiat 124 Sport Coupé and I take out my cameras and typewriter and one clean shirt. Wallace said I must travel light. The sun is warm. Birds are twittering in the park off the square. Stirling Moss comes out of the Hotel de Paris, jumps onto a tiny motorbike and scoots off towards the harbour. At a minute past eight I hear it. The rumble snaps the workmen's heads around too. Then we see it: a low, wide, mean red shovel on wheels.

It is easy to get into the Countach. The door swings lightly

AND THE REVS KEEP RISING

upwards, counter-balanced by a hydraulic piston, and you drop your backside down in first, pulling your head, arms and legs in after you. Wallace, urgent as ever, has the engine snapping back to life before I can pull the door back down, and we're off. It will be some miles before I can think about the seats and interior. It seems instantly comfortable.

We go briskly across the square with the suddenly silent workmen clearing a path. The Lamborghini rides hard on the pave surface, and inside there is the ever-present thunder of the 4.0-litre V12 and the urgent chatter of the twin Bendix fuel pumps. You notice them that first minute, then never again. A string of cars wants to come into the square as we want to go out. Wallace sits and waits as Fiats, an Alfa, a DS 21, edge past. The drivers take three times as long to slide past as they would normally. Wallace curses.

Along the winding road east to Menton he says it will take us a while to clear French customs, and then the Italians, but the 250-mile trip should take a little over four hours. The traffic thickens. We work along in second and third, usually with the tach around 1500rpm, sometimes running up to 3000 where Wallace will pick up another gear. A week earlier I'd been in an Espada and knew to expect unfussy flexibility from the V12. The Countach, legitimately, could have been less docile than the other Lamborghinis. But as we dribble along it's as docile as a lamb. The pull starts from the very bottom of the scale.

The engine is 'conventional' Lamborghini: the same format and size as the V12s of the Espada and Jarama. But it has detail improvements, particularly to the cylinder head ports, with the potential for a power hike. Wallace is working towards 400bhp by the time production starts. I concentrate on the noise for a while. It's loud, but not as severe as you might expect considering that the prototype doesn't have full sound and heat insulation. It doesn't seem as noisy as a Miura. There isn't the Miura's bombardment of different noises from exhaust, valves, cams, chains, fuel pumps. That V12 ran full length across your back. This one, prompted by Ferruccio Lamborghini's desire to reduce the noise level in the Miura's replacement, runs away from you, in line with the car

LAMBORGHINI COUNTACH LP400 #1120001

and not across it – a unique design with the gearbox ahead of the engine and between driver and passenger. The driveshaft runs out of the lower part of the gearbox and straight back through that huge tunnelled magnesium sump to the differential. This way, the axles are no further back than the distributor cap at the rear of the engine.

On Menton's pavé streets the car rides hard. It jigs, and there's a lot of loud thumping over the bumps. And yet it isn't all that uncomfortable: very firm but not jolting because it has a feeling of lightness to it. Not quite delicacy, but almost. The car *is* light. A great deal of work has gone into weight saving. Its chassis is space-frame: an incredibly complicated one, and super strong, but still quite light. Every possible mechanical component is magnesium alloy – the block, as usual, but also the enormous sump, the big gearbox housing, the long engine mounts, the oil filter and pump casing, engine pulleys, steering rack housing, twin-piston brake callipers, the suspension uprights, the shock absorbers. The wheels, too, of course. The body is aluminium. The total weight, Bob says, just over 2000lb. The benefits: sophistication, nimbleness and speed. The penalty: only cost.

I start noting the reactions of people on the streets and in the cars around us. One smartly dressed chap stepping along the footpath glances over his shoulder, stops dead, grabs his companion's shoulder and wrenches him around to stare, too. At intersections and squares I have time to study the faces more closely. The baker delivering to the cafe, the milkman lifting crates from his van, the mix of people on their way to work. They all stop and grin the tight little grin that everybody does when they see a car like this, and forget for a few moments what they're doing. A lanky young blade on a Honda 750 rips in, drops two gears and idles along beside us, looking down at me far below him. He stays there for a mile, peering in when he can, running his eyes over as much of the car as possible. Then we come to an open piece of road and Wallace runs it to six and goes *wharoom, wharoom, wharoom* through the gears and we leave the bike. He is taken by surprise, and he doesn't even try to catch up. This is a car that makes a farmer gathering violets

AND THE REVS KEEP RISING

beside the road drop his bunches. It stops a white-haired, stooped priest on a footpath in his tracks. I tire of looking.

The French border guards let us through in minutes. It takes longer a few metres further on at the Italian customs house. Wallace goes inside to sort it all out. I go around to the other side of the car, push through the crowd of blue-jacketed border guards already surrounding the Countach and get in behind the wheel.

Ever since the Countach was revealed, in its initial LP500 form, at the 1971 Geneva Motor Show, people have doubted that its lift-up doors would work. They work very well, leaving a gap that is easy to drop through and into the two suedette tunnels waiting inside. They're more like racing car tubs than road car seats. The only vehicle with an anything similar is the Lancia Stratos, which, like the Countach, had its design inspired by the first Bertone Stratos prototype. I once spent a day driving that car, finding its super wedge comfortable inside but hard to reconcile to the road because it was just so different, so space age.

The Countach is intriguingly similar. Bertone has pulled off a remarkable design feat. The seats themselves are curving devices that follow the flow of your spine and legs from neck to the knees. They slope back like canvas beach chairs. Again following the design of the original Stratos, the prototype's are upholstered in chunks that look like the pieces of a huge chocolate block. Mine, with the original thin chunks, is hard but comfortable. Wallace's is a new seat with much thicker, softer chunks and I sink into them now, feeling them hold me gently and firmly. The steering wheel adjusts in and out and up and down. The position Wallace has chosen is ideal. It faces you low and at a reach where your moderately extended arms drop to it completely naturally. Your feet touch the pedals in a similarly comfy manner. You feel immediately at home; that the Countach is a cosy thing.

The instruments in the LP500 were wildly futuristic. They didn't work. The replacement dials are similar to those of the Lamborghini Jarama, housed in a flat, oblong binnacle that ensures they don't reflect in the windscreen. The minor controls are worked by column stalks, which, I note quizzically, are the same as a Morris Marina's.

LAMBORGHINI COUNTACH LP400 #1120001

The heater controls lie just under the right edge of the instrument binnacle. To the right of them are six tell-tale lights for indicators, air conditioning fan, lights, and systems failures. In the console, just ahead of the gearstick, are air conditioning outlets, the temperature controls, and then a neat row of rocker switches for the lights, the extra radiator fans, the air conditioning fan and dash lights. There is one extra button with a tell-tale worked into it near the middle of the dash. It's Bob's check for the braking system. The gearshift sits high on the big tunnel. Its throws are long, moving well away from you in the reverse, second and fourth planes. But the lever is mounted close enough for it not to be a problem.

Wallace comes striding back. ''Kay, let's go.' We drop into our twin tubs, and it begins in earnest. He blips the engine twice as it fires, plugs the gearlever back into first, brings out the clutch hard into the revs and we rocket up the hill into Italy. I watch the tach. Seven, seven, seven. There is a bend. We are into it very quickly in fourth. The power goes down hard and decisively as we scythe through its apex. There is none of the movement towards an oversteer attitude that you might expect in a mid-engined car. It sits flat, too. The bends keep coming now, and keep disappearing. We are putting them behind us fast and effortlessly. That is how it feels from the inside. From a car trying to keep up it may be a different matter.

Wallace comments that we have 100 miles of bad road, of trucks, tunnels and road-works. So we are held back to a tame 100mph cruise on the first part of the *autostrada* along the coast to Genoa. The traffic is heavy and the tunnels treacherous because you hit their gloom from bright sunlight and more than likely there's a truck just inside the entrance overtaking another. Wallace approaches steadily, sensibly, occasionally flipping down to third, ready for anything, keeping the car steady.

The pods in the stubby nose are up now and the yellow tell-tale on the dash for the air conditioning is joined by the green one for the lights, and another that winks to say the indicators are flashing as we sweep past the slower cars in the tunnels' murk. For 100 miles it is like this. Sometimes we need the air horns to make an inattentive driver wake up and scoot out of the way.

AND THE REVS KEEP RISING

When the road finally opens out and we are able to nudge up the speed, I study the view the passenger gets as the car devours the road – in particular, as we come, at 6000rpm in fourth, up behind an Alfa 1750. I am lying relaxed in my tub, my left arm resting on the big tunnel that's almost up to armpit height. My right arm flops on the suede doorsill. In front of my eyes are only my knees, a few inches of the flat black dashboard and then the road. The windscreen seemingly has nothing in front of it. And it is so wide. The pillars rake down from above your head at an angle that spears both forward and out to the edge of the road so that you feel that you're behind a glass blade sweeping down the grey tarmac. You imagine that you could shovel straight under the cars ahead. We could flip them over the top of us like toys. Instead, breaking my reverie, there is the quick, strong pull backwards as Wallace's foot goes firmly on the brake pedal. A blast of the air horns to move the Alfa over, to let the Lancia Beta ahead of it know we're going past him too, and we are back into the clear.

We run at 120–130mph for a while. A red Ferrari Daytona drifts past, seemingly in slow motion. I start to realise that these cars rewrite the way you sense speed. Now it's only a five-letter word. We watch the Daytona clipping along, slowly pulling away. Wallace does not try to catch it. He just admires it and we talk about what a fine car it is. The last of the classic front-engined GT cars, from a different era to the Countach. It doesn't seem to matter that even if the Ferrari driver were flat out at just over 170mph we should be able to catch, flash, and pass him. Bob just sits quietly in the inside lane, steady and ever sensible, focused on the traffic as we shoot through tunnel after tunnel again. For some time I've been watching a Rolls-Royce 'way up ahead. Then I see there is a second one just in front of it. When I comment, Wallace says: 'There always were two. The front one has Rome plates, the second one's a Torino car.' We are still some way behind them. I smile: Bob's cool, unblinking eyes just go on watching the road.

His long, thin arm with the bony hand reaches out for the gearstick. The fingers wrap slowly, familiarly, around the palm-sized black leather knob and pull it back. Fifth. The movement is like all the other changes: never hurried; just a firm, positive movement. It's the same with the down changes. If you aren't watching the hand, the only indication is the change in engine note. The progress of the car is as smooth and relentless as ever. Relaxing. So this is the realm of the cutting-edge supercar, in the hands of its maker.

Just before Genoa, the traffic bunches, crawls, halts. We are caught in a jam for an hour. We have to push the doors open every time we're stationary because the sun is roasting us through the big windscreen, there is no insulation to counter the engine heat and the air conditioning can't cope. Bob knows the air conditioning will need to be a lot better for the production cars. But while *we're* hot, the engine is unruffled. The temperature gauge needle does not move. The twin side-mounted radiators, fed by the big ducts behind the side windows, do their job well. If the car doesn't overheat here, it never will. Again in this traffic I admire its flexibility.

One hundred miles later I'm admiring the other end of its performance scale. We have cleared the snarl and the trucks and the tunnels and are on the clear home stretch. We are sitting on 6500rpm in fifth. Bob slackens off to 6000rpm while he checks the road shimmering in the heat ahead. It's okay, and his foot goes down again and the surge forward is so strong you'd swear you were in second or third. He levels off again at 6500 and holds it for some time. I don't know exactly what speed we're doing. Clearly, we are getting along very well but the speedo isn't working. It is only later, when I work out that the car is geared for 308km/h at 7800rpm with the present diff, which means 39.5km/h/1000rpm, which at 6500rpm is 257km/h, which is 160mph. Without the speedo you wouldn't know.

I start thinking about why it seems so uneventful. I'm flopping back in my seat, occasionally making notes on the pad beside me on the suede sill while the tacho is still on 6500rpm. The noise has been long forgotten. After a while you don't notice it. And there is no wind noise. They key is the stability; the tremendous feeling of security even on the bumpy *autostrada*.

I ask Wallace if he's happy with the ride. He answers with his usual brevity: 'We haven't set it up yet. Haven't touched the spring or shocker rates so far.'

I say, surprised: 'The chassis must have been spot-on from the word go then?'

'It was pretty good,' Bob says. 'We had to change a few angles, that's all. Now we are about to work on the shocker and spring rates to remove that low-speed harshness and thumping.'

'Will the high speed ride stay the same then?'

'Oh yes. May get fractionally better.'

That's something to contemplate. It feels so secure already. Firm, but not too firm, always flat, the body just moving up and down over the bumps in a nicely controlled motion.

Then: at 120mph, just as we are lining up to pass a flatbed truck, it darts out to overtake a Fiat 500. The truck driver hasn't seen us and we've got nowhere to go! Bob jams his foot on the brakes and holds them at the point of lock-up, keeping us straight with tiny wheel corrections. The red nose edges deep under the tail of the truck until I'm looking up at the boards of its tray. We're so far under that, when the speeds match, our nose is almost beneath the truck's diff. Then Bob slowly and deliberately selects second and, as the truck starts to pull over, we surge clear. Through it all, the nose barely dips even though the braking force is pulling me forward almost out of my seat.

'The nose doesn't drop much, Bob,' I say in a little while. 'Is there much anti-dive in the geometry?'

'Oh, a little bit. But it's coming out. It's giving some bump steer. You can't have bump steer in a road car.' He shakes his head and grimaces.

Thinking about being beneath the tray of that truck and looking at the super-thin A-pillars a few inches from my head – our only protection – I ask: 'Do you fill the pillars with anything, for strength?'

'Actually, they're tubular, part of a roll bar structure around the entire cockpit.' I look. It is unobtrusive, hidden in the pillars and the roof edge and covered in the black suede. What about the two little handles sunk into the front and rear of the doors? Bob says: 'If

LAMBORGHINI COUNTACH LP400 #1120001

the car happened to roll over, preventing the doors from opening, you pull these handles and the doors fly off.'

A mile or so later he says: 'It's a pity you're riding in the car without its sound and heat insulation. But there's no point us putting it in while we're working on the car and having to pull it out every five minutes. So it's noisy and your arse gets pretty hot. We insulated it once, and it was pretty good, so we know it's not a problem.

'This car, the way the Countach will go into production, is completely different from the first car, the LP500. That had an integral floor pan chassis, different suspension, gearbox and engine.

'We'll do more work on the engine too. This one is close to how the production V12 will be but it only has 340lb/ft at 5000rpm and 340bhp at 7400rpm at the moment. The plan is to alter the torque and power curves to give nearer to 400bhp at 8200rpm. We'll lower the diff ratio slightly to aim for a top speed of 308km/h (191mph), which this engine can't reach with the present diff.'

'Is the car much less stable at that speed, Bob?'

'No,' and he has one hand off the wheel adjusting his sunglasses at 150mph as he speaks. 'It doesn't go all light or anything; doesn't move about. It feels very close to the way it does at this speed. It's pretty good, really.'

'Does it feel as small to you, driving at this pace, as it does to me sitting here?'

'Yes, small and manageable. That's one of the things we wanted to achieve.'

Near the end of the *autostrada* we strike a few long bends: curves at lower speeds, bends at this rate. And when we leave the motorway for the final run into Modena we hit many more corners. Down two, three gears and through them. And the Countach, as I began to suspect soon after we left Menton, seems to introduce a new dimension in handling. The thing that strikes you is the lack of the 'tightening up' effect you can feel in other current mid-engined cars, the prelude to an oversteer attitude. I'd expected to get it very much in the Countach.

But it doesn't seem to happen. Neutrality, grip and flatness seem

AND THE REVS KEEP RISING

to have a new level. I ask Wallace what it's like at really potent speeds. 'I'm not driving it hard now,' he says. 'But it really does stay neutral until you hit a pretty fast pace. And then the transition to oversteer is gradual anyway. At least it's safe and predictable.'

Into Modena, trundling back through town and watching people staring again – even in Modena they stare hard at the Countach – Wallace outlines the work still to be done. Where to relocate the cabin air outlet vents is a major problem. The cabin is going to be enlarged too, the firewall moved back a little, the footwells lengthened and the tunnel and sills slimmed down. These 'clap hands' wipers, which lift off above 120mph, will be ditched for a parallelogram sweeper. The final engine tune and suspension settings will be configured.

Soon Wallace is dropping me at my hotel, quickly hefting my gear from the boot and blasting off up the street. The Genoa traffic jam has made him an hour or more late. It's another hour out of the development schedule and he won't like that; he'll work on far into the night now. I stand and watch the Countach as it goes. Listen to it. The Miura stopped people in their tracks. This is something else again.

'MR FERRARI IS WAITING TO SEE YOU'

MARANELLO

1973

THE DOOR OPENED ONTO a long room. Enzo Ferrari sat at the far end, reading. It seemed such a deep, narrow room, and very bare – an unusual office. Or was it simply that the figure against the far wall drew my attention so completely that I lost perspective?

He looked older than even recent photographs had suggested. The familiar craggy features were drawn and frail. I saw with a start that the years – 75 – and recent illness were taking their toll. Only his eyes were untouched, and they peered fixedly down the long room to me.

They were hard, frightening eyes that glared pride and defiance. The eyes of a rugged old eagle watching an intruder entering his domain. They made you question your own confidence, even at that distance.

The shoulders were a little stooped as he leaned over his long desk. But the stoop, common to big men who are growing old, could not hide the elegant bearing of the man. The rock-steady eyes were not yet alone in their pride.

He began to rise as I moved into his room. Without the eyes moving from me, he pulled open a desk drawer and slid into it the magazine he'd been reading. Then he reached his full height and I saw how clearly his stature was fighting the years. He was still an impressive cut of a man. I reached his desk and stepped around the end of it to where he was waiting. Enzo Ferrari took my hand and his grip was as rock-hard as I now expected it to be. He pointed to the chair he wanted me to sit in, and we started to talk.

AND THE REVS KEEP RISING

The Ferrari factory is on the northern edge of the village of Maranello, and you go there from Modena, the bustling town where the main street, the Via Emilia, is as straight and true as it was when the Romans built it.

But visiting Ferrari is never straightforward. It usually takes several days of arranging and rearranging times, and getting the final go-ahead is rather like sitting around in a fighter-squadron mess hall waiting for the order to scramble. I got my go-ahead on the telephone in my hotel in Modena at 10 on a Tuesday morning. 'Come at four this afternoon,' said Dottore Franco Gozzi, Enzo Ferrari's public relations man and personal assistant.

There was weak sun as I drove the 20 kilometres south to Maranello, past streams of cyclists rhythmically pumping their way home. The road was flat and curving, passing through three or four villages and the tiny cheek-by-jowl farms that pack this part of Italy. At last Maranello, and there, at the end of the long straight into town, was a giant black prancing horse kicking boldly against its yellow background.

But that sign belongs to the Ristorante Cavallino, not the Ferrari factory. The real thing is across the road, marked by two much smaller signs on the fence either side of the main gates, and the single word 'Ferrari' on a building a few metres back from the entrance. I parked the Fiat 124 Sport in the restaurant's garden, crossed the road and stood bewildered outside the tall and green slatted-iron gates. They were shut tight and there was no-one about. No small side entrance open either. Presently, I caught the eye of a watchman in the building nearest the fence. He strode out, a grave look on his face, and I was afraid he was going to tell me to go away. A passage from Enzo Ferrari's memoir, *My Terrible Joys,* sprang into my mind:

'There is a constant stream of visitors. They arrive in coaches, by car and on scooters. We find them a big problem because they are distracting to the workmen and they take up the time of staff members who have to be detailed to act as guides. The only visits that I consider really worthwhile are those of engineering students from the universities or technical colleges, since what they see will be useful to them.'

MARANELLO

A side gate a few paces from me opened electrically and the watchman asked whom I wished to see. Dottore Gozzi, I told him and he said *si, si* and *uno momento* and I filled out the form saying who I was and why I was there. And then Franco Gozzi came into the gatehouse and took my arm and led me inside Ferrari.

There is nothing visually inspiring about the factory. It was built after industrial decentralisation was ordered in Italy in 1943, and Ferrari was forced to move out of his beloved Modena. He chose the unknown village of Maranello because it was close and he owned some agricultural land there. He had 40 people working for him and he set up the factory to make hydraulic grinding machines for the Italian war effort. The new plant was bombed twice; and then it was all over and Ferrari could drop the machine-making like a rock and draw up plans for motor cars: the first cars to carry his own name. Those that he'd run in his first 20 years as a racer and team manager had all been for Alfa Romeo.

Ferrari rebuilt the plant in 1946. Its construction is simple in the extreme. The brick administrative offices are neat but unpretentious. The factory buildings running out from them are efficient but shabby in parts. There are some broken windows and old odds and ends laying about outside, though the Fiat broom has swept many of them away. It is as if no-one worries too much about appearances; the focus is all on the building of cars. From the inside the factory is as unassuming as from the outside; an expression of Ferrari himself:

'I made no application to retain my title after the war, and am thus no longer a commendatore. Neither am I a commander, as I am sometimes called by foreigners. Others appear to think I should be addressed as ingegnere or cavaliere, but I prefer to be called simply Ferrari.'

The office of Dottore Gozzi did not have the anticipated plushness. It appeared once to have been a work or storage room; square, tall and drab, except that the walls housed a treasure trove of history from 27 years of motor racing. There were posters from famous races, scores of books, and groups of photographs with famous signatures

AND THE REVS KEEP RISING

scrawled across them. On one shelf was a melon-sized rock scuffed with red paint: the rock Jacky Ickx hit and which sent him crashing out of the 1973 Targa Florio. Franco picked it up and laughed.

From his office we went across into another bank of buildings near to the gate; through an office-like section and another door to emerge suddenly into a workshop of meticulous cleanliness and with an air of peace and stillness. There were two 365 GTB/4 Daytonas in there. One was on stands, wheels off, having a little chin spoiler tacked under its nose. Another, yellow and red with a stripe of Italy's tri-colours dividing the two, was beside it. It was almost ready to go. Like the first car, its wheel arches had been flared, but it still had its standard road wheels and not the fat racing replacements that would soon go on. Perspex covered its now-fixed headlights and twin megaphones leered out from under each flank. Inside each was a roll cage. The cars were the playthings of two very rich customers. They had asked the factory to prepare them for racing, and a handful of dedicated grey-coated men were doing just that.

Franco Gozzi led on through another series of doors and into the gloom of the foundry. The sight of so much fresh alloy was breathtaking. Gleaming and virginal, hot from the moulds it shone through the gloom. A pair of blocks stood end-up at my feet, waiting to be machined in the next phase of the creation of a 352bhp 4.4-litre V12. Beyond them grew a stack of 11 webbed and finned gearbox and diff housings for Daytonas. Against a wall leaned two long cylinder heads. Further over again was a pile, as high as my shoulders and as wide as the average family garage, of gearbox cases and diffs and sumps and pumps and blocks. Around them all a little old man was quietly sweeping. The day's work was almost over.

We went out into the light, and sitting there was the beat-up prototype Berlinetta Boxer. The very first one, its grey paint tatty now and chipped, scratched and knocked. How well it had done its job, pounding around the test track, up and down the *autostrada* and through the Futa Pass. Like the factory, it was used and battered. I climbed inside and saw the wear and smelt the sweat.

MARANELLO

Gozzi broke my idyll, beckoning me from the BB and across the yard. We rounded a long building and he introduced me to a dark and handsome young man named Paolo Guidetti.

Paolo was a test driver. Gozzi was acceding to a request I had made in his office; I wanted to go out with one of the test drivers. I glanced about as innocuously as I could, but there was no car in sight. I wondered what model it would be. A Boxer, perhaps? No – it was metallic blue 365 GT/4 2+2 that came out of a nearby doorway and drew alongside us. We settled in, Paolo snicked the gearstick forward into first and we moved off, through the back gate and up the road alongside the rear wall, through the village centre, and out onto the road up into the hills:

'I am much attached to this district where I was born – deeply emotionally attached to it. For tragic reasons connected with the destiny of my family, this is especially the case today. I worked in other places that had much more to offer than my birthplace, with its winter fogs and summer heat, its lack of any lake or seashore, with only a distant line of hills to break up flatness and the monotony. But I do not know whether I should have been able to achieve so much had I not returned.'

We ran quietly and smoothly for five or six minutes, clearing the village and the bikes. When the road was clear the speed crept up and up. As usual in a car like this, I didn't notice the pace. Insulated from the stationary world, and the world of ordinary cars, it was fun to try guessing the speed without peeking at the speedometer.

After cresting a hill we rushed flat in third down through a series of curves. But then the slow tail of a truck blocked the way, and we had to brake strong and hard and Paolo blipped back to second. For a few moments he steadied the car behind the truck on the V12's compression until I could tell him that the road was clear to pass (it was a right-hand drive car for England and he could not see to overtake easily).

As the power went down the car surged silkily forward. Not thrusting ahead like the lighter and more powerful Daytona, or the Boxer, but feeling exactly the car it was intended to be: a smooth, quiet and relaxing four seater still able to display flair and excitement:

'I don't know what will become of my works after I die, but to my successor I bequeath a very simple inheritance: to keep alive that constant striving after progress that was pursued in the past. I consider myself merely a builder of motor cars and am not cut out to be a large-scale manufacturer. The demands of mass-production are contrary to my temperament for I am mainly interested in promoting new developments. I should like to put something new into my cars every morning.'

As the engine ran right out in second and Paolo went into third, the tail dipping again and the four fat pipes cackling, two cyclists way up ahead swung off the road and turned around to look. They stood quietly and watched us sweep by, going now into fourth and once more settling back down to our relaxed and steady cruise somewhere well above 110mph. Paolo's smooth, capable hands guided the car gently through the bends. He shuffled the leather-bound wheel in practised, unflustered style with his grip low on the rim. The gear changes he made quickly, and they bit quickly, and the hand would glide back to the wheel. The car flowed on. Inside, there was an air of serenity, despite the speed.

The feeling through the bends was delicious. The tail would nudge out into an oversteer attitude as the power went on at the apex, demonstrating balance and responsiveness. We flew into a tight but visually open left-hand bend. Paolo swung the wheel early and one-handed. Raising his eyes and turning his head back to the right, he gazed half a mile ahead. *Yes*: the road was clear through the next few bends and he could commit the car fully to its line and bring on the power. The tail obeyed the throttle again and edged into its oversteer attitude.

The hands rested lightly on the wheel, feeling its messages. When the right answer was there, the foot took over and the balance was maintained by the throttle. It was the fine balance of a good car, well-driven.

Back at the factory I asked how Paolo thought the GT/4 compared with the 365 GTC/4. 'A much better car,' he said gesticulating. 'Better handling and roadholding and excellent balance. A fine car, this one.' Franco Gozzi chipped in that it was one of the new generation of Ferraris benefiting from the new design, development and production efficiency Fiat's involvement was bringing to Maranello. Franco then took me over to the big, bright and airy buildings that housed the production lines and I saw rows and rows of Daytona and Dino bodies, with occasional 365 GT/4 2+2s sprinkled among them.

The bodies, coming completed from Scaglietti in Modena for the Daytona and Dino, and from Pininfarina in Turin for the GT/4 2+2s, rested, wheel-less, on trolleys. The *carrozzerie* had built the bodies from chassis to final trim, and they had come on trucks to Maranello to have their engines, gearboxes, diffs and transmissions fitted.

There was an atmosphere of calm in the assembly plant, almost as if it wasn't a factory at all, but rather a giant storage room of sleek and glistening shapes. The reason for this contrast with the clatter and hustle of ordinary mass-production lines was the way the men worked, and the way the cars are put together. Alone or in groups of two or three, men leaned over, in or under the cars, fitting and bolting up the components.

It was more hectic in the machine room. On the floor were the revered billets of steel ready to be carved into crankshafts. As always, they had been left lying until their molecular structure had stabilised to eliminate the chance of faults later. Up and down the length of the shop were all the components of the V6, V12 and flat-12 engines, the steel or the alloy gleaming like mirrors now the machines had honed away the rough edges. As we moved away, I saw an awesome sight: rows of V12s, with downdraught Webers for the Daytonas and side-draughts for the GT/4. They were complete to the last shiny cam cover nut, and ready to go onto the test benches for final testing and running in:

'I had always liked the song of 12 cylinders; what is more, I must confess that the fact that in 1946 there was only one firm in the world – Packard – making such engines acted on me as a challenge and a spur. A few

AND THE REVS KEEP RISING

years later Packard abandoned their 12-cylinder engine and I was the only one making them. I came in for a deal of criticism; it was forecast that I was bringing about my own downfall, the experiment being judged too daring and presumptuous. There are initial difficulties with every new engine; but I never doubted we would win through both because I had faith in Giaocchino Colombo's design ability and because I again had the trusty Luigi Bazzi (both of whom had been at Alfa Romeo) with me and I knew I could rely on his skill in dealing with engines.

'That 12-cylinder was the ancestor of all Ferrari engines. There have been other smaller and bigger versions of it, but that first 1.5-litre example designed by Colombo is still recognisable in all its progeny.'

Franco Gozzi glanced at his watch and asked where my car was parked. Across the road in the ristorante's yard, I told him. We went to it and drove the half-mile or so to the Fiorano test track that Ferrari built in 1971. It is on the land surrounding the country house he bought so many years ago, and the £350,000 it cost to build the track came from his own money, not Fiat's.

The track's corners are replicas of some of the most famous and difficult bends from the Grand Prix circuits – here a corner from the Nürburgring, here a piece of Zandvoort, now a section of Monza. Electronic timing devices divide it up so that a driver's time can be analysed on each section. Ten TV cameras watch the cars perform, and feed the bank of closed-circuit screens in the control centre.

For Enzo Ferrari, it is a hobby as much as a technical necessity. He goes there and watches his drivers and his cars taking the corners and he checks their mistakes on the TV monitors. If there are any doubts it is all on video tape. 'It would have been madness to have gone on relying on the naked eye, especially when the eye has caught cold from being naked so long,' he said in one of those word-pictures that make his speech vivacious.

Fiorano was quiet as we went in; the day's testing had ended. So I drove around it with Franco urging me on and hanging on tight. It's a difficult circuit to learn. The corners are tricky, tightening up when you think they are going to open out and testing both car and driver. The Fiat managed quite well.

MARANELLO

At the factory again, Franco led me now to the engine test cells. In one, a new 3.0-litre Formula One engine had just been bolted down and an engineer was about to fire it up. He was running it in. It would be on the bed for 22 hours, like all Ferrari engines. Completing his preliminaries, the engineer turned on the switches and cranked the engine over. There was the high-pitched scream, and then the furious explosion as the 12 horizontally-opposed cylinders snarled into life. They were virginal no more, and they bellowed their anger. Running at low revs, the noise was like the staccato firing of light but savage cannon. But then, as the young engineer jerked the revs up it suddenly flattened out and over 5000rpm the noise blended into one prolonged roar as the thing began climbing onto its cams. And then came that furious Ferrari howl that you can always pick out even among a packed field of F1 cars. Somehow the Maranello engine is just that little bit louder and more ferocious than the Ford DFVs and BRM's V12.

The engineer, unafraid of the noise like me, bent over his charge and listened and then pulled again on the throttle. The read-out digits flickered and changed constantly as he took the tight and reluctant engine up and up. It showed 7544 for an instant; climbed again; levelled out at a neat 8000rpm for a few moments. Then he tugged again with a hefty blip and the engine argued back like a wounded bear. But the dial immediately showed 9672rpm. He dropped back to a steady 9300 and held it there... before kicking it again, and getting a little over 11,000rpm. Back down to eight; back up to nine, onto 11 for an instant, back down to eight. Then up to 11, hold it, drop it, blip it again. The brake was giving the readings he wanted, and the engine sounded healthy as a bull. Before it left the bed it would be giving 490bhp at 12,600rpm and would have been run to its limit of 13,000rpm. For engine and engineer it was going to be a long night.

When it was switched off for a few moments for adjustments, suddenly bringing ringing silence, we talked about the origins of it all. Ferrari had started with Alfa as a driver in 1920. Within a few years he was running the works team. Ten years later, Alfa decided to withdraw from racing and Ferrari bought the cars to form his own Scuderia Ferrari. Alfa supported him because they believed Scuderia Ferrari could keep their name to the fore although they did not wish to race themselves. Ferrari brought Alfa considerable success but in 1939 he broke with them, determined to return to Modena and build and race his own cars. In 1941 he built two cars but, because his contract with Alfa Romeo forbade him from racing activities for four years after he left them, he could not call them Ferraris. They were named simply 815s, and were handsome cars containing a lot of Fiat materials and using an eight cylinder 1.5-litre engine.

Ferrari couldn't make more cars during World War Two but continued to work on designs. The moment the war finished he was ready to start making them, with the assistance of Luigi Bazzi and Gioacchino Colombo who had joined him from Alfa Romeo. The first overall design was ready in 1946 and the car finished in May 1947. In its first race it was leading with only two laps to go... and then the fuel pump seized. But only a little while later the car won at Rome, and then gave the racing world a hint of things to come when it won the Turin Grand Prix. For Enzo, it was a poignant moment:

'I had applied to Fiat for a job and been turned down. Fiat was not a sufficiently big concern to be able to take on all ex-servicemen who were applying for jobs. It was the winter of 1918–19 and, I well remember, a very cold one. I found myself out in the street, my clothes feeling as though they were freezing to me. Crossing Turin's Valentine Park, I brushed the snow off a bench and sat down. I was alone, my father and brother were no more. Overcome by loneliness and despair, I wept. Many years later, in 1947 after Raymond Sommer had won the first post-war Turin Grand Prix with the 12-cylinder Ferrari, I went and sat on that same bench. The tears I shed that day, though, were of a very different kind.'

The engine started up again, the engineer bent to his task and we walked on, into the hallowed racing department. It's a strange place, in a way, housed in a very long but narrow section. But it's light and airy-feeling, with windows lining its outer wall. The cars to be worked on are strung-out, Indian-file, down it on stands or calibrated work benches and jigs. At first there isn't the myriad of equipment you might expect to see. But when you wander around, it is all there, either down the centre row with the cars or in the numerous little bays that run off the shop. The whole area has a sense of clinical cleanliness.

There was more urgency there than in the other parts of the plant, but still no great hustle and bustle. Instead, I was brought to silence by the obvious dedication and seriousness of the men working there, my footsteps slowing and lightening with reverence, though it is said that the dedication of the men and the efficiency of the department is no longer so intense as in pre-Fiat days. But the production capabilities weren't so good then:

'In Modena, there is a species of psychosis for racing cars that will eventually evolve into habits and create a breed of its own. Not only my own workshops are responsible for this, but also those of the other firms. The worker in these parts, whether of muscle or of mind', is extremely intelligent and very active. What is more, the people here are by nature of a rebellious character – they are not easy-going folk. In short, the union of blood and brain is such that the result is a type of man who is stubborn, capable and daring – the very qualities that are needed for making cars.'

Gozzi had reached the other end of the long racing department well before I had gone half-way down through the machines and the cars and the men. I looked up and caught sight of him across a prototype chassis. He beckoned and held open a door. Strange to be leaving so quickly I thought, when this is one of the most interesting parts of the plant.

We must hurry now,' said Franco – and spoke the words I will never forget: *'Mr Ferrari is waiting to see you*. He can spare you a few minutes.'

At the wing that holds Ferrari's office, there are two doors. The first admits you to a small antechamber where his personal attendant lurks, waiting upon Ferrari's every command. The second is a big wooden door that seems rather foreboding, creating a sense of

AND THE REVS KEEP RISING

anticipation. Gozzi stepped up to it and tapped twice. He waited for the answer from somewhere deep beyond it, and for a further polite moment, then reached in front of me and turned the handle.

The door swung back and there he was, the craggy figure at the end of the long room. As I reached him and held out my hand to his steely grip, a brief smile of welcome played on his thin lips. 'Buona sera,' he said and waved me to the chair across at the left side of his desk. Franco sat on the right.

The big desk was clean, now that the first of the week's motor racing magazines had been swept off it and into the top drawer. If Enzo Ferrari had had a trying day, there was no trace of it. He sat between his desk and the back wall of his office. The left-hand side of the desk merged into bookcases and shelves lining the wall near where I sat. Along the shelf, and placed easily at Ferrari's left side, was an electric control panel. With this panel, he controls his works with his fingertips.

I sat before him somewhat uneasily. The overbearing pride and confidence of the man – and his reputation – made me feel I should choose my words very carefully. One look at his face showed he was not a man who brooked fools or cared to have his time wasted. As I pondered this, and the seconds of silence seemed like agonising minutes, the old man regarded me almost quizzically through the dark glasses he had slipped on as he sat down. The famous dark glasses that let through just enough light to reveal his stony eyes. Eyes that took in everything, to be weighed up with judgement conditioned by experience.

'Signor Ferrari,' I asked, remembering him saying that his favourite car was the one he had not yet built, 'How disappointing is it to you that you may not be able to build a faster successor to the Boxer?'

The message was clearly evident in his reply. He said he held little regard for the American design regulations that were threatening to stop development of cars like the Boxer. They were the source of death of enjoyable motoring and inspiring engineering. Pollution had been blamed on the car and laws were clapped down on it before it was really proven that they were necessary. The same with many of

MARANELLO

the so-called safety rulings. It was only leading to bigger engines – five or six litres instead of four litres – to make up for the power loss, and for cars that were tanks rather than automobiles.

We talked backwards and forwards on the point for a few minutes, Gozzi translating and Ferrari sitting with his hands clasped and resting easily on the edge of his desk and fixing me solidly through his glasses as he waited for the translation to end. His disdain for the path fast cars were being forced to follow shone out in his eyes as well as in his speech. He gave the impression that he was able mentally to wash his hands of the situation and rest on the memories of the cars he had created in days free from restrictions. With the BB, he had done that anyway by refusing to attempt to meet the American design. If the Americans now weren't able to drive it, he said, then that was too bad for them.

Suddenly, Ferrari reached over and pressed one of the buttons on his control panel. In came the attendant from the antechamber. Ferrari leaned across to one side and spoke to the man in a voice of such sudden gruffness that it startled me. The man hurried off, and Ferrari turned back to me with a thin grin and continued. No, he said, he had no plans to retire completely. He was in a semi-retirement that allowed him ample free time. He was happy and feeling well. He would hope, as he had said many times, to work on until the end.

The attendant came back with something I couldn't see. Whatever it was, it was not what Ferrari wanted and he snarled at the man with a wrath that sent a further shiver up my spine. The man hurried away, and this time when he returned Ferrari took the thing sharply and passed it across his desk to me with a faint but warm smile creasing his rugged old face. There was a polystyrene box, about nine inches square and three inches thick. Still uneasy from the lashing the attendant had caught, I dared not look. Later – the moment I was outside – I saw it was a very large ashtray, yellow, with the rampant horse proud in its centre:

'The story of the rampant horse that I use as my trademark is a simple and fascinating one. The emblem was emblazoned on the fighter plane

of Francesco Baracca, the ace of WW1, who was shot down at Montello. In 1923 I made the acquaintance of Count Enrico Baracca, the hero's father; as a result I was subsequently introduced to the ace's mother who one day said to me: "Ferrari, why don't you put my son's rampant horse on your car? It will bring you luck."

I still have Baracca's photograph, with his parents' dedication in which they entrust the horse to me. The horse was, and has remained, black, while I added the gold field, the colour of Modena.'

I had not expected gifts, and there was a glint of interested pleasure in Enzo's eyes as he watched me tuck the ashtray at my side. Then we began to talk again. I approached the subject of racing carefully. The 1973 F1 season had been bad for Ferrari. It had not gone well with the Grand Prix cars, he agreed. But their performance had to be measured against the Ferrari victories of 27 years. Failure was a temporary thing and would not endure for long. Work and experience would see to that.

Who did he see as the most promising young driver? Was there someone on the way up with the potential to be a great? Ferrari hesitated a moment, and his expression did not warm nor his eyes flicker. Racing's greats had been his friends, and he had been their mentor:

'To the last, Tazio Nuvolari's technique remained a supreme demonstration of skill carried to the very bounds of human achievement and the laws of balance and momentum. Indeed, in all my years of racing experience I have seen it equalled only by one other driver, Stirling Moss.'

The stony look said that a newcomer was not going to get an ounce of the reserved reverence unless Ferrari felt it was justified. 'Perhaps,' he said after a while, 'there might be one. The South African, Jody Scheckter. If he learns to control his ambition so that it does not kill him, he could be very, very good. He has the most important ingredient – he is young.'

Just then Ferrari seemed to have something cross his mind. He reached again for the control button. The man hurried in, Ferrari spoke gruffly to him again and he came back with a big yellow book with the black horse on the cover and the title *'Enzo Ferrari, le briglie del successo'* – the reins of success. I knew what he was going to do, and I watched with gratitude as he swung the book open to its fly page and there signed his name in the venerated purple ink.

His mouth cracked into a ragged grin as he handed it to me and saw my delight. I put it down beside the ashtray. It was in Italian, a limited edition he had had printed in 1970 and not for sale. It was an updated version of *My Terrible Joys* (published by Hamilton in 1963.)

My next question had been side-tracked, and Dr Gozzi chipped in. The subject switched back to racing, and eventually to the sad discontinuation of the Targa Florio. Ah, said Ferrari, grinning widely and nodding with satisfaction – the Targa Florio! What a race! It was a race as he had known racing when he began driving. A race on roads and of skill and bravery and endurance, 44 miles through the Sicilian mountains. Ferrari first drove there, and came ninth, in 1919:

'In my first year of racing I was put to a decisive test as a driver in the Targa Florio. My team-mate and I left Milan for Sicily, driving down the length of Italy in the same CMN car with which we were to race. In the Abruzzi mountains we found ourselves in a blizzard and facing a risk we had never bargained for: we were chased by wolves! They were put to flight, however, by shots from the revolver which I always kept under the seat cushion.'

Ferrari laughed with knowing as I talked about the unforgettable memory of seeing his 460bhp prototypes roaring by the donkeys and the chickens and the peasants as they rushed around the circuit in the two full days of practice. Ferrari, still grinning, fetched out a copy of the Italian racing magazine *Autosprint* and opened it to a picture spread of the '73 Targa, run a couple of weeks earlier. He laid it out on his desk and we all leaned over it with him as he chuckled at the pictures of the Porsche Carrera RSRs, Alfa Type 33TTs and his 312PBs storming through the crowds, cheering unprotected, mere feet from their wheels.

AND THE REVS KEEP RISING

Ferrari said: 'The motorsport authorities must have a fit when they see things like that – not a barrier in sight. A real race that. The only proper race left in Italy. But of course Sicily is not really Italy. It's more of an Arab country.' In the light of that, I decided to ask if he'd heard the joke doing the rounds at the Targa that Sicily was the only Arab country yet to declare war on Israel. I looked at him with a hopeful grin while Gozzi translated. Then he lolled back in his chair and laughed hard, jiggling with mirth.

I caught Franco's eye and saw that it was an appropriate time to leave. I picked up my things and started to rise. Ferrari came up out of his chair, still chuckling, extended his big firm hand and said *arrividerci.* I bade him good evening and went.

At the door I looked back and saw him sit and return to the magazine. It was seven in the evening but I knew he would not leave until we were long gone. He would wait, as he does every night, until he is properly alone and then walk to the picture facing him from the wall. A lamp with three bulbs, in the red, white and green of the Italian flag, burns incessantly in front of the picture to light the face of Ferrari's son, Alfredo.

Dino died, just 24, in 1956 after suffering from muscular dystrophy. Everything Ferrari has done since has been dedicated to his memory. *'I am convinced,' Enzo once said, 'that the only total love in this world is that of a father for his son. I do not usher my visitors from my office first through politeness. It is just that I want to be the last one to look at Dino. I would be jealous if someone stayed in the room after I had gone out.'*

As the big wooden door closed behind me and I crossed the antechamber to go out into the evening air and back to Modena, I looked down at the yellow and black book, now adorned with the precious purple ink, that I held in my hands. In its introduction there is a passage that reads:

'My work has brought about some changes. Maranello for instance, was an unknown village; today it is many times bigger and there is a school which bears the name of my son. Along these straight roads, which I remember as dusty thoroughfares used by bullock carts, there today flash by strange, speeding shapes that are gone in an instant. So it is true that

MARANELLO

there have been changes. Have these been brought about, I sometimes ask myself, because I have at last realised my boyhood dreams? Have I done anything really worthwhile?

Many people know the answer to Enzo Ferrari's question: all those who have taken the best of his cars and driven them, properly, as he intended them to be driven. And watched them race.

TURNING ON TO THE TURBO
PORSCHE 911 TURBO
1974

LET ME TELL YOU about the Porsche 911 Turbo, the 3.0-litre car that blasts to 100mph in 12.8sec and has enough power its makers considered a five-speed gearbox superfluous. Let me tell you about this six-cylinder wonder that tops 160mph on low-octane fuel and takes 2+2 motoring into a realm previously attained only by the most exotic two-seaters. Should I mention also that it comes with a 20,000-mile warranty, requires servicing but once a year and can apparently return 22mpg?

Comprehending the Turbo's acceleration – it is to the 'ordinary' Carrera what that car is to the 911 – is taxing enough. The extra knowledge that, on the other hand, your wife could drive the kids to school in it because it's so flexible it will pull from 500rpm in top gear, calls for another round of head shaking. But then, turbocharging is the magic word. The thought of a road car with the devilish little blower causes people to suck in their breath in anticipation, mostly a result of the giant-killing successes of turbocharged cars in race series like Can-Am. Turbocharging has built up an aura of invincibility.

On the roads, it has transformed Ford Capris, Granadas and Opel Mantas turned out by Ralph Broad. It has turned BMW's 2.0-litre 2002 – the first production turbocharged car – into a bombshell. Now it has made Porsche's 911 into a supercar, bringing eager clients knocking impatiently at Stuttgart's door.

The Turbo looks the part. Its body is essentially the Carrera shell, but the wheel arches are wider and there is a different spoiler system edged in rubber at the nose. The rear spoiler is the big flat one, also tipped in soft rubber, from the Carrera 3.0-litre. Because this spoiler is so large, because the wheels and the arches are so obese, because the car hunches low over its tyres, it looks like a racer that's escaped to the road. It is mean, aggressive and declares its intention bluntly. On the road, other drivers can't get out of its way quickly enough.

The impact bumpers, fitted with recoil shock absorbers so that after a 5mph impact they'll spring back as if nothing happened, are standard. Hella's new high-power washers jut from the front bumper to clean the lights, and the familiar wiper is there on the rear window. Chassis changes are what you might expect. Spacers widen the front track 2in over the standard 911's and almost 6in at the rear. The front forged alloy wheels are an inch wider at 7 x 15 and the rears are up by 2in to 8 x 15. Front tyres are 185/70VR and the back ones 215/60VR. The torsion bars providing the springing have been uprated, the shockers are gas-filled Bilsteins and the anti-roll bars are much stiffer. Peer through the black wheel spokes and you'll see that the four brake discs are drilled axially as well as being vented; they're from the racing Martini-Porsche. Weight of the Turbo, at 2514lb, is 144lb up on the standard 911 and Carrera – but the power-to-weight ratio is still a mean 9.6lb/bhp.

The six-cylinder horizontally-opposed air-cooled engine uses the same 70.4mm stroke as the 2.7, but a bigger 95mm bore takes its capacity up to 2992cc. Onto this SOHC (per bank) six goes a KKK turbocharger, used in conjunction with the Bosch K-Jetronic fuel injection system – the first time a turbocharger and continuous injection have been mated in a road car. Bosch's new contactless electronic distributor is there too. Compression ratio is 6.5:0, but since the turbo pumps air in at almost 12psi the end result is effectively much higher.

From this comes 260bhp at 5500rpm with 253lb/ft of torque from 4000 to 5000rpm. That flat torque curve is what makes the Turbo, on the road, remarkable. At just 1000rpm there is 130lb/ft and at 2000rpm that's risen to 174. At 2300rpm you've got more torque than the 2.7 Carrera develops at its peak, and it stays that way until the 6500rpm redline. The curve climbs rapidly until it flattens completely at 4000rpm, developing that meaty 253lb/ft and

AND THE REVS KEEP RISING

holding it until five grand. It doesn't drop off after that either: at the maximum 6500rpm there is almost 200lb/ft. Meanwhile the bhp curve has been climbing like a rocket. With such oomph, and a wide power band despite the relatively low redline, Porsche believed a five-speed gearbox would not be necessary. As it is, the internal gearbox ratios are very high. Third is overdriven at 0.89 and top is a very leggy 0.65:1, with compensation coming from a low 4.222:1 differential. The end result is still a long-legged 25.8mph/1000rpm. As for strength, Porsche's 2140cc turbocharged race cars develop 500bhp and more power can be gained from the 3.0-litre just by turning up the boost screw. Importantly, the Turbo's low emissions and impact safety mean that it is the only one of the ultimate supercars that can be sold in America at present. That fact alone makes it a very significant car.

The six fires easily, not with the normal sound of a Porsche but with a deep burble more akin to a V8. The sound is aggressive but not loud. Relative quiet, as well as lower emissions are a side benefit of turbocharging. The idle is even, there is no fuss. The injection looks after it all. Nick Faure, who drives the AFN Carrera 3.0-litre race car, is in the driver's seat. I'm beside him, and we've come to a place where we can drive this car properly. It is the Turbo from the Earls Court Motor Show, the only RHD prototype. We're in it two months ahead of production and so far as we know this is the first time a Turbo has been taken on the road by outsiders to be driven to its full potential.

We move off. The solid torque is noticeable, the engine's willingness to rev unmistakable. Nick isn't using more than modest throttle pressure, we're still talking cheerily and we don't seem to be accelerating hard; only moving at a pace that feels briskly natural in the car. But a glance at the speedo shows that already, as we drift easily into mid-range in third, we're doing well over 90mph. We have merely moved away just as one might do in a family car, using the available torque to bring smooth, steady and sustained performance but not wringing the engine out. That is what the Turbo is like.

It isn't frightening performance, quick and all as it is. You

PORSCHE 911 TURBO

can feel the quick thrust of the power but it is smooth and fairly progressive; not like the BMW 2002 Turbo which is meek until 4000rpm when the turbo comes on and thrusts the car forward as if a second engine has cut in. There's not that kind of peakiness in the Porsche although you certainly notice that the pull comes steadily faster after 3000rpm. There are, however, certain things that must be learnt. From 3000rpm onwards the turbocharger keeps boosting so that even without increased pressure on the throttle the car accelerates. It isn't strong acceleration within the Turbo's capabilities, but it's potent by normal standards. Understanding this self-acceleration and knowing how to adjust to it is the secret of driving the Turbo. You're constantly backing off.

Hard acceleration? The car dips its rounded tail low and you're pressed hard back into the seat. And then, if you look not out the windscreen but out the side windows at the guide posts or other traffic, you really do know that you're reaching 60mph in five seconds and 100mph in just 12.8sec. At 6500rpm, Porsche's recommended maximum – there is an electric cut-out hidden in the red zone – the gears give 49mph, 85 and 124. Porsche says only that the top speed is 'above 155mph'. I am to learn that's not wrong.

But for the moment we're caught in a village and Nick is checking that 'self-acceleration' again, still learning about it. 'Say you put it into second,' he explains, 'and drop back to 2000rpm. You then stroke the throttle very quietly and the thing builds up to 3500rpm without any further pressure, and then it *goes* of its own accord! See, I'm not putting any pressure on it at the moment, and it's just going faster and faster. It's surprising how quickly you adapt, though, and I think the only time it would really catch you out is on a very twisty road. Even a very good driver could be tricked then. Say you're at 2500rpm in second, halfway through a bend with the revs building up. You hit 3500rpm and the power *really* comes on and you're caught in bloody big oversteer. You have to develop a technique where you back off at the right moment, instead of powering on, to achieve the same cornering balance as in an ordinary car.'

He grins: 'I learnt last night that on a greasy road the tail can

AND THE REVS KEEP RISING

come around frighteningly fast. Mind you, it comes back very nicely. But you have to be bloody quick – and that's by race standards! I drove it over a road where I regularly drive the Carrera hard. It's so much quicker than even that one, and very much more demanding because of the intricacies of the throttle control.'

We're on a motorway now, unrestricted, and running at a tame 130mph. He can't resist a gentle squeeze on the throttle. The car responds instantly, surging silkily forward, letting us feel the power in the small of the back. It wants to keep on going, and a concerted lift-off is needed. But then, stuff it, we go all the way, the Turbo *hurling* itself forward, speeding on to 160mph before traffic blocks our path. Even Faure is impressed: the top gear acceleration is equal to third gear in his racing Carrera 3.0-litre, and that has a five-speed gearbox. From 100mph to 130mph the acceleration is potent because that corresponds to the peak point of the torque curve. Right now, our 160mph is a shade over 6000rpm, and there seems to be more to come. From the feel of it, the 6500rpm redline should be obtainable, and that's 168mph. I wouldn't be surprised if owners find such figures registering on their dials.

The car is steady. Faure backs off totally and it doesn't budge. To reach this speed, you've been through a range of noises – the faint whine of the turbocharger as the power comes on strong in the lower gears, the burble you'd swear was coming from a V8 on a light throttle at around 3500rpm, and the low, sustained rumble that steadily intensifies as the throttle goes down. It never intrudes, mind you, merely serves as a pleasing background. There is, however, wind noise around the window edges. It could become tiring on a long trip at high speed, but it isn't loud enough to prevent conversation. The motorway ride is exemplary. Even at town speeds it is excellent, feeling little firmer than in the standard 911, and never making a sound as it soaks up the bumps.

Off the *autobahn* now and in towards a village. Faure doesn't bother to change down, simply backs off from 140mph and comes down to a 25-mph trickle in top with only 1000rpm showing. We go up a hill like that and the car doesn't grumble. It makes only a very low, exaggerated sort of Porsche noise up through the gearstick.

PORSCHE 911 TURBO

Next stop and we move a few feet in first and then it's straight into top at 500rpm. Again, no complaints. It pulls away cleanly.

Then it's the road we've been seeking, a good A-road, and in a moment the Porsche is pressing through its curling bends at a steady 140mph. There is no body roll, no effort from the driver other than moving the wheel very slightly and adjusting the throttle minutely to guide the car gently onto the precise line, straight-lining them. I casually continue making notes. A competent saloon like an Alfetta, I should think, wouldn't have felt fussed along here at about 90; one of the big front-engined V12s at around 120mph. Only a Countach, BB, Bora or Pantera would do it like this.

We try the brakes, and Nick ends up backing off from a full crash stop in case the tyres flat spot. The discs do not fade. Then the bends come quicker and tighter, and sometimes there are crests. Over one of them, in the middle of a kink that has become an S-bend at our speed, the car rises, sinks low on its suspension as it touches down and soaks up the impact as if nothing has happened and without any sound. It is at times like this that you appreciate the quality in the damping and the level of stability.

Nick is really into this car now, almost at ease with the power delivery, and he sights beautifully through a right-hander. The power goes on hard in second, the opposite lock is cranked on early to counteract it. It's precisely right and we exit in strong, full-blooded oversteer, tyres yowling and exhaust grumbling. I hopped out to see it from the roadside. Nick accelerated away hard, and all I could do was to stand on the grass verge and say *bloody hell!* as I witnessed the car's pace and heard its unique, riveting bellow. Watching it sweep sideways through the bends was awesome and educational. It looked just as flat as it had felt from inside.

We continued on for two hours, driving the car hard but not to its limits. Even Nick who owns two Porsches and races a factory car could not yet extend it that far. We both learnt certain home truths though: the Dunlop tyres ride well and aren't noisy but can be a little untidy in their actions; and there is about a 10th of a second lag in throttle response, so overtaking and power application in bends require anticipation. Back in London, we had a drink and

AND THE REVS KEEP RISING

tried to tell friends what it had been like. We'd blasted along two-lane roads at 140mph and seen 160mph on the motorway. But the speeds were all in perspective, worthy of note only for comparison's sake. We'd enjoyed hundreds of miles of supercar motoring that only two other cars can achieve at this point in time. And still the Porsche had more to give.

The production Turbos will come with heating that maintains cabin temperature at a pre-set level, leather interior with tartan inlays, electronic speedometer, stereo radio/cassette deck with four speakers, headlight washers, rear window wiper, heated windscreen and rear window, electric windows and tinted glass. Owners will get a 20,000-mile/12-month warranty and their car will require nothing more than normal 12,000-mile Porsche servicing. They should achieve 18 to 22mpg in everyday driving. Buyers will want for nothing. Porsche wants them to feel they're getting something special. One day out like mine in this superlative machine will be all that's needed to convince most that they're getting something *very* special indeed.

TAKING A BATMOBILE HOME TO MUNICH
BMW 3.0 CSL
1975

THE TASK WAS SIMPLE: deliver a BMW 3.0 CSL to Munich. The point, however, was more esoteric. The days of cars so ostentatiously aggressive, so obviously spawned by motor sport homologation rules, so downright phallic as the big-winged CSL, have gone. Were they worth the bother as road cars? Could they take two or three people across Europe any faster, more safely or any better than a less pretentious-looking or performance-oriented coupé or saloon? Would a standard BMW CS do the job just as satisfactorily? Moreover, do the speed limits descending on Europe deliver the *coup de grâce* to high performance cars? And do they consume fuel so fast they're a liability, even if you do ignore the police?

We left London on a Wednesday, threading through the cold pre-dawn drizzle for the first cross-Channel ferry out of Dover. Eighty-odd miles around London a day or two before had sucked the top from the fuel supply, but no longer did we bother to top up before *ca-clonking* onto the ship. A quick check had shown that 74p for a gallon made British fuel the most expensive in Europe, apart from Italy's 90p rip-off. Better to fill up in Belgium, even France or Germany.

The French coast brought sunshine, the makings of a magnificent winter's day. Striking out from Dunkirk to the new *autoroute* that slices south of Lille and Brussels to Aachen on the German border, we began to settle into the rhythm we wanted. There wasn't much traffic but the slow and steady pace at which everyone was travelling was testimony to the diligence of the police. Take a risk?

AND THE REVS KEEP RISING

Open the BMW up and hope to spot the traps? No; play it cool and ignore the car's potential for now, no matter how much it cried out to be used. Better to benefit from its abilities at a slow, almost dream-like 70mph and savour the day, not the law. Our caution paid dividends. Not long after we crossed into Belgium an Opel Commodore GSE flashed past. Behind it came the police, and when we saw the two parties beside the road a little further on, the cop's stony face showed no mercy.

The CSL had been in Britain as part of BMW's UK test fleet. By rights, it should have been sold off months ago – it had logged a high mileage and no longer fits the image BMW want to portray: racing is dead for now; compact luxury is IN – but somehow had evaded the hammer. Simply by being in Britain, the CSL also avoided losing its three spoilers. They're outlawed in Germany; BMW supplies them in the boot of each CSL and it's up to owners if they want to defy the police and fit them. Not only the police: during the height of the fuel crisis in Germany, to drive something that looked as if it guzzled fuel brought unsavoury reactions from other motorists. There wasn't much temptation to fit the spoilers unless you considered them essential to the CSL's performance. But more of that later.

The CSL was and is the fastest BMW road car. It is based on the CSi coupé, but the familiar six-cylinder engine is bored an extra 4mm and stroked very slightly to increase its capacity from 2985cc to 3153cc in line with homologation requirements for the 430bhp racing coupé. Ford produced the Capri RS3100 with a similar capacity for precisely the same reason. Compression is untouched at 9.5 and so is the electronically controlled Bosch fuel injection, but the power goes up from 200 to 206bhp at 5600rpm and there is a more than worthwhile increase in torque, developed at slightly lower revs. The transmission and final drive ratios are as for the CSi, but the CSL is armed with a limited slip differential. There are suspension differences: the body is dropped 0.8in to lower the centre of gravity, an extra degree of negative camber has been cranked on to the front wheels to improve stability and handling, the coil springs are stronger and more progressive, and Bilstein gas

BMW 3.0 CSL

pressure shock absorbers take over from the standard dampers. This new spring/damper combination allows the front and rear stabiliser bars to be flung away. Fat 7in alloy wheels carrying the excellent Michelin 195/70VR14 XWX radials replace the normal 6in rims and lesser tyres and the steering is uprated to the ZF-Gemmer worm and roller system with a slightly slower ratio than standard.

Part and parcel of the CSL is a weight shedding job in which alloy door skins and bonnet replace the steel ones, the front bumper is tossed away in favour of the deep chin spoiler, the rear bumper is replaced by a black plastic imitation bumper and the windscreen is made from special Verbel laminated glass. The chin spoiler and the small one at the lip of the boot lid, along with the black rubber air guides on top of the front mudguards, are part of the basic CSL package. The extra, outlandish spoilers – the deflector across the rear of the roof and the 'Batmobile' wing that rises up from the boot – are supplied with the car so that, BMW says, owners who want to go racing full time can bolt them on or part-time racers can put them on for weekend sport and take them off again to run around the streets, keeping the police happy.

Apart from running the risk of being booked in Germany, what happens when the spoilers, developed for the European Touring Car Championship racer, are in place? Drag is reduced by 16 per cent, improving penetration as greatly as if the car had an extra 50bhp, BMW reckons. Fuel consumption goes down, straight line and cornering stability is improved thanks to a solid slug of downforce, and so is crosswind resistance.

The Bosch injection makes the CSL fire up immediately and idle easily. Even in the cold at 5am there is no hesitation as the clutch comes out and the 2567lb coupé (that's *562lb* down on the CSi) moves away. It's smooth. Fuss-free. No trace of meanness, no hint of high-level tuning. Now, running along this motorway towards Germany, the thing is turning over as sweetly as ever and you're settled back comfortably in the rally-type bucket seat. There's no backrest adjustment, but the arrangement is as close to perfect as most drivers would want it: distances to the wheel, pedals and gearlever are precisely correct, vision is excellent, instruments and

AND THE REVS KEEP RISING

controls located for easy reading and reaching. The leather-covered, drilled-spoke wheel is mounted high, in an old-fashioned sort of way. But it is comfortable and, when the time comes, will permit appropriately deft applications of opposite lock…

Meanwhile, the fuel tank reads dangerously low and there's been no hint of a motorway service area. Playing safe, we swing off into pleasant, sleepy Tournai, and fill the CSL. We've logged a surprising 22mpg, including the running around London. For the most part, we've been touring at 75mph, maybe 80 when the chances of being caught look remote. The next tank, taken near Frankfurt, confirms the figure – 22.2mpg this time, and we've been travelling at 90mph since we've been in Germany where the 80mph limit is advisory only, occasionally logging 100mph or more. There is no doubt, then, that the aerodynamic aids fulfil this part of their promise. You will not see such figures in a CSi or an ordinary CS.

The border guards, as we'd passed into Germany, eyed us with quizzical friendliness. The fins might have been illegal, but they still made the car look dramatic and exciting, made our journey look purposeful, and we were given the impression that it was good luck to the mad Englishmen for disregarding the whole fins affair. Bolting back out onto the *autobahn*, winding the CSL right out in first and second to slip into the traffic flow, listening to the well-mannered rumble from the SOHC six and watching the tachometer needle spin to its 6400rpm red line (where you get 38mph in first, 65 in second and precisely 100mph in third) revealed an aspect of the CSL I hadn't been able to explore much before: the acceleration. It isn't earth-shattering, for this is not one of the big stick supercars. It is still, however, thoroughly fast, getting to 60mph in 7secs and pushing driver and passengers deeply into the seats as the bonnet lifts and the growl from beneath it deepens. The car may, for the most part, feel refined and even docile, but it has its fair share of the mailed fist/velvet glove ingredient and, when asked, it responds. Most of all, it feels especially well balanced: engine to chassis to brakes.

Although the German speed limit is advisory, it's quite obvious from the steady 85mph progress of almost everybody that it doesn't pay to take too much advantage of the situation. Roadside radar, prowling patrol cars and predatory helicopters complete the message. So we stick to 90mph, a speed we think will be safe enough, and the cruising is pleasant. The slightly greater speed than we'd dared use in Belgium sharpens driver concentration, and, indeed, the car. Up to 90mph, the CSL feels pretty much like any big BMW: supple, smooth, fairly precise but not notably so. Above 90, things begin to change and above 100mph you really know about those spoilers' good work. You feel like praising them aloud. The CSL tautens, much as a professional athlete might suddenly turn on for a race rather than simply jogging around the park. The steering goes solid, pin-sharp, but not heavy. The ride stays comfortable but seems to firm, too, and hurl away any trace of wallow. You can really feel the thing sitting down on the road, everything clicking into place. It's one of those special 'fingertips and seat-of-the-pants' feelings that make real motoring in a fine car such a high. You feel confident, but not aggressive; safe, but not shut off from the reality of the road.

And so the miles disappear with increasing ease. The top speed potential remains unexplored, except for one burst to 130mph where the rock-like steadiness is even more apparent. But the benefit of having such speed and power reserves (100mph is 4500rpm, just above the torque peak) is that a quick prod on the throttle thrusts the car past trucks on the narrow two-lane *autobahns*, and out of harm's way.

All three of us – for I had two passengers, both travelling quite comfortably: the thin backs of the rally buckets improve rear legroom – were developing considerable respect for the CSL as the sun at last began dipping. That was an interesting development because our journey had started with modest expectations. I have always disliked the big BMW coupés. They're disappointing after the 3-litre saloons. The CS isn't a coupé version of 3.0-litre saloon: it's based on the decrepit 2000 chassis. Careful development, however, as in the CSL, can cure no end of ills.

Our map showed a side road leading from the *autobahn* down to a series of villages on the River Main, about 40 miles past Frankfurt.

AND THE REVS KEEP RISING

We chose well. Marktheidenfeld, where we stopped, is a quaint and quiet little wine town on the river bank, full of very old houses, wine cellars and pokey streets as well as an enjoyable hotel called the Anker where the landlady was good enough to direct us to a restaurant called Mainblick – Mainview. It looked onto the river and moored barges, and the food was as excellent as we'd been led to believe. What's more, the bill, including a good deal of lager, totalled £2.30 each! The hotel was £3 a head, so don't think you can't travel cheaply in Germany if you stay off the main routes.

We were within 200 miles of Munich by now and our plan for Thursday was to drive through the mountains into Bavaria seeking locations for Mervyn Franklyn's camera. Again, the weather was clear and bright after a night that brought very thick frost. The CSL, on the soaking and slippery back roads, was surefooted. One did not feel inhibited by its power. When we reached the high country, however, we drove into mist, icy roads and snow. I hate black ice, and proceeded very cautiously, using only third and top. But after several miles, it was obvious that the CSL had an unusually high level of road holding, and the handling to match if the grip did break. Soon, even in those grim conditions, I was driving the car full out, snuggling back in the rally bucket, getting precise responses from the engine to the movements of the throttle and lapping up the fluidity of the steering. We found a bend for photographs, a tight and constant uphill curve. After a couple of exploratory runs, it was being taken full power at 60mph in second and there was no hint of the tail creeping more than a few inches out of line. That bend sealed my faith in the CSL.

It was all downhill running after that: literally because we crossed the range; and figuratively because I felt so much at ease with the car that it was unbridled enjoyment without needing to spare further time for familiarity. We completed our journey by streaking along the pleasing and almost deserted roads that snake through the hop fields close to Munich, and switched off at our hotel in the city at 6pm. We could, had we wished, have completed the trip the night before if we'd pressed on down the *autobahn*. But that would have been to deny ourselves a day of far more enjoyable motoring than anyone has a right to deserve in such wintry conditions.

The CSL *was* worth the bother. The fins and wings may be passé now; they have done their job. They did it well. Is a car of the CSL's capabilities redundant though? No way. To eat up the miles so competently, to provide such driving pleasure and to do it with an average fuel consumption of 21.17mpg (better than a 3-litre Granada would return in the circumstances) is more than desirable.

BIG WIND, BLOWING HARD
MASERATI BORA
1975

IT ALL CAME TOGETHER in one bend in Kirkcudbright. A smoothly curving ess, wide and well cambered and with perfect vision because the pines, almost as if in anticipation, had chosen this very spot to withdraw a respectful distance from the road. We came to the bend down a long straight that had been capable of taking the Maserati flat-out in fourth, its four fat exhausts booming at the pines and shaking the valley as thoroughly as thunder. We entered the bend hard, the Bora heeling over with the *g* as it swung onto line, balanced against late brakes and tyre grip and with the gearlever coming back from fourth to second in a toe-and-heel shuffle. A dip in the road, hidden from view by shadows, did its best to fling us offline but failed, and we reached the apex of the first curve, a right-hander, with the nose still steady as it scraped low to the road under the last ounce of braking pressure. The tail was beginning to get that familiar light feel that says *enough*: come off the brakes now; you're in as deep as it's possible to go. Take it a fraction more and your traction is gone. Get back on the power – but *smoothly*, as smoothly as the braking had had to be executed.

The power flicked the car straight, lifting it from the razor's edge and driving it like an arrow through what was left of the right-hander. It was then lined up for the ensuing left-hander, and the exit. Open the throttle more progressively now: the way is clear. Feel the full bite of the power as the V8 sings to 6000rpm. In second gear that means *real* oomph and you know the tail is going to come around. A moment of doubt! It's a left-hander, remember, and you've good reason for trepidation about left-handers. Will it be

MASERATI BORA

here that the thing finally bites you as the sickening climax to a trip that has been the ultimate in love-hate relationships?

No; indeed not. The tail comes, and comes big and fast. But it's caught and held by a quick twist of opposite lock, a slight adjustment with the throttle pedal, and you swing out of that bend in glorious power oversteer to snatch third when it's almost straight and surge forward again. We exclaim in unison: "That's it!" and brake and stop and Phil Sayer gets out to take his photographs. I am to dash through these curves again and again while he shoots, given a reason without really needing one. And each time it is better. Each time the high is heightened. Each time the balance and the feel of the car is more delicious. It's addictive; you just don't want to stop extending this £12,000 delight to its limits and beyond and reaping the rewards – rewards made all the sweeter by the dramas of the miles that have gone before; the love and hate and, yes, the mistrust of the car. At last, the promise that those self-same miles, despite the troubles, had held was fulfilled. That gracious bend and the final, simultaneous escape from all the restrictions had done it.

The Maserati Bora is something of an enigma within the supercar world. It has the power, the speed and the specification of the ultimate performance car layout. It has sophistication, and anyone who has driven a Bora in a worthwhile manner won't hesitate to list it amongst the finest cars built. And yet, the Bora lacks the charisma of its Italian opponents. The Lamborghinis and Ferraris – first the Miura and the Daytona, now the Boxer and Countach – stand in the limelight with the Bora tucked away in the wings. To some extent, that can be explained by its nature: it doesn't have the rawness of the Miura, or quite the pace of the Daytona. Its performance is eclipsed now by the Boxer and Countach and it lives in a niche about halfway between them and the new generation of less powerful mid-engined cars like its own sister the Merak, Lamborghini Urraco and Ferrari Dino 308. Another reason is that mainstream exotic interest had all but bypassed Maserati in the years immediately before the Bora appeared. The Ghibli was appealing but not dramatic; the Indy was staid looking and awful to drive. Maserati did not have cars that upheld the dash

AND THE REVS KEEP RISING

and glamour created in its racing days. Less aggressive and well-organised marketing than that of Lamborghini and Ferrari must have contributed to the Bora's low profile too.

At the end of 1974, the Bora stood with one foot prematurely in the grave. A victim of the fuel crisis, it was presumed around Modena that Maserati would let it fade away quietly – just as demand for big supercars had done. But the Bora's reputation had grown strong enough to save it. Orders have been trickling in from America, Canada and Britain and the Citroën-owned factory is now set to build a further 200 Boras and expects that to rise to 400. The Bora lives.

Although strictly a two-seater, the Bora has certain design and mechanical features that set it apart from other mid-engined cars. For instance, its engine is a V8 that develops peak power at revs that are almost indecently low by Italian standards yet it has quad cams and four dual throat Webers and is mounted fore and aft in the chassis. Sophisticated high-pressure hydraulic systems that would appear more at home in a Citroën than in one of the fastest mid-engined sports cars control major functions. Another thing: there is considerably less compromise about its interior than in any other mid-engined two-seater. A little luggage locker behind the passenger's seat is one of the things that distinguish it from its contemporaries.

You sink into the Bora's driving seat, gripped by the substantial lateral supports and extend the left hand to two black toggles on the dash just to the left of the steering column. The toggles activate hydraulic systems: one to raise or lower the seat, the other to slide the pedals forwards or back. Combine this facility with a steering wheel that adjusts for rake and reach and you achieve a perfect driving position, quite different – because it's almost conventional – from any other mid-engined car. The minor controls and instruments look formidable but dipping into the fat and detailed handbook reveals the logic with which they have been integrated into the dash or onto the steering column. The shorter of the two stalks on the right works the indicator; the longer one, swinging through three positions, selects parking/lights, dipped

MASERATI BORA

beam/flashers or high beam. A little toggle at the right-hand edge of the dash commands the lights to rise hydraulically from their stowed position. The lone stalk on the left of the column controls the wipers and washers and, strangely, the interior lights if its knob is twisted. A dash-mounted rheostat backs up this main wiper control by allowing variable duration intermittent wiping. Rocker switches set neatly into the dash work fog lights, hazard flashers, rear window demister, heater fan, electric windows and instrument lights. Two small toggles operate the electric radio aerial and emergency parking lights (in case the main lights can't be raised). Instruments are straightforward but complete, and are backed up by an elaborate system of warning lights. Everything is easy to see; everything is easy to reach. It is one of the better cockpits.

Next to the heater control – one of the vertical slides at the left edge of the control panel – is the choke. Crank it right on, twist the key and hold the throttle down about halfway. After a churn or two, the over-square 4719cc alloy V8 barks heartily. Provided it's had enough choke, it displays no cold weather temperament. It's as eager as the driver to get going. It warms quickly, with the careful choke location and its smooth operation allowing precise control during the initial running period. The Maserati engine does not have the ultimate smoothness of a V12, but there is abundant torque and superb flexibility (the 310bhp is developed at 6000rpm; the 340lb/ft of torque at 4200rpm) and it makes the Bora a highly appealing car around town. It will trundle along on seemingly cruelly low revs, the up-changes coming at 2000rpm or less, and it will work in fifth at traffic-flow speeds if you like. It is an effortless car here, displaying no hint of temperament and showing more sophistication than one might have anticipated from a vehicle of its capacity-versus-performance potential.

And it's nice to find that the gear pattern is of the old style where first is out and back on the left of the H, intended for starting only, and leaving the top four gears for the real work. It is worth dallying a moment longer on the Bora's performance in congested areas. A combination of its torque and flexibility, its engine and road noise insulation, its ride quality, seats and driving position, complete

AND THE REVS KEEP RISING

equipment list and aesthetic appeal to its occupants make it seem more like an outright luxury car than one whose real forte is very high performance. It is these things, this obvious sophistication above and beyond that normally found in such cars, that make it special.

When the Bora's throttles are opened, there is likely to be a flat spot about mid-range, as if the four Webers have been caught out momentarily. But the V8 just coughs, catches again and revs with biting fervour. It displays an impressively flat torque curve; there's no peakiness, just sustained and potent pull. A pity, though, that it ends at 6000rpm, the recommended maximum; one gets used to the 7000 and 8000rpm limits of the V12, V6s and V8s of the other Italian manufacturers. The Bora, for the most part, feels fast in a somewhat docile if torquey manner; but should the driver give it a big bagful of revs after it has begun moving (*ie*, once the clutch is fully home) it will snarl and flick dramatically sideways and prove that no matter how tame it can be on the one hand, it's all there if the tap is flung right open. By ultimate terms the acceleration is not mind-blowing. Within more common contexts it is exhilarating. You'll be given 0–60mph in 6.4seconds, 0–100mph in 15 dead. But more than the pure rate of acceleration, it's the magnificently sustained manner in which the Bora surges forward that is really addictive. The gear ratios – running, at 6000rpm to 48mph, 82, 120 and 147 – are so well matched to the V8's torque, and so excellently stepped, that the acceleration all the way up to fifth is one long and meaty progression broken only by the blur of your hand on the lever and an accompanying alteration in note from the barking exhausts.

I left London for Glasgow on a Friday evening in the Bora. I had sworn to cruise at the legal limit to see just what it's like to run one of the finest and fastest supercars within the confines of Britain's motorway system. I also wanted to see what the fuel consumption might be when the car was driven so quietly. At 70mph, the Bora was not really much more comfortable than scores of lesser cars. There was a pleasant but somewhat removed burble from the exhausts, the impressive ride, the strong stability; the omnipresent impression that the thing was so far within its limits it was like

MASERATI BORA

relaxing in front of a screen showing a film of a motorway. The only effort asked of me was to try to keep to 70mph. There, the Bora is well below the pace at which it feels most natural and where its cohesion is reached. Nevertheless, the car showed a remarkable mile-gobbling ability, even compared with its contemporaries: somehow, the distance seemed to pass amazingly quickly. The fuel angle? At a steady 70mph the car returns 15.1mpg. It is actually more economical if it is cruised at 100mph, where it will give 16mpg. I can't pinpoint the overall consumption more accurately than at 12mpg because 250 miles out of London the speedo cable snapped. It was to be the first of many such events.

Now I knew what life in a Bora was like at 70mph I couldn't hold off any longer. And pulling out of a service area after a 10 minute coffee break and with a full tank again, I gave into temptation. There was nothing ahead of me on the on-ramp or out on motorway and I did that thing I'm sure we all dream about whenever we pull out of a service area: flattening it, and hitting the redline in each gear; letting it all go. When you do that in the Bora, the note of the quad-cam V8 at your back shifts from its guttural burble to a harder, deeper, thrilling rumble. All 300-odd horses lunge. Its nose lifts and tail squats and it *bolts* forward in its own rather magic way. *Here* is the steel in the Bora's velvet glove. It's an enticing reminder that, amid all its sophistication, refinement and comfort – born of its peculiar half Maserati/half Citroën parentage – there's still a big dose of old fashioned hairy-chested spirit.

At high speed, the Bora moves about on the road like a Porsche, sort of walking and jiggling about its steering. You let it, merely maintaining gentle guiding pressure on the wheel, for it is simply selecting its own path through the night and if it appears unstable or nervous at first it is in fact glued steadfastly to the road. Give it a long, fast bend like those in Cumbria and it almost grins with pleasure. It responds with a sophisticated precision that consumes the curves as if they aren't there. Only the weight of g on your body tells you the speed. What's more, with the speed – with the sharper feel that the car has taken on as it travels in the way that it prefers – it shrinks around you, feeling more like a meatier Ferrari Dino

AND THE REVS KEEP RISING

246. How I revelled in this feeling, eating the miles with contempt, but feeling sorry because soon there weren't going to be any left.

And then… *bang!* In a nasty bend, the left-hander of a downhill S, a back tyre blew. A hunk of metal or wood ripped out the wall. I was doing 70mph, in the midst of savouring the balance, and then the back went twitch… flick… twitch.

I thought it was an isolated patch of ice and said so as I corrected. Then the second tail wag came and I knew otherwise. I stopped as soon as I could, hearing the £50 Michelin XWX flop-flopping to destruction as I looked for somewhere to get off the road.

That night then became a nightmare. It had made not the slightest difference to the Bora's grip beforehand, but I now found it was raining heavily. I was drenched even before I had the spare wheel out from under the big lift-up rear panel. But then the zipper on the cover stuck fast and as I struggled with it in the headlight beams, the battery went dead. So I had no light (my torch, usually never out of my bag, had been lent to a friend). Nor was there a jack handle or a wheel brace. The plush toolkit contained everything but the two most important items! A friend, dragged from his bed to drive the 30 miles to me, was the rescuer. But besides changing the wheel there was the matter of restarting the Bora with jump leads and it was 5.30am, hours after the blowout, that I got to bed.

Finding a new tyre for a Maserati Bora in Scotland on a Saturday is not easy. The Maserati dealers are 180 miles to the north, at Elgin. However, luck and goodwill were on my side. Ninian Sanderson, the Le Mans winner who now runs Dixons, Glasgow's main Citroën dealership, told me about a friend called John Haston who owns a Daytona and has had two Boras. Mr Haston was almost embarrassingly hospitable. There I was, still tired, and with a filthy Bora on my hands, imposing on his hospitality on a Saturday and hoping to purloin one of the spare Michelins I'd been told he kept handy. He didn't hesitate to part with one of what he claimed were the only pair in Scotland. The afternoon was memorable for the tales he told of owning nothing but Ferraris and Maseratis for 15 years. He loved the Boras, but he's staying with the Daytona now (he's 63) because it's a classic front-engined GT.

MASERATI BORA

It was on my way home from Mr Haston's that the Bora bit me again. I was driving it briskly but not all that quickly along a B road. I passed a couple of cars under acceleration, went enjoyably through a couple of right-handers and then came into a left-hander. Within an instant I was dramatically sideways. My reactions must be better than I imagined, for the tail had come around so quickly that by rights I should have spun. It was when I stopped to gather my nerve again that I realised what I'd done. A cardinal sin: I'd forgotten that the virginal spare tyre, now on the right rear corner of the car, had not been scrubbed in. It was slippery and the moment any real strain was placed on it, as that little left-hander had imposed, it was going to let go. So I tip-toed home, cursing and wary.

The Sunday was relaxing; I didn't dare drive far for fear of another puncture since I hadn't yet been able to get Mr Haston's XWX fitted to the rim. But I needn't have presumed that my jinx had let up: the indicator stalk stopped self-cancelling on right-hand turns and, not long after, when I squeezed the stalk to wipe the windscreen, it came away in my hand. I went home and locked the car up.

And so I was somewhat wary on Monday morning as I picked Phil Sayer up from Central Station and headed south for Kirkcudbright and the road I chose to provide Phil with good photographic locations and me with some real motoring. I cringed at every left-hander; used every control with the lightest touch. At least, now, we had a proper spare, thanks to the staff at Glasgow's Central Tyre Service. But what else would go wrong? We ran south through Ayrshire, trundling along with the traffic, the Maserati again feeling so damned nice on the road, so tempting. Overhead, the sky began clearing; our luck was changing. And it came full-circle when we hit the minor road I'd selected and we ran hard down that mile-long straight and arced into that S-bend.

There was a fleeting moment of doubt as the Bora flicked into the bend's left-hander but the new tyre was well and truly scrubbed now. All the pressures had been checked and rechecked and I'd had 100 miles to regain my confidence and settle into the car once more. Now it was just like it had been before the tyre blew on Friday night.

AND THE REVS KEEP RISING

Now the bellowing beast was again balanced beautifully, giving me back the exquisite message through fingers and backside. It cocked sideways with the power full on in second, sneering at the S-bend and coming out in the most magnificent oversteer. This was it at last and I relived it a dozen times more while Phil shot it.

He clambered back in and we set off down the road; a confident new purpose in my driving and the Maserati giving of its best. I now knew precisely what it was capable of offering, and the road was up to asking it of the car. I shall not forget that morning. We braked hard and solid into the bends, at times coming *blap, blap, blap, blap* all the way down to first with the help of that abnormally fine gear change and then blasting out again to the tune of all that sonorous V8 could give. The Bora showed exceptional balance, tenacious grip, delightful response. It demonstrated remarkable stability even by supercar standards over the potentially hairy crests. It rises then falls, softly, and storms on ahead as if nothing had stood in its way. Its all-wishbone suspension soaked up the bumps with disdain. None of them could edge it from its line. Nor is there any change in attitude as it nears top speed – which, when the car is given its head for long enough in the right conditions, is a full 6000rpm in top and a speedo reading of 168mph.

We rejoined the motorway and settled back for the 300-mile run home. Nothing more went wrong. At the end of the day, we were left with the feeling that the journey had been despatched with the utmost purposefulness; that we covered the miles with a reassuring precision and an ever-present sense of competence oozing from the car. That, simply, is known as Grand Touring. It mattered not whether the road be a tortuous back route or a top-grade motorway nor whether the distance be 50 or 500 miles. And at the end of the journey I was left in no doubt that the Maserati Bora is one of the finest two-seaters available.

It is set apart, even within the supercar realm, by its exceptional sophistication, especially within the cabin. It can be as docile as to become just another car in the city, or it can be potent and big-hearted enough to satisfy a demanding driver on the open road. It doesn't have many faults but those it does have are infuriating –

MASERATI BORA

minor controls prone to breakage, or pitiful finish under the skin (for example, the steel framework that keeps the spare wheel in place was breaking away on the test car and there were patches of surface rust on the tubular sub-frame). Such patchy finish, where Maserati think the eye won't see, contrasts with the generally impressive finish of the bodywork and the interior. You may not like the high-pressure Citroën braking system either; I don't, for it robs the driver of finite judgement when braking ordinarily, let alone in a crash stop even though the car does pull up in short order. It also makes late braking into the apexes of bends more difficult than it should be and reduces the pleasure of doing so because of the automatic release of pressure and then reapplication.

But those points do not weigh so strongly when stacked against the Bora's virtues. No-one is happier than I that is has survived the gloom of the fuel crisis, or more ready to envy those few hundred souls who have had the wisdom to tell Maserati they want to include a Bora in their future.

A WELSH ODYSSEY
LAMBORGHINI URRACO 3000
1975

CALL IT THE FINAL fling of an idyllic summer. Call it decadent. Call it logical. Call it what you will – but we just opened the map, picked a spot in Wales and said *there* for no other reason than to drive the Lamborghini Urraco that had fallen into my hands for a few days. What other reason is there for having a Lamborghini than to drive far and fast?

But wasn't there a certain purpose among my thoughts as I fired up the compact V8, resplendent in all its alloy under that dramatically slotted cover, then listened to its burble as we eased through London's deserted streets in the cold dawn? Yes. It had been two years since I'd driven a Urraco P250 and then just enough to suspect that it was a thing of sweetness. Since then, I'd had only a colleague's word that the 3.0-litre Urraco was something special.

There was only one way to find out for myself, and I poked the lever through the gate into the next gear, heading west, and my photographer friend Richard Cooke settled back with the map book on his lap. I had picked up the Urraco the previous evening and was surprised because I seemed to recall that it had an awkward driving position. And yet, after slipping the leather bucket back a notch and adjusting the backrest, I found myself quite at home. Legs splayed just a little, but pleasantly; arms straight out to the wheel. Ah yes: that ever-pleasant sensation of just twirling it, with the arms working in parallel from the shoulders and hands fixed on the rim. It always seems so purposeful and efficient.

In fact, around town, to negotiate right angle bends, you're forced to shuffle the wheel through your hands, because the steering, while smooth and consistent is low geared. Irritation subsides as your

LAMBORGHINI URRACO 3000

attention switches to the precision and relaxed efficiency of it. Here is your introduction to the special charm of the little Lamborghini.

And yet, even as you are beginning to respond to the gentle touch of the Urraco's chassis, you are also discovering that it is offset by a certain savageness from within the 3.0-litre V8 that's beating away, sideways, behind your head. It's easy to underestimate the power and performance of the smaller Italian exotics. The original 2.5-litre Urraco and Maserati Merak, if not the Ferrari Dino, *were* undernourished and have come to maturity in the shadow of big brothers like the Lamborghini Countach, Maserati Bora and Ferrari Berlinetta Boxer. But the impression lingers. After all, don't the Urraco P300 and Dino 308 GT4 only have 3.0-litre engines.

Indeed they do – but what engines! Both brim with ability, starting first twist of the key whether hot or cold, displaying spirit and breeding but not temperament, and offering marvellous flexibility and responsiveness coupled to top-end bite that will take both to 60mph in just over six seconds. And that puts them close enough to the ultimate of the species, even if it is less notable than the performance of the old 2.7 Porsche Carrera.

Of these two small V8s, it is the Ferrari's that is the most impressive. It manages to be even smoother than the Lamborghini's, even more responsive, has even more power and torque that it delivers even more tastily. But, outputs aside – 255bhp versus 250 – we are talking of minute differences, perhaps just personal preference, and the Urraco's 3.0-litre has quality enough to make most drivers happy. It will lug down to 1000rpm in fifth without fuss or drive-train judder and then re-accelerate hard as long as the four Webers aren't opened so wide that they drown the engine. You need watch it only up to 2000rpm. From then on the V8 takes every drop the carburettors can give, fairly flying around to 7500rpm where it hits maximum power and where you should change up – except that going on to 8000 is even sweeter still.

The full-bore bellow then is the culmination of the sounds the V8 makes as it goes about its work. They are magnificent sounds. More insulation than the 2.5-litre car's has eliminated rowdiness. Now, there is only music. Twin belt-driven overhead cams per

AND THE REVS KEEP RISING

bank instead of the single cams on the 2.5 V8 mean an entirely new orchestration. It starts out with a deep burble from 1000 to 2000rpm that would be typical of a V8 were it not for a sharpness that makes it sound more spirited and responsive than usual. As the revs rise – at 2000rpm you can *feel* the engine flattening out, as well as *hearing* it – it changes to a sort of mellow howl as the spinning cams and sucking Webers add the top notes while the booming exhausts deliver the bass. From then on it is a whopping, spine-tingling sound, rising in pitch and purpose until you change up at eight. Within a mile of picking the car up I had my window down and was looking for alleys and underpasses where I could blip the engine to hear as much of it as possible. I found myself accelerating gently so the tonal changes played out slowly and I could savour each one before inducing the next.

So despite the cold Richard and I had the windows down as we headed north west, revelling in the burble as I eased steadily up through the gears and waited for the oil temperature to climb. Our next stop was in North Wales for a latish breakfast. It rained for most of the journey. Just drizzle, but enough to make the roads very slippery. But, after seeing how much power I could apply in first and second before the wheels spun – a lot – and then being delighted when I realised how fast we could go through roundabouts, I was able to ignore the drizzle. The Urraco's grip was the best I have yet experienced.

On the motorway, it was impressively stable, thrusting through the spray and feeling easy and relaxed in the hands; master of the conditions. On the back roads, it could dart along extraordinarily quickly. It was easy to forget about the weather until the rain became so heavy it restricted vision. Both of us looked back over our shoulders as we walked away from it to the cafe for breakfast, and then couldn't help peering at it admiringly through the rain-spattered window, along with the tittering Welsh ladies, and then paid our bill quickly so we could get going once again.

The rain stopped a few minutes before we finished eating and the ensuing sunlight made the roads glisten like chrome while it dried them out. It was then, slowly but steadily, that I began to explore the upper reaches of the Urraco's ability. That steering, pleasingly light at parking speeds, becomes no lighter even at full clip, and while you are not dramatically conscious of the feel you just know, almost subconsciously, that it is there. So this is a car with decorum: you aim it where you want it and it just goes there, mostly neutrally but if you have a lot of speed on and have left your braking a bit late you'll detect mild understeer. Instinctively, you ease the pressure in your right foot a shade and the nose tightens. And then you power out, hard, and marvel at the simultaneous gentleness and precision of the change in attitude. Inevitably you will be in the right gear for maximum acceleration because, although the fat spread of torque means that it is never entirely necessary, you'll have come down through the 'box to the gear that seems correct for the sheer pleasure of it. It isn't a super-slick shift: the lever is sturdy and you need to move it through the gate with deliberation and a fair bit of force. But there is something special about the way it combines with the clutch and the brake and the throttle, inviting you to go down *blam blam blam* as often as possible.

Perhaps, as I think about it, the point that makes driving the Urraco so pleasurable and makes you feel so confident is something you don't notice unless you don't have it: stability. The Urraco has it in spades, into the bends as well as out of them, and under brakes as well as under full power. There is no brake dive to speak of, just rock solid feel and a progressive action that lets you know subtly and gently what the car is doing, how much effort you need and how far you can go. This absence from dive and the stability makes for an ongoing smoothness that, coupled with instantaneous acceleration out of the bends, means fatigue-free travel over long distances on arduous roads.

We found arduous roads around shores of lakes, lonely and cold. We wound around them, the Urraco's sound beating through the trees and, once, bouncing back at us from a long dam wall so that we were moved to screw up our faces in delight. We found roads across bleak sheep country that were full of potholes and crests and dips, roads I would have kept only for Porsches before, and

AND THE REVS KEEP RISING

discovered that Lamborghini's ability to give its cars outstanding rides is epitomised in the Urraco.

Then we came over a crest and in front of us a deep and inviting valley cleaved the hills. A twisting, dipping, beckoning ribbon of road ran for two or three miles down its northern side. I dropped Richard at the top with his cameras and went howling off to the bottom, turned around impatiently and charged back up. Most of the run, I could see for close to two miles ahead, so the only limits were my own, and the Urraco's. At last it was flat in first and second and third *and* fourth, pelting up that thin ribbon, gripping like a leach. I was ready for understeer over the bumps to some of the tighter bends; but I needn't have been because the Urraco didn't waver. Only once, when I had full power spitting from the V8 in second as I left a hairpin, did I need to worry about oversteer. Even then it was just a quick flick of the wheel, hold it on and feel the car coming straight again utterly obediently. Only when I reached the top and peered back did I think about the 500ft drop at the edge of the road. The sound of the V8, Richard said, howling flat up that valley and going on for minutes was pure joy.

Then we were out of the big country onto a fast and open road with bends that could be taken flat in fourth. There is no roll from the Urraco at times like this. You just point it, squeeze open the long-travel throttle, feel the little leather-rimmed wheel murmuring in your hands, note the presence of the *g*-force and feel, through your backside, the flexing of the wall of the outside rear tyre. Slower bends appear. Down to fourth to third to second. *Blap, blap, blap.* Hug the bank tight. Power out hard when the exit is visible. A straight with kinks – bends to the cars ahead of us and now entering them – is next. A mile or more of vision. Take two of the cars on the approach to the right-hander, reaching for fourth as you leave them behind. Sprint hard up the short straight to the next one – a Celica GT in a left-hander – and dart easily, confidently, safely around him and onwards.

I could describe every inch of that trip from then until we switched off back in London. Highlights included the red Alfa GTV driver who saw us closing on him at almost twice his speed as he approached a long, visually open S with a quaint stone bridge at its centre. He clung tight to the left of the right-hander that led to it as we bore down on him, waved us through with glee and we took him just before the bridge, still accelerating. A little curve to the left then preceded the big, final one to the right. Open and fast. Take it flat in fourth and seek the Urraco's limit. Yes, there it is. Feel the nose run just a little wide. Feel it right through the car, not just in the steering, and lift off for a fraction of a second, feeling the chassis come back instantly, precisely and somehow softly.

Later, in a similarly-demanding left-hander I tried *hard to* get oversteer but at high speed in a high gear there wasn't enough power to induce it that way and the grip wouldn't let that the pace alone do it. How does Lamborghini manage to winkle such grip from a simple MacPherson strut suspension and contain body roll while allowing generous suspension travel and thus achieve a comfortable ride?

We rejoined the motorway after driving full-out, effortlessly, for score upon score of miles. One magnificent, full-throttle burst to 7600rpm in fifth, and then we slowed to saunter along with the rest of the traffic. When we filled up for the second time we found we'd logged a bit over 15mpg, satisfactory enough considering the distance, the time elapsed and pleasure given, albeit not up to the Carrera's exceptional 19mpg.

Cruising into London, we were still relaxed and comfortable as the final miles rolled beneath us, the strongly offset pedals having bothered me less than I'd expected. The minor switch gear, on top of the shallow panel in front of you, is easy enough to reach, but there should be stalks for washing and wiping the windscreen and I suppose there are those who would find the speedo (10 per cent fast) and tachometer mounted at opposite ends of the panel inconvenient. Everyone, I'm sure, would like the rear 'seats' to be capable of carrying people instead of a small person squashed in sideways for cross-town hops. The boot is roomy but the proximity of the exhausts and no insulation means that heat sensitive luggage must go in the cabin.

So, with 641 miles under our belts in just under 15 hours we

AND THE REVS KEEP RISING

were home again. Richard assured me he felt as fresh as I did, and I picked up my girlfriend for dinner only an hour after the suggested time. I left the Urraco's parking lights on while we dined; somehow, that made me feel it stayed alive. I ate in silence, thinking about it all, and wasn't hard pressed to conclude that the Urraco 3.0-litre is the most enjoyable car I have driven so far. It isn't only its outstanding handling and roadholding that, like Douglas Blain and LJK Setright, I think is surpassed only by the Countach's and Boxer's. It's the *feel* and the sound and the exceptionally forgiving character; it's the enchanting balance between gentleness and potency that makes me think it's worth every penny.

'SIGNOR, YOU GO MORE SLOW, EH?'
FERRARI 308 GTB
1976

THE CARABINIERI WERE WAITING at the top of the pass. They were hidden in a farm entrance around a tight right-hand bend, and I didn't see them until it was much too late. Damn it: where had the radar trap been? How was I going to worm out of this? Their ears would have told them everything. They'd have heard the wailing of that superlative little V8 rising and rising and rising as it wound through four gears to culminate in a bellow as it touched 7500rpm. And then there'd have been the pause and the smack as the next gear took up and it was all repeated, again and again. Amid the wharoom… wharoom… wharoom of the downshifts there'd have been the occasional squeal of a punished brake as the car was hauled down hard, Michelins scrabbling, for one of the tighter hairpins.

For close to 11km, by my reckoning, they must have been treated to this, and they must have been in no doubt that the red Ferrari now trickling to a stop at their command had been going very fast. It is possible that once or twice, had they perhaps needed visual proof or sought to heighten the experience, they might have caught sight of it as it devoured the mountain below them, racing into their arms, a red streak against the lush green of early summer.

I got out. The younger policeman took charge: 'Documenti, signor?' I gave him the wad of papers Ferrari had provided for me, hauled out my licence and told him what he already knew: that this little devil of a Ferrari 308 GTB was out on test from the factory now more than 100 miles back through the mountains. He studied the papers for a long time, going slowly over each document. Then

AND THE REVS KEEP RISING

he replaced them carefully in their leather folder and handed them back. I made to get back in the car, but he waved me back with his ping-pong bat, and it was then that I thought I was in real trouble.

But no; he just wanted to peer inside, and then to walk slowly around it, admiring it from this angle and that. He said only one word, 'Magnifico', held out his hand and invited me to retake my place behind the little leather steering wheel. When the V8, after that high-pitched wheeze from the starter that so characterises Ferraris, burst into life he summoned me to blip it several times, and he shook his head slowly with appreciation and respect. 'Buongiorno, signor', he said, with a nod of his head. 'Arrividerci.' And then, with a grin, in the best English he could summon: 'Signor, you go more slow, eh?'

He stepped back waved me forward with a happy grin, and raised his ping-pong stick in salute as I brought up a few revs and released the clutch. I will never know if they had taken a reading of my speed – and at times, even up that steep snake of a road, the car had been flat in fourth at 112mph – or if they were merely there to stop everybody because bandits had raided a bank in the area or if they were simply checking for stolen cars. I do know that the Carabinieri, respected rather than feared for their integrity and efficiency, looked at and listened to the newest Ferrari with pride as well as admiration. Say what you like, a Ferrari is a Ferrari.

In fact, the 308 GTB does not sound especially good from the outside. The 308 GT4 2+2 from which it is derived mechanically is not noted for its musical ability, but it is rather more pleasing than its new sister which has the misfortune to sound more like a Lotus than a quad-cam V8. There is a reason: the exhaust pipes, in two bunches of four, are collected into two main pipes and these in turn feed into the one large silencer; the gas and the sound is then forced to emerge through only the one paltry outlet to meet external decibel regulations. But, in the cabin, it's a different matter. Even if Ferrari tried to keep the engine's natural music from the driver's ears, it would stand little chance. The 3.0-litre V8, sitting there transversely, is even closer to the occupants' backs than in the GT4. Top it with twin cams on each cylinder bank, feed it with four twin-

FERRARI 308 GTB

choke Weber carburettors, build most of it from light alloy, let it rev to 7700rpm and tune it to provide 255bhp and you get an engine that will not – should not – be silenced. The exhaust note might be lily-livered, but the rest of the sounds that provide your first clue to the excellence of the Ferrari 3.0-litre V8 are all there, even down to the just-audible sucking at the mouths of the air intakes just aft of the doors.

Whereas the 308 GTB bears a strong physical resemblance to its much-loved 246 predecessor and is mechanically almost identical to the 308 GT4, its construction is different from them and all previous production Ferraris: it is fibreglass-reinforced plastic over a tubular steel chassis. Ferrari doesn't feel the need to mention this fact in the 308's brochure. Nor, I suppose, should it. It is the finest plastic bodywork I have yet seen, and most people would not suspect it isn't metal.

The facts that emerge when one compares the three Ferraris – Dino 246, GT4 and new GTB – show that the 308 GTB represents a swing back to the concept and character of the beloved 246: a small, light, fast and intensely personal two-seater. Gone is the compromise of the 2+2 GT4 but present are the lessons of sophistication and practicality gleaned from it. Dimensionally, in all but width (where it is broader by a mere half-inch anyway) the 308 GTB is actually fractionally smaller than the Dino 246. It is not lighter although of course it has a significant weight advantage over the 308 GT4 – 2403lb compared with 2576lb. And since both 308s have the same engine, the GTB has a decent edge over its 2+2 sister in power to weight ratio: 9.4 against 10.1 (the 195bhp Dino 246's was 12.2).

Translate this into on-the-road terms – into the rasping of the exhaust, the howling of the cams, the sucking of the carburettors, the chirp of the tyres and the slap of the thin metal gearlever in its clinical metal gate – and the 308 GTB pushes firmly away from the GT4. It covers the standing quarter in 14.1sec instead of 14.4; it emerges from the standing kilometre at 136.7mph after a 25.4sec run instead of 131mph and 26.2sec.

There's another hint of the way Maranello – and indeed the market place – has been thinking to be found in the gearing. The

AND THE REVS KEEP RISING

final drive and the first four ratios in the gearbox that nestles beneath the V8 are identical for the two 308s. Take both to 7000rpm – the power peak but not the absolute rev limit – in those first four gears and each will provide you with a lusty 41, 59, 83 and 112mph. But in the GTB, Ferrari, freed from the need to make the GTB achieve a higher top speed than the GT4, has raised fifth gear to provide instead for more economical cruising. The GTB's weight advantage means it will still accelerate quicker in top anyway. The difference in the final gearing in fifth isn't great at 21.6mph/1000rpm rather than 21.08mph but at the identical top speeds of 156mph you'll have 7250rpm on the GTB's tachometer while the driver in the GT4 is showing 7400rpm.

Does the 308 GTB really do as Ferrari claims? Of course it does. After being given carte blanche by the Carabinieri, and being waved on by another group a couple of hundred kilometres later as I pelted through the Futa Pass – what joy! – I rejoined the *Autostrada del Sole* back to Modena. After watching a Daytona closing steadily on me as I sat on a relaxed 130mph and then seeing him disappear into the distance at, I'd guess, well over 160mph, I opened the GTB right up. It answers like the thoroughbred it is. It surges forward with spirit, the tachometer and speedometer needles climbing in unison, and the sound behind your head growing more intense, until there is just no more to come. In fact, the speedo was reading just over 160mph but the tachometer said it was incorrect. At this speed the 308 GTB, like the GT4, is admirably stable. It doesn't move from the path you have selected, goes unmolested by crosswinds and sits on the road with a security you can feel through your backside. It's a good feeling.

So too is the feeling of security when the GTB is flat-out through a bend or thundering through a dip, as it was for kilometre after kilometre on the way from Maranello south through the mountains, down the other side towards Florence and then back again along that magnificent driving road called the Passo della Futa. Like the GT4, the 308 is very easy to drive. It puts you at ease. There is the same taut but undemanding drive train, with a clutch that has plenty of firmness to its springing but not too much weight and

FERRARI 308 GTB

a gearshift that moves with the sort of chunky, metal-to-metal deliberation one has come to expect. There is the same lack of fuss from the 3.0-litre V8, the same instant response and magnificent flexibility. There is no flab about any of the functions. You just get into the GTB, feel at home, and get on with the job.

The driving position is low, but quite 'normal'. There's the usual Italian rake to the wheel, but the positioning is fine and the distance from the seat to the rim and to the pedals makes for immediate comfort. The instruments are arranged differently from the 308 GT4. A rather tall, deeply hooded binnacle juts up from the fascia. Big, simply marked speedo and tachometer reside there, along with oil pressure, water temperature and fuel gauges. A clock and the oil temperature gauge are tucked away on the lower extremity of the dash where you won't see either in a hurry. Visual access to the main instruments is excellent, but Ferrari spoiled it by failing to eliminate reflections on their faces.

Three stalks operate the minor controls. Toggles for the auxiliaries, the air conditioning knobs and the heater/ventilator slides sit on the little central console just behind the gear lever. The cabin is very much like the Boxer's but perhaps a bit neater. There is an unusual appeal about the way the long, thin armrests on the doors mate at their forward ends with the edges of the dashboard and although the cabin isn't very big there is an air of adequate spaciousness to it thanks to the pleasant trim materials. The vision creates no problems and combined with the other well-considered aspects makes the GTB's passenger cell an accommodating place.

The plain leather seats prove to be comfortable and to have sufficient grip as you begin driving, in this instance a few familiarisation laps around Ferrari's Fiorano test track over the way from the factory. Nicest of all, as you begin, is the steering. Light and smooth and pleasantly geared; the sort of steering that lets you work the wheel through the hands with a soft, almost caressing motion, taking the messages through the skin of the palms and the tips of the fingers and thumbs. And yet, when you strike surface irregularities there is enough feedback to remind you just how directly the wheel is linked to the front wheels.

AND THE REVS KEEP RISING

The GTB comes smoothly and effortlessly into the bends. It has more of a softness about it than the 308 GT4, a gentleness; even more poise. There is a manifest feeling of sweetness, and you tend to trust it implicitly from the outset for you can sense how well-balanced it is. You begin to go faster, unable to resist that track with its corners copied from the world's Grand Prix circuits. There is a gentle pushing out at the nose into the very tight ones. A modest easing of the throttle stops it and, with the steering still so light in the hands and the car feeling beautifully poised, it sticks to the line you have chosen, and you can then really push the long-travel throttle and let the V8 propel you forward pleasingly fast.

With such an introduction I was ready for the mountains ahead, and something close to 300 miles. Except for the few kilometres on the *autostrada* that took us between the two passes we chose, and then back to Maranello when we had left the hills behind, we were in series after series of bends, some hairpin-tight, others long and open and fast.

Most of the time I drove at a fast, steady pace so that Richard, my passenger, wouldn't have to put up with too much lateral force. Even so, it was quick enough for him to remark how extraordinary it seemed to be able to cover so many miles so quickly, easily and securely. This little Ferrari is like that: you feel relaxed in it. There seems to be plenty of time to position it correctly, to brake, steer, and sweep through the bends. You remain unflustered, even when you decide to use still more of the performance; to take it to 7700rpm out of the bends and come in to the next lot hard and fast, approaching the limits of the roadholding to see if the balance will be upset. It isn't. The GTB merely goes faster, swinging from one lock to the other with swift and clean response. Its poise is never lost, its stability never upset. It feels so safe all the time.

The GTB seems to have decidedly stronger roadholding than the 308 GT4 and notably better balance. When it is going to let go it gives you warning, loud and clear, where the 2+2 doesn't. And it is easy to catch. This one is a honey; a sports car par excellence. Ferrari's recipe for performance car motoring a level below the Boxer is delicious. Its approach to furthering the appeal of its

FERRARI 308 GTB

cars, if this one is typical, is enticingly thorough. If the 308 GTB has faults it is that the zip-on cover for the luggage compartment is fiddly and above 120mph there is too much windnoise around the trailing edges of the doors. Otherwise, the profound beauty of its shape, its character and its ability make it a jewel. It leaves me with only one hard question: how to choose between it and the Lamborghini Urraco?

SINGING IN THE RAIN
MASERATI MERAK SS
1976

THE RAIN WAS PELTING down and driving on the *autostrada* was like dicing with death, so we turned off at the next exit and headed for the hills. If anything the weather up there was worse. Half the time we were in and out of swirling, dank cloud. But at least we were rid of the trucks. Up there it was just us, the car and the elements. Bright yellow on shiny black and lush, dripping green.

It didn't take long to appreciate the effectiveness of Maserati's changes to the latest Merak. Adjustments really: a little more front wheel castor, a shade more rear wheel toe-in and an increase in the body's torsional stiffness. Nothing else, except that the Merak SS has a good deal more power than the initial model... the one that drew the admiration of many people for its sophistication and good looks only to have them draw away because, with 187bhp, it didn't have *quite* enough performance. The Merak was nice but not successful. When Maserati collapsed the uprated 217bhp SS had only just gotten going. The engineers, suddenly free of Citroën management, were able, under new owner Alessandro de Tomaso, to return to making what they think Maseratis should really be like. They swiftly did what they thought necessary to put the seal on the SS as a driver's car, and make it competitive at last.

We reached the top of the mountain, surprised by how much of its power the Merak had been able to put onto that streaming road as we'd climbed up. For a while the cloud broke, and it was possible to see where the road ahead went. Curving and dipping and twisting around the mountain to the river far below. Around and through the odd vineyard, skirting the occasional farmhouse. Dropping in a whole series of bends at a time then flattening for

MASERATI MERAK SS

a little way before dropping into another set, even tighter, until eventually it reached the valley bottom.

While we were at the top, I darted out to clean the headlights and nearly fell flat. There'd been no rain for weeks, and the asphalt was slippery as ice. I made a mental promise to be very careful until I knew more about the Merak. It took a few moments with the fan blowing hard to demist the car again. It was wet but not cold and the car fogged up fast. The air conditioning finished its job, and I reached for the starter again, snicked the Citroën SM-style lever into first and pressed gently on the throttle.

There was something, though, that told me that perhaps I did not need to be as timid as seemed prudent. I don't know what it was: perhaps the ease with which the Merak had offered itself to me as we left the gates of the Maserati factory and wound through the streets of Modena to the *autostrada*. Perhaps it was the way the car felt so much more positive than the earlier Merak as we accelerated away from the tollgate up the slip road to the motorway. It was going hard then, sitting down its back wheels, heeling a little through the curve and feeling lively, willing and stable. It could have been the way it darted so easily, without being opened out in any one of its five gears, to a steady 120mph as we headed south past Bologna – with Radio 2 telling us what was happening back in Britain on a fine summer's day. It might well have been me, and not the car, tensing when the rain came down harder. The Merak did not deviate from its path; it tracked as accurately as before, with as much feel reaching my hands, and two long black lines on the road behind to show where its Michelins had flung the water out of their way.

So, around the top of the mountain and down I used an extra thousand rpm in second than I had in first, and was into fourth with no sign of slippage before the first serious bend demanded that the pace be slackened. The Merak is not light. There's a certain heftiness to its feel. And yet while one notes this feeling of chunkiness it is not a problem to place the car accurately. There's a cold precision to it, an interesting contrast to the precision of the 3.0-litre Ferraris and Lamborghinis. Theirs somehow feels clothed in gentleness.

AND THE REVS KEEP RISING

The Merak swung into that first curve, with the braking incomplete until the car was a good way past the entry point, and simply going where the little four-spoke leather wheel told it to. There was enough speed to induce some body roll but the nose did not want to run wide. It was poised; steady. Encouraging. The exit appeared and I pushed the throttle fairly hard and the V6 answered with its sharp, rather menacing growl. There was a push in the back that you wouldn't have had in the old car. This Merak has life. It did not take many of those exits to show that the SS has enough performance to take it close to the 3.0-litre Urraco and the Ferrari 308 GTB.

Before the descent's halfway point, the Merak was whipping down the mountain as if the road were dry. I had no fear that the car would betray me. I was coming into the bends hard enough to need most of the braking power, staying just this side of lock-up. As soon as the brakes were off, on with the power again. Not all of the power in second or third. That would have induced too much oversteer. But enough to have the car working hard and revealing extremely good balance, particularly in four very literal hairpins. The balance gave the sort of control that is neither throttle-off nor throttle-on. You know: that hint of throttle in a bend that stabilises the car and holds it steady as you hug the bank, rather like keeping just enough pressure on the reins to keep a good horse in a canter without it going into a gallop. That control comes to you readily in the Merak now. It didn't before.

By the time we swished across the bridge at the bottom of the valley I couldn't have cared less about the rain. There was another road climbing a higher peak and I attacked it with all of the Merak's go. Twice, when the curve, camber and speed were just right, I did what I've never before attempted in a mid-engined car: pushing the tail out under brakes coming into the bend to enter slightly sideways and then powering through in an arc that clips the far side of the road. I was surprised at the ease of it. There was only some raggedness when the body dropped back as it came off opposite lock. Again, that slightly heavy, fractionally dead feeling.

At times, the Merak came out of those uphill bends so hard, with

MASERATI MERAK SS

the tachometer needle hitting red at 6500rpm and all 217 horses charging, that it was in hefty, happy oversteer for a long way. Red-blooded stuff: a Maserati in full cry; a Maserati that no-one, ever again, need label an old man's car. I went back to one corner and did it again for Richard Cooke's camera and people came out of their cottage on the corner and watched and loved it, as they always do in Italy. And then we went on, driving more tamely and getting pleasure from that. The miles went down quickly and easily. We reaped the pleasures of travelling quickly and safely in difficult conditions in a thoroughbred sports car.

What makes the Merak so appealing, gives it a character all its own among the 3.0-litre coupés, is the fact that it not only now goes, stops and handles well enough to give a Ferrari, Lamborghini or Porsche 911 owner a rude shock but that it has an air of real sophistication. The Bora, its V8 sister that shares the basic body shell, has that too. The influence from previous owners Citroën is present in the cabin: the big egg-crate air vents, the gearshift, the central console with its sliding-top ashtray, the soft cloth trim of the seats and their careful shaping. As a result, the Merak has a slice of luxury that the Dino 308, 308 GTB, Urraco or Porsche don't, beautifully trimmed though they might be. Their accent is on sportiness, with an almost stark efficiency. Nothing wrong with that. It works in all four instances. The Merak, however, is different. Like the Bora, it has its own special appeal.

Unlike the Bora, though, the Merak's driving seat moves on conventional runners rather than remaining fixed while the pedals move hydraulically at the touch of a button. The Merak's wheel adjusts for rake and reach and, as has long been the case in Maseratis, the driving position has none of the common Italian quirks that ask for familiarity. The vision is good enough for fuss-free town driving and easy placement on the open road. The instruments – the two plain dials straight in front of you – are clear but blighted by reflections. The minor gauges are strung out across the centre of the fascia making a quick check of your oil or water temperature harder than it should be. It's a comfortable cockpit for two, but not three. It is possible for a tiny person to ride in the

AND THE REVS KEEP RISING

space behind the seats but they won't be happy. It's best for odds and ends.

The overall impression of civility is heightened by the high-pressure French hydraulics for the clutch and brakes. Somehow, it seems easier in the Merak to get used to the fairy-light brake pedal pressure than it did in the Bora. The gearchange is fair. It has modest feel and relatively short movements but is not a source of great pleasure as in the Merak's contemporaries. The seats provide a lot of under-thigh support, and their backs are shaped for adequate lumbar and lateral support. The ride is very firm at low speeds, and transmits a lot of road noise. This disappears with speed and while the ride is good enough it's not as impressive as the Ferrari's or Urraco's. Above 120mph the Merak is quietest, though. It has an advantage in storing luggage too. The nose compartment will take a satisfactory load. The spare wheel is stored aft, behind the V6.

The grossly oversquare V6's dimensions give it a capacity of 2965cc. It's a successful engine if not an inspiring one. It doesn't have the magic of the similarly sized V8s from Maranello and Sant'Agata Bolognese; not quite the smooth, solid urge with which they delight their drivers. The Maserati V6 substitutes a feeling of bite and sharpness instead, while the four cams and three twin-choke Webers at least give it the right sounds. It's capable, Maserati says, of tuning for close to 300bhp.

But – and this may seem an odd thing to say – I'm not sure the Merak really needs all that much more power. It is now a very well sorted and balanced car. It does its job beautifully, with a panache all its own. It may well be better suited than its rivals to an owner who wants more than just performance, but it is now capable of satisfying someone whose priorities lie the other way too.

900 MILES IN 11 HOURS: A GRAND TOURER AT WORK

LAMBORGHINI ESPADA

1976

EARLY SATURDAY MORNING, MODENA, northern Italy. Nine hundred miles to the French coast at Calais, ferry to Dover and on to London. I want to be home tonight. A Lamborghini Espada in the hotel garage. Keys in my hand.

I've been in Modena all week seeing Ferrari, Maserati, De Tomaso and Lamborghini. Ubaldo Sgarzi, Lamborghini's genial sales director, needs an Espada, the dramatic-looking 154mph four-seater, delivered to London by Monday. I'm – *ahem* – happy to take it.

At 6am I fire her up, wend quietly from the hotel through Modena's empty streets to the *Autostrada del Sole* and head north. For the first 20 miles I warm the 4.0-litre V12 carefully then ease up to a steady 130mph and begin whipping past the sparse traffic as if it were standing still, swooping through the *autostrada*'s long sweepers as if they weren't there. Parma, Piacenza, Milano and Novara come and go.

Beyond Aosta we start the long climb on two-lane road to Courmayeur and the entrance of the Mont Blanc tunnel. The Espada soars up through its bends, running out hard in second (69mph at 7500rpm) and third (94mph), and hitting fourth's 125mph peak on some of the handier straights. Such is the Espada's grip and performance – it'll hit 60mph in 6.5sec – that it blasts past the trundling semi-trailers without bother. Three hundred and fifty horsepower at 7500rpm removes us from the clog of the traffic on this clear autumn morning. The finesse of a great grand tourer is at work.

I'm driving fast and enjoying myself, but needing to expend

AND THE REVS KEEP RISING

remarkably little mental or physical effort. My passenger is asleep. Down the other side of Mont Blanc into France the Espada's poise into bends, the accuracy of its steering and the clean bite of its four disc brakes – coupled with the precise and pleasurable gearshift – come to the fore. Can't help but be impressed by the ride, too. If there were four of us on board we'd all be just as comfortable.

The descent is as inspiringly smooth and satisfying as the ascent. Out of the mountains and eventually picking up France's lovely *Autoroute du Soleil,* the Espada goes back to straightforward mile-gobbling. She sits happily on a neat 140mph and I ease back in the seat to let her do the work.

The 300 miles to Paris slips by amazingly swiftly and then there's just the final leg to the coast. It's not enough. For the last 100 miles I swing off the main road to take a back-road through the farms and villages because, even with all that distance behind me, I want to enjoy more of the Espada on the most satisfying roads I can find. It's glorious, and I come into Calais and onto the ferry, and dinner, sated but not tired. The 900 miles has taken precisely 11 hours' driving time and 13 hours elapsed, including clearing customs at the French border and stopping for fuel and a lunchtime sandwich. *What a drive.*

IN THE CLEARING STANDS A BOXER

FERRARI BB 512

1977

THIS IS FOR THE man who said there was no such thing as a wonderful car, and he a Citroën owner. This is for the man who said that one simply couldn't *use* high-performance cars any more, could one, and he a Porsche driver. This is for the man who said no car could be worth £25,000, and he an artist. But most of all, this story is for those who do not understand the indomitable spirit of Modena for they are the people who would ask *why* Enzo Ferrari has just raised the capacity of the Berlinetta Boxer to 5.0 litres to make what was perhaps the world's fastest production car even more powerful.

Even more powerful? Didn't the plush brochure for the superseded 4.4-litre 365 GT4 BB say it had 380 horsepower? And doesn't the equally elaborate brochure for the new BB 512 say that it has a mere 360bhp? Indeed so – and Ferrari now admits that the 4.4-litre's rating was exaggerated by 50bhp! It was an 'untruth', they say in Maranello now, swiftly insisting that the listing of 360bhp for the 5.0-litre Boxer is genuine.

Compared with the 4.4, the 5.0-litre flat-12 has a bore of 82mm instead of 81mm and a stroke up from 71mm to 78mm. The new displacement is 4942cc but there is more to the upgrading than that. Compression ratio up from 8.8 to 9.2:1, maximum power point chopped from 7500rpm to 6800rpm, redline backed off from 7700rpm to 7000rpm and higher gearing reveal a shift in emphasis if not in character.

So the BB 512 has more torque and more power at lower revs

AND THE REVS KEEP RISING

but the advent of a 3.21:1 final drive ratio instead of 3.46 means that the gear maxima remain very close to those of the old BB, and that the through-the-gears performance and top speed are little different. In fact, the respective brochures, while quoting gear maxima of 54, 80, 108, 138 and 188mph at 7000rpm (that's where the warning sector preceding the 7700rpm redline began) for the 4.4 BB, and 58, 81, 107, 141 and 188mph at 6800rpm for the 512, suggest that the acceleration is identical for both models: standing quarter mile times of 13.7sec and standing kilometre in 24sec, which means that in the space of 1056 yards you have gone from standstill to 154mph.

But with yet another shrug about the brochures, the good people at Maranello say that the 512 does in fact accelerate more quickly through the gears than the 4.4 BB, and is rather quicker in-the-gears. The same data sheets suggest that, despite its extra 30 horsepower, the BB 512 labours against a power-to-weight disadvantage because it is, at 3084lb, more than 360lb heavier than the 'little' Boxer. Ah yes, but the weight for the old car, wrong in the brochure anyway, was given without air conditioning, electric windows and a stereo system because they were then optional. Now they're standard, although it is almost impossible to find a 4.4 BB without them. So in the end the 512 emerges with a power advantage.

It also benefits, at last, from wider tyres on the rear. They're still Michelin XWXs but the rears are now 225/70VR15 rather than 215/70 so the Boxer is no longer the only mid-engined supercar without wider rear tyres. The rear track is wider by 1.7in now, and the width of the car, thanks to arches with more pronounced flares, is up by 2in. An increase in the length, by a little over 1.5in, is more difficult to understand until you look closely at the rear body moulding. The way it meets the central body section has been changed, and it looks better. The tailpiece comes back slightly further and there are subtle changes to the way the buttresses join the tail. There is more extensive venting in the flat panel above the engine and the mesh that filled the central part of the tail panel has been ditched in favour of slats. Three tail lights on each side have been reduced to two, like those of the 308 GTB, and

FERRARI BB 512

four relocated tailpipes sprout where once there were six. Ferrari's aerodynamics studies in Pininfarina's wind tunnel revealed the need for big air scoops in the flanks to feed the rear brakes, and for a spoiler beneath the nose. Apart from the wider rear wheels and tyres, Ferrari specifies no suspension changes, saying only that the engineers have been 'fiddling about'.

But take the BB 512 out onto the road and all this confusion disappears as rapidly as the other traffic. The changes to the body and suspension, however subtle, add up to a significant improvement. And, impossible though it might seem, so do those to the engine. This is an even more sophisticated car, easier to drive, even more appealing. This is a Boxer with more charm as well as more fight; more poise as well as more spirit. Funnily enough, it's the gearshift that provides the first indication of what's to come. 'Like a good switch, it is,' said the man from Maranello Concessionaires with enthusiasm, and he was right. I'd never found much to grumble about with the old shift. It was positive and pleasantly, solidly, definite in its six-slot gate and you moved it with solid, positive action, getting pleasure from the smack that greeted your ears and which you felt through your palm as it went home, especially on the up changes. But some of the customers didn't like it: too much effort around town they reckoned. Ferrari has changed it by removing most of the pressure on the shift mechanism. And now that long steel shaft fairly flicks around its gate… just like a good switch.

It's not so much that the changes can be made lightning fast: that is somehow out of place in a car with this much power coming through the transmission. Rather, the removal of the pressure on the shift means that the changes are smoother, especially when made full-cry. The jerk that introduced an unmistakable manliness to the proceedings before, as the power came off with the disengagement of the gear, is all but gone. The clutch, too, is lighter and the throw seems shorter. And if the steering isn't actually lighter than in the 4.4, then it certainly asks for no more effort from the driver than does the gearlever. So this BB glides away from the kerb and into the traffic with even more aplomb than the old one.

AND THE REVS KEEP RISING

It's so easy to manage, so very undemanding. You're underway and moving quickly before you've had time to contemplate the problem of applying 360bhp to streaming wet roads – a prospect that had seemed daunting.

Just a few miles on back roads and then a few more on the motorway demonstrate that the 512 is more positive than its predecessor. You notice it most over the little crests on the back roads, through the long bends taken with a decent amount of power on, and from 90mph to 110 or so on the motorway. Side winds at these speeds made the old Boxer weave a little and feel slightly unstable before it gained absolute steadiness from 140mph upwards. The 512 always feels steadier and more purposeful, more secure, and therefore makes life that much easier for the driver as well as more rewarding. The revised aerodynamics play a major part in the way the Boxer now spears through the air. Under hard acceleration, the nose barely lifts at all. Before, you were well aware of its rise and fall. But there seems to be a distinct new positiveness from the suspension itself as well. The quality of the ride – always an impressive part of the BB's make-up – has not deteriorated, but the traces of waywardness seem to have been contained.

Steady rain, too many patches of mud on the roads and grim visibility stopped me pressing the 512 to its limits. But there was barely a moment among those hours when I wasn't surprised by the new level of grip and by how much of the 512's performance could be employed. Once you're moving, you can apply full power in first and second gears, with a steady push on the throttle rather than a snap opening, and get no trace of wheelspin. Unless there is such a difference between the roads over which I last drove a Boxer in the rain and those I covered in the 512, the extra grip of the fatter rear tyres is enough to cope with it all. In the corners, you're left in no doubt about their contribution: a tight roundabout entered quite hard in second with the revs well up brings mild, consistent understeer that you feel with a delicious communication from the leather of the little wheel to the skin of your fingers and palms that didn't seem to be there before either. The front isn't so much moving off line; it's just telling you that the limit of adhesion

FERRARI BB 512

is being reached and you need to ease the throttle slightly. The message in your hands changes, the grip is all there again and when you're heading for the exit you can bring on all the power and nine times out of 10 you will get no reaction other than the most marvellous acceleration out of the bend. On the other occasions – and for me they numbered no more than three or four in a day's hard driving – the application of all that power brings a nudge of oversteer no greater than the touch of understeer on the way in has been. Again, the messages come in the same sure, gentle way, with everything so very positive. It is here that the BB 512 is subtly better than its predecessor. The nose lift is reduced and so is the roll and the squatting of the tail over the wheel taking the load. Things are a lot flatter now.

Without losing anything by way of civility this is a tauter, tidier car: a wide, heavy and powerful car that now feels small and handy. Conditions that allow the car to be extended as far as it will go may yet reveal that the slight waywardness that made one treat the 4.4 BB as something of a point-and-squirt machine may still linger but from my experience on those sodden roads, I'd be surprised. This one has grip in a straight line where a solid push on the throttle in second or even third would bring instant wheelspin in the old car. This one does not ask for the caution that one soon learned was necessary in roundabouts taken at the same sort of speed in the 4.4, and the lurch into pronounced oversteer, with the weight and suspension inadequacies making itself apparent as you corrected, never come. This car, even in conditions so miserable and difficult, is much more satisfying to drive.

And that engine! It's as easy to manage as ever, a tiger so subject to your will that you may forget its potency until you look at the speedo and find that the most gentle progression up through the gears, using no more than a few revs it would seem, has taken you up to three figures. Even when you push the throttle pedal through its long travel to tug the butterflies in the four triple-choke Webers wide open, you seem to do nothing more than flow forward at a very fast rate. There is no great thump in the back, or jerkiness, or a feeling of ferocity. It's a sustained thrust that goes on and on

AND THE REVS KEEP RISING

and on. Such is the smoothness and magnificence of this 5.0-litre engine that it's a while before you even think about trying to pick the differences between it and the 4.4. It doesn't immediately feel a lot more potent; the higher gearing takes care of that. But after a few miles of accelerating up through the range and working within the gears as the bends come and go or traffic impedes your progress and is then despatched, you notice a new meatiness. Through the gears it makes the acceleration feel even more effortless. In the gears, there is an extra dollop of strength that makes the mechanical heart beating behind your back more awesome than ever. Changing up earlier, if anything, makes the 512 seem more relaxed without removing any of the pleasure from running the flat 12 out to maximum revs.

The noise is still there, of course: the high whine of the Dinoflex electronic ignition from just behind your head when you turn the key; the grunts that greet the starter when the engine is cold; and then, after you've kept your foot flat to floor for long seconds, the wail of those 12 cylinders and the marvellous tenor, behind them, of the exhausts. On the road though, the BB 512 is quieter than the 4.4, subdued to a point where you might actually contemplate turning on the radio or listening idly to a tape as you work along back roads at 70 to 80mph, for that is the speed you will find yourself logging even in conditions as foul as those I experienced and even when driving cautiously, with eyes peeled for mud and the tractors that put it there.

You feel very safe and relaxed, satisfied to be in a car that feels far within its capabilities. Inside the cabin, very little has changed. The feeling of airiness is still there, and the vision that is so surprisingly good for a mid-engined car. The driving position is notably un-Italian, the minor controls are worked by column-mounted stalks, with a host of knobs, toggles and little levers on the tunnel between the seats for things like the air conditioning, heating and ventilation, the separate fans for driver and passenger, hazard flashers, fog lights, the choke, and the electric windows. The instruments still have red figures on black backgrounds and, annoyingly, the rim of the wheel that feels so dainty and smooth in

FERRARI BB 512

the hands still masks the most vital sector of the tachometer. The finish of the Boxer seems more impressive than ever; enhanced, owners should find, by the substitution of black leather on the top of the fascia instead of the suede-like material used before and which faded alarmingly in an embarrassingly short time. The problem of where to put luggage still exists, perhaps heightened by the wider rear wheels which steal even more of the scant space under the bonnet should one need to be swapped with the bicycle-like emergency spare normally resident there.

You may say that a car costing so much should be faultless. Of course it should – but none ever are because people make them. The advent of the BB 512 means that the compromise chosen by Maranello for the 4.4, wherein it was a very fast car but just a shade too soggy in its attempt to be effortless to drive, has been reduced. The engineers have chipped away until they've achieved a poise the old car needed but lacked. This car feels subject to your will and your actions all the time; indomitable but never dominant. It's lost nothing of the Boxer's virtues but gained a new balance, more ability and gives you more control. Its character has such appeal it borders on the irresistible. You are aware that a very careful – and necessary – process of refinement has been carried out, and the result is a truly wonderful car, Mr Citroën owner; a car whose gigantic performance can be used so effortlessly so much of the time, Mr Porsche buyer; a car that, provided you can spare £23,868, will give you the sort of pleasure that seems beyond price, Mr Artist.

CONVOY!
FLAT OUT ACROSS EUROPE
LAMBORGHINI COUNTACH, URRACO AND SILHOUETTE
1977

IT HAD THE UNREAL quality of a dream. That strange hyper-cleanliness, the dazzling intensity of colour, the haunting feeling of being suspended in time and motion: sitting there with the speedo reading beyond 160mph and two more gold Lamborghinis drifting along ahead. Not even those surreal driving scenes from Claude Lelouch's film *A Man and a Woman* were like this: the pale grey ribbon of motorway stretching on until it disappeared into the sharp, clear blue of a Sunday morning in France, mid-autumn, and those strange, dramatic shapes eating it up. What a sight from the few slower cars as that trio came and went. What a sight from the bridges and the service areas – watchers there would have seen the speed. So would the police, of course, those same *gendarmes* who, one after another, parked their Renaults and motorbikes and stood beside the road to drink it in; to savour it as an occasion rather than intercept us.

We hadn't intended to travel so quickly when we left Modena, in the heart of northern Italy, with near enough 1000 miles home to London ahead of us. But given the build-up, the crispness of that morning, the perfection of that road and those cars, it was inevitable. And not to have run so hard and so fast would have seemed appalling afterwards. Only a few days later the French brought in their 130km/h motorway speed limit.

But to go back to the beginning... We arrived in Modena on Thursday night, spilling tired from an Avis Fiat rented from Milan

LAMBORGHINI COUNTACH, URRACO AND SILHOUETTE

airport. For some reason, all the hotels in Modena were full. But Roger Phillips had a trump card: a key to the flat of Rene Leimer, the owner of Lamborghini, and we set off in the tired Fiat again, weaving along the lanes until we stopped at a trattoria in a village near Sant'Agata Bolognese, near the Lamborghini factory, about 15 miles east of Modena. It was two in the morning, but the place was still in full swing. Carlo, the owner, treated us like long-lost brothers, and in moments we were starting an excellent four-course dinner. No bill: there would be a grand reckoning when it was all over. And with that we tumbled off to Monsieur Leimer's beds, thankful that he was in Switzerland and thus spared the embarrassment of four unexpected and uninvited guests.

We were there because Roger Phillips, Britain's Lamborghini concessionaire, had come to pick up his latest batch of cars. Next morning, about 10, he phoned the factory. 'Ah Phillips' – it was almost possible to see sales manager Ubaldo Sgarzi shrugging – 'your cars? Perhaps this afternoon, perhaps tomorrow morning.' The little Urraco P300 was ready. Even the Countach was ready. But the Silhouette was still being painted. Now Roger had been there before, countless times, on similar missions. So had David Joliffe, London's main Lamborghini dealer. So had Steve Brazier, Britain's biggest Lamborghini service agent. And so had I. We knew what to expect when it came to dealing with the supercar manufacturers, whether Lamborghini, Ferrari, Maserati or De Tomaso. We sauntered off for lunch at another of Carlo's establishments, a place of superior tone. Besuited this time, he waited on us personally, recommending this, tut-tutting over that, sweeping away dishes not to his approval before we could even taste them and replacing them with others. For three hours we ate and drank gloriously.

And then it was off to the Lamborghini factory, that long fawn establishment among the Lambrusco vines on the Modena side of Sant'Agata. It was Friday, so no Gian Paolo Dallara, wizard creator of the Miura; part-time now. No Dottore Ingegnere Franco Baraldini, the wiry little engineer who runs the factory and controls the engineering. He was in Munich updating BMW about the progress of Project E26, the 24-valve, 3.3-litre, in-line, six cylinder

AND THE REVS KEEP RISING

mid-engined coupé that Lamborghini will soon begin making for them. Down on the factory floor, the third strike of the day was over and the business of building Lamborghinis was underway once more. Ah yes, there was our Countach and there was the Urraco, waiting to go. On its own down at the end of the line busy trimming Countachs – including an incredible blue one with gold-painted engine, cockpit and wheel arches, apparently bound for Haiti – was the Silhouette. Around it clustered a team of men and women, buffing and polishing the fresh bronze-gold paint, painstakingly fitting the last bits and pieces. They'd be there for hours yet so there was no hope of our getting away before nightfall. The cars had yet to be checked and 'sealed' by the customs man from Modena, too, an event that experience said was rather dependent upon his whim, his lunch and the weather. Better to shrug with the Italians and wander around the factory, soaking it all up again.

In and out of the Olivetti milling machines and all those marvellous, glistening alloy castings being bored and trimmed and drilled to make blocks, cylinder heads, transmissions and suspension uprights. Most impressive of all was the Countach sump with its fine, full-length cooling fins and big holes in each end to allow the driveshaft to run through from the transmission, ahead of the engine, to the differential mounted behind it – unique, imaginative and magnificent. Sauntering past the rows and rows of plastic parts bins, each in its clearly marked spot. Ducking under the four production lines, with Espadas and Urracos, Countachs and Silhouettes all in various stages of completion, their bodywork carefully protected by big quilts, their undersides shining with new nuts and bolts. Peering into the dyno rooms, where the freshly finished engines are run in, mile after bench-mile. Watching the test drivers going through their checklists with the mechanics after completing their 50-mile circuit out on the road, with never a wheel or a rev wrong, and no pussyfooting. Leaving the spotless, spacious, unfussed factory to sneak across into the advanced engineering shop to talk to Umberto, the chief body-man, lovingly tending an old 350GT returned by a respectful owner to the factory for restoration. Running a hand over the smooth, sharp, hyper-

LAMBORGHINI COUNTACH, URRACO AND SILHOUETTE

economical lines of the prototype Bravo, about to start on the developmental path that Lamborghini hopes will eventually take it into production with a resurrected Miura 4.0-litre V12 sitting sideways between its flanks.

Apart from Ferruccio Lamborghini himself, the only element missing was Bob Wallace, his lanky 6ft 4in frame doing its best to fit into the traditional blue overalls, leaning low over a prototype, brow furrowed and taciturn as ever. The legendary Kiwi development engineer, who went to Italy to work for Ferrari and fulfil a childhood desire then crossed the tracks to Sant'Agata with other romantics like Dallara to build the Lamborghini dream, is gone now, settled in Arizona, where he maintains Italian exotics for American enthusiasts.

The trip down memory lane, the buzz of soaking up the atmosphere and detail of an inspiring factory, came to an end. We set off to dine again at the good Carlo's and did ourselves no disservice at all. The grand reckoning was remarkably reasonable: about £25 for each of us for three excellent meals and a lot of wine. We availed ourselves of M Leimer's unwitting hospitality yet again, but at an early hour this time. We were anxious to be on the road early next day: the serious business of ferrying three Lamborghinis back to London would begin.

The noise of 28 cylinders, 12 cams, 14 sucking carbs and eight howling exhausts rent the damp, still morning. *Oh God* I'd thought when Phillips tossed me the keys to the Countach. *Not the Countach to begin with!* Not that one, right-hand drive and no usable mirror on the left, to go through the villages and the narrow streets of Modena. Not that awesome beast, with its awkward cabin, daunting visibility and 360 horsepower. I tugged off my boots to have maximum command of the pedals and, while I was messing about, the others were gone in a flurry of sound and exhaust vapour. I reached the factory gate, stopped to check the exit then eased on some revs and let the clutch out. The V12 coughed and sputtered. I flung the clutch in and pumped the throttle. The engine picked up again with a roar as the car straddled the centre of the road. The clutch came out hard and we were away with a chirp from the fat

AND THE REVS KEEP RISING

rear Michelins and a quick waggle from the tail.

By the time I'd caught the others filling their tanks at the garage just up the road, I'd learned once more that my trepidation about the Countach was unfounded. How good it was to be back behind that outlandishly raked windscreen, with the little leather-bound wheel between my knees and the solid metal gearshift in its big, chunky, metallic gate beneath my left hand. The first mile – yes, as little as that – had brought it all back: the feeling of supreme stability and purpose, and the sheer precision of a car that has no purpose other than to spear down the road as far and as fast as possible. That feeling is so strong in the Countach it can take your breath away. And there was no trouble with the pedals. I put my boots back on, those big clumpy Fryes, and never gave them another thought. With the tanks full, we fired up again, darted out into the traffic and flowed with it until we reached the motorway north towards Milano, the Alps, and France.

Even mild throttle and modest revs took us scampering past the rest of the traffic as we accelerated away from the entry tollbooth and settled quickly into fifth for a steady 80mph cruising speed for the most, but varying it now and then to let the engines work at different revs for their first few road miles.

Running in with the Italian supercars – with an engine that's been bedded in on the dynamometer – tends to be more driver discipline than the engine's asking. They just feel ready to go, and indeed, within two hours, our speed was creeping steadily upwards until we were sitting on 110mph, with the Fiats and slower Alfas and Lancias moving swiftly out of the way as this extraordinary £52,000 convoy sprang into their mirrors.

The pleasure to be had merely from sitting there conducting the Countach at that steady, restful, seemingly slow speed was considerable. Again, it's the overwhelming stability that comes through strongest, and the absolute decisiveness of the car. The steering is not heavy, just *solid*. Turn it with the thumb and forefinger of one hand, s-l-o-w-l-y, and feel the car alter direction without a millisecond's hesitation. Feel it change direction at precisely the tempo and to precisely the degree you have

LAMBORGHINI COUNTACH, URRACO AND SILHOUETTE

commanded. Swing the wheel back and grin with pleasure as it returns just as precisely to its heading. There has been no roll, nothing more nor less than you asked for. Feel too the messages being patted into the palms of your hands. I watched the Urraco and Silhouette, a little way ahead, riding over the bumps. The feel of the Countach said it was dipping and rebounding even less than they were. And yet its ride is never uncomfortable. Yes, it's firm – about as firm as that supplied by a modestly padded steel office chair resting on thick carpet when you jiggle up and down on it – but never uncomfortable. It simply feels honed as finely as every other component in this most exotic of supercars.

We stopped for fuel and food. The first of many crowds gathered around the cars and stared in silence. We swapped keys, and I drew the Silhouette, which Roger had pronounced surprisingly and interestingly different from the Urraco, even though they are essentially the same mechanically. He was right. Especially after the Countach, but even compared with the standard Urraco, I was startled by what appeared to be slack in the Silhouette's steering. It seemed very soft at the straight-ahead. Turning it brought accurate response once the rim had moved a little way, but it just didn't have the sharpness of the other 3.0-litre. The explanation lay with the Pirelli P7 tyres. They were allowing the rims to move above their treads before responding fully. The capability is there – even more so – it's just that the Silhouette feels a lot softer. Its ride is similarly affected, and I lounged back in its tall tombstone seat and watched the Countach now snapping over the bumps in front of me, its tail barely bobbing. The differences in the performance were brought home too. Where Roger was accelerating relatively mildly in the V12, we had to prod the V8s decisively to keep up as he shot off from the tollbooths and past slower traffic. There was no disputing which car was boss.

In the bright sunshine of the afternoon, we swapped again, and Roger removed the Silhouette's roof. I switched to the Urraco with Steve at the wheel to try and take pictures. We were surging up the Aosta Valley now, heading for the Mont Blanc tunnel. The air was clean and fresh and the sight of those two cars behind us, as I

AND THE REVS KEEP RISING

hung out the Urraco's window with my camera, was magnificent. A wide, clear road, mountains topped with snow rearing on either side and the soft light of the dropping sun. I stayed out there until the cold wind of 90mph made it impossible to hang on longer and then asked Steve why he'd gone so fast. 'Sorry cock', he said in his London accent, 'didn't realise.' I knew what he meant. We returned to a more natural 120mph.

Not so far from Aosta, we stopped for enough fuel to take us into France. I changed back to the Silhouette and buttoned up my coat. The lack of buffeting with the roof off was surprising. We were soon running at 140mph on the almost-deserted *autostrada,* and even at that speed there was little noise or wind intrusion. Mont Blanc loomed ahead, the sun was low and dropping fast and the air was getting cold. The heater, full-on, warmed my legs and chest while my face froze. But what an evening: flowing so quickly and effortlessly up that mountain and finding that the Silhouette and its Pirellis had more grip than I might have imagined. Alone again in a real sports car with the power to eat those bends and catapult past the trucks.

For I know not how long I endured perfect pleasure. I didn't realise how cold I was until we stopped at the customs control at the entrance to the Mont Blanc tunnel. Like a fool, I volunteered to be a passenger again for the descent, although I suspect I gained nearly as much reward from watching the Countach and Silhouette darting through the endless downhill bends ahead as I might have from driving myself. There was scarcely a car on the long, quick *autoroute* up to the Swiss border, and we covered it at a steady 140mph cruise, the cars hardly seeming to work. Night was coming quickly, and we wanted to be within reasonable striking distance of the Mâcon–Paris *autoroute* before stopping.

After we'd stopped for coffee at a bar whose owner claimed that his front door was in France and his back door was in Switzerland, the Silhouette was mine again, and we covered the bumpy back roads taking us across the Rhône and on towards Nantua with the sort of ease that can be had only in a true grand touring car. It's at times like these, with several hundred miles under your belt and

LAMBORGHINI COUNTACH, URRACO AND SILHOUETTE

the going getting more difficult and tiring, that you appreciate them most. They are so very much in control; so much within themselves. And their reserves are your reserves. We came over a crest and there, on the wrong side of the road with no hope of making it, was a bumbling, juddering, wound-up Citroën 2CV trying to overtake a truck. There was a small pull-off area, and the Silhouette darted into it as the Deux Chevaux sailed past. David and Steve saw the dust and followed suit. The rock wall lining the road resumed again and, no doubt, so did the 2CV driver.

We stopped at the first likely hotel, and that's how we discovered France's answer to Fawlty Towers: an intriguingly decadent place called Château du Pradon that was terrorised by two mad cats called Antoinette and Voltaire. It had wallpaper tacked on with tape and decidedly curious plumbing but comfortable beds, humorous staff and an impeccable restaurant. The Urraco went into the garage, and so, barely, did the Countach, but the Silhouette's chin spoiler was just too low to clear the ramp. It stayed outside and at six the next morning, with the other cars already throbbing out of the courtyard, I found that its windshield was covered in ice.

While I was still scraping the screen clear, the others were through nearby Nantua and gone. Despite the cold, the V8 had come to life as easily as ever and, after warming it up carefully, I was ready for an attempt to catch up. But was there ice on the road? The first few bends suggested not, just as they also again suggested how much roadholding was available in this new little Lamborghini. And what a road on which to exploit it: running along the side of a lake and then climbing up through first one range of hills, dropping, then rising and descending through two more over a distance of about 50 miles, and barely a straight anywhere. Without the car being taxed in any way, it simply devoured that road. Keeping the V8 in mid-range and occasionally giving it its head for a moment coming out the bends brought more than enough speed. Despite those curves, the pace was rarely below 70mph and frequently around 100. The bumps in mid-bend (often severe) could not throw the Silhouette off-line. Wet patches encountered under braking into hairpins did not make it budge.

AND THE REVS KEEP RISING

Ah, how well it could all be felt through that leather-bound wheel and the pliant but beautifully controlled suspension. To experience it is to understand just how good a car can be; to know how swiftly but safely you may travel, with never a wheel out of place or a trace of drama. There's just pleasure.

The others were waiting, dawdling along, on a straight preceding a vital junction. The road from there took us over yet another set of hills. As we reached their peak, we looked down upon a sea of mist filling the river valley below. It was eerily beautiful. Phillips, in the Countach, knew I would want to stop for pictures and before I could overtake him to call a halt, he sped up. Until we ran into the mist ourselves, those three cars tore down through the bends, each of us keeping close so we could listen to the engines of the others' cars as the gearchanges came thick and fast; each of us watching the progress of the other cars through the bends simply for the delight of seeing how flatly and tidily the gold beasts obeyed their drivers' commands.

We reached Bourg-en-Bresse as the mist began to ease. On the pavement in one part of the town huddled a group of men. One of them saw us coming. He stepped out to the edge and pumped his arm furiously to summon his companions. They lined the road and watched in awe as we wailed past, whatever they were doing instantly forgotten. Leaving the town, we came upon a Citroën GSX2. It was sitting on a steady 100mph and brought me back to reality. It was much easier for us to hold that speed, and we had a great deal more in hand – but here was this little 1200cc sedan, kids and all, scooting along at the maximum speed that vision would permit. Its *pilote* could drive too, and we were content to sit behind him until we had really clear road ahead of us where we could let the Lambos have their heads again.

The Countach reached the *Autoroute du Soleil* west of Mâcon first. And after such a stirring early morning warm-up, who would have been able to resist giving such a car its head? Roger took it hard up through the gears. I dropped my window to listen and could still hear it above the sound of the Silhouette's V8. Steve and I did our best to catch up, running onto 165mph, only to see the Countach

LAMBORGHINI COUNTACH, URRACO AND SILHOUETTE

still disappearing into the distance – and into the unobstructed vision of a *gendarme* sitting on his motorbike beside the motorway. He watched us come, one by one, turning his head after each of us. We pulled into the rest stop a kilometre or so up ahead; and so did he. But he just parked his bike and wandered over to look at the cars with a nodded hello. A whole busload of *gendarmes* pulled in and came over, and so did another two motorbike cops. Word had spread. We watched them looking over the cars from the restaurant's windows as we ate breakfast.

And then the police watched us go, accelerating away at a pace merely briskish for us but very fast to an onlooker. By the time we reached the motorway, we were each doing well over 100mph. None of the *gendarmes* moved. Somehow, we knew we were going to be all right, and for the rest of the day our speed stayed around 120mph, with some spells at 140 and some at a little over 160mph. And so we flowed along that silver-grey ribbon of road, disappearing north into a blue, blue morning. It was a big, wide-open feeling – lulling and warm. You felt relaxed, hand just resting on the wheel, the car reaffirming its poise and arrow-like direction every instant. It made you feel *sharp*, provided you with an alertness that lasts hundreds of miles at a time. Even nearing their top speeds, these cars feel free from stress, and so do you.

We ran on and on and it really was like a scene from a film, with first the Countach flowing out to pass a slower car and then peeling in again, and then the Silhouette, and then the Urraco. We stopped for fuel and a quick break on the way to Paris, and then again on the stretch up to Lille. After that came a sort of climax; a defining moment. I was with Roger in the Countach. We were running at around 120mph. In the mirror Roger saw a Jaguar XJ-S closing fast. Cold bloodedly, he changed down to fourth and opened the Countach right up. It surged ahead with force and, precisely as the Jaguar came alongside, we had matched its speed at 155mph. We went into fifth gear again as 8000rpm came up, the throttle still open, and we left the XJ-S as if it were standing still. When the clock was showing 185mph, we were forced to lift off and as we slowed I saw that both the Silhouette and Urraco had come past

125

AND THE REVS KEEP RISING

the Jaguar too. The pain was more, apparently, than its driver could bear. He caught us up, took a long look and then pulled off into the inside lane and proceeded at something like 80mph. If our taunt sounds irresponsible, I would in principle be forced to agree. But the road was clear and Roger hadn't blocked the Jaguar's path. The Countach had too much in hand for that. I can tell you that even at an indicated 185mph, a Countach feels solid as a rock, never twitching from its path, while behind your head is this incredible, ferocious noise: the V12 in full cry.

It was all something of an anti-climax after that, although the pleasure went on. I took over the Countach again and was able to enjoy the V12's potency as we worked down to Calais on the minor roads, hanging back as the lead car with its sightseeing passenger set the pattern for overtaking, and then blasting through in second or third and being both thrilled and amazed by the acceleration and the ease with which it can be used and controlled. By five o'clock we were on the ferry, and it was all coming to an end. There was just the customs clearance at Dover, and then the tame run up to London on the beleaguered roads of a misty Sunday night.

We were not tired when we stopped at last, just as I had not been tired a few months earlier when I'd driven an Espada 900 miles in 13 hours, including stops, over much the same route. You just switch these cars off, get out – and begin to relive it all. I'm still reliving this trip. I always will be.

Postscript: Countach's sad farewell...

High up on London's A40 Westway, just where it climbs away from Marylebone Road and heads west over the rooftops for Oxford, a metallic gold Lamborghini Countach was being smashed to pieces. Some fool had chopped across its path mid-bend. It started spinning in great big arcs, thumping into the barrier on one side of the road and being flung back to smash against the other side. The nose was pounded back to the windscreen in the first gyration, taking the front wheels with it. The side had already gone and, as it slammed into the barrier for the last time, the tail was flattened to the engine – that glorious V12.

LAMBORGHINI COUNTACH, URRACO AND SILHOUETTE

I happened to be driving the other way, into London, and saw it happening right there on the other side of the motorway. I couldn't believe it. I shouted with anguish… horror… anger. Even in the blur of the destruction, before it had stopped and I had parked to run across and see if the driver was all right, I knew it was *my* Countach. We'd only had 48 hours together a couple of weeks earlier. But each hour, every single minute, was a jewel that I, and the three others who'd shared the experience, will treasure forever. That Countach, along with the Silhouette and Urraco, was the one that had whisked us halfway across Europe in our epic high-speed convoy.

Its occupants were able to swing the doors up and step out, shaken but uninjured. The windscreen hadn't broken, even though the nose had been so hideously flattened and the severity of the impact, I'd learn later, had cracked the alloy of the crankcase and transmission. In death, as in life, that car was magnificent.

A PORSCHE TO MAKE THE TURBO TREMBLE

PORSCHE 911 KREMER

1977

KEITH JARRETT IS A pianist. One of his best albums is called *The Köln Concert*. There's just him, alone on stage. He begins playing, building his melody from a few notes. They are sweet, enchanting. He starts to move along, expanding into one riff and then another, all linked, and all built up from those first few notes. And what notes they are! Clear and ringing, each pregnant with beauty. And his timing! He climbs, almost tentatively, almost feeling his way, and then, after the merest and most perfect hesitation, tumbles into long, exquisite runs. He goes on building until, about half-way through the first side of the first disc, everything that has gone before is co-ordinated into music of such pendulum-rhythm, of such melody and delicacy and yet such decisiveness and control, that its beauty engulfs you. And the flow of it is such, as it sweeps you along, that – like Jarrett himself – you have to cry out for joy. And that's how it was in the Porsche Kremer. In a series of bends, on a quiet afternoon, somewhere deep in Somerset.

But this was a very special Porsche, for a very special Porsche customer. He won't mind if I call him a Porsche freak. He could have ordered a Ferrari Boxer or a Lamborghini Countach or anything else he wished. But not for a moment did he think he had an alternative. He'd dreamed since childhood of having a Porsche, bought one as soon as he could afford to and, when his business was sufficiently successful for him to contemplate a replacement, it had to be what he considered the ultimate road-going Porsche. A Turbo? Too easy, and there were too many of them; and they didn't

Race-bred Chevvy-powered Holden Monaro GTS 350, above, was ideal for fast open roads in the Australian bush, like the dash from Nyngan to Bourke, NSW, where it despatched 125 miles in an hour on an unrestricted road. Ford's revered Falcon GT-HO Phase III, centre, was even faster. Uwe Kuessner's back-seat picture, right, of Nichols flat out at 141mph in the HO is Australia's most famous motoring photograph.

Brian Redman roars past, above, in the Ferrari team's Dino 246 reconnaissance car on a Targa Florio practice day while Nichols, perched on his Fiat 124 Sport's bonnet, snaps Sicilian road sweepers who wanted their picture taken. Nichols later did a lap in the Dino with Redman. After swapping cars with Autosport's *Pete Lyons, Nichols punted Pete's 1973 Corvette, below, around the never-ending bends of the 44-mile circuit. The Stingray acquitted itself well.*

Bob Wallace refuels the Lamborghini Countach prototype, above, at Sant'Agata Bolognese for another day's hard test driving. Bob's height emphasises how low the Countach was. Wallace took Nichols from Monaco to Modena rather rapidly. Enzo Ferrari, below, invited Nichols to his office several times, always keen for feedback on his latest car. The painting is of the Merzario/Munari 312PB winning the 1972 Targa Florio. Great honour to have a book signed in the legendary purple ink.

Maserati Bora, above, was an unusual mix of performance and refinement – marvellous for long, fast trips. This one wasn't without problems on Nichols' run to Scotland though. A day's hard driving in a Lamborghini Urraco 3000, left, in Wales showed how beautifully Bob Wallace had developed the car's ride and handling – it was impeccable. It wasn't only the Carabinieri who admired the Ferrari 308 GTB, below, during Nichols' test run in the hills south of Maranello.

Maserati Merak SS – a Bora minus two cylinders – provided an inspiring day's driving despite rain and mist in the Italian mountains, above. Lamborghini Espada, right, proved just what a superb grand touring car it was on a dash from Modena to London. It was one of Nichols' best-ever drives. Pictures like this of the Ferrari BB 512, below, helped set CAR magazine apart. Good photography took effort but it was always worth it.

BMW 3.0 CSL 'Batmobile', left, ran fast despite challenging conditions on its trip home to Munich after ending its UK test stint. The first RHD Porsche 911 Turbo, below, with Nick Faure at the wheel. Its speed was an indicator of what turbocharging would soon do for cars' performance. But this 911 built by Kremer Racing for a CAR reader, bottom, was even faster than the Turbo and scintillating to drive.

Never-to-be-forgotten trip with three Lamborghinis in convoy, above, from Italy to London before there were speed limits in France. Here the Urraco is showing just over 160mph, a true 154mph. The cars felt relaxed spending long periods at this speed. Mighty Countach went to another level with S version in 1978, below. The hot factory test car hit 194mph on Nichols' run. A later journey by Silhouette, bottom, from Modena to London brought its own pleasures.

And The Revs Keep Rising

Pink Floyd drummer Nick Mason has one of the world's most enviable car collections. He lent Nichols first his Jaguar D-type, above, then Ferrari 250 GTO, below, and Ferrari Daytona, below right. All three are fabulous, but most especially the GTO, often hailed as the greatest Ferrari of them all. Nick drove his daughter through the snow to school in the hugely valuable GTO one cold day when none of his other cars would start.

PORSCHE 911 KREMER

have quite enough performance. So he ordered a basic 1977 model 911, silver metallic, and asked for it to be delivered to Kremer Racing in Köln. 'Please build me,' he instructed Erwin and Manfred Kremer, 'the optimum 911 for road use and occasional club racing.' The Kremer brothers' reputation is impeccable. They have been building racing Porsches, and cleaning up on the track, since 1962. They haven't built many road cars. But when they have, the results, it's said, have been quite magnificent. My friend could not resist.

To the basic 911, through the official Porsche options list, he added right-hand drive, a limited slip differential, 6in wide forged alloy wheels, rear window wiper, five-speed transmission, black trim instead of chrome, a centre console, electric sliding roof and a Blaupunkt Bamberg stereo system. That came to a total, without tax, of £9418 at current exchange rates. The Kremers had made their recommendations, and my friend had responded with a few more of his own: electrically operated and heated mirrors, 100-watt Cibié driving lights, the best Recaro seats with stereo headrests, and an anti-theft cut-out device. And could the bumpers be left in their natural, 5mph crashable state, please?

Kremer removed the engine, and, keeping only the original block, crankshaft and conrods, took it to 3.0 litres and increased the horsepower from the standard 165 to 250. They replaced the standard wheels and tyres with 7in and 8in wheels wearing 205/50 and 225/50 Pirelli P7 tyres and fitted Carrera rear mudguards to cover them. The front suspension's torsion bars and stabiliser went untouched, but the rear torsion bars were replaced by thicker ones, a special rear stabiliser system was worked in and the four standard shock-absorbers were ditched for a set of Bilsteins. A Group Four racing spoiler almost brushing the ground and incorporating the driving lights and the big-capacity oil cooler went under the car's chin, and the familiar 'whale's tail' spoiler went on to its bootlid. The whole lot was tuned, adjusted, tweaked. It came to £10,625, of which £5884 went on the engine and another £1000 on the wheels and tyres.

I must admit that I did not share my friend's faith that the car would fulfil his expectations. What tuning firm, however good and

AND THE REVS KEEP RISING

for whatever price, could do a better job than Porsche itself had done with the Turbo? Think of the noise and fuss. Think of the lack of flexibility around town. Think of the harsh ride and the effort asked of the driver. Not even the excited message from a mutual friend, formerly as sceptical as me, who'd gone with our Porscheophile to Germany to pick up the 911, could raise my enthusiasm. 'It's good,' he said on the phone when they'd returned to London. 'It's *bloody* good. Wait 'til you drive it.'

Three weeks later we were at the beginning of the long straight at a test track. The Porsche's owner was crouching at the back of the Kremer, still grimy with the dirt of the miles it had covered around Germany while he ran it in before taking it back to Kremer for final tuning and then heading for England. I watched, intrigued, while he unscrewed a heavy steel cap blocking off the last of the three stubby exhaust pipes poking through the rear bodywork – visible evidence of one compromise, at least, that Kremer had had to make for the car's dual roles. In city centres or areas with a low decibel ceiling the Porsche runs with caps on two of the three pipes. It then makes about as much noise as a normal Carrera albeit slightly more savage. For everyday road use in the suburbs it sheds a cap and instantly gains another 20bhp. The third cap comes off, releasing a further 20bhp, for racing – although who could not resist screwing it off for a long hard drive cross-country?

That last cap was coming off now, unwillingly because in three weeks a heavy carbon deposit had built up, cementing it in place. Then it was off. I reached inside the cabin and turned the key. There was a violent, shattering new roar – the roar that you get from a proper racing Porsche – and the heads of the few people in the vicinity snapped around. It wasn't only for their benefit that the blipping and crackling went on for a few moments. The cobwebs came spewing out until a few more blips brought nothing but a twitch from the body and that Teutonically purposeful sound.

'Please drive,' said my friend, and we buckled ourselves in. The clutch, from Porsche's own RS racer, came out beautifully, steady as you like, but short and positive in its action, full of feel and without any heaviness. The nose rose but a fraction, the tail barely twitched

PORSCHE 911 KREMER

and with the three pipes blaring their mighty song we tore down the track. When we stopped, the watches said we'd reached 60mph in 6.0sec and 100mph in 12.6sec. And we hadn't been trying! This was just a practice run, the first time the car had been opened up, the first time I'd so much as sat behind its wheel. We lined up again, with a few more rpm for the take-off and ready to hold each gear to the full 7300rpm that Kremer had set as the change-up points. That gave us 5.5 and 12.1 seconds… and there was more.

It had become apparent that revs on take-off were critical. Too few and the grip of the squat Pirellis was enough to bog the car down a little; too many and there was too much wheelspin. The right figure, it transpired, was precisely 3300rpm. Slip the clutch then and the Porsche was away as clean as a whistle with wheelspin for just a few feet and the engine firmly into its power band. But I kept getting it wrong, thrown by such readily available wheelspin in a Porsche (you can't get it in the Turbo because, at the very high revs necessary, the clutch slips), and fearful that the loss of traction was at the clutch and not 'twixt tyres and road surface. But then I got it just right, and we were looking at just 5.0sec and 11.6sec. Kremer had given my friend the edge he sought over the Turbo, and the Boxer, and the Countach. That the clutch felt that it would never give out only added to the feeling of effortlessness accompanying the performance. There was a tremendous responsiveness to it all too, and an enticing mixture of lustiness and spriteliness.

The 307lb/ft of torque might be developed at 5200rpm but there must be a great deal of it available really low in the range, and there is no suggestion of a big jump higher up. There is no peakiness: the camshafts are from the standard 3.0-litre Carrera. There is no hesitation in the delivery of fuel: the injection pump is from the Turbo. This engine just performs, smoothly, willingly and powerfully, stopping at 7300rpm only because the electronic cut-out stops it going further. And such is the speed with which the engine reaches those revs that it would take a brave man, at those prices, to remove the cut-out. As it is, at 7300rpm the gears provide 45, 77, 108 and 136mph, with 169mph theoretically possible in fifth.

AND THE REVS KEEP RISING

But more than the undeniable race car response, and the scale of the performance, more than the speeds attainable in those gears, it is the ease with which the car can be driven, the sheer lack of fuss, that makes it especially impressive.

As chance had it, I was in possession of a '77 Carrera 3, and to put the Kremer into perspective we ran performance figures on that one too before leaving to get on with the real driving. The clutch, not surprisingly, soon showed that it did not wish to take too many standing starts, but not before we'd clocked the excellent times of 6.0sec to 60mph and 13.9 to 100. It had seemed fast, though not quite *that* fast. But it felt noticeably slower than the Kremer. We left the Carrera where it was and set off in the Kremer, and as we wound our way to the motorway it was interesting to consider the behavioural differences between the two Porsches. The Kremer required no more effort from the driver than the Carrera; it was just vastly more positive, more purposeful, and better to drive. There was a lot more noise in the Kremer, but the ride was actually better than the Carrera's. Firm, communicative but not harsh. The amazing Pirellis seemed actually to help the Bilsteins' damping while still providing excellent communication and mighty grip.

And then there was the stability provided by both the suspension and the aerodynamic aids. Where the wheel of the Carrera had jiggled in the hands, in the usual Porsche fashion, the wheel of the Kremer was dead steady. Where the Carrera walked about on the road, in the usual Porsche fashion, the Kremer was positive as a bullet. Where the Carrera 3, without the benefit of the spoilers and dampers of the Kremer or even its 2.7-litre predecessor and the current Carrera Sport above it, felt far too lively – unstable, even – at fast speeds, the Kremer did not budge. The difference was quite staggering and when the Kremer swept over a certain crest in one right-hander that can be taken at about 90mph, its body did not lurch and force the car into roll oversteer as the Carrera had done. It just stayed flat, neutral and perfectly tidy. Even though a lot more power was reaching its wheels, it did not snap dramatically sideways like the Carrera when, on a damp stretch of road, I pulled out to overtake and trod down hard in second.

PORSCHE 911 KREMER

But was the comparison really valid? The Carrera 3 has on one hand been endowed with a great deal of power and on the other been robbed of the correct suspension and spoilers out of deference to buyer demand, and it has taken the car back several years. It is the worst 911 in recent times, upset and often upsetting. Where, on the motorway, this awkward car had moved disconcertingly in the crosswinds at fairly modest speeds, the Kremer Porsche stormed on as unaffected as an express train, better even than the Carrera 3 Sport and the Turbo. A 100mph cruise became a doddle, and at that gentle pace the noise was trailing gloriously behind to leave the cabin quiet enough for normal speech.

When we reached the tight streets of the villages of the west, however, and in the confined lanes, there arose a foible that my friend is going to have to accept. With the three pipes uncapped, there is a severe exhaust resonance – a droning boom that overwhelms the car – from 2000 to 2200rpm. Or, in fourth, from 37 to 40mph. You go back to third or up to top to avoid it. And while the Kremer certainly has the flexibility to take 1700rpm, or even less, in fifth, it loses the addictive feeling of responsiveness that it has from about 2000rpm upwards. You'll have to ride through the boom again as you accelerate in fifth anyway so to avoid it altogether you need to slip back to third when the chance to pick up speed arises. It's a rather frustrating upset to the flow. Thankfully, the boom is reduced when the first cap is in place, and all but eliminated by the second, although that of course curtails the performance.

We stopped for a quick sandwich and a tank of fuel – we had logged 13.6mpg – and it wasn't long after that we found the sort of roads we'd been seeking: curving, but fast and visually open. The traffic had thinned to one or two cars every now and then. The Porsche, settling into one of those grand touring-car paces that builds up and up until there's an intoxicating driver/car rhythm, gathered them in and swept past to leave them nothing but a shrinking tail and that stunning noise.

The Recaro, adjustable under the knees and across the small of the back, held me snugly and comfortably, with the same

AND THE REVS KEEP RISING

sort of purpose displayed by everything else in the car. Set-up so comfortably and yet in such a business-like manner, secured by a full harness, with ideal reach to the pedals and the wheel, and with the gearshift slipping easily through its pattern beneath your left hand, you feel perfectly established to devote full attention to the road and placing the car on it. This Porsche, as it flung the miles behind us, was easier to place than any I had driven previously. Sharper than the Turbo, more positive, more responsive, it swung instantly and precisely into the bends and then maintained its line with perfect balance. There wasn't even so much as the gentle tug from the Pirellis, relayed through the steering in the Turbo, to let you know that you were riding through a touch of designed-in understeer. This Porsche just changed direction to exactly the degree asked of it, whether by steering alone or with help from the throttle. There was no roll, no diagonal movement under hard brakes into tight bends or under hard power coming out of them. Just absolute control and poise. Erwin and Manfred Kremer had given my friend power: they had also given him a chassis that allowed every last drop to be used and enjoyed. We encountered roads still wet from showers, and even they did not incite the car to deviate.

Slowly, surely, delightfully, it was all building up to a magnificent afternoon's driving. It's always best when it happens like that. You start out low-key, warming up with the car, establishing a harmony with it, working towards real rhythm. Precise, controlled movements, almost of the brain rather than hands and feet, that elicit an answer in smoothness from the car. And after 200 miles, superb in themselves, of this sort of build-up came 25 miles or so of the most idyllic road. Everything was perfect: the harmony was there, and the Porsche simply slipped through the bends. Certain now of the Kremer's grip, aware of the excellence of its handling, the precision of its steering and its throttle response, and the power of its braking as well as that of its engine, and aided and abetted by the feel and the sound, I started using it all.

All but brushing the banks under brakes on the way in, holding tight, tight, tight to the apex until the tail was almost ready to creep and then coming off that hard little pedal and back onto the throttle to open up that engine: it was as if there was no break in time at all between the hard braking and the smooth, devastating acceleration. There was no mechanical flab to interrupt the flow and with its tearing, stirring wail the car would be surging forward for the next bend. Almost always there was room to run second gear to its limit, and sometimes for 7300rpm to come up in third too. And then there'd be the push on the brakes again for the next bend and a repetitive process.

Some of the corners under the trees were wet but even then the full force of second gear only once edged the car into oversteer. And it required nothing more than the swiftest flick of the wheel into a few degrees of opposite lock, with the throttle still hard down, to bring the car straight again. It had never deviated from its line, never faltered. Glorious! When there were crests, the Porsche just flashed over them, still so surefooted. In the dips, it never crashed onto its bumpstops: the vagaries of the road surface were simply dealt with, disdainfully efficiently.

And so we went on and on rocketing through those seemingly endless bends, curving this way and that in a captive rhythm. There was such a feeling of control and safety and sheer speed and pleasure that, like Keith Jarrett caught in the grip of his music, I had to yell out with joy. It really was that good. So much performance so obediently on hand; such an impeccably accurate chassis. This car seemed unable to do anything wrong and although its character was pure efficiency, somehow it was not cold – solid, but not heavy in the hands.

There was a chance, if I continued much further, that I'd spoil it. And it had all been so perfect. So I stopped and my friend took control of his car again. He drove it magnificently and it was not in fear or concern that I asked, after a while, if we'd been travelling so quickly when I'd been driving. 'Maybe faster,' he said, and it seemed impossible. From the passenger's seat the sheer pace was brought home.

Back in London, we weren't tired, just very happy. My friend because it had become patently obvious that his car was indeed even better than he had imagined. And me because a bright and unexpected new gem had been added to my motoring experiences; one that would be brought to life every time I played *The Köln Concert*.

Postscript

After this story appeared in *CAR* March 1977, Pete King, who was Ronnie Scott's partner in the famous Soho jazz club Ronnie Scott's, rang me up. Pete raced Escorts at the weekends. He said, in his gruff Bow accent: 'Pete King from Ronnie Scott's 'ere. You've just written about the two things I love most: jazz and cars. 'kin brilliant. Come down the club any time you like. Just ask at the door for Pete.' I was thrilled.

Reader Ronnie Somerville told me this anecdote: 'I was hitchhiking in Germany with my girlfriend and we got a lift from a couple of longhairs in an old Beetle. Stuffed in the back with our rucksacks we chatted and after a while they put on a tape of solo piano music while we traversed a mountain pass. I hadn't heard it before but after 20 minutes or so I thought that it must be the piece you had described. Indeed, it was *The Köln Concert*. At the time I thought "Mel would be pleased!" and always meant to contact you.'

ROAD AMERICA AND THE SILVER TRASHCAN

MERCEDES-BENZ 450SEL 6.9
1977

SILVER TRASHCAN INDEED! THE call sign was as unlikely as it was inappropriate, and it caught the imagination of our fellow travellers from one side of America to the other. 'That sure is some trashcan!' they'd yelp delightedly into their CB radios as we rolled by, sometimes at a legal 55mph and sometimes at as much as 130mph. Such tomfoolery! Who would be wag enough to call a four-door saloon capable of such speed, a car with 6.9 litres of alloy V8 under its bonnet, hydro-pneumatic suspension, and a Mercedes star on its nose… who would dare dub such a car a *trashcan*? Daimler-Benz can thank the wry mind of David E. Davis, Jr. for that. *I* can thank him for his friendship and generosity, for his love of cars and his country; for it was he who took me to see America. Los Angeles to New York. Deserts to forests. Plains to mountains. Tranquil skies to awesome storms. Fizzy beer to rich Californian wines, pancakes and eggs over-easy to roast beef and home-made biscuits, raunchy motels to elegant southern homes. Ocean to ocean, one world to another… seven days and 3500 miles.

For the most part, it was executed with the sort of spontaneity that had led to my inclusion in the adventure of ferrying a top-of-the-range Mercedes-Benz. 450SEL 6.9, new in America, from the West Coast back to New York. A casual telephone conversation developed into an invitation to join in, and then there was a plane from London to Los Angeles. Iceland glittered white in that cold, slow blue sea, and grey-green Canada stretched vast and flat.

I'd thought we might head east as soon as the plane landed and

AND THE REVS KEEP RISING

I – tired but excited; I hadn't been to the United States before – was safely in the big Mercedes. Waiting for me had delayed David and his wife Jeannie by more than 24 hours. But no: we joined the evening peak hour traffic streaming along one of those amazing Los Angeles freeways and went south to Newport Beach to dine with Dan Gurney. He doesn't race anymore; he builds cars for others to search out their limits, and he enjoys family life. Dear dead friends, painfully lost, grin out from the walls of an otherwise happy trophy room. Dan converses in quiet, warm tones, laughing a lot, talking of racers past and present, and wondering whether he and Jackie Stewart really will egg each other into going racing again, *I-will-if-you-will*, just once.

We began driving at seven o'clock the next morning after a night at what would prove to be an abnormally expensive motel. The cashier got $34, and we got no breakfast because there was a long queue for tables even at 6.30. Americans begin their business early. So we took to the road, beginning near the famous Briggs Cunningham automotive museum in Costa Mesa that I would like to have seen, and picking up the Newport Freeway that would sweep us swiftly through the Santa Ana Mountains, and Orange County (the name tells the story) to Riverside and San Bernadino where we'd pick up Interstate 15 to swing north for the desert. As we climbed away from Los Angeles, into foothills that looked scruffy to me, we were being released from the smog that the mountains force back upon Los Angeles. Down in the basin it was warm but dull. Up here it became hot, bright and sparkling. It was if we'd climbed out of a gigantic pot of hot dirty mist.

A slip road took us into a garage and restaurant, as just about every eating house in America is called, tucked away in the trees. 'Eggs any style' means precisely what it says. You can concoct just about any mix of eggs, sausages, pancakes, toast, fresh fruit or big, inviting-looking home-made pies. For swift service and fairly good food but awful coffee (unfortunately typical) we paid just $8. We'd be doing better in other places, but my expectations of terrible food were on the way to being dashed.

The first of many tanks of lead-free fuel went into the silver

MERCEDES-BENZ 450SEL 6.9

Mercedes. We were close to the Interstate that would take us directly north before spearing across the desert in a direct line for Flagstaff, Albuquerque, Oklahoma City, Little Rock, Memphis and Nashville. The Interstate road system is relatively new, essentially crossing the country from west to east at several latitudes, but with dozens of north south links too, and forming part of Uncle Sam's defence system as well as giving road transport fast, toll-free motorways. Beautifully engineered, the Interstates usually have two-lanes in each direction, but they're separated by wide spaces which provide safety as well as the room to expand to three or even four lanes. The signposting is clean and logical. A blue and red shield denotes the Interstates, a white shield shaped like a US marshal's badge designates normal federal highways and the state roads have white oval sign plates.

At San Bernadino, we had a choice of roads. Interstate 15 leading to 40, or I-One-Oh (remember CW McCall's *Convoy)'* which sweeps across the far south through Phoenix, Tucson, El Paso, Houston and around, just north of New Orleans, to the eastern side of the Gulf of Mexico. But David had chosen I40 because it would take us to a special canyon in Arizona that he had in mind, and then to the Fort Apache Indian reservation. I was soon to find out that it would have a touch of romance about it too; for most of its length it runs over the path of Old Route 66. The Rolling Stones' song (with apologies to Nat King Cole) plays on your lips, images from the old TV series flip through your mind. Years of books, songs and films have turned America into a heavy case of *deja vu*.

We cleared the San Bernardino Mountains, rearing above us to 11,000ft, full of both summer and ski resorts, and still with a little snow at the peaks. We climbed up and up through the Cajon Canyon pass, the Mercedes eating the sweeping, climbing curves, until we dropped again and emerged into the Mojave Desert. The man-eating country was beginning.

We had cause to feel the intensity of its heat – and this was early spring – when we were forced to stop not far from a place called Barstow. There'd been a Highway Patrolman running behind us for a while but he'd turned off onto the old road and, steadily, Jeannie

AND THE REVS KEEP RISING

had been letting the Mercedes' speed build up on the straight, flat and almost-deserted road. The policeman had anticipated perfectly. He picked us up a few miles further on and by the time Jeannie spotted him in the mirror it was too late. He was courteous and pleasant as he wrote the ticket, for 65mph in fact and not the 75 she'd really been doing, and he asked why we weren't using our Citizens' Band radio. 'The truckers out here are on channel 21, and it's 19 for the cars,' he advised. We appreciated it too; but we had a problem with the CB: it would plug into the cigarette lighter for power and switch on OK, and the magnetic-base aerial would cling to the roof without trouble, but when we tried to speak we were greeted with cries of: 'Hey buddy, your mike is screamin' its head off!' We'd switched off until we could find a CB shop to check it and connect up our radar detector. As it turned out, that wouldn't be until the following afternoon, a long way on.

So a sedate but safe 60mph took us on across the desert, rising out of one grey basin and into the next. The mountains closed in around us as we headed into the south-eastern reaches of the Mojave with its weird, wild, awesome formations, like Pisgah Crater where the NASA astronauts practised moonwalking because the surfaces were so similar. In the middle of it all, a town called Essex. A few hours further on, a sign loomed out of the desert: 'See London Bridge'.

It's at Lake Havasu, a little south of where we stopped for lunch, at Topock, just over the Colorado River that separates California from Arizona. Las Vegas was behind and to the north of us. When we had been fiddling with the CB radio, we'd heard the truckers talking about various adventures there.

At Topock, with four hours of desert driving behind us, and a time change that lost us an hour the instant we crossed the river, we found our way down a dusty road to a dumpy brick place carrying the inevitable restaurant sign and hoped for the best. And it was all right: cool and shady, overlooking a lagoon where ducks and water rats went about their business and a humming bird, frail and fast as a horsefly, fed from a dispenser on the veranda. The hamburgers weren't terrific but the beer was icy cold. Polite

MERCEDES-BENZ 450SEL 6.9

questions about Britain, lots of well-wishing, $8.35, 1.55pm, and we were underway again.

It was a little too early in the season for the expanses of wild flowers that bring the desert to life. But now and then there was a splash of orange among the dull, green Greasewood bushes: little red cacti. It would have been a mistake to imagine that hard, gravelly country barren and dead. Apart from the vegetation – and the cacti will provide a man with enough water to stay alive – there are quail (blue and a little bigger than European ones), jack-rabbits, coyotes, wild cats, foxes and mule deer (named for their big ears). Signs to ghost towns, pointing off into the hills along rugged old roads, dot the highway here and there. It made me long for more time and a four-wheel-drive vehicle to go and investigate. The cleanliness of that intensely dry heat and the feeling of space make it hard to resist.

And I was sorry when, within hours, we began nudging out of the grey, bright, powerful desert into less severe country actually covered in light, pale grass, with that relentless road rushing on to disappear against the walls of a vast range of mountains rising straight up ahead of us. Flagstaff was on top of it all, and a look at the map showed the city – still 170 miles away – to be at almost 7000ft. Even the desert we'd been in was at something like 4000ft, which later helped explain a curious event.

The climb into those towering ranges was surprisingly gentle. We were moving more quickly now, for the radio was providing us with enough reception to pick up the information on the Smokey Bears – policemen. The Interstates are marked every mile, with the numbers starting at each state line and running east. West-bound drivers tell the east-bounders where the police are, and vice-versa, quite apart from providing weather information, news of road conditions and emergencies. And of course there's a certain amount of chit-chat between new friends and old with just one thing in common: they're all on the road at the same time, a vast transient population.

After an hour's steady climb – perhaps the tireless energy of the Mercedes had made it seem less severe than it really had been – we were in vast plains, with banks of scrub here and there. And there

AND THE REVS KEEP RISING

on our left, 100miles to the north, was the Grand Canyon, those famous walls like a purple scar in the earth. We could see herds of cattle now, and we started looking for pronghorn antelope, their tails like white splashes against the fawn grass and, with their vision the equal of a man with *20/20* sight using eight-power binoculars, certain to pick you up before you get near them. A little later, a princely bald-headed eagle sitting on a pole beside the road brought us to a stop. The sun was getting low but it was still searingly hot out of the car. Big, red rock bluffs rose up from the plains: we were in Arizona all right. Yet another long blue-and-yellow Santa Fe train eased by. Essentially, we were following the old Santa Fe Trail, one of the most arduous for Indian attacks and difficult country. The Comanche and Apache had such tremendous places to launch raids and wait in ambush. The desert behind us was perfect for that too. A man on horseback could disappear in an instant in those draws.

Fairly soon we were into tall stands of pine trees, climbing again, to beyond 5000ft, and the air was growing crisp. At a place called Williams, some way short of Flagstaff and named after one Bill Williams who founded it in 1876 for who knows what reason, we stopped. It was a place with just a main street and a couple of blocks, the usual cafe and stores and garages and, up Fourth Street on the south side, a shop with AMMO! We passed it as we swung off I40/Route 66 to make for the place that was at the top of our list: Oak Creek Canyon. A few miles out of town, in the sort of heavily pined country that you'd expect in Canada or Montana, snow lay in big patches. The thaw hadn't finished. Williams and Flagstaff are sometimes deep in snow in May. Only a few hours before we'd been in the intense heat of the desert.

The little road, which soon became well-graded dirt, took us south along the ridge of the range, losing altitude until there was no more snow, just a magnificent sunset across the plains and canyons and eventually desert that dropped away to our right. Mule deer leaped away into the trees at several points as we interrupted their evening feeding, for we were the only people using the road that crisp night. Jeannie, driving once more, wheeled the Mercedes expertly along the twisting, dipping road as it began to drop into one canyon after

MERCEDES-BENZ 450SEL 6.9

the next, the trees receding again and the rich red dirt kicking up behind us. Soon it was dark, and in 50 miles we would see only one ranch house, although the quaint wooden signs, like something out of a boy scouts' book, pointed the way clearly enough. The road got pretty rough in parts but the Mercedes handled it with sure feet and plenty of ride comfort, although not free from the suspension bump-thump common to all models in Stuttgart's range.

For the last 20 miles, it was obvious that we were edging around the side of a vast canyon that must have been stunning in the daylight, and we cursed that we'd reached it so late in the day. Still, we'd covered a lot of ground. At 8.30pm we plopped out of the wilderness into a strange hillside town called Jerome, full of tall timber buildings with verandas and buckets of charm but not many people. The place we'd thought would take care of us for the night was all but a ghost town with 400 inhabitants where once the mines carried 15,000. But Sedona wasn't far away and we soon found a motel there with comfortable rooms. The landlord, dragged away from his TV set, wasn't too friendly. He wanted $22 (£13), which seemed over the odds but not offensively so because Sedona is justifiably popular, and not just with Hollywood film crews. David's hunch that there was a reasonable restaurant a few miles back down the road paid off, and we dined on big steaks and a bottle of 1972 Almaden Pinot Noir from California that was very good indeed for $6. All up, our bill was $26. We left the piano player – 'straight from the nightspots of Las Vegas' – tinkling away to drown a croaky voice in the cabaret room next door and toddled off to bed.

I woke at 5am and drew the blinds back from the full-depth window to behold a breath-taking sight. The sun was filling the red rock canyons, four of them, running out like the arms of a star from the town. The view from the back door was just as glorious. The world was bright blue and red and purple and fresh and clean. You want to take deep breaths. I went walking for an hour, and somehow the multi-coloured signs of Sedona didn't look out of place: nature was bigger than them all. No wonder so many films have been shot here, and that so many people spend large chunks of their year out here (one of Wall Street's biggest stockbrokers has

AND THE REVS KEEP RISING

an office in the shopping centre). Sedona, at the entrance to Oak Creek Canyon, is a picture postcard town, modern and appealing, and something of an art and culture centre.

Even at 7am, television was in full swing. One channel was showing a startling event called the RTL Club, which I think was coming from Phoenix, away to the south. It was a phone-in prayer programme, with a wound-up, chubby-faced compere who could have sold Chevrolets to Henry Ford rattling off long prayers for the lady with sclerosis of the liver and the man with cancer of the colon and the shopkeeper whose young wife had run off with his eldest son and the accountant with his second coronary. 'Friends, we are here, at the other end of your telephone line, to help you in your hour of need…'

After breakfast (I braved a stack of pancakes with eggs, sausages and maple syrup, just like the locals) we searched in vain for a CB shop. But in the camera store we turned up a greater treasure. The owner was sporting a big Indian turquoise bracelet, and he told us about Don Hoel, up the canyon a little way, who had, he reckoned, the finest range of Indian jewellery in the country.

Mr Hoel's house nestled in the pines, beside the stream and with the canyon wall rearing up behind it, red and yellow. He took us into a room, packed with local Navajo, Hopi and Zuni artefacts. In the space of two hours, once he realised we were genuinely interested and would be buying, Mr Hoel showed us piece after piece of the most marvellous jewellery, more magnificent and far more expensive than I'd ever have guessed. Big, solid silver settings carry deep blue turquoise stones, formed into necklaces, bracelets or belts. I had to fiercely resist going deep into hock for an old, magnificent belt priced at $600. The turquoise, expensive and mined in several parts of Arizona, Colorado and New Mexico, has been used by the south-western tribes since about 500AD, but it wasn't until the 1850s that the Navajo, now the biggest of the American tribes with 75,500 people, learned to be silversmiths. Their early work was influenced by the roaming Mexican craftsmen who taught them. And thanks to the Spanish, there are influences from people as distant to the Indians as the North African Moors.

MERCEDES-BENZ 450SEL 6.9

The Zuni, a 5500-strong New Mexico tribe who live south-east of the Navajo, began in 1890 to inlay silver with stones, developing their own distinctive style of jewellery. It is more delicate, more artistic than the Navajo work; some of it mosaic-like and some of it scores of pieces of turquoise or coral mounted individually to form elaborate brooches, bracelets and rings. Mr Hoel wanted $300 for an inlaid brooch I liked. Jewellery by the Hopi (there are 6500 of them living inside the Navajo areas in the central north of Arizona) is a lot simpler, with patterns that look Scandinavian cut into solid silver bracelets or pendants. They are patterns developed from the distinctive designs on the pottery they've been making for centuries. The Zuni also carve tiny animal figures called fetishes from antler, stone or turquoise that are of prehistoric origin and are believed to carry spirits that will help the wearer in war or when he's hunting. They're drilled and strung and usually have six strands to a necklace. The finest in Mr Hoel's possession (or at least that he showed us) was $18,000, all top quality turquoise. He showed us a glorious Navajo rug, 90 strands to the inch, made of nothing but black and white undied wool rolled 'together to make up various subtle colours. It had taken a 90-year-old woman three years to weave, and he was asking $11,000 for it. From a side room he produced a bracelet like no other: Navajo, very old, silver and turquoise, ebony and mother-of-pearl, big and chunky, and weighted to the lower part of the wrist. It suited Jeannie as perfectly as it fitted her, and just before we were leaving David gave Mr Hoel $500 for it. We tore ourselves away before we spent more money we didn't have.

The rocks, many of them world famous, towered above us until the road finally began to climb out of Oak Creek Canyon. There were tight uphill bends, one after the other, and David, who can drive, started using the Mercedes. It was here that the car displayed its *raison d'être*. Until then, we could have been just as comfortable in some of the better American cars costing a 10th as much as the Mercedes. I must admit that I had been having thoughts about it being over-engineered for the smooth roads of the United States. But the 450SEL 6.9 is a driver's car and not a limousine: you take it and open up that big silky V8 and it gets up and responds. It shrinks

AND THE REVS KEEP RISING

around you and is perfectly behaved, edging into power oversteer where you want it, or staying neutral where you'd prefer it that way. So you're paying $40,000 (£23,00 in the UK) for on-the-road ability with this Mercedes, not extreme comfort or luxury or status. It needs a better temperature control system, less bump-thump from the tyres, rear cigarette lighters and a less stark interior.

Out of the canyon, north to Flagstaff, a pleasing city in among the trees, and east again picking up I40/Route 66 once more. Big plains, with tumbleweed. Tumbling too, for we were running into thunderstorms. The plains were as grey as the sky, except for white patches of sand whipped up by the air currents. Dull, uncomfortable country, with the town of Winslow – immortalised by The Eagles in *Take it Easy* – right in the middle of it: just a long, wide main street, swept with wind and sand, crammed with signs, and the feeling that the last thing you'd want to do would be stop. David told the story of how he once had an immaculate TR2 stripped to the metal in a sandstorm out here, and whisky wasn't enough to drown the frustration.

We had the CB on all the time by then, getting updates on the weather and the Smokey Bears. 'Breaker one-nine for an east-bounder runnin' for Holbrook on I-four-oh. What's back over your shoulder, good buddy?'

'You got an east-bounder, and you got Smokey Bear takin' pictures westbound at the 260-mile marker.'

'I'll thank you kindly for the information, good buddy.'

High-pitched new voice: 'Whah doan chew try doin' 55?'

First trucker, soft and despairingly: 'Oh boy, there's one in every crowd.'

As the traffic passes, the updates go on. The CB range is usually about 10 miles, but a west-bounder might have given the east-bounders information for up to 100 miles ahead. Asking for an update, should it not have come unprompted as they usually do, in 20 miles or so will determine whether the Bear is still in position or if he's moved, and if so where to and what's he doing. Weather and road condition reports come just as quickly and seriously as they do for the police.

MERCEDES-BENZ 450SEL 6.9

'Breaker one-nine – if there's a Smokey Bear listenin' on this channel, the flags on them there roadworks at the 320 marker are blowin' away in the wind. Can you tell the construction people?' A policeman answers instantly and thanks the trucker for the information. By the time we get to the roadworks, the police are helping the workers get the warning flags and drums back into place.

The weather was freaky, but the rain, and hopefully lots of it, was welcome. Drought had hit the western states: 6.8 million acres of Oklahoma alone had been blown away, so the man on TV had said. In Texas, a CBer says, there's been the good news of two inches of rain overnight, and big storms coming. The map suggested that Holbrook might be as miserable as Winslow. For some reason, not quite, although it too has one of those highway streets with forests of neon signs and gas stations and motels, shops and the police station. It was windswept too but not as depressing. We found a CB shop. The problem had been in our aerial lead. While the young bloke from the shop fixed it ($6 for parts and $6 for labour, including wiring up the Super Snooper radar detector) we ate a miserable lunch in a cafe that had changed hands since David was last there. On the way out of town, while we were stopped for petrol (14.5mpg, compared with 14.3 and 13.4 at the previous two fill-ups), the kid running the pumps walked over to pick up a .44 pistol from a friend who'd driven up in a Jeep. He took it and put it in his office. Guns are second nature out here. People have racks of them in the back windows of their pick-ups.

Snowflake, a town in a dip at the edge of a vast, grey, dull, scrubby plain, on Route 77 that we took south from Holbrook, lived up to its name. The wind and sand storms gave way to a fully-fledged blizzard just before we entered the town. No sign of it letting up, so the CB told us, and we ran on through it to Show Low, a town so named because a pioneer, gambling with a ranch at stake, challenged another to 'show low'. He won, and named the place accordingly before eventually giving it to the Mormons who built the town.

The snow stopped by the time we'd run on down State 73 to the Fort Apache Indian reservation in the White Mountains

155

AND THE REVS KEEP RISING

(stopping for thick, terrific boysenberry pie and ice-cream and coffee at the Hon-dah – Apache for 'welcome' – Motel; on the radio the man was talking about the latest government measures to combat the drought). There are three tribes of Western Apache, the San Carlos, White Mountain and Tonto Apache. It was from the hills and valleys of the Fort Apache area that Apache raiders operated so successfully and justifiably, after the treatment they'd been given. The Apache could never understand how, in 1853, the United States could lay claim to their territory when neither they, nor the Spaniards or Mexicans had ever defeated them. Many Apache refused to be confined to reservations and went on raiding, as the finest of guerrillas, until 1890. Fort Apache, on a bluff above the White River, was built in 1870, and the black cavalrymen who eventually wore the Apache down, operated from there. Essentially, the Indians were left land no-one else wanted. They had, and are having, the last laugh. The 12,000 White Mountain Apache have turned their 1.7 million acre reservation, their traditional territory, into a thriving and beautiful chunk of Arizona. Apart from being successful cattle ranchers, they have massive pine forests and they've developed the natural beauty spots of the White Mountains into attractive resorts for skiing and fishing. The reservation is run to a corporate charter by a 10-member elected council.

As we wound through the reservation with its big plains, deep valleys, majestic red rock outcrops and fine timber stands, it began to snow again. We were waved down at a bridge. Did we have CB? An Apache woman coming the other way had understeered straight off at the curve onto the bridge and plunged down the creek bank. Neither she nor her two kids were hurt, but they needed help. A couple of calls for a Smokey Bear monitoring the channel proved fruitless; we were too deep in the valley. But a woman answered our third call, and from a higher position passed the word along to the police and a tow truck operator. We gave the woman and her children a lift to a garage to escape the snow, and passed on the message of her whereabouts. The CB involvement went on. Rolling on towards Show Low, someone said:

MERCEDES-BENZ 450SEL 6.9

'Breaker one-nine for that silver Mercedes.'

David: 'You got the Silver Trashcan.' How long he'd had that handle – as call signs are dubbed – in his mind I didn't know, but evocative it certainly was.

Voice: 'This here's the Sniper, in that green motorhome up ahead of you. The snow's getting thicker up here. Take it steady.'

And so it went on, everybody keeping each other posted about the constantly changing road conditions, and watching for people in trouble.

We almost had it as we ran down a long hill out of the reservation. A Datsun 180B pulled straight out of a side road in front of us. We had to brake hard, thankful for the Mercedes' poise and traction, then accelerated by when the Datsun eased over.

David: 'This is the Silver Trashcan. I just about got me a little blue Japanese thing for a hood ornament back there.'

Squawky woman's voice: 'Oh no you didn't. I had my eyes on you, and I kept over. If I'd stopped on that snow I wouldn't have got going again.'

The sun was almost gone by then, a cold pink glow among the White-draped pines and alpine timber houses of the pretty villages. We determined to go on another hour to a place called Springerville, 13 miles from the New Mexico state line, for the night. It had a Ramada Inn that was more than reasonable at $11 for a big room with another of those kingsize beds, well-fitted bathroom, TV and radio. Nor was $6.95 bad for a whopping T-bone. We retired for a few of Mr Davis's fine Armagnacs before crashing into bed. Had we really come so far and seen so much already? Out in the main street, tin-top cowboys dragged away from the traffic lights. Springerville, now a shopping and service centre for timber and cattle industries, wasn't always so peaceful. In the 1870s and '80s it was one of the roughest towns in the southwest, packed with fugitive rustlers, horse thieves and outlaws.

Saturday, 6.00am: Fine and clear. Snow still on the ground. Another sleepy, wide main street, glistening in the sun. Eggs, bacon, hash brown potatoes, thick toast and coffee for $2. One of the ranchers, in the motel for breakfast after an hour's work

AND THE REVS KEEP RISING

already, says *he* had 4in of snow yesterday. Doesn't expect it to melt for another two weeks. 7.00am: Hit the road, east on US60, through grazing land sprinkled with snow. 7.10am: Into New Mexico, straight road climbing gently and dropping over low hills every 10 miles or so.

7.11am: David: 'Breaker one-nine for a west-bounder on this Route 60.'

'Go breaker.'

'What's over your shoulder good buddy?'

'It's clear all the way to Socorro.'

'Thanks friend. We're east out of Springerville and you're clean and green right on through there.'

The Mercedes surges on to a smooth, quiet 130mph before the aerial's magnets give up their attempt to hold it upright on the roof. No damage. Settle for a more sedate 120mph. Almost no traffic. 8.05am: Radar detector starts bleeping. Crash down to 50mph. No Smokeys, only a radar relay for aircraft on a hill a mile away. At least the thing works.

'Big country!' we all chorus as we top the rise and look down and ahead of us. Heading into the sort of land where Billy the Kid killed and was killed. 8.30am: The wide sky ahead turns filthy grey. We're running into rain. Cross the Continental Divide, 7796ft, just another crest in the road, but from here on all the rivers will run east. 8.35am: Spectacular Datil Mountains rear up on the left, a string of silhouettes. The rain hits us hard. It turns to snow. 9.10am: It stops. 9.45am: Socorro, bright and open, but no tape in the hardware store to make sure the aerial stays on the roof. Run north on Interstate 25 towards Albuquerque. CB warns of Bear activity. Set the cruise control to keep us on a steady 65mph. 10.00am: Turn east onto US60 again. Cross the Rio Grande, a narrow stream of water here in a wide, sandy riverbed with scrubby bushes. Run along the flat before climbing the long, sweeping road into a place called Mountainair where there's not much beyond a couple of gas stations, a hairdressers, Farmer Jones restaurant, a grass patch for the local Chev dealer, a drab adobe building housing the library on one side and police on the other. Trashcan takes 22.8 gallons of

unleaded for an 11.69mpg readout. Running at upwards of 100mph takes its toll.

10.45am: Still on US60, east again cross flat country, big-sky country, storms gathering at three or four separate points. Share it with a mile-long Santa Fe train. Now and then small, dreary adobe towns like Vaughn, Encino and Yeso slumber either side of the road. Clear the 'city limits' and reactivate the cruise control to take the Trashcan up to a neat 100mph once more. It has so much pickup from 60, 80 or even 100mph, and speed makes no difference to the way it feels. Fierce rainstorms drift across our path every 20 miles or so. 12.30pm: Pass a '67 Dodge Charger, running about 80mph, with three big whip aerials bending back in the wind. Tell him he looks like a tuna boat and he tells us he's pulled 'em off his truck and is working out which is the best. There are masses of different aerials giving widely varying results.

12.35pm: Tuna Boat: 'Silver Trashcan, you still out there?'

Trashcan: 'We're here.'

Tuna Boat: 'You must be movin' – I can't see you any more.'

Trashcan: 'Well, we're doing a corrected 55mph. We just check the speedo, add in a little fiddle factor, keep one eye on the Snooper and listen real close to the CB, and we call that a corrected 55.'

He's broken one of the unwritten CB rules: never suggest that a specific car or truck is travelling quickly. 12.55pm: Word comes down the line that there's a Smokey Bear just outside Fort Sumner. One mile before we're due to reach him, we knock it off and waffle by at 60. A good time to stop for lunch. The number of cars outside it makes Jeannie pick Tito's Cafe, and she hits the jackpot. A truly excellent Mexican lunch of tacos, enchiladas, rice and refried beans and some big puffy pastry envelopes to fill with honey all costs $9.10 for the three of us.

1.45pm: Pull into the Billy The Kid Museum at old Fort Sumner, where he copped it at Pat Garrett's hands in 1881, and spend half an hour looking at a motley collection of relics, including, for what it's worth, the boots The Kid was wearing when he was shot, and gory old pictures of local hangings and bunches of desperadoes. The lady in charge, pedalling cheap imitation Indian jewellery but who

AND THE REVS KEEP RISING

knows the real thing when she sees it, nearly falls over herself to get a look at Jeannie's bracelet.

2.50pm: The usual long straight road but with dips and crests quite often, and slightly greener country – have they had good rain here? – the Super Snooper (watchdog, in CB jargon) bleep-bleep-bleeps, and sure enough a mile further on there's a Tijuana Taxi travelling east with his radar on. The police can use their radar from a stationary position, in either direction when they're on the move, either behind or in front of them, approaching or going away from you. They also have handheld 'guns' they can aim at individual cars in a stream of traffic. We spread the word on the CB.

3.15pm: Roll into Clovis, New Mexico. Stop outside a western shop. Spend half an hour with friendly, helpful people in a well laid out place buying cowboy boots, belt and Stetson for me, hat band for David and some moccasins for Jeannie. 3.45pm: Coming out of Clovis, a pleasant town with interesting buildings and an intriguing old cinema, the Snooper sounds again. The Smokey Bear is hidden in some bushes in the median strip. Saved again. We're into flat farmland now with vast cultivated fields for wheat and cattle fodder, and mammoth silos alongside the railway that accompanies the road.

In a few minutes we cross into the Texas Panhandle, losing an hour as we change into the central time zone. Long irrigators keep huge fields watered. Everything's big here: the silos, the Santa Fe trains hauled by four whopping diesel engines (piggy-back truck containers on flat-bed cars mean new-life for the more progressive railways; the others are sliding into bankruptcy) and especially the enormous, unique cattle feed lots. They're thousands of acres of corrals packed with cattle bought and being fed by agents forwarding them, usually with price speculation, to slaughterhouses. Conveyor belts bring the feed out from central processing plants that look like chemical installations. It's a seething mass of black and red and white shapes stretching into the distance. The stench is overwhelming.

6.55pm: Near Amarillo, as we rejoin I40. CBer: 'Uh, that Blacktop headin' south – you got your flashers going.'

MERCEDES-BENZ 450SEL 6.9

Blacktop: 'Yeah I know good buddy. I'm pushin' along, tryin' to get to the hospital.'

Woman's voice: 'Good for you buddy. Good luck with the new baby.'

First CBer: 'He didn't say anything about a baby, lady.'

Blacktop: ''Preciate you folks' interest. But she's right: I'm gonna have a new baby!'

7.30pm: A motel sign in a town called Groom gets us and we pull in. It's $15, smells a bit and passing trucks will shake the walls most of the night. We eat in a steakhouse up the road, successfully, admiring the features and the outfit of the elderly sheriff at a nearby table, finish with pecan pie and drive back through the rain to turn in early. We've covered 600-odd miles for the day. Test my boots and hope they'll break in.

On Sunday we set ourselves an even greater target: Nashville, 1000 miles east, with what's left of Texas, all of Oklahoma, Arkansas and half of Tennessee between us. We're on the road at 5.30am in the grey dawn drizzle and run for a couple of hours before stopping, deep into Oklahoma, for breakfast, this time with biscuits – sort of sweet scones – and the usual watery coffee. From the road, Oklahoma, Arkansas and Tennessee are red and green states: deep basalt earth topped with lush, light green foliage, with fat Herefords and Anguses in place of the straggly-looking cattle of the west. They're hot, steamy places made worse for us because the Trashcan's air conditioning isn't working properly. We see increasingly quaint wooden farmhouses and those dull red barns straight out of picture books and movies, spring flowers, and farmers in the restaurants in blue denim overalls and striped peaked caps.

We were in and out of rainstorms most of the morning and they made the mugginess worse. We had to laugh, though, at the guy on a big motorbike. He wasn't in wet weather gear so, once he'd cleared a deluge, swung his legs out into the breeze for miles to dry his boots and trousers. He was having a ball. When he turned his CB back on – he'd switched it off in the storm because he was scared it would short out – we learned that he'd been wandering around in Arizona and was heading back to Okie City. He stayed with us for 50 miles or so, at a nice comfortable 85mph, with the

AND THE REVS KEEP RISING

CB information coming regularly enough to reassure us and the watchdog on the dash filling in the gaps.

By 10.30am we'd crossed into Arkansas and about lunchtime were running just north of Little Rock. The CB went to bits: the air was full of Sunday drivers, with the mike generally in the hands of women passengers, chit-chatting endlessly and awfully and making it impossible for serious motorists to break in even for Bear Reports, the magic words that normally shut everybody down. They had really imaginative handles like 'Sexy Momma' and 'Foxy Lady'. Their inane gossiping crippled a vital form of communication. We turned the radio down and slowed until we were well clear of Little Rock and the traffic thinned.

Just before 5.00pm we crossed the wide, grey-brown mass of water that is the Mississippi and were at once into Memphis and Tennessee. A few river boats downstream, and tower blocks, with the unmistakable look of '30s architecture and thus like something out of old comic books or gangster movies, rising up like a clump of trees along the river's eastern bank. A pleasant looking city, the sort that makes you want to get into it and investigate. We had to keep driving, and within five minutes, the interstate had swept us over the city and on towards Nashville. After the Snooper had given us early warning of a Bear planted in a bus beside the road we joined forces with the driver of a yellow Datsun – King Bee. He offered to run back-door for us, passing on the word that the run to Nashville was likely to be fairly easy except for the possibility of Bear at the 108 and 190 markers. He made the trip every Sunday night. We checked with each other every five minutes or so, until the Trashcan's greater speed had carried us out of reach, and then our messages were relayed by people in between. Our unlikely handle was paying off. As it turned out, we went off at exit 108 (they're keyed to the mileage) for fuel. And as we started to head back onto the motorway the Snooper went wild. Sure enough, there was the Bear, sitting high up on the run-on ramp, lights off, taking pictures of the folks heading east. We spread the word that our dog was barking, picked up the King Bee and confirmed his tip. There was another one at the 190 marker, just like he said.

MERCEDES-BENZ 450SEL 6.9

In Nashville, on the complex freeway system, we got lost looking for the Hilton Hotel and in response to our request on the radio for local information we were soon put straight. It was 9.00pm. We were hot and tired, but we had better than 1000 miles under our belts, and today we'd passed the half-way point in our cross-country run. A vast room in the Hilton, with the ubiquitous air conditioning, colour TV and well-fitted bathroom was $21. In the parking lot, Cadillac after Cadillac. Posters told us that, as always, there were plenty of country-and-western musicians in town but Sunday night is their night off. So we ate well at a restaurant David knew out in the suburbs and zoomed back along the freeway to our beds. The Trashcan's ability to cover the miles without fatigue, although the rear seat was not ideal, was immense.

Madison Smith *naturally*, as his sign said, turned out to be not only Nashville's Mercedes dealer but a pretty fine driver as well as an Alfa Romeo freak. He'd just sold his Alfa and Citroën franchise to his partner, and was continuing alone with Mercs and Ferraris. His service department replaced the line that had come adrift in the air conditioning with speed and efficiency, and he tested their workmanship personally, hurling the Benz into a sweeper onto the freeway at 90mph and accelerating, delighting himself with its handling. He hadn't seen a 6.9 before: there were only four in the US so far, and he was itching to get his. It was a less brutal, more appealing car than the old 6.3, he reckoned as he saw us on our way. Somehow, I hadn't imagined Madison Smith, in deepest Tennessee, as an Alfa and Citroën lover.

Shortly before midday we crossed, going north, into Kentucky. The country began to roll more, with smaller, quainter farms and lots of those white timber fences. Kentucky is a relatively poor state. For years, coal mining was its key industry. There's been more now but large tracts of the state are rocky hills that won't grow anything. By 12.30pm we were, however, into green and beautiful dairy country that looked prosperous enough. We worked our way along little valleys, with 'hollers' running off them, David enjoying the tidiness of the Merc in the hills once more. Just as we were about to show a determined kid in a Camaro what it was all about a

AND THE REVS KEEP RISING

Tijuana Taxi appeared and we let the kid go while we checked to see if the policeman flip-flopped. David took us to Cumberland Lake, a huge water catchment in the hills, formed when they dammed the Cumberland River, and now stretching miles and miles back into the Appalachian Mountains. There aren't many people there, for it is harsh rocky country beneath the close trees, and mules are still valid transport. This is the land of the oft-depicted backwoods. Later on, we'd stopped for some real *Kentucky* Kentucky Fried Chicken and found it just the same as Col Sanders anywhere else. I was intrigued to learn that this whisky-producing state is, for the most part, dry. Some counties sell liquor, but in most you have to drive across the state line to buy so much as a can of beer... unless you have a tame bootlegger to keep you stocked with moonshine. What the church doesn't see doesn't hurt it, apparently.

Short, green, dense, rounded trees on lots of rocky hills made the area north of Cumberland look a lot like Stuttgart, ironically enough. But we headed north out of those hills for the college town of Berea, a special place, all but post-card perfect. Appalachian youngsters who would otherwise be deprived of a tertiary education come down out of the hills to Berea. The system dictates that they must work 10 hours every week, either in the hotel or the crafts shops or on crafts to stock them, to help pay their way.

The crafts are indigenous to the Appalachians, and at Berea they are passed on with skill and caring. Tradition is upheld in a country so eager for history. The furniture, made at the college, to period designs, is exquisite, both in the rooms of the Berea College Hotel, where we stayed for $21, and for sale in the crafts shops. So too are the quilts, not made by students but by women, some in log cabins up in the hills. A very good one, strikingly beautiful, costs about $300. On the wall of the best shop there was one for which the owners had been offered $1500, but they weren't selling.

In the dining room of the hotel, staffed by college students, most of the other guests were retired couples heading west or north again after wintering in Florida. It wasn't hard to see the attraction of Berea for them. Apart from its excellent, traditional hotel, it must have been like a trip back to college days for them,

MERCEDES-BENZ 450SEL 6.9

with wholesome America on display. We enjoyed an interesting and excellent meal for $7.40. Relishes to munch on, then terrific boiled ham, something called mustard greens, sweet potatoes and chocolate satin pie, washed down with ice water (because Berea is dry) in that big, 19th century dining room. We were thankful for our reserves of Armagnac and whisky upstairs. We basked in the charm and treasures of Berea rather too long the next morning. I managed to tear myself away from the quilts but Jeannie couldn't. She got a bargain: a $245 quilt for $95 because the lady who made it, up in the hills, had asked the shopkeeper to shift it quickly: her husband had been ill all winter.

And so we moved deeper into blue grass country, heading north to enter Ohio at Cincinnati. A pleasing city built on the hills above the Ohio River, and with a distinct German flavour about it: a surprise. Another surprise: Ohio was over-run with traffic police. The CB was pinpointing them every few minutes. 'County Mounty takin' pictures northbound at the three-five marker.' 'Local Yokel rollin' south at four-nine.' 'No sir, he's just done a flip-flop – watch out you north bounders.' 'Bear in the Air at seven-five.' We stayed on 60mph, like just about everybody else, and wondered at the cost of maintaining such intense patrols.

It was flatish, gentle farming country, warm in the spring sun, and free from the sultriness of the south. Around 4pm we pulled in for a hamburger and then took to the back roads through land not unlike England's West Country, but with the neat white-board houses, set back from the roads and without fences, of apple-pie America. At 5.30 we reached David's parents' home at New Pittsburg, Ohio, and from charming, eloquent, witty people I learned about American antiques and heard tales of hunting before a fine dinner of roast beef, succotash (lima beans and corn boiled together: excellent), boiled beets, rhubarb and raspberries and scrumptious home-made biscuits, followed by apple pie and angel cake. Late in the night we moved on, east again, past Akron, to get within fair striking distance of New York. By rights I should have been there to catch a plane at 9.00am. No way.

Yet another Ramada Inn came to our rescue, with rooms vacant

AND THE REVS KEEP RISING

at 1.00am for $15, not too many trucks rolling across the carpet and a 6.00am wake-up call. Ten minutes after setting off we were in Pennsylvania with 3121 miles behind us, and a bit over 400 to go. We'd be in New York just after lunch. While we ate a Howard Johnson's breakfast, the mechanic over the road tightened the pulley on the Trashcan's transmission coiler pump. We'd heard it making a noise when we stopped for petrol. Lo and behold, when we stopped again, 200 miles on, there it was again, but worse. We were at a garage deep in the Appalachian conifers, as pleasant a place to break down as any, but remote. The guy on duty nudged the Trashcan onto the hoist to try and tighten the thing up again, and no sooner had he cranked pressure into the hoist than we remembered: the air suspension! Too late. He dropped the car and sure enough it was flat as a tack, its front wheels disappearing up into their wheel arches. We ran the engine at idle, as the book said, but the suspension didn't want to know about jacking itself up again. And the rubber chocks, to be installed in just such situations, were not to be found. The nearest Mercedes dealer, about 40 miles away in Williamsport, said they'd come immediately but the 6.9 was just as new to them as it had been to Madison Smith *naturally*.

David rang *Flying*, sister magazine to his magazine, *Car and Driver*, and asked if their aeroplane was free. I was now booked on a 9pm flight out of JFK. Another look at the handbook suggested running the car at fast idle for a long time. We did, hoping the pulley wouldn't fly off, and after three or four minutes the SEL drew itself up to a respectable height again. Jeannie lit off into the nearest town in the garageman's pick-up truck for some steaks, and while the Mercedes mechanics secured the errant pulley sufficiently for us to reach The Big Apple, David barbecued the steaks on an amazing portable grille that looks like a three-part folding bucket into which you toss a sheet of newspaper. It worked, deliciously. With the makeshift repairs completed (back-up systems in the transmission meant that the pump could be safely disconnected should the pulley come off) we got under way again, running at a gentle 70mph and shakin' the trees for a fellow who called himself the White Rabbit, who was raking up the leaves at the backdoor for

MERCEDES-BENZ 450SEL 6.9

us. Ideally, you get yourself in the rocking chair, with someone out in front and someone else following, so that you're guarded for up to 10 miles in either direction.

By 4.30pm we were into New Jersey, the road still edged by much the same deciduous woods, blooming with the spring, that we'd enjoyed in country a lot further away from New York City. There was still a feeling of being in the wilds. There were deer grazing within sight of the road. Not what you'd expect at all. The traffic slowly began to thicken in both directions until we were into a four-lane system both ways, each lane full and whipping along at 60 to 70mph. Getting closer in, the roadway climbed above the trees, and nestled among them were the houses of suburbia, whole towns even. We were swept on until the battered cars pressed hard around us, speeding over the bridges that link the various parts of this intense, aquatic metropolis. We struck rougher roads than we'd found anywhere in the desert. The driving was savage and aggressive; stimulating if you like competitiveness, distressing if you cherish the idea of your car lasting more than a year or two.

We'd driven 3553 miles to reach this wilderness. It was frightening, but exciting too, like no other city I'd ever been in. We enjoyed a quiet beer at David's East Side apartment. Then he and Jeannie showed me briefly around Manhattan – just enough to whet my appetite – and it was time to get on the jumbo. The passengers around me settled down to watch the movie. I couldn't. It couldn't compete with the kaleidoscope whirling in my mind, one image after another. Bright, intense, alive – like America itself.

FROM BLACKPOOL WITH BITE
TVR TAIMAR TURBO
1977

IT WAS NO PLACE to be: Blackpool on a sodden day in summer; close and seamy, sordid and depressing, gross and awful. Even the seagulls were morose, and the people dishing out what is reputed to be the world's best fish and chips were just plain cantankerous. The souls who'd come on holiday, those of them braving the deluge, looked glum and lost, sitting eating scones in little huddles in tram shelters or clutching deck chairs they'd hired in hope of sunny hours on the sands. They watched us and we watched them, and a few wandered over and looked at the car, grey and wet as the weather, and wondered about its make and origin.

It was a TVR Turbo, and it had come not three miles from the little factory that has been in the Blackpool suburbs for so long now; *in* Blackpool, but not entirely *of* Blackpool, and yet in its own way belonging there too, for just as the town – through its extremes of vulgarity – is unlike any other, so is the TVR unlike other cars. Their common bond, the town and the car, is individuality.

Individuality is the key to TVR, its *raison d'être* and the reason, years after the car's creation, that it is increasingly in demand. Is that not an anachronism by any other name? While the TVR people confirm that, they also put it into perspective. They know precisely what they have on their hands, and why they believe they have to go on having it: a car in the mould of the Morgan, a car that has gone on through the years without much change to become a classic in the eyes of its beholders. They are buying it precisely because they see it as just that in a world now all but

TVR TAIMAR TURBO

devoid of traditional sports cars. 'We've found our place in the market,' says company owner Martin Lilley. 'We understand it and we're sticking to it.'

He's a cheery man, but careful, quick and deliberate too; at ease with himself and his little company and the anticipated £1.8m it will turn over for him this year. Perhaps another Ferrari to accompany his Daytona Spider now that the 308GTB has gone, or a Shadow II to replace the old Roller as the mobile boardroom? Such a turnover comes from building 10 cars a week. TVR hopes, when the expansion it is now working towards comes to fruition, to lift production to 15 cars a week. The customers are there: Germany and Holland form the backbone of its European market, and things are going sufficiently well in North America to give TVR a Lotus-style three-sector market, hedged bets against something going wrong.

The factory – unassuming really is the right word for it – blends with those around it on an outskirts area that's as close as Blackpool will probably get to an industrial estate. There's a pleasing northern bluntness about it: Lilley's office, one for the receptionist/secretary and another for deputy MD Stewart Halstead and one thin corridor are all that stand between the street and the little team making cars amid the familiar smell of fibreglass and fresh paint. There is a cheery informality to it: naked plastic bodies, piles of trim, people in jeans crouched over just-finished chassis within feet of others detailing complete cars ready for despatch to customers, and all of it in a space not much bigger than a typical business office. Just outside the back door, in a little tin shed, a man in a spaceman-like suit sprays the just-welded chassis gleaming black, and on an adjoining patch of land where soon the factory will grow, there are strange shapes among the scattered body shells, for TVR's expansion – within the confines of their confirmed approach – *will* be with additional models and not just increased production.

The informality, the pride and the confidence, the family feeling, revealed itself in another way when the time came to get on with the driving. For photography, we had a choice of models and colours

AND THE REVS KEEP RISING

and chose a silver grey Taimar Turbo. It matched the day. But for driving, for a blast through the rain and puddles up into the Lakes conveniently near to the north, Stewart Halstead had a customer's Turbo ready. It had covered 18,000 miles in nine months and had come in the day before for servicing. They'd asked the owner, a local engineer with offices in Belgium and something of a commuter route in between, if he minded if I drove the car; and he didn't. Any reserve was mine, not his. And if, as the TVR staff say, most of their customers become close friends, they also work at it. Halstead has a man on the road doing nothing but visiting customers – there are now about 2000 TVR owners in Britain – to talk about their cars and their problems and their likes and dislikes. 'That's one of the reasons we know we're on the right track and that we shouldn't deviate too far,' he says.

The last car I'd driven with the benefit of tuner Ralph Broad's turbocharged breath was one of his own Granadas: a fine car indeed, refined as well as fast. That the TVR Turbo would be fast I had no doubt. But refined? Hardly the image evoked when a car belonging to another era is endowed, at a stroke, with 230bhp and 273lb/ft of torque and a 145mph top speed. If it were to be anything more than a potent blast from the past, TVR would need to have been more successful at the conversion than MG was, for instance, with the MGB V8. But is such scepticism fair? The Porsche 911 endures in constantly more powerful forms, and the Morgan V8, the ultimate anachronism, is no monster. And after all, the TVR has a rather better base from which updates may stem than many cars. Its backbone is a tubular steel chassis in open-box form that mates up with full box frame at the rear and spreads either side of the engine at the front to go on to provide strong pickup points for the suspension as well as absorbing the required crash forces. Outriggers run between the front and rear wheels so that there is support below and behind the glassfibre body's sills. The suspension front and rear is by wide-based upper and lower wishbones, not unlike those of most racing cars, welded up from tubular steel. The dampers run inside the four coil springs, and at the back the differential and its independent axles are enclosed

TVR TAIMAR TURBO

within the transverse box-frame. But the pertinent point about the TVR is that its engine – the 2.5-litre Triumph six is still available but the accent is on the Ford V6, and soon in its new 2.8-litre injected form – is mounted so far back behind the front axle line that the car is virtually mid-engined.

Before Mr Broad gets to work on the V6, it delivers 142bhp at 5000rpm and 172lb/ft of torque. The Holset turbocharger increases the power by 61.9 per cent and, significantly, the torque by 58.7 per cent. Not surprisingly, a lot more horsepower is available but TVR's brief was for Broadspeed to develop a very strong, flat torque curve for potent, consistent pull from low revs so the turbocharger is set to peak at 8.5psi. The aspiration is by twin choke Weber carburettor rather than the injection that Porsche and Saab, for instance, use but the carburettor is enclosed in the very clever airbox that Broadspeed developed and which is one of the reasons why its method of turbocharging works so well. The ignition is electronic, a refinement not found in the basic V6. The Turbo's suspension is set slightly differently from the lesser TVRs too, and it runs on 195 section Michelin XWX radials on 6in TVR alloy rims.

The TVR's cockpit is as personal as ever. This is an old-style sports car, a tight coupé for a driver and an interested passenger. Getting the luggage in was a problem until the introduction recently of the Taimar version with its lift-up rear section. Previously, and in the standard model, the luggage had to be hefted around behind the seats to be put on the flat rear platform. Quite a lot of gear (there's so much room ahead of the engine that the spare wheel lurks there) can be packed in – much more easily in the Taimar of course – if you're prepared to lose your rear vision, but neither model has anything to stop the luggage sliding forward under the strong braking of which the TVR is capable.

The car is low, and the doors narrow at the top. You have to sort of duck down and in, dropping into a narrow bucket squeezed between the sill and the vast central section that covers the backbone chassis. It splits the car into two monocoques. So the character of the TVR is thus established as strongly inside as it is from the outside. The windscreen is shallow, the steering wheel

AND THE REVS KEEP RISING

upright, the scuttle rises up in front of driver and passenger and dips between them. It has a flat padded facia, with big conventional instruments set into it symmetrically. The outward sweep of the chassis as it goes forward and past the engine forces the pedals to lay over to the right; and they're small. The extreme rearward mounting of the engine means that the gearbox and its short shift lever are very well back. Your left arm lays along the top of the central tunnel, working a lever that is level with the front of the rib cage when it's forward in the first and third positions and level with the back of the ribs when it's in second and top. The Turbo's standard equipment is fair, running to things like a Sundym laminated windscreen and Sundym side glass. But an external mirror is an extra, and so are halogen headlights at £39. Leather seats cost an extra £250, electric windows are £226, a sun roof £80, and if you want a side band to proclaim to the world that you're driving a Turbo or a Taimar it'll cost you another £56. That's on top of £8150 for the ordinary Turbo and £8832 for the Taimar.

Is that too steep? The Turbo soon speaks for itself. It is an instantly easy car to drive, and an appealing one. It feels small and easy to handle, but it is wider than its long bonnet would lead you to expect and it takes a while to place the nearside wheel as accurately as you would wish – and indeed, will need – to. Looking forward, the vision is adequate but the low header rail means that there is a slightly claustrophobic impression, the constant awareness that you *are* in an old-style sports car with plenty up front and the bare minimum when it comes to cabin space. To the rear, the Taimar's big back window changes the aspect, and makes reversing simple.

The Turbo's steering is sort of dead – accurate and consistent but dead. But it asks little of the driver, and takes the car where he directs without fuss once he has learned to judge his wheel placement correctly. Nor is there much to be learned about the pedals beyond the first few moments of familiarity, for the clutch is of reasonable weight and predictable take-up. If the distance between brake and throttle is a little further than ideal, toe and heeling is easy enough if you roll the edge of your foot onto the

TVR TAIMAR TURBO

throttle while the ball of the foot does the braking. Your left arm comes back further than is really desirable to operate the gearshift but you can rest it along the top of the central section, and the Ford shift is light, short and unobtrusive enough once you've come to grips with its location.

The engine beneath the one-piece bonnet is equally unobtrusive. It is smoother than the standard V6. It pulls the car away from very low speed without any fuss and it will lope along in any gear you choose as you mix it with the traffic, or talk, or daydream. Top is geared for 21.6mph/1000rpm but the engine is happy enough to come right down to that point should you ask it to. It picks up again silkily, and from 2000rpm there is some reaction on the boost gauge. By the time the tachometer is showing 2800rpm, the turbocharger is at full boost and the car is really beginning to move. In top gear, that's around 60mph, and from there on you have enough acceleration to embarrass a Porsche Turbo doing the same thing in top gear (well, a 3.0-litre Porsche Turbo anyway). As in the Porsche, the increase in power and performance does not come with a sudden thump, as it did in the BMW 2002 Turbo. The accelerative rate just gets stronger and stronger, and you don't truly appreciate the full force of the thrust until you break the power train with eased throttle and depressed clutch pedal to change up, or simply to shut it all down if you run out of road. You jerk forward in your seat then. Such is the smoothness and unobtrusiveness it makes you think of a turbine or very powerful rotary engine. You'd never know there is just an ordinary Ford V6 down there with an ordinary turbocharger attached to it.

But it is that simple combination that will take you to 60mph in 6.0sec if you want to lay it on, or from 70 to 90mph in top in well under 5.0sec when you wish to overtake without a downshift. In third – which will run to 100mph; first goes to 44mph and second to 72 – the time between 70 and 90mph is a mere 3.7sec, and that is *handy.* Keeping your foot down, with a full-bore change into top at 100mph and the 6500rpm redline, the car goes on pulling to 145mph. It is as unperturbing a speed as 70 or 100mph are. There is no feeling of strain, no directional instability to make you grip

AND THE REVS KEEP RISING

the wheel and get ready to counteract some sudden deviation. Nor is there all that much racket, for the TVR is impressively low on windnoise and there is never much beyond a pleasing exhaust burble to give the engine's power away. But nor, at more common cruising speeds, is it a quiet car: the rear axle is too close to you for that, and if there is the slightest maladjustment in the drive line you'll be riding with enough grumble just behind your backside for it to become annoying. There are not, however, the rattles and bumps that one might expect, even in a car with 18,000 miles under its belt.

Although the suspension is set firmly it was the ride that most surprised me. The spring and damper rates seem spot-on, providing a well-controlled and properly comfortable ride, with, of course, the required roadholding and handling. This is notably better in the Turbo, whether through its suspension settings or the fat Michelins, or a combination of both. The body roll seems less noticeable than in the normal TVR 3.0-litre, too, and the return to normal attitude after oversteer has been corrected is tidier. Even in the wet full power can be applied most of the time, certainly in the higher gears. If there is going to be loss of traction, look for it at the front end if you come too hard under brakes into bends that drop away from a crest. The outside wheel will lose its grip then and you will be dependent upon your own skill to keep things in shape. It is best to go into bends with some caution and then let the engine have its head when the way out of them is clear. You will probably be surprised time and again at the refusal of the tail to wag as the 230bhp gets on with the job of whisking the car forward to the next one. In an area like the Lake District you will also have to be careful of crests and dips, for the TVR is low enough to thump its exhaust pipes on the tarmac in a shower of sparks.

But that is fairly small penalty for what the Turbo offers. As we streamed along through the Cumbrian rain, along those winding and dipping and diving roads, the confidence with which the Turbo went about its job impressed me greatly. There is an especially appealing integrity about the Turbo that the ordinary 3000M seems to lack. Perhaps it stems from the smoothness and response of the

TVR TAIMAR TURBO

engine. There is none of the anticipated rawness about its character and yet it does have plenty of the desired individuality. Nor is there anything nasty about it. It makes no bones about the fact that if you push too hard it will understeer under brakes into a wet bend, or go into rapid roll oversteer if you manage to get around. It tells an attentive driver that clearly enough, and he knows to allow for it either through avoidance or correct response.

For my liking, the seats are too flat and don't have the right sort of lower-back and under-thigh support, but there is nothing wrong with the ride. And, mercifully, there is no bumpsteer. Indeed, the car is so well-balanced and has the sort of properly-sorted handling that will allow hard braking right into the apex of a dry bend, dropping into the road to fractionally tighten its line the way a keen diver will wish it to. It is a fast car that can be driven fast with ease and pleasure. The finish of the cabin might look somewhat amateurish to and the ventilation is terrible (air conditioning is both essential and underway). But overpriced? Certainly not.

DAY OF THE D-TYPE
JAGUAR XKD 516
1977

IT'S SITTING IN A garage in North London, its stubby black nose pointing to the door, its tail squatting near the flank of a green Aston Martin Ulster, and I'd go again to see it at the drop of a hat. Again to walk around it, pressed into silence. Again to run a hand over its smooth alloy, an eye around its snug cockpit. Again to swing up its little door and sit in it, feel it, and perhaps even start it and *hear* it. Ah, but would walking away again be too much to bear? Even were the money to be immaterial – £35,000, in all probability – it could never be mine. Enough people have already offered Nick Mason at least that much for it, but he won't sell. He had fortune enough for it to fall into his hands – a 1955 Jaguar D-type, unspoiled, uncrashed, untouched – and he isn't letting it go. But if I must envy him I must also thank him, for one day this autumn that garage door opened and I was the one who drove it out, roaring and spitting, black and beautiful, fierce and frightening. They were *my* hands that guided it through the streets and the shoppers and the traffic of London, and they were *my* eyes that saw the motorway disappearing beneath its bulging bonnet for mile-after-mile. And when the chance came, it was *my* foot that pressed down hard on that steely throttle pedal to give a Porsche Turbo the come-uppance of its life.

The 911 Turbo had come sweeping down the motorway, growing steadily in the Jaguar's quivering mirror. And then, with the D-type merely sauntering in third, the Porsche was alongside and its driver was braking hard, shifting down and leaning sideways in his seat to get a better view. How incongruous the Jaguar must have looked: a black triumph from the past rolling along amid the everyday traffic,

JAGUAR XKD 516

with a fool in a flat cap and a thin jumper and string-back gloves at the wheel on a grey and cold day.

The Porsche driver drank it in then began to accelerate again. For me, the curiosity was too great. Here, alongside me, was the measuring stick for the D-type's performance. Three litres of turbocharged and fuel-injected '70s flat six against 3.4 litres of '50s inline six fed by three fat Webers; about 250 horsepower and four-speed gearboxes apiece. Down went the D-type's throttle, and flick-flick-flick went the spindly tachometer needle as it climbed in that big old-fashioned dial. The staccato bark of the exhaust swelled to a solid snarl as the engine began to climb onto its cams, and as the needle flicked past 3000rpm the thrust forward – rather as if a turbocharger had cut in, ironically enough – seemed to double in an instant. For a little while we ran neck and neck. And then, about the time my rev limit appeared and the long white needle snapped down from 5000 to 4000rpm, stopped, and began its upward flicker once more in fourth, the Porsche drifted backwards from my peripheral vision. It reappeared a few moments later, shrinking slowly, in the frail little central mirror that trembled in the pressure of the wind. I was trembling too. Despite my glasses and the tiny Perspex windscreen, the buffeting was extreme enough by the time the car had reached 5000rpm in top to turn my vision to a blur. So I should have worn a helmet and goggles after all! Enough: I backed off. The still-steaming Porsche closed the gap and pulled alongside again. It hesitated a moment, its driver stared hard, and then it was gone, followed through by a Bentley Continental, ton-up, its driver tooting and waving with delight.

But the D-type has always had its accolades. This one, as it turns out, was not one of those that immortalised Jaguar's name on the racetrack. The number on the brass plate riveted to its scuttle pinpoints it as XKD 516. The original build information and test reports that Jaguar so easily and willingly found for me in its archive say that it was the eighth of the proper production D-types, and the third despatched to a private owner. It was cream then, and after its stringent series of tests it was sent, on October 12 1955, to Commander J Rutherford in Palm Beach, Florida. But, Jaguar's typed and hand-written file reveals, the tests weren't without their

AND THE REVS KEEP RISING

problems. Like the other D-types, XKD 516 was driven hour after hour at the MIRA test track. Some cars did as much as 850 miles before Les Bottrill, the test engineer, considered them sufficiently good to be handed over to their owners. Whether they raced them or used them as road cars… well, that was up to them.

The first test for XKD 516 showed that the suspension settings were slightly out, that its throttle stop was not where it should have been and so full power was not being obtained, that its clutch adjustment was not right, that the rear axle seals were leaking, that the gearshift was stiff, and the breather clip was fouling the bonnet. Some of the riveting in the body was defective, some of the panel gaps awkward. And the nearside valance was fouling the steering rack bellows and the shock absorbers. The second test revealed that the gearshift had not improved: a new gearbox was fitted. The third test pinpointed a few further flaws. The fourth, on September 26, 1955, narrowed the remaining jobs to refitting of the air box lid, fitting hub blanks, changing the front wheels because of tyre wear, checking the stone damage incurred during the testing, and cleaning out the interior. 'Note,' said a hasty paragraph at the bottom of the final test sheet, 'gearbox still slightly stiff – may improve with use'.

And so XKD 516 went off to Florida. But a few years ago it came home, brought back from the US by an English enthusiast. And it was from him that Nick Mason bought it, a jewel in his growing but already mouth-watering collection: three pre-war Astons, three Ferraris and an A-type Connaught. In fact, it was Nick's Ferrari that led me to the Jaguar. LJK Setright and I were at Goodwood for a Ferrari day that Modena Engineering had organised and Nick's Dino 246 and Daytona were among the cars we drove. Suddenly, out among the Ferraris came this immaculate black D-type, in all its glory, with Nick's father Bill (who made the marvellous *Shell History of Motor Sport* films) at the wheel. And when I dared to ask whether, one day, I might try the D and fulfil a dream, I was pressed into grateful silence by Nick's cheerful agreement, for I had asked not to drive it on a racetrack but on the open road.

Before that happened, there was one more pleasant surprise in store. The building in London's Kentish Town where Nick Mason's

JAGUAR XKD 516

Astons and the Jaguar are housed is more than just a garage. It's called Morntane Engineering and it's run as a fully-fledged business, with former Connaught works engineer Derrick Edwards restoring and maintaining not only his own cars and Nick's but those of customers too. The place is a palace of glorious, glittering cars, gleaming engines, and orderly rows of tools and parts. But whatever the attractions of the other cars, I could not swing my eyes away from the Jaguar for long. For me, its beauty vies with the Ferrari 250 GTO's. Its body is so short and efficient but so perfectly proportioned and so breathtakingly sensual. I see the D-type as the height of William Lyons' and Malcolm Sayer's achievements.

Its visual splendour extends beyond its alloy bodywork. Undo the straps and tilt the one-piece bonnet forward and you look at a mass of shining alloy: the firewall, the cylinder head and its cam covers, the fat Webers and their gleaming trumpets, the radiator and its separate header tank, the oil coiler, the dry sump's catch tank and its big flip-top cap. Such a mass of it, so bright against the black bodywork. Look closely and you see also the excellence, the purposefulness, of the engineering. Those beautifully sculpted wishbones, clean as polished conrods, for instance; none of your pressed metal or welded up tubing here. It's such an intriguingly built car too, with that rigid central monocoque shaped around the driver and theoretical passenger and ending behind them just as abruptly as it begins ahead of them. A tubular steel frame (magnesium alloy in the first works racers of 1954) shaped like a broadhead arrow bolts up under it and extends forward to allow the engine to perch, cocked over eight degrees to the left, between its arms. It also carries the suspension and the bonnet. The rear suspension simply fastens up to the strengthened rear bulkhead, mere inches behind the driver's back, and the rear body panel, quite unstressed, is bolted on to it too, hiding within it the twin flexible fuel tanks that provide a total capacity of 37 gallons, and the spare wheel. The springing front and rear is by torsion bars, two working with the lower wishbones at the front, and one big transverse one, fastened at its centre, at the rear. Upper and lower steel plate trailing links (the lower pair connected to the torsion bar) locate the live rear axle, and they too are in torsion during cornering. A central A-bracket controls

AND THE REVS KEEP RISING

the axle's lateral movement, and the telescopic dampers (acting on the lower trailing links) tilt forward and inwards to mounts on two upright box section members fixed to the bulkhead. The four-wheel disc brakes are largely as they had been for the C-type Jaguars, but rid of the faults that plagued them in the early days, and servo assisted. The rack and pinion steering is much the same as it was for the XK140 that was a contemporary of the D-type.

The engine, too, is much as it was for the normal Jaguar saloons and sports cars: that famous in-line six introduced in 1948 and still going strong almost 30 years later. But in the D-type, in its 3442cc form, it has a cylinder head derived from the C-type casting with bigger inlet valves, cams with pronounced overlap and a complex system of breathers in the cam covers. The three 45mm Weber carburettors, mounted to compensate for the tilt of the engine, overwhelm its right side. On the left, the two cast exhaust manifolds with their pronounced branch shaping spear almost straight out from the head, descending to fat silver-ripple flexible pipes that run to the expansion box mounted along the lower left side of the body, for all the world to see. The result of all this, and a fairly modest 9.0:1 compression ratio, is 245bhp at 5750rpm and 242lb/ft at 4000rpm. It goes to the four-speed all-synchromesh gearbox – new for the D-type – through a triple-plate, hydraulically operated clutch, the housing of which, with the starter motor ring gear, takes the place of a true flywheel. Jaguar offered nine differential ratios; XKD 516, and most of the production cars, left Allesley with what was considered to be the standard ratio – 3.54:1. That allows the car to reach 138mph at the maximum 5750 revs in top, with 64, 84 and 108mph in the lower three. At Le Mans, the D-types used either 2.79 or 2.69 differentials so they could reach the high maximums that took them so often to victory. All of this capability is contained, of course, within a car 12ft 10in long, 65in wide, a mere 31.5in high, riding on a wheelbase of 90in and weighing just over 1900lb… and costing, in 1955, £3878.

They say the D-type cockpit is rather better for the driver than it was in the C-types. Lifting up that tiny door and climbing over the gunwale, stepping on the seat cushion and then dropping your legs down into the footwell puts you in a snug metallic cubbyhole.

JAGUAR XKD 516

The Perspex screen, attached to the bodywork by a neat row of bolts, curls around from shoulder to shoulder, rising to a point just below eye level. The later long nose racers got the more protective full-width screens. The reach to the pedals is fine. The distance to the big drilled and riveted alloy and wood wheel is about halfway between old and new styles, so your arms are almost straight out but some bent-elbow shuffling is still needed. The curve of the monocoque behind your back, rather than any sort of formal seat, provides the lateral support, for there are only those thin pads. The high sill – the side of the tub – pins you on the right, and the tunnel that covers the transmission, driveshaft and the central part of the tubular framework locks you in from the left. Tough leather covers most of the tunnel and the strange little bulge just ahead of the gearlever that allows for the starter motor, which sits on top of the gearbox. The gear lever itself is strange: long and capped with a slim machined alloy knob, and it lays forward at an angle that would make most people mistake it for the handbrake. That is even longer, and mounted on the left side of the tunnel. It's a fly-off device, which, like most of them, doesn't work terribly well.

On the plain, black, metal panel that forms the dashboard, there are two small dials to the right of the steering column, the lower of the two and the more easily visible, is the temperature gauge. The upper one monitors the oil pressure. On the left of the steering column there is the huge white-on-black dial that is the speedo, reading to 180mph and graduated every 2mph. Above it is a little shrouded lamp – black like everything else – and near its lower left edge there's an old-fashioned foot-type dipswitch that's easily punchable. And then, hidden under the panel that covers the cockpit but easily visible to the driver when he glances down and left, is the equally large tachometer, reading to 8000rpm and running, again like the speedo, from two o'clock around to 10 o'clock. It carries a thin red line at 5750rpm, and a tell-tale that will indicate driver indiscretion. Five grand, Nick Mason ruled, with only half a grin. There is then just the small key, the little starter button, and three more switches for the side, head and panel lights.

'If you have to start it from cold,' Derrick Edwards said when my

AND THE REVS KEEP RISING

cockpit check was completed, 'open the bonnet and have someone stand by with the fire extinguisher.' You give it two dabs on the throttle, then press the starter. But if it doesn't fire first time there is the likelihood of flooding, with petrol pouring from those six big trumpets and, unless it's mopped up, perhaps a fiery flash-back the next time you try. But the Jaguar was warm. Rick, the mechanic who gave up a career in chemistry to join Nick and Derek at Morntane, had started it earlier. Just a touch of the button and a swift dab on the throttle and there was the torque-induced twitch of the body and the amazing, magnificent snarl of the exhausts. What a sound! I got ready to move. 'Crikey,' I said. 'A real clutch!' They all laughed, and I left.

That snappy little clutch pedal, so bullish and travelling through what seemed like a mere inch or two, was out and the D-type was away down the narrow lane. But I fell foul of that long first gear. Not enough revs pulling out into Highgate Road, that sudden clutch, and I stalled. The six fired again immediately and I gave it a boot full and with a swift chirp from the 16in Dunlop Racing covers and a waggle from the tail we were away, the exhausts' thunder stopping the pedestrians and the other drivers in their tracks.

As the car went on through the suburbs in search of the motorway I was overwhelmed by the attention it drew. Everybody, just everybody, stopped and stared and marvelled. I played the part of course, and not just for cheap thrills; all that blipping really was necessary if the engine wasn't to stall again. But it was the clutch I was really worried about. There seemed to be so many red lights on so many hills. I dreaded every take-off. Each, with the revs needed to make the car move in that high first gear, brought that familiar, evil smell of stressed clutch. But it never grew worse and I was soon more concerned about the way the temperature gauge was climbing as the traffic thickened and eventually forced me to a crawl. Nick had said to tug down the knob under the dash to turn on the fan when the needle reached 70 degrees. But that didn't stop it touching 90 degrees when the going became really slow. A side street began to look like the only escape. While Nick had once had the D to 100 degrees and back without damage, I wasn't prepared to risk it. But it stabilised, the traffic cleared and with flowing air it dropped back to 60 degrees. In a few minutes I was within sight of the motorway.

Out of the last roundabout, pulling 4000rpm in first and second and rocketing past the Cortinas and Marinas and trucks, taking third and, running full-out on the approach road, the D dashed to freedom, with its exhausts in full, terrible cry. It seemed to cut a swathe through the other vehicles on the motorway. Those who saw it in their mirrors dived out the way whether it was bearing down hard on them or not. And those who didn't see it approach swerved with surprise and interest when it went by. Buses tooted and lorry drivers waved. In the tiny cockpit, it just felt so purposeful; so controllable and yet so raw. The feeling came from the noise, from its curvy compactness, from the wind bashing me in the face, from the nuts and bolts and rivets all around me, and from the immediate positive flick of the tacho needle when the throttle pressure changed (it's one of those old-style tachometers that moves in 100rpm steps, like a doctor's blood pressure gauge). I settled for a steady 70mph on that vast speedo, and was intrigued to find that the bark of the exhaust, so loud at lower speeds, disappeared altogether in the wind or was simply left behind when cruising in top. There was a sort of lonely, windy silence. And if the comfort of the ride continued to be surprising, I had long since discovered that, while the exhaust beat levelled out at a little-over 2000rpm, the cams weren't *really* biting hard until the revs reached 3000. Then there was a sudden, smooth surge forward – more of a quickening of the pace, for it was not jerky or violent – and the car really began to move.

Such perfect spirit! So I changed down to third and to second whenever I was overtaking in order to revel in the power and the exhaust roar that went with it. But, poor fool, when Ian Dawson and his driver in our photographic car caught me up I learned that what the Jaguar's old speedo said was a steady 70mph was really more like 90. Thank goodness there hadn't been a policeman within eye or earshot. Like the noise, your natural judgement of speed is lost in the wind, for despite the relatively tall racing windscreen your face is buffeted hard and glasses and cap need frequent repositioning. Cold? Yes I was cold, but it was the sort of exhilarating cold that

AND THE REVS KEEP RISING

goes with the pleasure of being free in the wind and with a spirit as captivating as this Jaguar's; the pleasure of being in a real sports car. I hadn't had that feeling so intensely since a hard drive in an Austin-Healey 100S years ago.

The Porsche and the Bentley Continental came and went and I had a perspective on the performance the Jaguar could offer – and even if it was without using all of its power. According to *Road & Track* figures from 1956, it will reach 60mph in well under 5.0sec, and do 0–100mph in 12. Moreover, it's such a pleasant car to drive fast. Once you're moving, that clutch is as satisfying as everything else. A swift, solid stab and it's in and out, working with a gearshift that is light, almost delicate and very mechanical. XKD 516's 17,000 miles have removed the stiffness the factory testers found. But you must shift it very deliberately, for it will deviate from its plane unless you're positive with it. Do that, and you have quick, clean changes. Even into first gear there is deft synchromesh, and a lock that won't allow first to be disengaged without the clutch being depressed for it was a ratio very much in use at Le Mans.

The steering, too is essentially light. It's slightly… well, loose… at the dead ahead but the impression of slack is gone in an instant once you apply pressure to the wooden rim. Then, the D's response is as positive and precise as the engine's is to the throttle. The brakes have the same sort of 'old' feel about them but they are rock solid. If your foot is on the pedal, the pads are on the discs. That's the sort of communication you have and *feel* in the D-type. Yet it's such a gentle sort of communication too, and while the immense ability of the D-type can leave you awestruck the good-natured feeling that goes with it will set you on the path to adoration.

Just how far along that path the Jaguar was to lead me I did not suspect until I left the motorway and took B roads to a Royal Navy airfield with a perimeter road two miles long and a commandant who is an enthusiast. He stood atop his control tower to watch, and all around the airfield people stopped what they were doing to look and listen as the D-type took charge. I'd been there with dozens of cars before, all of them new and most of them interesting, but the firemen and the helicopter mechanics and the fitters and the grasscutters rarely noticed. One lap and the D-type had brought them all from their tasks to stand by the roadside in reverence.

As it swept around and around, how small and how personal the Jaguar seemed. And how controllable, for the rain that had made the motorway greasy had spared the airfield and the Dunlops were biting hard again. How faithful and how trustworthy, words that before I climbed into it – and in the first few miles as I learned to adopt the older style of driving that it demands – I hadn't thought I'd be applying to it. But when it flicked sideways on the join in the tarmac at the centre of the first fast curve, it never flicked too far and asked for nothing more than a quick snip of opposite lock. It even went most of the way towards regaining its own composure. When it nudged into understeer in the long, long off-camber bend that scouts around the end of the main runway, it fed the information willingly and steadily to my hands and gave me the choice of lifting off or neutralising it with the throttle. I had long since learned that if I asked for power I would jolly well get it, instantly and precisely.

So the long drifts began, the car sitting flat and never making me feel that I was on the edge of disaster. If the rear did move out just a bit too much the message was delivered to my backside in an instant and again there was time to choose throttle or steering correction. In a tight right-hander taken almost flat in second, I thought I had it as sideways as I dared it. But it went some more, and told me, and answered the extra, urgent snap of lock and tweak of throttle with the sort of meaty obedience that was so pleasurable it made me want to yell with delight. From there it was into third and flat all the way through an uphill kink and on to 5000rpm and into fourth, with that engine – far too potent to be called simply silky – roaring away. When it's flat it makes itself heard above the wind whatever the speed. And there it was: 5000rpm and a proper 120mph in top for a glorious, wind-battered half-mile before hauling down all the way to first for the 90-degree left. There I learned about the power of the brakes and the pedal effort they demanded. There was, too, a significant amount of heft needed at the wheel, making you well aware of the Jaguar's indomitable character: it doesn't fight you, but it doesn't knuckle under either. It just asks that you match its

AND THE REVS KEEP RISING

positivity and integrity. Best of all, even when it is accelerating as hard as it will go, it never feels threatening or as if it is going to get away from you. You can simply indulge in its speed.

But as the airfield's straights and the frequent sharp bends at the end of them soon showed, you cannot think of the D-type as anything but a period piece. You've learned that you have to push hard, hard, hard on that brake pedal twice as early as you would in a quick current car. And that, while its handling might be deft and rewarding, where the D is scrabbling for grip in a bend or has long since passed its limits, something like a Lotus Esprit, and very definitely that Porsche Turbo, would hardly be trying. The limits of a live axle were reached long ago and tyre technology has advanced far beyond the level of those once autarchic Dunlops.

But the D-type is a period piece like a Spitfire or a Sabre jet are period pieces; and the very last thing I wanted to do that afternoon was to stop pelting it around and around that airfield. I did sally forth once more before we left, to show the Lt Commander what it was like. Problem is, although the removable panel on the passenger's side allows you to carry a friend, the lack of protection from the wind will soon make them so cold and distort their faces that it inhibits the driver. No: the D-type is not a car to be shared. It is so overwhelmingly a personal car, one that makes you want to go off and be alone with it and never get out of it. It is the epitome of the true sports car, the ultimate in escapism. It is a racer for the road, brawny but not brutal, delicious but not dainty, irresistible, unforgettable and, of course, all but unobtainable. These are the sorts of thoughts that were buzzing about in my mind as I took XKD 516 back along the motorway – a police Range Rover admiringly alongside for 20 miles – and, with new zest, back through the London traffic. An easier clutch in traffic – well, a more durable one – is all you'd wish for. Even then you'd think twice, for a very large part of the appeal of this car is its originality and the depth of the beauty under its skin. I walked away from it with the knowledge, oh so gloriously gleaned, that the D-type is more magnificent, more desirable than I had dared imagine. Nick Mason… my thanks.

...AND THE REVS KEEP RISING

LAMBORGHINI COUNTACH S
1978

THE STRAIGHT IS RUNNING out and we're rushing at the bend. Stanislao Sterzel's foot stays flat to the floor and the V12 behind our heads – almost between our heads – goes on snarling. The tachometer needle keeps climbing: six-six... six-seven... six-eight. Even at those revs in fifth and with the speed already beyond 170mph we're still being pressed back into our seats, prisoners of that mighty engine. Such harnessed savagery! Such thrust! When will it stop? Is it running away with us, sweeping us beyond control as surely as if we are in the clutches of a rip? I guess it will probably abate somewhere between 7300 and 7500rpm. But not on this straight; not before the bend takes the road left at something like 30 degrees. Surely Stanislao will lift off soon: we are almost on top of it.

But no: his foot stays hard down. Six-nine... seven... seven-one. And then we are into it. His hands roll the wheel a few inches to the left. The nose changes course instantly, flatly. The loading on our bodies switches to an immense lateral pressure, our rib cages pressed against the sides of the seats, and we can feel the suspension tugging against the tyres. The communication is intense. It says that the tyres don't intend to surrender their grip upon the road; that Stanislao indeed hadn't needed to lift off – and now dare not. It says we are riding over surface irregularities but a brawny jiggling will be the only result. The lateral pressure isn't easing. It just feels as if I am sitting in a firm steel chair with a glued-on cushion and, with my torso pressed against the arm and the backrest, I'm jerking

AND THE REVS KEEP RISING

my hips sideways. It feels as tied down as a roller coaster.

We are into the next straight. The throttle is still wide open and the revs keep rising, so swiftly, to 7500 before the clear road runs out. But those revs mean, if the tachometer is accurate and the gearing figure Lamborghini has given me is correct, that we have reached 194mph – and that we went through that bend at 183mph. What an introduction to the Lamborghini Countach S.

It has been a long time coming, this second generation Countach. Like most Lamborghinis, it has not been done overnight; like most of them it has been the subject of intense speculation. It is for instance about 18 months since engineers Gian Paolo Dallara and Franco Baraldini confirmed that they were redesigning the chassis of the Countach to take the Pirelli P7 tyre. Even before that, Formula 1 player Walter Wolf had had Lamborghini build him a Countach sporting Bravo prototype wheels wearing P7s, with black wheel arch extensions to cover them, and a massive rear spoiler. Rumours soon spread that it also had a 5.0-litre engine (it did), the size originally mooted for the Countach but not put into production because of development costs, and on the assumption that the 380bhp of Lamborghini's existing 4.0-litre V12 was adequate. So it had also become common belief that the next iteration of the Countach would have the bigger engine lurking between its loins.

It does not. The LP 400S is to the Countach what the SV was to the Miura, an improved model with the modifications centring around tyres and suspension induced by the march of technology and available components, and through experience gained with three years of production. Equally, it would be naïve to think that the modifications would not stand the Countach in good stead for more power should Lamborghini decide to put a 5.0-litre version of the V12 into production.

Meanwhile, the changes conceived under Baraldini and brought to fruition under his successor as Lamborghini's director of engineering, Marco Raimondi, have taken the Countach closer to its original concept rather than away from it. From the beginning, it was intended that the car would run on very wide low profile tyres. But the car was ready before the tyres and it had to be

LAMBORGHINI COUNTACH S

developed and signed off on the widest Michelins available, even though they were narrower than the engineers would have liked. As it happens, the Pirelli P7 arrived shortly after the Countach went into production. But years of development – remember, Lamborghini canned the first chassis because it wasn't strong and light enough then designed and developed a completely new one – over hundreds of thousands of miles couldn't be ditched overnight just because a more advanced tyre had finally come along. Instead, consultant engineer Dallara chose the little Bravo prototype, unveiled by Bertone at the 1974 Turin Motor Show, to introduce the revolutionary Pirelli to Lamborghini. Dallara and his colleagues did 40,000 miles of development work with the Bravo before the project was scrapped. He put the lessons learned to good use in the creation of the Urraco 3.0-litre-based Silhouette.

At the time, Dallara said he regarded the P7 as the greatest single breakthrough in motoring history (!) because it freed chassis designers from constraints that had restricted them for so long. But Dallara also preferred to wait and gain a wealth of P7 experience before committing the fastest Lamborghini to them. He felt there were under-appreciated subtleties to working with them; that it was not desirable to change over to them for the sake of fashion and without capitalising fully upon their advantages.

So the Countach became the third car that Lamborghini designed around the P7. Almost at the same time, BMW contracted development of the mid-engined E26/M1 to Lamborghini so its chassis design, too, was a direct product of the experience gained with the Bravo and the Silhouette, and from observation of the handful of other cars using the P7. Thus the Countach S and BMW M1 have been developed side-by-side, with both benefiting from the experience gained with the earlier projects and from cross fertilisation.

When I spell out for you the changes to the Countach you will be tempted to say *so what*. But keep in mind that the use of Pirelli P7s requires the utmost understanding of suspension geometry; of the stresses that their grip imposes upon suspension components and that the changes made to accommodate them usually do appear as

AND THE REVS KEEP RISING

modest as they are important. It is also important to understand that you are dealing here with a hot-bed of engineering integrity where the goal is the highest possible automotive standard within the limits of the technology of the day, and where idealism can and does exist because, at the price asked for a Countach, customers really do seek the ultimate in capability.

And so if you look at the Countach S you will see that it has the same body as before except for flared wheel arches covering 205/50VR15 Pirelli P7s at the front and 345/35VR15 P7s (the Michelins were a mere 215/70VR14!) at the rear, mounted upon those alloy Bravo-type wheels that look rather like the barrel of a gigantic Gatling gun. The production S will also have a nasal spoiler missing from the developmental car, a concave skirt that wraps around the snout and extends almost to the ground with twin ducts for the brakes. Customers may also specify a small rear spoiler. It is very small because the nasal spoiler so increases the downforce of the Countach's body that with both fitted there is almost too much. There is an assessable gain in stability at maximum speed, at the expense of that maximum being lowered by 700rpm. It is up to the customer to decide which he prefers: absolute speed, or absolute stability, with not much between either and probably little chance of finding out. You will see big black mirrors upon the developmental car too, mounted further forward on the doors than the smaller mirrors of the old car. They are prominent mirrors, and you may find them notably ugly. They also provide the Countach with much better rear vision, are electrically adjustable and don't cost much aerodynamically.

None of these changes hint at anything different under the skin. But the mass of steel tubing that is the chassis has revised suspension pick-up points, and the wide-based A-arms that previously ran out from it to carry the cast alloy uprights have been replaced by rigid parallel arms. They have the required strength and work through arcs that extract the most from the P7s. At the rear, their advantage is the elimination of toe-in as well as most camber change: the tyres are kept running as straight and upright as possible. A simple aim and simple ends, yes; but the geometry and the bushing are critical. At the front the most significant change is to the steering. The rack has been widened and the tie-rods shortened and strengthened so that they cannot flex. At the same time their joints have been redesigned so they move more easily through a much longer vertical arc. Don't ask me how (and Lamborghini aren't much interested in divulging the high theory of it just yet) but that eliminates bumpsteer and the slight straight-ahead vagueness that until now has been part and parcel of driving on P7s. When the BMW M1 appears soon you will find the same arrangement, for it has been tuned just as intensely to the P7 with, apparently, equally good results. The new Countach's brakes are more potent, their diameters up by a little less than half an inch, and the pads are meatier, a side benefit of the larger diameter wheels that go with such low profile tyres. Nor are those five big holes moulded into the wheel there simply for looks: they suck air across the brakes with gusto. Inside, the car is just as before except for the unseen but welcome benefit of more efficient air conditioning.

Chief experimental engineer Fiorenzo Fiorini finished explaining all this and I was barely into the passenger's cradle before tall, dark Stanislao Sterzel, who has taken over from Bob Wallace as chief test driver, had the V12 snapping and barking. An instant later the nose was darting for the gates and the road through Sant'Agata and on towards the open farming country, leaving poor John Perkins and his cameras and Fiorenzo to folio on in our Alfetta 2000 as best they could.

Do you ever get used to the raw excitement of a Countach? It was as if I'd boarded some extreme fairground machine and been instantly whisked away, enslaved by its power. We had to drop the speed down for the village but then there were no restrictions – the familiar Emilian haze was not intense enough to limit vision and Stanislao was running out to 8000rpm in all the gears, calm and relaxed, smooth and positive with his movement (reassuring: I hadn't driven with him before, and by following Wallace he has inherited large shoes). Out of the factory and through the village, the car had immediately spelled out certain differences brought about

AND THE REVS KEEP RISING

by the changes. The ride is now *really* firm, knobbly and jiggling and joggling and yet carrying neither noise nor harshness with its extreme communication. The authority of the damping is not lost with speed, but the knobbliness is left behind. You soon forget the ride: it is lost to the positiveness and precision, the stability and the function of the motion – and the speed. We had soon run out of revs in fourth and were into fifth, rolling at a steady and effortless 6000rpm which brought not only that unabated, glorious howl from the engine but 155mph as well. There were a couple of bends: not extreme but enough to subject the rib cage to strong pressure as we darted through them. If the old Countach responded swiftly to the helm, this one is even more precise and more accurate. And if the old one was noteworthy for its lack of roll, this one is amazingly flat. It is an altogether more deliberate car.

A little further and we were on to a long straight that speared across the Emilian plain, a long grey ribbon that disappeared into the haze. Stanislao had gone back to fourth for the preceding bend. Now he went for fifth again at yet another spitting eight grand, and this time the revs just went on rising and it rather looked as if my Countach experience was going to climb to another plane. The quickest I'd run in one before was just on the top side of 180mph. As we reached that speed, and as I looked at the corner looming ahead of us now, I was trying to recall the old car's stability at the top end. Not quite as solid and pressed down as this. There was something so nuggety about this one. What must it be like with either or both of the spoilers? I waited for Stanislao to back off, tensing, reassuring myself that he knew the road and what he was doing. Then it became obvious that no lift-off was likely. As we went through the bend there was that solid, slight, gutsy jiggling from the rear of the car; the impression of sheer grip. There was very little lock at the wheel and absolutely no correction, and we were through and running on to 7500rpm. And if I thought that would see the Countach out, I was wrong. The engine was still straining onwards and I was not only taken closer to 200mph than I might have dared to expect but given to suspect that the car might well have gone on to nudge its 8000rpm limit even in that grossly

LAMBORGHINI COUNTACH S

overdriven top gear. And that would be 206mph. But surely that couldn't happen. Road cars don't do that. Nor will the Countach S unless you order the special diff ratio that our developmental car happened to be running that day. The standard diff will be 4.09:1, which will give the car 23mph/1000rpm – and thus 184mph at 8000rpm – rather than our 25.8mph/1000rpm.

It wasn't long after that that we stopped and Perky and Fiorenzo caught up and we got on with taking pictures. We found a 90-degree bend and after a few runs through it at just on 90mph, flat out in second, I got out of the Countach to watch and listen up on the bank with Fiorenzo. It was a spectacle I did not want to miss. And how I wish you could have shared the sight and the sound with us. The silence, until we indicated that the road was clear. The door of the little red blob 'way off in the distance swinging down, and then the snarl as Stanislao started up, blipped the V12 a few times, ran through first into second, flat, into third, flat, braked hard, down to second, reapplied the power and ripped through the bend. The noise was loud, magnificent and awesome. Hard as I looked, I couldn't see the car moving off line, front or rear. It just went around the bend, and with barely any body roll. We'd asked Stanislao for oversteer. He'd shrugged as if I were joking. And try as he might it was only on the last three of 15 runs that he managed to edge the tail out, 380bhp doing their best to overcome the Pirelli's grip. The tail stayed out for an instant. In the cabin, Stanislao had to snap on a small and swift dose of opposite lock. And then it flicked back, shrugged as the Countach straightened up, and was gone. Even Fiorenzo, who's worked day-in day-out with this car, found the spectacle awesome. Even for Stanislao it was hard to overcome the traction, and he is a promising World Sports Car Championship driver. But it was pretty much like that on the road with the old Countach: you very rarely got it sideways.

This new one? In the normal scheme of things, I'm not sure that you would. I can only go by the miles we went on to cover that afternoon, incredibly quickly, and never once with understeer or oversteer. The capability of the car is such that it corners with intense precision at speeds far greater than one can usually reach.

AND THE REVS KEEP RISING

Lamborghini has never pretended that the Countach was anything but a car for drivers who wanted to cover long distances at maximum speed with minimum drama. If the world had caught up with the old Countach, it's going to take a while to catch up to this one.

SAD SWEET SONG OF THE LAST SILHOUETTE
LAMBORGHINI SILHOUETTE
1978

FOR MOST OF THE afternoon, I was upstairs in the big glassy offices talking to René Leimer, Pier Luigi Capellini and Ubaldo Sgarzi about the state of despair that has befallen Lamborghini. I left John Mason, my friend and photographer, wandering with his cameras in the factory below. He had not seen it before. But when we were together again, heading away from Sant'Agata Bolognese in the silver Silhouette we'd gone to collect, I did nothing more than enquire after his professional fortunes. Had he gotten some good pictures? I kept the emotion, the sense of awe and wonder – subdued this time, of course; dampened by concern and anxiety – to myself. I did not expect it to have touched John; after all, he is not a car enthusiast. He photographs cars as he photographs people, jewellery, clothes and places: professionally, and well. Yes, he said – he had some good pictures. And then he was silent. He was listening, as the Silhouette finished going up through the gears and settled down in fifth, to the bellow of the V8, now a solid, low wail. He caught sight of the speedo. We were doing a sedate 80mph. It surprised him: without seeing the dial he'd have guessed we were doing 50mph. It seemed to crystallise his thoughts.

'Christ, man,' he blurted. 'I understand these things now. I saw what they're all about today in that strange factory miles from nowhere. The people working away at all that metal were really putting something into it – they were actually enjoying themselves. They really *care!*

'I'd looked at cars like this through socialist eyes. I saw them

AND THE REVS KEEP RISING

just as awful indulgences in luxury. *Everyone should have Volkswagens, mate!* But that's not what they're all about. They really mean something to those people. You can hear it and feel it in the car. This is something I didn't know existed: mechanical purity. This is the automobile as an art form!'

I knew it. I had the leather of that Silhouette's wheel against my palms, the cold alloy of its gear lever against my kneecap, the precision of its pedals beneath my feet, and its horsepower at my command. I could feel it all, just as I had been fortunate enough to do many times before. I had long since become a believer, and here I was, at ease in my Mecca, happily agnostic as we entered Modena itself and looked down from the flyover upon the Maserati factory, then wound around past De Tomaso and into the lanes that would take us out to Ferrari at Maranello. It would be different there: John would see scores of cars pressing down the lines, spilling out into the yards as fast as the transporters could carry them away. Ferrari would be building something like 160 cars for the month; Lamborghini would be lucky if it made six. But if, in the midst of such gloom – the greatest Lamborghini has known in its 15 years – a pagan could be so swiftly converted the message must be indeed divine.

But is it faith or raw Italian optimism that is keeping Lamborghini alive? It should be dead, and yet one can't even say that it is dying; only that it continues to exist. Weighing up the odds, it is likely that, as a factory making cars it *shall* survive. The real question is whether resurrection will take place before Lamborghini enters a state that the Italians call *amministrazione controllata* – controlled administration. It is similar to, but not as extreme as, receivership. It is a legal procedure to, as the Italians put it, 'show the authorities that a company is honest but has no chance of surviving in its present form'. Debts are suspended but trading does not cease while a solution – hopefully a buyer with enough money to get the company on its feet again – is sought. The period of grace may last two years. Will a prospective buyer be attracted to Lamborghini under controlled administration, or would he prefer to see the company plunge into full bankruptcy and pick it up from there, stigma and all? Or can Lamborghini's owners, René Leimer and his

LAMBORGHINI SILHOUETTE

partner Georges-Henri Rossetti, persuade someone to buy them out in whole or in part before controlled administration or bankruptcy are no longer avoidable? That is their race against time, with the factory in something approaching a state of limbo.

For Leimer and Rossetti, once mere owners of Lamborghinis rather than Lamborghini, it has all gone terribly wrong. It began going wrong in 1973, not long after Rossetti paid around £800,000 to Ferruccio Lamborghini for 51 per cent of the company's shares. Ferruccio's tractor business had run into trouble (a programme to sell 5000 tractors in America collapsed). He was going broke so he sold off the majority share in the car company – the most appetising of his three concerns – to save himself. Not long after, Lamborghini sought to sell his remaining shareholding and it was another one of his Swiss customers, Rosetti's friend René Leimer, who was persuaded to buy. With an investment of around £450,000, Leimer arrived in Sant'Agata Bolognese in the summer of 1974. By then, the factory was well advanced with the scheme that was to lead to its downfall, mass production of the 2.5-litre Urraco. Lamborghini had been told by its American importer that he could sell 500 Urracos a year and gleefully programmed a production run of 3000 cars. Like Paolo Stanzani, then factory manager and 'father' of the Urraco, Leimer enthusiastically endorsed the project. But the 2.5-litre Urraco didn't have enough performance and was afflicted by maintenance problems. The American arrangements went sour. Cars piled up at the factory. So did the parts inventory, and invoices from suppliers. By mid-1975 the factory was on the verge of collapse. Leimer, who had taken charge and was spending three days a week in Italy and the other two with his pre-fab and construction businesses back in Switzerland (Rossetti has always been 'sick'), called in Pier Luigi Capellini. He had been with Lamborghini in the early days before going to be Alessandro de Tomaso's right-hand man. Capellini went straight to America, sacked the '500-Urracos-a-year' importer, and opened an agreement with a new concessionaire from whom he obtained a letter of credit, good for three years, for £275,000. Lamborghini was to supply him with the more realistic figure of 140 cars a year.

AND THE REVS KEEP RISING

By this time, Lamborghini just about had the much-needed 3.0-litre version of the Urraco ready. It had somehow managed to shift almost 700 2.5s, and came up with the tax-dodging 2.0-litre version for Italy to use up some of the remaining parts, and was working on the ostentatious Silhouette – aimed directly at the Americans. But then the company ran into serious cash flow problems again. Late in 1976 and in the early part of 1977 it gained some liquidity again but it wasn't enough. By autumn 1977, Lamborghini plunged deeply into trouble as the debts overwhelmed it – the trouble from which it will not, in its present form, recover. For 1977, the Silhouette was the only car actually homologated for the United States but again the factory couldn't supply enough to make it worth the importer's while.

Lamborghini soldiered on selling in Europe, South Africa, the Middle East and Australia. Capellini tried to find a financial lifebelt. Franco Baraldini, that energetic young engineer, roamed the world seeking other projects that could occupy Sant'Agata's under-utilised production lines and workforce. He forged links with Mobility Technology in California for the Cheetah off-road project, and got the deal for Lamborghini to build the BMW M1 underway. It looked as if the answers had been found. In his search, Capellini even went so far as to find a buyer for the company: Walter Wolf, the Formula One team owner. A contract was drawn up. Wolf would pay £660,000 to Rossetti and £440,000 to Leimer. But the Swiss wouldn't sign. They didn't think the offer substantial enough and Rossetti, Leimer says, 'was fond of the company and did not want to end his involvement'. When the deal evaporated, Capellini was able to borrow £1.1m from the Italian government, enough to keep the company going and to provide for the BMW project.

But while Lamborghini had built and developed the M1 prototype to their and BMW's satisfaction – and everyone connected with it says it's superb – there wasn't enough money left to get production underway on schedule. Too much of the government money had been channelled towards the Cheetah. That caused a serious split in the camp: Leimer and Baraldini, who were enthusiastic about the Cheetah project, against Capellini who considered it ill advised and ill timed. Baraldini left, and his place as director of engineering was taken by Marco Raimondi – an appointment that, as we'll see shortly, had serious consequences for Britain. Now, Capellini and Raimondi have gone too, leaving Lamborghini without a managing director/financial controller and a chief engineer. The politics of it are intense. For instance, Capellini and Raimondi and three of their former associates at Sant'Agata are joining forces in a small company called Ital Engineering. BMW is among their first clients: Ital Engineering is finding and organising the supply of the parts BMW needs to have the M1 built by Bauer in Stuttgart.

Tall, serious, intelligent, articulate Capellini says: 'I put everything into trying to keep Lamborghini afloat, and for three years I succeeded. I was shattered when I saw that the deal with Walter Wolf wasn't going to go through. That was our big hope, and I gave a piece of my heart to its organisation. After it failed I struggled on and got the money from the government – as recognition of my struggles they made me *Cavaliere*. But it became impossible for me to stay on. The situation is now so bad that there is no option but controlled administration, take-over or bankruptcy. And if the company is taken over by someone with both the money and the know-how to make it work – as I sincerely hope it will be – they would not want to keep me on. I am sorry it has ended like this: I really loved Lamborghini. But the whole history of the company is full of mistakes, each one linked to the next, and my task, coming in when the factory was on the verge of collapse, proved to be impossible. For 18 months, Leimer, Baraldini and I worked well together. But the Cheetah came between us and fractured the relationship.'

According to Capellini, Lamborghini's liabilities are now around £3.25m –around £0.5m owed to the local bank, £1.25m to the Italian government, £0.75m to suppliers and £0.75m in overdue social security payments. If the company goes down, another £270,000 or so will be due in redundancy money; if it is rescued, there will need to be at least £500,000 available in cash to enable even very modest production to be resumed. If those are the figures involved, and if the company's assets stand at around £2.2m, the value of Messrs Leimer and Rossetti's shares is a highly debatable point. Nor is the

AND THE REVS KEEP RISING

matter even that simple. A complex situation in the holding of the Rossetti shares exists between Georges-Henri and his uncle.

Portly, ebullient, indefatigable, ever-optimistic Leimer says: 'We have to be realistic – we are going to have to take what we can get for Lamborghini. We lost a lot of money by simply investing Swiss francs in Italy anyway. We are talking with several interested parties but we are not yet near to making a deal. We are ready to sell all or part of our holding.

'Yes, we have made mistakes. I now know that this company should build very few cars and sell them at very high prices. It is a mistake to try to build a car like the Urraco in relatively big numbers and sell it for a relatively low price. In the beginning, I thought that the Cheetah could be made here but it was impossible to produce without the help of a big weapons manufacturer. I am still trying to convince a weapons company to enter into a joint agreement to make it. With the BMW, £500,000 would have been enough to buy the parts and get the production underway but we just didn't have the cash left. We asked BMW to lend it to us, but we understand that their controlling body long ago laid down a rule that no money whatsoever was to be invested in Italy. They told us that if we'd been in any other country they'd have been glad to lend us the money.

'Perhaps our hopes of getting some of our money back are now in vain but I'm optimistic. Whatever happens to us, I think that production of Lamborghini cars will go on. They are the base of the company, and always will be. They deserve to go on being made, and I think they will survive this crisis as they have others in the past.'

As he spoke, down on the factory floor there were very few Lamborghinis being made that Thursday. One Espada was halfway along the line, getting its suspension. One red Countach S was just a few days from completion (the new car for Armin Johl, a customer in Germany: his first Countach S had been written off when it was at the factory for servicing and an old man in a truck pulled out into its path while test driver Valentino Balboni was checking it. Lamborghini built him another in six weeks). Another S, a marvellous deep bronze, was being readied for collection the next day. Our own Silhouette – well, the Silhouette we were to bring back

LAMBORGHINI SILHOUETTE

to England for Charles Choularton in Cheshire – was next to it, being buffed and detailed after its final test run. Among the new cars – indeed, easily outnumbering them – were customer's cars back for repair or restoration, their metal being worked, their interiors refitted and their engines pored over with the same loving care. There was an air of peace rather than a sense of doom; but pathos too: Number One line bore a proud, still-fresh sign saying 'BMW'.

Eventually, the Silhouette was ready. They parked it near one of the big blue doors for me, and while the customs man from Modena affixed its seal for the journey back to Britain, I went down among the drilling machines and glittering alloy blocks and sumps and gearbox casings to find John. He was lost in a new world. Neither of us spoke as we popped our bags into the Silhouette, checked the paperwork and made ready to leave. I was to learn later what was in John's mind. My own thoughts were confused. There was *concern:* the story I'd just heard. *Perfidy:* would we still have time to get a Ferrari? *Curiosity:* how would Ferrari react when we arrived in a Lamborghini? *Anticipation:* the 1000 miles home ahead of us. *Gratitude:* that I had been entrusted with this car in which to cover them. *Melancholy:* that, for the foreseeable future, it would be the last time it would happen.

You see, this was the last Lamborghini the law will allow to come to Britain: Lamborghini's homologation for the UK has now expired. The paperwork necessary for compliance with the new type-approval regulations was neglected in the turmoil at Sant'Agata in the past few months. Type-approval was Raimondi's job; too much of his attention was diverted when he had to take over the factory upon Baraldini's departure. And now, of course, he too is gone, and Lamborghini's troubles are far bigger than lack of type approval for Britain. For Roger Phillips, Lamborghini's long-time British importer, it is a disastrous turn. He could sell something like 60 Lamborghinis a year in Britain, if he could get them. At least he is once more independent after running (at Leimer's instigation) the importers as a factory subsidiary company for the past two years. Somehow, he hasn't lost faith and from his premises in Whyteleafe, Surrey, is carrying on a full Lamborghini parts and service operation as well as selling used Lamborghinis. Indeed, it was with Roger's manager, Martin Billing, making one of his regular treks to Modena for spares, that we hitched a lift.

He was ready to the leave the factory, loaded up, at the same time we were. We followed him out the gate in the Silhouette, waved, and headed for Maranello. What a contrast, there, to hear of Ferrari's run of success. It will make more than 2000 cars in 1978 and sell more than 200 in Britain. Boxers and 400 automatics and 308 GTBs and Spiders are rolling steadily off the lines. But the Ferrari people were more interested in the Silhouette than talking about their own cars. Engineers and line workers, salesmen and the gate men packed around it and peered in it and under it. Wonderful, they said. 'What a tragedy that things are so bad for a company that can make cars like this,' said my friend Franco Gozzi, slowly shaking his head. And when we left after our meeting, a crowd gathered at the big green gates to listen as we accelerated along the straight.

We ran easily up the *Autostrada del Sole* with the evening traffic, letting the car settle, and found a fine little hotel incongruously called Tiffany's near the western Milano *tangenziale* and after a quiet, reflective but excellent dinner and a bottle of first-class Grumello, we sauntered off to bed. We had business at Alfa Romeo next day; and it was to be 3pm before we were back in the Silhouette, heading west through steamy summer drizzle to pick up the *autostrada* into the Aosta valley.

The Silhouette would, if I wished to make a point of it, take full torque without a trace of traction lost between those wide Pirellis and the road. It would also accept the full power of the four disc brakes without doing anything other than squashing itself into the road. So the headlights went up and the wipers went on to high-speed and with the spray streaming out behind us we knuckled down to a business-like 110mph cruise in order to reach the San Bernardino pass before too much of the Friday evening traffic.

I needn't have worried. When we reached the rough, narrow road that replaces the motorway out of Aosta and takes you climbing towards Switzerland, *there* was all the power and security, the old feeling of real ability, that allowed me to come out alongside the

LAMBORGHINI SILHOUETTE

trucks and the campervans and the plodding tourists' saloons, have a look, and *go! There* was the grip and stability that allowed me to come steadily and safely into bend after bend at mile-gobbling speeds. *There* was the carefully calculated suspension geometry that allowed me to feel the bumps in the worst bends but which wouldn't let the wheels be deflected off line. And *there* was the power to push on relentlessly up the hills into the next one. How good it was to fall back into the rhythm that such a car allows a driver: that state of alert equilibrium, the eyes working 'way ahead to feed the brain with a steady stream of information; and the brain working with an unhurried efficiency to elicit precisely the right movements from the hands, fingers and feet at precisely the right moment. I began to appreciate something I hadn't pinned down before: a car like this allows you to take unusual pleasure in your own functions as you drive. It isn't sensuality; it's an awareness of your own precision, your own mental and physical control. They give you *yourself* as well as *themselves.* The automobile as an art form, indeed, John Mason: the automobile as a medium.

'I don't believe this,' John said quietly when we were somewhere near the top of the pass and its tunnel. 'I came along this road a few weeks ago in weather as bad as this, and it was hell. I hated every minute of it and swore I'd never drive down here again in such rotten conditions. To this thing, it's nothing.' We saw nothing of the grandeur of the pass. The mountains were shrouded in cloud and rain. We should have felt miserable. We just got on with the job of coming home, wondering how far we'd get before we stopped for the night. Would we make it into France?

The rain cleared for a while on the Swiss side of the mountains, enough to give us dry surface for the marvellous road down the Val d'Entremont. And, happily, John asked, at the top of its most exquisite series of kinks and hairpins, if I'd mind driving up and down while he took some pictures. He was entirely correct: here at last we had some dry weather, even if there wasn't much light left, and we had no way of knowing what tomorrow and France had in store. I'd have swopped places with him, you know: from his vantage point at the top of the run he could see it and hear it.

AND THE REVS KEEP RISING

But what pleasure it was to *drive* it, searing up and down that road without really pushing the car, knowing that I had to go seriously quickly to reach its limits, seeking my rewards in working smoothly and gently with it and not against it. Hearing and feeling the V8 climb up through its power band, and still with 2000rpm in hand, for I didn't want to run it right out yet. So I watched for my self-imposed limit of 5500rpm and then reaching for the lever and pushing it through the big gate and hearing and feeling it *ka*-chock into the next gear, with the wail of the cams and the groan of the Webers and the blaring of the exhausts providing the soundtrack. There was the cleanliness and control of the engine on the over-run, the feel and the precision of the brakes – not that I had to use them hard – into the bends and then the gentle tug of the big Pirellis against the steering and then against the rear suspension. This was not tedious. Not even for John. 'Jesus man – you should *hear* it from up there.'

We had spasmodic rain for the rest of the run to Montreux and then along the narrow, clean Swiss motorway to Lausanne. We went slowly out of deference to that efficient Swiss radar. Ah, but then we picked up the small road for the border, direction Pontarlier, and the speed with which the Swiss were pushing their Renaults, Simcas and Citroëns and BMWs and Volkswagens suggested that there was nothing more to worry about. So we clipped along with them, and passed them. But oh dear, if we weren't delayed by the most disinterested border guards in Switzerland we had dallied too long with our pictures for we reached Pontarlier precisely at nine. And in the dining room of the Grande Hotel de La Poste at 9.02pm we were bluntly told that this was not England and that restaurants in provincial France shut at 9.00pm. There was a pizzeria around the corner for people like us. There was also a brasserie across the road and John's French secured us a more than passable meal.

We were up at six and breakfasted and gone by 6.30am. The V8 had started to the first turn of the key and a fully depressed throttle, no doubt shattering the slumber of the guests still enjoying the Poste's comfort. It certainly brought the staff to the courtyard windows. The rain was bucketing down and, we soon saw, the

LAMBORGHINI SILHOUETTE

roads were often inches deep. It wasn't only to warm up the car correctly that I began slowly. The road was rutted and irregular, many of its corners beyond crests, and off-camber, and if I knew both the Silhouette and Pirelli's P7s well, I hadn't worked with either in water as deep as this. But they both had some lessons in store, and within 30 miles our frequent speed had risen to 80mph come rain, crest or corner. It was so *easy!* Only once, on a glass-shiny patch of road, drastically off-camber and mid-bend, was there a nudge into understeer as the front tyres let go, and then a tiny wag from the tail as I played games and applied more power than I really needed to neutralise it. The Silhouette is like that: it tells you what you can do. A Renault 30 came pressing upon our tail along one great long straight between a glorious avenue of trees. We were doing 100 and might have done half as much again had I cared to ignore Saturday morning's tractors and farm entrances. He passed us and pressed on. We were on his tail half a dozen bends later, past him out of the next one and when, miles further on, we stopped for petrol we'd filled up, paid, wiped the windscreen and were checking the oil before he went past. That is the difference between a good contemporary car and a great one.

We pressed onwards and suffered with the rest of the trucks and traffic around Dijon, the rain still heavy. But something moved me to throw caution mildly to the winds when we picked up the *autoroute* for Paris and I sat the Silhouette on 110 again. How would the gendarmes react? My luck was in. We saw none, and it was at that comfortable pace that we journeyed on toward Paris. It was on the same *autoroute* that, 18 months ago, we'd cruised for hours at between 140 and 160mph in that incredible Countach-Silhouette-Urraco convoy. The only convoy we ran this time was with Mr H Napier's Scottish Volvo F88 articulated lorry. We hailed him in a service area and he was pleased to have John clamber up into his mate's seat to shoot down on the Silhouette running alongside him in the rain for 10 miles or so. There was the awful, blind aggression of a Frankfurt-registered BMW 633i driver on the *Périphérique* and we cringed on the inside lane while he lunged at the Citroëns' tails in the dense afternoon traffic. We hoped he wasn't heading for Lille.

AND THE REVS KEEP RISING

We were, and with just one more stop for fuel and a swift snack were painlessly onto the new spur motorway for Calais in less time than we'd thought the conditions would permit, with plenty in hand to catch the boat. I used the car on that last leg of jammed, crest-ridden A-road from the end of the motorway to the coast. I ran it right out hard in the gears several times as we howled past the dawdling convoys. *There* was the full force of 260 horsepower at 7500rpm, and *there* was all the acceleration they could provide. *There* was the extreme purposefulness the Silhouette could provide. I drank it in, and hoped like hell that it really wouldn't be for the last time.

Our agent did his best to clear us quickly through customs in Dover, but we still had a four-hour wait. So there was plenty of time to collate thoughts. How on earth, through the turmoil of the past five years, have Lamborghinis – the cars – gone on as they have? There have been the Countach and then the Countach S, the 3.0-litre Urraco and then the Silhouette. The Bravo got a long way down its developmental road. The BMW M1 has gone all the way, and from the test drivers' reports it's fabulous. The one thing that has not foundered at Lamborghini is the standard of engineering. It's hard to explain the remarkable continuity of design and developmental and manufacturing that goes on come hell or high water. Thank goodness it does. Right now, there are not more roadable cars in the world. Ask Armin Johl, for one. Besides the Countach – his third – he has a Ferrari 400 GT, 308 GTS and a 275 GTB/4. Yet the signs of the difficulties are there in the cars too. The Silhouette is not developed as fully as it should be. Its instrument panel is awful – although that's just bad design – and when you open the doors in the rain, water pours from the roof onto the sills or your legs. Nor, you'd assume from hearing the creaks and groans over kerbs, is the body rigid enough, which suggests the doors will probably drop with time. No; it would still be the plain Urraco 3.0-litre for me and I'd try not to remember that the Silhouette has stronger roadholding and more formidable wet weather performance. It'd be nice to hear what *you* think, Mr Choularton. After all, the last Lamborghini to reach Britain for what may be a long time is now yours. I'm glad that I could steal at least 1000 miles of its precious life.

SIX DAYS ON THE ROAD WITH ENZO'S GREATEST HIT

1962 FERRARI 250 GTO
1979

'YOU'LL BE TIRED WHEN you get there,' they said, grinning; and I was. But what a tiredness! Alone through the night with a Ferrari 250 GTO, blazing over 100 miles of taxing and deserted roads, the exhausts whooping and snarling and barking and wailing, the V12 both gentle and savage, the steering sharp and alive, the gearshift sweet and steely, the cabin cold, loud and intimate, the concentration intense; the experience fatiguing but overwhelming. And, tired or not, I couldn't leave the car alone when I arrived. There was too much of it, too much in it, too much to be had from it.

I warmed myself by the fire, ate a little and then had to go out into the night with it again, anxious to share its extraordinary pleasures with an appreciative friend; unable simply to slip it into the garage. And nor, in the face of such inspiration, was sleep to come quickly when at last I settled down. There were too many moments to relive and too many more to anticipate: the GTO was to be mine for another six days. The legend was within my grasp at last.

For me, that legend began with a picture on a school friend's wall in Tasmania. It was a picture of a red car so beautiful and yet so purposeful that we looked at in awe. On the other side of the earth, in southern England, a young man named Nick Mason stood awed before another red GTO as it swept to victory one Sunday at Goodwood. He vowed that it was the car he would, one day, do his utmost to own. Becoming the drummer in a band called Pink Floyd would make it possible.

AND THE REVS KEEP RISING

It was Nick, all these years later, who, right there at Goodwood, handed me the keys to his GTO. It was a moment heady with excitement and sombre with apprehension. I knew he'd refused £75,000 for the car only weeks before. I knew how long he'd searched for it and I knew that, when it was finally his, he'd discovered that it was the selfsame car that had captivated him at Goodwood in 1964.

Why *is* the 250 GTO so special? It was the last front-engined Ferrari racing car, the crowning glory in that incredible array of gentleman's racers, the 250 Gran Turismo Berlinettas, that, between late 1955 and 1965 won more races (three World Championships among them) than any other series. They were the cars that did most to carve out the Ferrari reputation. They were created to contest the GT category – set up to separate the enclosed cars from the true sports cars in the mid-'50s – but some were also to be sold as road cars to customers prepared to sacrifice a few creature comforts. Altogether, there were about 350 250 GTs of varying types; 39 of them were GTOs – 36 with the original '62/'63 bodies then a further three '64 models with redesigned bodies that made them look more like 250LMs.

According to Jess Pourret's fine book *The Ferrari Legend: The Competition 250 GT Berlinetta* (John W Barnes Publishing/Patrick Stephens) the racing world in 1962 thought that, after seven indomitable years, the 250 GT was at the top of the tree. But the best was yet to come. Strong challenges were looming from the lightweight Jaguars, Aston Martin Zagatos, Cobras and Porsches. And Ferrari, at the end of 1960, had begun developing the GTO from the familiar low, nuggety, short wheelbase 250 GT – itself derived, in 1959, from the original long wheelbase GT, the car that soon after appearing in the mid-'50s put paid to the Mercedes 300SL.

Enzo Ferrari knew that the 250's engine could meet the challenge. His faith in that omnipotent Colombo-designed sohc 3.0-litre V12 had paid off handsomely. It was sensible, simple, beautifully made and reliable. More power could be drawn from it without endangering that reliability. The chassis was old and ᵔlatively crude but it too was sturdy and reliable and could be

1962 FERRARI 250 GTO

made to hang on for another couple of years. Importantly, since more than 100 short wheelbase cars had already been built around the chassis, new bodywork could be used without the need for fresh homologation.

It was the bodywork that had to change. The 250 GT SWB's blunt nose limited its speed to 155mph. Beyond 149mph it grew very light at the front and the short rear bodywork couldn't keep the rear wheels down. Ferrari wanted 180mph to keep his growing army of opponents at bay. Ferrari's engineers hadn't concerned themselves with detail aerodynamics: their engines had always been powerful enough to overcome any drawbacks. But the puny-engined Lotuses, Panhards and Alpines at Le Mans had shown what good aerodynamics could do. So, in 1961, with various hacked-about Berlinetta bodies, Ferrari spent a great deal of time examining penetration, drag, lift and adhesion. Many of the tests were conducted on the *autostrada*, others on the track and still more in the wind tunnel. Step-by-step, the GTO's body evolved.

It was never really styled as such but the final shape was and is exquisite. It's born entirely of purpose and yet that purpose is combined with an extraordinary beauty, a classic example of the Emilian engineers' aesthetics. Beyond admiring the shape, to look at a GTO now is to be bemused. Here is a racing car with chromed windscreen wiper arms and chromed surrounds for its windscreen, back and side windows, dainty chromed clips to hold its forward-opening bonnet in place (along with those little leather straps), locking door buttons, beautiful hand-beaten surrounds for its headlight covers and a prancing horse delicately carved from light alloy mounted so as to float in its elliptical snout, itself outlined with chrome. There were slight variations to the GTO bodies but most were like Nick's car (chassis no 3757GT, delivered to the Belgian Ecurie Francorchamps on June 14, 1962) with rectangular foglights set into the nose either side of the central opening, then the twin brake duct openings and with the sidelights jutting from the curving bodywork half under and half beside the headlights.

And then there were the three extra vents in the nose, the three scallops that made the GTO so instantly recognisable. You undid their press-and-twist Dzus fasteners and lifted off the covers to increase the cooling at low speeds. There were, too, those Plexiglas scoops over the inlets on the cowl that fed air to the cockpit, and the slashes in the flanks that released the air channelled to the brakes (the forward vent) and air from the engine compartment (the after vent). All the GTOs came out of the factory with just these two side vents, but many owners swiftly added a fashionable third. Ecurie Francorchamps did. Another vent in each rear mudguard released air from the rear brakes, and on the tail there was, for the first time on a GT car, a spoiler. Initially, the spoiler was riveted on. Later, it was faired into the bodywork. All these things were distinctively GTO, but most of all it was a car with a very low nose and low waistline and it had all the penetration that would allow a 2220lb car of only 3.0 litres to reach 180mph.

The engine's height helped there. For its new role it was given a new dry sump made of magnesium that not only helped the lubrication but also meant that the engine was shallow, permitting the low nose and bonnet line and helping the engineers obtain the lowest possible centre of gravity. The V12, its block cast in Silumin with the cylinder banks at 60 degrees, was made to extremely close tolerances with enormous skill. The crankshaft was, in familiar Ferrari fashion, machined from one steel billet. So too were the con rods. The cylinder heads had the biggest valves the combustion chambers could take, and all the gas conduits were beautifully polished, with each intake/exhaust port matched against the other. The rocker arms were milled for spring clearance and they pivoted on needle bearings. The cam covers were magnesium, again to save weight.

Nestling between them went six twin-choke downdraught Webers topped only with stubby trumpets with their flanges carefully Siamesed. The precise capacity, from an oversquare bore and stroke of 73 x 58.8mm, was 2953cc. The compression ratio was 9.8:1, and if each engine did not develop between 296 and 302bhp at 7500rpm on the test bed it went back to the racing shop for rebuilding. Only where the required figures were registered

1962 FERRARI 250 GTO

and the engine fully tested was it installed in the car. Coupled to it went an all-synchromesh five-speed gearbox and any one of eight differentials ranging from a low of 4.85:1 (which gave phenomenal acceleration against a top speed of 129.3mph at 7500rpm in fifth) to a high of 3.5:1, which meant less acceleration but a top speed of 175.9mph. It was enough, when the GTO began racing at the beginning of the 1962 season, to hammer the opposition.

The chassis of the GTO was very similar to that of the old 250 GT. The 94.4in wheelbase was retained, and the frame was made up from the same sort of tubular steel although some of the tubing itself and the position of many of the bracing members and mounts for things like the body, fuel tank, Watts linkages and dampers was different. There were forged unequal length A-arms, coil springs and new adjustable Koni dampers at the front, along with a hefty anti-roll bar. The rear axle was live, located by stiffer leaf springs than had been used before, and by four track rods, the two Watts links and another pair of the new Konis. There were disc brakes all round, with special alloy callipers at the front and a little pump to boost the braking effort to the front wheels. The steering was 17:1 ZF recirculating ball. The 35 gallon fuel tank, hand-riveted, went behind the rear axle: the five gallon oil reservoir was between the chassis rails just behind the passenger's seat. Both were protected from stones by an aluminium shield slung beneath the car that was also cunningly contrived to use the airflow beneath the car to assist high-speed stability. The wheels were Borrani, with alloy rims and steel spokes, 600 x 15 at the front and 700 x 15 at the rear carrying either Dunlop R5s or R6s. Those tyres would last nine hours at Le Mans and one-and-a-half hours at Goodwood.

It was a crisp, clear winter afternoon at Goodwood when it became my turn to open the door of a GTO, drop into the little leather bucket and snap on the racing harness. The door, you note, feels light and almost dainty and yet it shuts with a no-nonsense *thunk*. There is no more flab on it than elsewhere in the cabin. There isn't even a door handle inside, only a cord to pull when you wish to get out. Your eyes pick up plenty of the black-painted tubing of the frame work: in the footwells, running up inside the pillars, close beside your seat,

AND THE REVS KEEP RISING

and even diagonally across the passenger's foot space, forcing one shin to go under it and one over it. The plain tunnel that splits the cockpit has flat sides and top. On its left side there is a little leather-covered pad, a buffer for the driver's right knee.

From the top of the tunnel juts the box holding the gearlever and its open metal gate: big, meaty, meaningful; beautiful. The lever itself rises high, so that its round, glistening alloy knob is almost at the level of the steering wheel boss – or, for someone my height (5ft 10in) at a point that allows the arm to be run almost straight out from the shoulder. In first it is less than a hand's spread from the wheel rim; in fourth, where it is furthest from you, it is at a full arm's stretch and around 120 degrees to the plane of the chest.

The wheel has even more appeal. Straight ahead of you, polished wood bonded to an alloy rim and with alloy spokes and, dancing in its centre, the black-on-yellow horse. Your hands drop on to it perfectly, not quite at full arm's reach. Through it, mounted in a frugal black crackle-covered metal panel that is shrouded no more than it need be, you see a huge, clear tachometer that reads to 10,000rpm. Its tell-tale is set at 7500rpm. Around it there are five smaller dials: on the far left the fuel gauge, at 11 o'clock to the tachometer the fuel pressure gauge, and at seven o'clock the water temperature gauge. The oil pressure gauge is beside the upper right edge of the tachometer, and the oil temperature gauge is directly below that. It is a neat grouping, each dial nicely chrome-rimmed, and all but free from reflections. There is an indicator stalk (from a Lancia Fulvia, one suspects) on the left of the steering column. Arrayed across a thin little panel tacked on to the main dash cowling to the right of the wheel you find the tiny ignition lock, the knurled headlight knob and then three tiny alloy toggles. The nearest to you is to switch the fuel pumps on and off, and next the wipers and the next the fog lights. Finally, there is another knurled knob with which you adjust your panel lighting. There is a wide slot cut into the centre of the top of the dash. Through it peep three pipes. They provide the demisting and the ventilation. You can supplement them on a hot day by tugging back the sliding Perspex side windows. The air is swept from the cabin through a hole,

1962 FERRARI 250 GTO

shielded by another of those clear scoops you find on the bonnet, in the rear window which is itself acrylic.

Lift your eyes beyond the dashboard and the view is luscious. It is rather like looking down an E-type's bonnet but it is shorter and the curves more sultry – though not as pronounced as the D-type's. There is the seductive curve of the wing on the left, flattening out low and smooth ahead of the windscreen to disappear below the point where your left hand rests on the wheel. Were you to guide the car close alongside a white line, the wing would curve out over it at the front but it would become visible again where you glance down through the lower corner of the windscreen. Voluptuous curves or not, the GTO can be placed tight, tight, tight into a curb because it provides its driver with tremendously good vision. Swing the eyes across to the centre of the car and there is a flat section and then the bulge that covers those six carburettors. Another flat section and then the full curve of the right wing. The acrylic scoops and the chromed bonnet clips, gleaming in the sun, are the icing on the cake. If this car looks menacingly beautiful from the outside, from inside it is merely sensational.

Adjust the mirror, squeeze down on the throttle, turn the key in its neat lock and then push it. There is a wheeze and then the roar. This engine has the lightest of flywheels and the most precise of throttle linkages. You've pressed too hard and the revs are soaring. Now you know about its responsiveness. Pull the tall gearlever over and back into first, and feel the gear engage. Ease the clutch out. How extraordinarily sweet and accommodating it is. The GTO rolls forward, bumping across the grass, jiggling and joggling. What will it be like on those long, everyday roads away from the circuit, this car that ran third at Le Mans in 1962, won the 500km race at Spa in 1963 and set a new lap record of 127mph doing it, then went on and on building its race record? Didn't Jess Pourret say he'd driven 25,000 absolutely trouble free miles on the road in his GTO; and didn't Nick Mason's little logbook list journeys in his first 18 months with the car as diverse as a run to the Nürburgring for a historical meeting and taking his daughter the two miles to school through north London streets?

AND THE REVS KEEP RISING

The GTO was warm. It had been running hard around Goodwood all afternoon. Modena Engineering and some of their friends were having an owners' day. The Ferrari swung on to the track, empty now since most people had gone, and began accelerating. Clean, hard – and loud. All the legendary sounds of the Ferrari V12 were there: the solid suck of the carburettors, the whine and thrash of the cams and valve gear and a constantly changing exhaust note that sounds more marvellous than one might think possible from a mechanical object. The first shift left me in no doubt about the pleasures that were going to come from that movement of the gearlever in its big, slotted gate. And the steering, into the first corner, swiftly showed that it, too, had more than enough to offer. It was quite light, quick, full of feel and there was no doubt that the car would react to it instantly and accurately. There was the slightest understeer, and then, in response to a little more from the engine when I cared to ask for it with my toes, a swift shift to neutrality. Moments, mere moments, were enough to demonstrate the integrity and balance of a car that's so exciting and dramatic and yet so comforting and reassuring to drive – until, says David Piper, who raced GTOs often, you seek the last half-second and then it can become very difficult, prone to sudden breakaway that's difficult to catch. It was soon apparent that all the performance could be used; and how glorious it was to hear the engine howl around – *so quickly!* – to 7500 in fourth, those exhausts thundering out their music, and then get that stupendous change of note with the shift, flat, into fifth.

Running hard like that, climbing beyond 7000rpm and 140mph in top but resisting going on to the 7500rpm limit and the 147mph it would bring, nothing seemed intimidating or difficult about the GTO. It just went lunging, yowling, forward: light and easy in the hands, rock stable, lifting very slightly at the front but stuck down hard at the rear. You *knew* it was stuck down hard; you could feel it through your backside. Then it was time for the brakes, and they required a strong, sustained push, the leg straining against the pedal and the results modest. So that was it: allow plenty of space, more than in almost any contemporary car, and then push hard with the

1962 FERRARI 250 GTO

ball of the foot, dabbing at the throttle with the smaller toes to blip up the revs for the downshifts. The stability was all still there, and when the foot came off the brake the car just turned perfectly into the bend and went sailing through and away ready to go up through the gears again. In a few more laps, when it had demonstrated its poise to the full, I was able to begin drifting it, and it was there that it was sufficiently delectable to make me tingle with pleasure. That link between buttocks and rear axle said everything. The tyres shifted sideways and the feel of them nudging across the surface came through immediately. Flick the wooden wheel and the tyres came straight back into line, and with a superb tidiness. There was so much purpose to it all but so much feel and character too, and within those few laps the car had me firmly within its spell.

Out on the road, it was no less captivating. The ride was very firm and ever-joggly and it would, as Nick and his pals had said knowingly as they saw me off, tire me by the time I'd completed the 150-mile journey that lay ahead. From time to time, the racing tyres made the car tug against the wheel and dart about. But it was not unexpected and never awkward, just part of driving a racing car of another period on the road. It had, more than anything else, the highly animated feel of a race car going slowly. The motion wasn't exactly discordant but all the ingredients were not flowing silkily together to create the optimum. Yet there was great pleasure to be had from driving the car slowly like that, feeling and examining all those ingredients, savouring each, and occasionally blending them with a concerted blast through an inviting series of bends or with full acceleration past slower traffic.

It wasn't long before I was in thick traffic, for my journey was taking me right across London, and any fears I might once have harboured about the GTO's behaviour there were despatched at a stroke. That smooth and positive clutch was never anything else; that potent V12 demonstrated that its heart was as big as its soul, moving off without fuss and idling along in the snarls without a hiccup or complaint. It would, if you cared to test its flexibility, potter down to 1000rpm – 20mph – in fifth and pick up happily again. Drive the GTO in the city? Absolutely.

AND THE REVS KEEP RISING

Ah, but how extraordinarily satisfying it is to drive on open roads. By the time I'd cleared London there was little traffic left on the unfolding roads and I was ready to string those GTO ingredients together as best I could. So that I could hear the sound and revel in the acceleration – around 11sec from 0–100mph, and more than enough to press you hard back into the seat – I ran to 7500rpm in the gears as often as possible. Fifty, 74, 101 and 126mph, with fifth to come. Empty roundabouts challenged me to get the braking exact, to match the downshifts perfectly, to select the correct line and then to take the Ferrari through, wailing hard and balanced on the edge of adhesion. Mild though the angles were, I could feel it heeling slightly, nose lifting and tail dipping, with the power. Sometimes, sweeping out of the final curve with the V12 giving its all, the tail would nudge quickly and yet somehow gently into flat, positive oversteer. The feeling of catching it, simply by flicking the wrists, with the wheel light and delicate between the fingers, was as intense as it was beautiful. On smooth roads, when you get it right, the GTO is like that. It flatters you with the poise and the balance special to a terribly good front-engined car.

It might have tugged against the wheel and jiggled at loping speeds on the back roads that quickly followed the dual carriageways, but it sharpened into a clean, flowing projectile beyond 100mph – often possible with such strong acceleration on hand. Everything blended to deliver the goal of covering the ground quickly, effectively and securely. It just ran straight and hard, but still with all that communication pouring through. Under hard brakes into the tighter bends it did not dodge and dart as you might expect a car of its age and type to do. Its approach was smooth and sure. Nor was it much deflected by bumps mid-bend, and if I wanted the slightest gain or reduction in power from the V12 to adjust the line or attitude, I had it.

The steering was the same. There was a little lost motion, common with recirculating ball steering, at the rim in the straight ahead position, but move it more than a fraction of an inch and you had instant and fluid action. Those lingering, sensuous gearshifts of the miles in town became swift purposeful movements, the hand

1962 FERRARI 250 GTO

helped by near-perfect spring loading, the clutch ideal for in-and-out jabs. And there was that furious noise all the time from the carburettors and the cams, the exhausts and the wind. Near the top end, the roar of the wind past the little side windows was like a turbine. Cold air rushed in between those Perspex panels and from between the doors and the wings, for there are no niceties like rubber seals. Nor was the heater, simple as it is, working and I shivered as I trundled through the villages, thankful that it wasn't raining. The GTO would not be so much fun then.

So – cold, tired by the noise, the liveliness of the ride and the degree of concentration, but exalted by the experience – I arrived at my destination to be greeted by friends who, from within their house, had heard the GTO coming through the night. I went out and drove it again later that night, unable to wean myself from its remarkable character. In the ensuing days I drove it whenever I could. Any excuse was enough: taking a child to the church fete, nipping down to the butcher's, volunteering to go and pick up the bread, insisting that a far-flung antique dealer had a piece worth inspecting, arguing falsely that a certain beer was only available in an off licence 30 miles away. Each time, the GTO fired perfectly from cold in response to three prods on the throttle and then idled without fuss. It would take a long time to warm up, and the gearbox was stiff until it did, but giving it that time and respectful treatment was just part of the pleasure of being with it.

So too was to roll gently through the higgledy-piggledy villages, listening to the burble bouncing back off the walls, or to be caught in a stream of traffic, having to meander up and down the lower part of the rev range, soaking up the constantly varying music. There would be a pronounced burble up to 2000rpm before the sound grew sharper and shriller, rising through a proper 'tearing calico' period around 3500rpm. In the higher gears you could feel the engine climb properly onto the cams at that point, but proper peakiness was not part of its behaviour and nor was hesitancy. Just a mild caress of the throttle would have the car surging forward. Should you have to back off without being able to wind the engine right out, there'd be a tremendous rumble on the over-run, laced with a sort

AND THE REVS KEEP RISING

of cracking and popping, in the range between 3500 and 4000rpm. From the cams would come a really shrill whine. Accelerate again and that whine would rise until it became a solid, exciting thrash. The exhaust note would be rising too, and at about 5000rpm it'd combine with the engine's tones to create the bellow that, by the time you'd reached 7500rpm, had become so beautiful it was hard to believe. A friend, who stood and listened as the GTO blasted flat out along a lonely forest road then came right down through the gears as it neared him, said that if you were asked to imagine how the world's best racing car would sound – perfect, powerful, magnificent – then you would imagine something like this.

Were you to establish an image of classical handling, you would probably find that the GTO fitted it perfectly too. Savour its cornering power and balance though I might, I never felt I had fully extended the car. I knew it to have finite balance well beyond me. And yet it never treated me with cruelty or disdain. Once, coming hard enough through a bend for all of the road and careful balancing of throttle and steering to be necessary, I encountered a mole right where, in an instant, the GTO's left front wheel would be. There was a moment of pity and panic but then somehow I knew I could drive around him, and the car let me to do it. Once, almost flat in second and pushed hard back into the little leather bucket by the power, I encountered a patch of mud on a normally safe crest and the tail snapped around far enough for me to look, wide-eyed, out the side window. The car allowed me to collect it cleanly and easily. What it had done was to remind me that, gentle though it was prepared to be – 'It always feels as if it's on your side,' Nick had said. 'That's why it's so special' – those 300 horses were alive and very well.

Beyond relating that knowledge to the prevailing conditions, and beyond allowing something like double the braking distances one would in a modern high-performance car, the GTO insists on little from its driver. But he is not doing it justice if he does not try to perform every function as perfectly as he is able. It feels old, a survivor of a previous era, but it rises far beyond that era and mechanical limitations like a live axle and leaf springs. As a car of

1962 FERRARI 250 GTO

its time and type it is everything, to heed LJK Setright's contention, that the Cobra is not.

Sorrowfully, on the sixth day, I took the GTO from the garage for the last time and, heading south again, ran it hard where I knew I could run it hard and trundled with only minimally reduced pleasure where I had to trundle. Just to be in the car, feeling it and hearing it, was to be enthralled. In London, I picked up a pal for the final run down to the GTO's home and, like everyone else who rode in the car, he too was reduced to speechless awe when, clearing town, I let it all go for the last time.

I have driven many cars that, given the benefits of tyre and suspension developments – and mid-engined layouts – will corner more quickly and cover bumpy roads in less time and greater comfort. But I have never driven a car in which the ingredients blend so sumptuously to provide the driver with such enormous pools of pleasure, a car where purpose is backed by even greater degrees of soul and character; yes, and manners too. Do not, however, think of the GTO as servile. It is a proud stallion of a car, the Ferrari epitomised, and the six days I spent with it have enriched my treasure trove of motoring pleasures beyond anything I could have dreamed when I looked at that picture of the GTO on David Stubbs's wall.

LIFE IN SUPERCAR CITY
AMONG THE MODENESE
1979

IN SO MANY WAYS it was the classic visit to Modena. We arrived sufficiently early on a Sunday evening, after a stirring run down through the Brenner Pass – deep snow but clear roads and the sun shining in a bright blue alpine sky – to check into the friendly little Hotel Castello out among the Lambrusco vines and Parmigiano factories and then slip back into the heart of Modena in time to secure a table for dinner at Fini.

Ah, Fini! What a restaurant! You duck under some weather beaten colonnades and go through double glass doors into a hushed lobby. Have you blundered into an exclusive apartment building by mistake? No; the real entrance to the restaurant winds off to the left at the end of the lobby – who knows what *is* up the stairs – and when you're through the second portal you're in a softly-lit, elegant series of rooms, escorted by an immaculately dressed and efficiently polite waiter to a table bedecked with a crisp pink table cloth and set with expensive cutlery.

Half-past seven. Few other diners yet. Anti-pasti? Of course. And Lambrusco? Of course. This is the home of tortellini. He'll have his *in brodo*. Arrosti misti or bollito misto? An amazing selection of roasted or boiled meats, carved with panache directly onto your plate from vast, gleaming warm-trolleys wheeled briskly around from table to table. Or should it be one of dozens of other equally enticing main courses? Impossible to resist the mixed roasts. And the atmosphere. Sunday evening at Fini is special, and it wasn't long before the tables began filling with a fascinating array of people. Quiet, aristocratic-looking Modenese couples. Middle-aged men with girlfriends less than half their age dressed to the nines and showing it all off.

AMONG THE MODENESE

Marvellously eccentric families with parents in volatile discussion and teenage daughters who'd seemingly spent hours making themselves up to look like pre-Raphaelite beauties; the younger ones, studiously bored, occasionally endeavouring to pin down a male at another table with their eyes. Groups of friends with each member trying to outdo the others in his or her affections. A woman in her late 20s with pallid make-up and black orbs of eyes, savagely bleached hair and a black silk dress slit from neck to navel and, in the skirt, from ankle to thigh top; her man-friend, who had no intention of removing the camel hair coat draped over his shoulders, or the sunglasses pushed up on to his grey-streaked coiffure. The face of another girl nagged at me. Then I remembered. She was Danish, one of the hostesses imported to lure Modenese rakes to one of the city's more infamous clubs, and met because, along with the other girls from just about every country in Europe, she'd been living at the Palace Hotel when I'd stayed there during my first magical visit to Modena in the spring of '73. My friend Pete and I had struck up a friendship with them: lonely, brave-faced girls not quite sure where they were going, or why they'd come. The Danish girl had been intent upon hitting it big in Rome. Now, here she was in Fini on a Sunday night six years later, make-up noticeable on skin once so fresh it hadn't needed it, the figure a little fuller but still enough for her entrance to have turned most of the heads. Across the table from her a young and seemingly well-to-do young man obviously devoted to her. Dreams of Rome had faded in place of comfort, and a role in this unnervingly Fellini-like scene in Modena. Fascinating. The cost of admission for Richard Davies and I had been £10 each for exquisite food and an evening unique to Modena. We went back to the Castello, mused over one last grappa, and sank happily into our beds. We were due at Ferrari at 10 the next morning.

You never know quite what to expect, of course, except a warm welcome from Franco Gozzi, the ebullient public relations officer and Enzo Ferrari's personal assistant. My plan, outlined in the customary shower of letters, telegrams and phone calls so that there would be some chance of it actually happening, was to spend some time talking with Ferrari engineers whom I'd managed to miss on previous visits,

AND THE REVS KEEP RISING

perhaps to talk with Mr Ferrari and perhaps to take a 400 GT out for a few hours in the hills. Despite the clear, bright sunshine, the weather put paid to that scheme: it was -3 degrees C with ice thick on the ground. Staying on the road in our faithful Peugeot 604Ti was difficult enough. It wasn't the day to play with a 340bhp Ferrari.

But there was dear old Franco striding up to us as we parked the Peugeot inside the famous green gates with the rampant horse kicking over them. Joyous handshakes and much backslapping. Then, as he led us to his office, Franco wrapped his great arm around me and declared: 'You lucky man – you lucky, lucky man.' It transpired that in just a few hours Ferrari was to unveil its new 312T4 Formula 1 car. Enzo Ferrari had made the decision suddenly the previous Friday afternoon and Franco had been on the phone all Friday evening and Saturday morning, summoning journalists from all over Europe; but many of the motor sport journalists had already left for the first Grand Prix in Argentina. 'What a weekend!' said Franco. What luck, thought I. In all my visits to Maranello I'd never attended a launch of a new F1 car – the subjects dearest to Enzo's heart. 'The Maranello town hall at 2.30,' said Franco. 'Now go and talk to your engineers – they're waiting.'

Among the points I was anxious to raise with Dottore Ingegnere Angelo Bellei, a Ferrari man for 30 years and director of product design and development, and Dottore Ingegnere Giuliano De Angelis, 16 years at Maranello and head of road car engine design and development, were the power outputs and claimed top speeds of the two Berlinetta Boxer models so far produced. The first 4.4-litre 365 GT4 BB, shown in 1971 and put into production two years later, had been accredited by the factory with 380bhp at 7000rpm and a top speed of 188mph.

Its successor, the 5.0-litre BB 512 introduced at the end of 1976, was attributed with 360bhp at 6200rpm and, initially, the same top speed, although its brochure now gives that as 176mph. I'd asked Franco about the discrepancies when the 512 was introduced. He rolled off the explanation that the 4.4-litre engine's power had been exaggerated by 50bhp, and that the 512 was in fact faster, and if it still didn't make a lot of sense I forgot one of his classic, jovial

AMONG THE MODENESE

comments of the past: 'I promise with all my heart that I will do exactly what you say – but then, I am a terrible liar.'

No one seems to have run a 4.4-litre Boxer right out. The best I ever had the chance of seeing was a little over 170mph, with more in hand but not the road. And, try as they might, *Autocar* testers were unable to get a BB 512 beyond 163mph. According to Dr Ing De Angelis, who designed the BB's flat-12 engine, and Dr Ing Bellei, who masterminded the entire project, the first prototype BB *had* been developing 380bhp but in the final juggle of power against emissions and drivability, that was cut back to 360bhp for the production 4.4-litre Boxers. That same prototype had attained 188mph but the production 365 Boxers would not exceed 180mph. And the true power of the 5.0-litre engine is not 360bhp as its brochure claims but 340bhp at 6200rpm, with 331lb/ft of torque at 4300rpm. The highest top speed a 512 has ever reached is 176mph, Dr Ing Bellei says, and most of the production cars are a fraction down on that. So that explains a few things. Next for the Boxer? Possibly fuel injection if emissions rules disadvantage the carburettors too much. Ferrari is also well into studies with turbocharged engines, but with smaller capacities; perhaps one day…

Meanwhile, Ferrari is pumping out more cars than ever. All the models now benefit from a new paint and finishing plant, which means that the chassis are now electro-phoretically dipped – unheard of and just about undreamt of among Italian exotica! – as well as being better-painted and detailed. We strolled through the factory, and again I was awed by the sight of all the gleaming alloy castings for the V8, V12 and flat-12 engines and transmissions, the swoopy body panels, and simply by being there.

Suddenly it was time for lunch, and as we went out through the big green gates we saw that dozens of people had begun to arrive, and they too were spilling across the road to the Cavallino restaurant where a cheery, vibrant atmosphere was already firmly established, the unperturbed owner darting about the tables to ask what everyone would like and somehow seeming to bring everyone the same thing. Franco strolled in to check his flock, capping a hand on a shoulder here or greeting somebody else in French as fluent as

AND THE REVS KEEP RISING

his English, there. Jody Scheckter threaded his way between the tables, followed by two tall Italians we'd seen him with earlier. He'd been changing out of his immaculate grey suit into driving overalls bearing the name of new sponsors while a fat Italian photographer in a flat cap strutted in front of him trying to work out some sort of a picture. Eventually he sat Scheckter down on the wheel of one of the old T3 racers in the reception area. Nikki Lauda, it said on its side. Now the photographer panted along behind as the racing driver led the way to a table. To hell with the pictures. The real business was about to begin.

Around 2.15 the party began to break up, everyone delighted to find that Franco was picking up the bill. We were just getting into the Peugeot when he came rushing out of his office, shouted 'follow me!' leapt into a Fiat and tore off through the gates. At the Maranello town hall, half a mile away, a small circular auditorium, tables laden with more food and lined with bottles of Ferrari champagne (from Trento, no relation) had been laid out. In the centre of the floor a strange shape lurked beneath a cover. But as the gesticulating and animated conversations grew, the excitement was too much and somebody tugged it off ahead of schedule to reveal the dramatic new T4 with its weird boat-like upper bodywork, Lotus-like skirts and driving position so close to the sharply dipping nose. Cameras began flashing and popping, bodies pressed hard around the car and the hubbub grew even more intense. Television crews tried to weave their way between the bodies, elbowing first and apologising later. I watched from high up among the deserted seats: a fine scene of wonderful Italian chaos. In an hour or so it had settled down. Scheckter and Ferrari's racing boss Mauro Forghieri had posed good-naturedly by the car, had champagne glasses pressed into their hands, had talked into dozens of microphones. The rope barriers around the car had long since been tugged down so that the keenest could peer right in under the T4 to investigate its suspension or examine its skirts. Ing Nozetto, one of its designers, had said it would corner at around $2.2g$. Scheckter, doing his best to be patient, tried to escape but was cut off.

Then he lost the spotlight. Enzo Ferrari had arrived: frail, older,

AMONG THE MODENESE

but dignified as ever. He refused to be dragged into the main throng and sat instead in a quiet corner, his aides around him, talking quietly with those who were prepared to go and stand reverently for their turn, like the faithful kneeling before the Pope. I pressed a T4 brochure forward and asked if he'd mind signing it. That cold, hard look and then a touch of a smile and nod of recognition, the famous flourish, and a handshake as he gave it back. Firm, but not as firm as it once was. In a flash, more brochures appeared for him to sign. He talked as he wrote: he was feeling fairly well; he thought the T4 had great potential; it was the result of almost three months' work in the Pininfarina wind tunnel; it might even be faster than the Lotuses…

Then he was off, moving swiftly, grinning easily, joking animatedly as he said his farewells and then, incongruously, shielding his face against the cameras. As he emerged from the building, the crowd that had heard what was happening and cheered and roared when Scheckter and other personalities walked out went perfectly still. People stayed hushed for a moment then began clapping politely. Ferrari walked through their ranks with a few little nods, a prince among his people. A few minutes later Gozzi told the mechanics they could wheel the car out, and it was bedlam again. Back at the Castello later on, we watched the fun and games on that evening's TV news.

In the morning, we journeyed out to the other side of Modena, and when we got to Lamborghini – unannounced but greeted with as much friendliness as ever – we found sales manager Ubaldo Sgarzi in the big office that had once been Ferruccio's, phone clasped in one hand and the other gesticulating furiously. No sooner had he finished the conversation than it rang again, and he went on like that for 15 minutes before he had a moment's peace. One of the calls was from the new court-appointed administrator, Dr Artesi, who was tied up elsewhere; another from Ing Alfieri, formerly of Maserati, whom Artesi had put in charge of engineering at Lamborghini. Both appointments had pleased the long-surviving Sgarzi, and he went on to outline the bold new plan for Lamborghini to build 350 cars this year. Down on the floor (you could still eat your dinner off it; this is still one of the most orderly factories you'll

AND THE REVS KEEP RISING

find) they were indeed making cars, the first of the new Countachs baking in the paint shop and another four on the line.

But it was a yellow Urraco that caught my eye. There it was, over near the test bays, wearing Pirelli P7s and the Countach-type flared arches needed to cover them. Development tests had begun but it was uncertain whether production Urracos to such a specification will be built. More certain was that the more powerful new version of its V8 engine would go into its open-topped sister, the Silhouette. Possibly, Sgarzi said, the hotter bits would filter back to the Urraco once the Silhouette S was well underway. Anyway, the fat-tyred Urraco looked good with new meatiness and a harder image.

Just beyond it, over a bay with a mechanic working on its suspension, was the Bravo prototype. It's hard to decide whether it's a successor to the Urraco or more of a pint-sized Countach – and perhaps not so pint-sized in the long run either: apart from the 3.0-litre V8 in the prototype, the 4.0-litre V12 transverse power plant from the Miura will slip straight into the Bravo. That would make it go.

We ran the Bravo outside to get a better look. It's a visual delight: incredibly compact, chunky, and striking. But it's difficult to get into because the main part of the door opening is very small and when you're in your shoulder line is aft of the door pillar. It'd need modifications before production. Sgarzi, concerned that we were missing out on lunch, came down to check before he slipped off to the pleasant, airy dining room above the gatehouse.

While Richard carried on with his Nikons I went for a little wander among the snow to the rear of the experimental shop. I hadn't been around there before. I was swiftly in Lamborghini's graveyard. There was a Miura reduced to a few barely recognisable panels and then a clutch of the most extraordinary prototypes for the old 350GT, Espada and Urraco. They were just there on blocks rusting away quietly but at least Lamborghini has them.

A cursory examination of the road through Sant'Agata revealed too many ice patches, so I reluctantly eased the Bravo back inside the factory. If the day before had not been the time to drive a Ferrari, this certainly wasn't the moment to meddle with a next-to-priceless one-only prototype.

AMONG THE MODENESE

It was into Modena itself the next morning and down the Viale Ciro Menotti to Maserati. No sooner had we been greeted by ever-cheerful, ever-helpful Ermanno Cozze than a truck rounded the corner carrying two new Quattroportes. They were pilot build cars, put together by hand, going back to Innocenti – another of Alessandro de Tomaso's concerns – in Turin for checking. Down in the factory itself Ermanno proudly showed us workmen busy installing the new Quattroporte production line. The target is for 300 this year. Merak, Khamsin and Kyalami production was underway as merrily as ever and I wasn't going to miss an opportunity to wander in and out of the pits – for Maserati build sits cars in a strange unitary sort of way, moving them sideways along a platform with service station-like pits either side so that the fitters can get in underneath. What a happy lot. The grim days of three years ago when the workers were picketing the shut-down factory demanding their jobs back seem miles away. Now there's just talk of the increasing production.

Good to his word, Ermanno had a pristine Kyalami with the 4.9-litre V8 that Maserati has begun slipping into it above the standard 4.2. The roads were a little clearer so we set off on a loping run down towards Bologna, stopped for a cup of coffee and then came back, able to run steadily at an indicated 150mph most of the way home. You notice the extra urge of the bigger V8 in the lower gears – there's some bite now – but it's in the higher gears that the extra urge becomes most valuable. Lift off cautiously to clear a few trucks, for example, and a dab on the throttle will soon have you whisking back to the redline on the tachometer in fifth. The Kyalami rides very firmly by Jaguar or Mercedes standards, but it's a comfortable, positive sort of ride with plenty of pleasing information feeding back. There is no wind noise, but the exhaust maintains a low, steady throb. You are being reminded, subtly and pleasantly, that you are in an Italian car. The engine retains that mystical Maserati appeal. It's a strange V8, very responsive and accurate to the throttle, and somehow different from all other V8s; smooth but slightly too masculine to be dubbed really silky. The car handles with a gentle touch of understeer unless you wish to push the power right on and then you'll get modest oversteer; the

AND THE REVS KEEP RISING

two are easy to balance. Flat-out, the directional stability is very good. A swift, elegant, conservative but appealing car with plenty of thoroughbred feel to it made more likeable by the big engine. The Bora, from whence the engine stemmed, is not yet dead either. Ermanno, shrugging this way and that, says that he'll probably make 20 for devotees this year. *They're* not silly people.

We got Ermanno back to the factory somewhat later than intended, and he apologised about the lack of a luncheon invitation but he had to do something at his son's school. We weren't much concerned about lunch. It was market day in Modena and stalls were spread end to end through the ancient streets. All sorts of things from marvellous confectionery to good cheap leather goods and friendly stall-keepers ready to do business in just about any language or currency you wished. We grabbed some barbecued sausage sliced into unleavened bread and rambled for an hour.

If Maserati is in an old factory in an old city, De Tomaso, Maserati's new parent, is in a new factory in a new industrial area on the outskirts. We rolled up after our ramble. Ing Aurelio Bertocchi had had to rush away to Innocenti but had deputised Giorgio Montagnani to look after us, with appropriate assistance from Bertocchi the elder – old Guerino, the race driver who'd become chief test driver at Maserati and left to join his son at De Tomaso when Citroën arrived in Viale Ciro Menotti. The usual bundle of brochures and posters, issued with great ceremony and enthusiasm; the regulation tour of the tiny factory that steadily turns out Panteras, Longchamps – whence sprang the Maserati Kyalami, under Ing Bertocchi's guidance – and four-door Deauvilles; and a potter through the array of old De Tomaso racers and prototypes; then an animated discussion about which car we might like to go out in first. Guerino Bertocchi was clutching his age-beaten little test bag containing his gloves, Prova plates and a few rags to wipe the windows. All very well, I thought, but how to keep him off the back roads with all this ice about? Well I knew his attitude to the throttle pedal. 'A Pantera GTS with P7s,' I suggested. I wondered what sort of job Aurelio Bertocchi had done in slipping the Pantera onto the new Pirellis. Soon, Guerino returned, beckoning furiously.

AMONG THE MODENESE

He'd turned up a near-new GTS belonging to a Yugoslav diplomat stationed in Berlin that had come in for servicing and been pronounced fit as a fiddle. '*L'autostrada, per favore,*' I muttered and away we went. What a surprise. Here's this old mid-engined two-seater with its hulking Ford V8 and steady series of updates taking its place with the best of 'em. It goes hard and handles really well. But more than that, it rides well – firmly, as you'd expect, but very well – and with practically no transmission or road noise. We came hard out of the tollbooth at the start of the *autostrada* to the Brenner Pass and ran up to just beyond 150mph before the old man had to back off for some trucks. Impressive straight line stability too, and damned good under brakes when, a few moments later, he needed to get on them hard *and* allow for patches of slush at the same time. Some of the Pantera's rawness has gone, but it's still a brassy sort of a car with big, obvious spirit.

What it has now is a fine edge and touch of refinement that weren't there before, and that blast amid the trucks, slush and ice, with old Guerino in his peppery mix of Italian, French, English and German all the while relating stories of the most outrageous journeys, has given me an unexpected new enthusiasm for Alessandro's Italian–American hybrid. Further exploration may reveal that it has taken to the P7s better than just about anything else! Back at the factory, Guerino continued his tales, backing them up with frequent flashes of his current Formula 1 driver's licence of which, at 71, he is very proud; lord knows how he gets hold of it every year. I was grinning less at the outrageousness of the stories – some I knew to be true – than the man himself. As much as anybody else, he epitomises the indomitable spirit of Modena.

Before night could come down, and with our Peugeot's washer bottle full of a special Bertocchi concoction of anti-freeze, alcohol and something else we couldn't quite fathom but which he swore would prevent our washers freezing as they had on the way down despite anti-freeze rated down to -40 degrees C, we headed north again, our motoring spirits revived and our palates itching for another spell in Modena come spring. Detroit, Birmingham, Stuttgart, Munich or even Milan and Turin somehow just aren't the same.

A RATHER GENTLEMANLY (FAST) CARRIAGE

ASTON MARTIN VOLANTE

1979

THERE WAS NO SUN and it did not matter. We lowered the roof just the same and swept through the gently lit lanes with the trees intertwining above our heads, and the V8 gently burbling, almost murmuring, in the natural tunnels.

Was such gentle travel, such elegantly *superior* motoring, the embodiment of the indulgence that is, and that is allowed by, the Aston Martin Volante? Or was that exemplified later when we slipped back to the motorway and asked the Aston to sprint rather than lope so that it whisked us swiftly to 130mph, the four of us sitting there with our hair barely ruffled and the sound from the radio still reaching our ears? Is *that* the real indulgence of the Volante? Should you be inclined to opt for the former, categorising the car as an elegant open carriage for four, best employed at modest speeds in gentlemanly touring mode, could you deny that it is a true sports car because, with roof down and passengers enjoying their passage through the air, it *will* exceed 130mph?

It is indeed tempting to swiftly establish a clear vision of the Volante, but it is not so limited as that. This is a car that impresses itself – favourably – upon your mind for the way it blends its abilities (yes, abilities; not extremes, because they don't clash) and for their unique total.

The Aston Martin V8, launched in 1972, is an old car that I never liked. It felt out-dated, awkward and unaccomplished alongside its contemporaries. It had a lot of performance and was built with an appealingly English quality. But that was not enough. It was let down by a geriatric waywardness. It felt so much like a car whose makers had stopped progressing or even keeping in touch. That began to change in the wake of Aston Martin's acquisition by Peter Sprague and George Minden (later joined by chairman Alan Curtis) in 1975. They brought spirit back to Newport Pagnell. It wasn't so much that they brought in fresh know-how, beyond their managerial skills, but that they relit the fires beneath a great cauldron of experience and dedication that lay within the company. Initially, steps were taken to improve production quality and to make it consistent, so that, despite its dynamic limitations, the familiar V8 coupé could at least be seen as a car of considerable quality and individuality. The Lagonda project was laid down, and then attention turned back to the V8. The high performance Vantage was developed from it, a car that above all felt hefty and manly and which, at a stroke, was rid of the imprecision and awkwardness of the standard coupé.

It demanded effort from the driver but rewarded that effort with vigorous performance and, in its heavy way, an adroitness of handling and ability on the road that immediately took it into the ranks of the great cars. The pity was that if you drove a standard V8 coupé within minutes, or even days, of driving a Vantage it seemed like a vague high performance truck, veering alarmingly from the straight ahead if you backed off suddenly at much beyond 90mph, only to swing back the other way in response to the reapplied torque when you opened the throttle again. In corners, it felt wayward – sort of loose – even though it had pretty strong grip upon the tarmac. But Aston kept quietly beavering away with its development, and with creating the Volante. Thus Aston, in the space of a few years, again had a range of cars to sell: the much improved V8 coupé and, derived from it, a convertible, an ultra high-performance model, and the dramatic Lagonda saloon (itself using the potent all-alloy V8 and the main suspension components from the coupé).

The convertible Volante is the new boy in the troupe. Fundamentally, it is the coupé with the roof removed. There is a lot more to it than that, of course, because the body had to be strengthened to compensate for the loss of rigidity caused by the removal of the steel roof, and it can't have been easy to devise and

AND THE REVS KEEP RISING

install a folding roof as aesthetically pleasing, efficient and, when lowered, unobtrusive. Visually, the metamorphosis from coupé to convertible is extremely successful. The Volante's profile is smooth, clean and rather hippy in keeping with the style at the time of the basic car's conception. That endows it with a certain maturity. There is a natural grace too, a flowing of line despite the car's 3800lb bulk. Roof up, its expansive rear quarters create an intimate, private sort of look. Roof down, there is just a tidy gathering around the rear of the cockpit, with the folds of the roof covered neatly by a half-tonneau. Most of all, roof up or down, the Volante is a substantial-looking car that exudes quality and taste and, perhaps through its obvious visual link with the past, a sense of breeding.

Underneath, it is Newport Pagnell as we have known it for a decade and a half. There is the 5.3-litre V8, moderately oversquare with a bore and stroke of 100mm by 85mm, that carries a balanced crankshaft forged from chrome molybdenum steel and which is aided by a torsional vibration damper. Its block is cast in aluminium alloy, and it sheaths its cast aluminium pistons in centrifugally cast chrome vanadium iron top-sealing wet liners. Its heads are cast in aluminium alloy, with fully machined hemispherical combustion chambers. The valves are inclined at 64 degrees, should you care for such detail, and the guides for the exhaust valves are in direct contact with the coolant water. There are two overhead camshafts per cylinder head, driven by Duplex roller chains. The engine is fed by four Weber twin choke downdraught carburettors. We don't know how much power it develops. For all the years Aston has been making it, it has never revealed its precise output. You may rest assured that it is somewhere around 350bhp, and that there is abundant torque. Buyers may have a ZF five-speed manual gearbox that is no nicer now than ever it was, but in the Volante and the plain V8 coupé they'd be better specifying the three-speed Torqueflite automatic Aston buys in from Chrysler. Rightly, it's regarded as one of the world's best transmissions. The manual transmission runs a differential ratio of 3.54:1; the automatic's is 3.07:1, giving it longer legs.

At the front, the suspension is a conventional upper and lower wishbone system, with co-axial coil springs and dampers, and an

ASTON MARTIN VOLANTE

anti-roll bar. At the rear, there is a de Dion axle located by parallel trailing arms, a Watts linkage, coil springs and piston type dampers. The steering is power-assisted rack and pinion; the brakes are big Girling discs, all ventilated. The slotted cast alloy wheels are 7in wide and carry GR70VR15 Avon radials.

It fires easily, that big V8, and it is ready to whisk you away without fuss the moment it does so. Just press the button in the top of the gearlever's knob and tug it back to the *Drive* position and then glide away. You are aware of the power that is present within the engine. It's that husky but well-mannered power that pulls you away and gives you a feeling of purpose. You feel that you can be as subdued in your use of the power and performance or as dramatic as you wish. It engenders a feeling of superiority. Out of town, if you keep your foot hard down, the full-throttle change from second to third will be as swift and smooth as the first-to-second change and the acceleration goes on with a vengeance. You will soon be at 100mph, and not all that much later the speedo will be reading beyond 130mph. Still the engine is smooth and unfussed. It is one of those engines that, despite its size, feels 'light' – low on internal friction, finely balanced and able to spin cleanly. That is a pleasing and expensive feeling.

With the top up, the Volante is snug and mechanically pleasantly quiet. But there is too much wind noise from around the leading edge of the roof and the sealing points with the side windows. Up to 80mph it is all right. Beyond that, the noise rises dramatically although it's never too much to be tolerated.

It's with the top down, though, that the Volante shines. Here is another dimension; here, the improvements that have made the current Aston V8s so much more enjoyable and respectable than their predecessors are aided and abetted by the pleasure of comfortable top-down motoring. The car's ingredients come together to create a special and endearing whole.

Dropping the roof is easy. It's electrically operated. You just release the two catches securing it to the windscreen then press the button on the dash to have it fold down into its recess, then snap its fine-fitting tonneau into place. And roof down, there is

AND THE REVS KEEP RISING

so little buffeting that, if the sun is hiding, you need not fear for your enjoyment. Given even mild air temperature, you may waft contentedly through the lanes admiring the trees overhead and relishing the smell of the countryside that you will rarely sample in a closed car, and delighting in the sounds.

Waft? You will probably find that your genteel progress is in fact at 60 or 80mph, even on quite narrow and winding roads. It is the smoothness of the Volante – its natural refinement and aplomb – that makes it seem so sedate. It rides so very nicely. While its dampers exert careful control, its springs are quite soft so you're aware that you're riding on a very comfortable suspension. You are also aware that there is considerable grip although you're unlikely to be inclined to throw such a heavy and wide car around. More likely, you'll drive steadily and cleanly, and find that the Volante handles admirably neutrally. Should you get a nudge of understeer now and then, the car does give you the option of inducing oversteer with power. But that would spoil your passengers' idyll.

And therein lies a special virtue of the Volante: it really can carry four people. The rear space may look to be occasional but big men can climb in and sit there happily enough, cossetted by the leather like their confrères in the front. And while they are likely to be delighted by the ride comfort, they won't, if they're enthusiasts, be disappointed by the pace. Dignified the Volante may well be but it is decently swift too. So you have a lot to enjoy as you languish in the Volante's sumptuously appointed, tastefully designed and beautifully constructed cabin. It's a wondrous blend of wood and leather that is unmistakably British.

Indeed, the whole car is a fine blend of abilities that's distinctively British. It is not an all-out supercar, but nor is it a boulevardier like the Rolls-Royce Corniche convertible. It is not a thoroughly modern and dynamically impeccable transport tool, but nor is it a relic from a previous era. It is perhaps rather like a pair of Church's shoes: obviously hand-crafted and expensive, noticeable for its taste and quality rather than its outright style; notable for a quiet ability that its user will come to appreciate, respect and admire, and entirely able to make him feel very good indeed. Indulgent? Perhaps not.

THE CAR THAT TIME CAN'T TAME

FERRARI 365 GTB/4 DAYTONA
1980

WE CAME OVER THE crest and into the valley and there ahead of us lay an open, loping stretch of road. It dropped gently, ran flat and diagonally across the valley floor and then rose again towards the valley's far rim. Before it reached the top a bend flicked it to the right, so that it ran up to cross the rim square on.

The Daytona had been in full flight for miles. This was more grist to its mill, and we swooped down into that pretty little valley with the nose lifting and the V12's yowl bellowing behind us. Second ran out at 86mph, third gave 116mph at the same 7700rpm redline and then we were pushing forward furiously in fourth.

The bend, the high-speed kink, loomed. We'd be doing around 130mph when we reached it – 6800rpm or so in fourth and around 340bhp pumping from the engine. If I kept my foot flat, there would almost certainly be oversteer. But how much oversteer? How suddenly would it come? How savagely? What *does* a Daytona do when it lets go at 130mph? What happens if you can't cope with it? How do you ring its owner and tell him you've overcooked it and his Daytona's lying shattered at the far end of a field? Should I try it or not? My mind raced with apprehension.

But there was something, something discovered in the days and miles between the expectation of driving the Daytona and attaining comfortable familiarity with it, that said it would be all right; and I could not resist. The throttle stayed flat, the six Webers wide open, the exhausts thundering, and very soon the car was at the turn-in point and there was no longer time for anxiety.

AND THE REVS KEEP RISING

There was an obvious line and the Daytona came onto it with now-familiar but ever-impressive alacrity: you just need a firm mind-set and hands firm upon the wheel. The inside wheels clipped the apex. The nose began to drive outwards again to the far side of the road. And in the same instant, there it was! The rear tyres let go and slid, and in the very split second that they let go, I knew. The message was delivered to me as clearly as if it had been the seat of my trousers itself that was touching the road. Somehow, even as it happened and spanning such a tiny slice of time as it did, I had time to wonder how much the wheels might go on to slide. But then there was the quick flick of the wrists to wrap on a twist of opposite lock at the leather rimmed wheel – just the one quick, instinctive, parsimonious flick – and the tail came back, as flatly and precisely and positively as it had broken away. In my peripheral vision I'd seen Colin Curwood's right hand snap out to grasp the grab handle, and then withdraw again as he too felt that it was all right. We didn't even need the full width of the road for the exit. The Daytona just swept a couple of feet out from the road's inside edge, lined itself up as the wheel was neutralised, and stormed onwards, heading straight as a die for the crest, with fourth, too, almost running to its 146mph limit before there was call for the brakes.

There were other sublime moments, plenty of them, during my time with Nick Mason's 1972 Ferrari 365 GTB/4 Daytona, 35,000 hard and trouble-free miles into its life. There was the awesomeness of the ease with which, when the traffic cleared momentarily on the motorway, it whisked me to 165mph and so obviously had more to give had I not been forced to lift off. There was the pure thrill to be had, so many times, of unleashing the sort of power that brings up 60mph in 5.5sec and 100 in a little over 12sec. There was the satisfaction, after a long fast drive, of switching it off and remaining in it, listening to the ticking metal cooling down, and recalling the miles. There was the prolonged, adrenalin-filled high of balancing it finely, against the wheel and plenty of second gear power, through one of the long and open bends we found that looked so good for photographs. But the climax was that lone right-hand kink. There, for me, the Daytona told its story. There, it despatched the

FERRARI 365 GTB/4 DAYTONA

last of the suspicion that had been implanted in my mind by the mythology that has accompanied its passage through the '70s and into immortality. A monster, a great big old brute of a thing that goes like crazy and must be treated, the myth had it, with extreme caution if not downright trepidation.

But the Daytona is not like that. It arrived late in 1968 to a mixed, even mildly disparaging reception. Some acclaimed its styling as a masterpiece. Others criticised the wide glass panel that covered the four headlights as silly and impractical (later, mostly for legal reasons, the arrangement would be changed to the twin sets of pop-up headlights that stayed with the Daytona until its demise in 1974). But most of the reaction against the Daytona stemmed from those who had expected Ferrari to follow the path of the little Dino 206 GT and to answer the challenge of the Lamborghini Miura with an all-out mid-engined two-seater. The ultimate Ferrari, they pouted, should be of the ultimate technical form.

But Enzo Ferrari has often lagged in his adoption of technical novelties. Maranello's path, so often, has been a traditional one pursued to the upper reaches of development, with the wind of change growing irresistibly strong before the course has been altered. Perhaps the Daytona's critics didn't care to consider perspectives: that the 4.4-litre 365 series engine had been developed for use in an assortment of front-engined cars, that there was considerable lead time, that Maranello's engineers had an engine and chassis design that they liked very much and a body styled by Pininfarina to which they were also very attracted. There are many clear and supportable reasons why Ferrari laid down the Daytona the way it did. But when it's all boiled down, the core of the matter is that in the mid-'60s, for its big grand touring road cars, Ferrari's belief rested firmly with the front-engined layout, its development and its refinement. So there would be one more all-out front-engined Ferrari two-seater of the traditional mould. And it would have enough capability to deal with the upstart Miura from the other side of Modena, loudly hailed as the machine that had taken the wind out of Ferrari's sails. A neat 300km/h – 186mph – had been claimed for the mid-engined Miura, but around 172mph was nearer the mark until the SV came

AND THE REVS KEEP RISING

along later. Ferrari just said that the Daytona would reach 280km/h – 174mph – and it wasn't to be all that long before independent testers proved that it wasn't exaggerating.

There is as much purity as individuality in the Daytona's styling. Nothing else conveys the long bonnet, small cabin, chopped tail slingshot look as dramatically, and if the proportioning looks uncomfortable then walk up close and let the eye feast upon the deliciousness of the car's detail, the sultriness of its curves and the way they go together to make the whole. Stand back again and consider that this car, weighing 3500lb dry, is sufficiently slippery to permit not only a top speed of 174mph but upper-end acceleration in fourth and fifth that is still unequalled in a road car except perhaps by a perfectly tuned Countach S. And consider that, without a trace of a spoiler, the Daytona is impeccably stable.

The Daytona replaced the Ferrari 275 GTB/4 (made from 1966 to 1968), and was very much a development of it. Its steel body, built by Scaglietti to Pininfarina's design, was bolted onto a similar tubular steel chassis frame and the wheelbase, at 94.5in, was identical. But the Daytona benefited from wider 56.6 and 56.1in tracks. Its suspension is Italian conventional, a system proved time and again to work exceptionally well: upper and lower wishbones with coil springs, telescopic dampers and an anti-roll bar at the front, with another set of upper and lower wishbones, more coil springs, telescopic dampers and another anti-roll bar at the rear. The steering is worm and nut, the brakes 11.4 and 11.7in ventilated Girling discs with twin circuitry and servo assistance. The classic wheels, to become known as 'Daytona-pattern', are cast alloy, centre locked onto splined axles, carrying 215/70-15 Michelin XVRs.

To help balance the car as finely as possible, Ferrari mounted the engine a long way back in the chassis. Almost all of it is behind the front axle line. The engineers went further: the transmission was despatched to the rear, in unit with the differential, and linked by drive shaft and torque tube to the engine and clutch. All five gears are indirect, running from first's 3.07 through a 2.12 second, 1.51 third and 1.25 fourth to a 0.96 fifth. The final drive ratio is a well-balanced 3.3:1 giving 23.7mph/1000rpm in fifth.

FERRARI 365 GTB/4 DAYTONA

The Daytona's engine is a member of Ferrari's classic road-going V12 family, and descended directly from the 3.3-litre four-cam 12 of the 275 GTB/4. The angle between the cylinder banks is 60deg, the bore and stroke 81mm by 71mm, giving a total capacity of 4390cc. The crankcase and block are cast in Silumin, with shrunk-in liners, and the fully machined crank runs in seven bearings. The compression ratio is 9.3:1. There are two camshafts on each cylinder head, six downdraught Weber carburettors, twin coils and distributors, and a dry sump. From this engine, running on 100-octane fuel, comes nothing less than 352bhp at 7500rpm. And from it flows massive torque. It peaks at 318lb/ft at 5500rpm but the curve is so flat and hefty that even at 1000rpm there is almost 190lb/ft, and everywhere from 2000rpm to 7000 more than 260lb/ft is available.

The Daytona is long and fairly low – 14ft 6in by 49in. You hook a finger behind those strange little catches on the top of its doors, swing them out and drop down into seats like old-style racing buckets that hug the body cosily and say that they will keep you in place when the car is going hard about its business. The driver is faced with an alloy-spoked and leather-rimmed wheel, with a large metal boss that encircles the vaunted black-and-yellow prancing horse horn button. It is connected to twin Fiamm air horns. The wheel, whose flat spokes are drilled, is moderately raked, somehow very business-like and yet somehow casual too. The hands just drop onto its rim comfortably; perfectly.

Through it, enclosed within one oval and deeply hooded pod, are the instruments – the vast matching tachometer and speedo, with the four most important minor gauges grouped between them. You see all of them well enough. Best of all, you are never in any doubt about the whereabouts of the tachometer needle. In the corners of this big binnacle are two final gauges: on the driver's left, the fuel gauge and on his right a clock. All the gauges are black-rimmed, standing out from the metal panel that carries them. They reflect a little in some lighting conditions. Overall, they have a certain flair and appeal that does not interfere with their efficiency. They are less stylish than some Ferrari gauges but they are also more efficient

AND THE REVS KEEP RISING

and easily read than most. A small stalk on the steering column works the indicators. A larger one behind it controls the headlights. A stalk on the other side of the column activates the two-speed wipers and electric washers. Three of those Italian sliding levers in the centre of the dash control the heat supply to each side of the car and regulate the temperature. Toggles below them switch on the heated rear window and the hazard flashers. On the flat-topped central console, down near the base of the gearlever, are rocker switches for the electric windows. Like the radio, the cigarette lighter and ashtray are dropped into the tunnel cover – not afterthoughts, but given a casualness that indicates their standing in this cockpit.

The tall, spindly, unbooted gearlever sprouts from one of those marvellous open Ferrari gates. Its height means that the arm need simply extend to it, not drop, and that the hand does not have to move far from the wheel's rim to grasp it. When the arms are comfortable at wheel and gearlever, the legs extend forward with just a little bending at the knees to big, manly, business-like pedals. The clutch does not travel very far, and while it is not light it isn't ridiculously heavy either: it is simply what you expect. Put the right foot on the brake pedal, and feel with its outer edge the tall throttle pedal. Heel-and-toeing is perfect.

There is a closeness about the Daytona's cabin that helps the driver feel in tune with it, part of it. The roof is small above the head, and the windscreen and side windows curve well in to meet it, so that at the same time they feel as if they curve in around your head. You wear this car. And if the long bonnet appears from the outside as though it will be ungainly and difficult to place, it is not like that from the driver's seat. You can't see all of it – just to a point beyond those outlet vents – but it doesn't matter. It does not take long to sense its extremities and to feel at ease with them. And nor – and this is the truly marvellous thing about the Daytona – does it take long to know, understand and feel at ease with all its extraordinary performance. It is there to work *with* you (if not exactly *for* you, for it could never be obsequious, this car) but it is not there to intimidate you.

FERRARI 365 GTB/4 DAYTONA

Pump the throttle a couple of times on a cold morning, even one with ice on the ground, then turn the key and the V12 will fire immediately. From its first beat it runs evenly, without snapping or popping or missing. It is ready to be driven away, asking nothing more than due respect by way of warm-up. The gears need to be shifted slowly and deliberately, for the oil stays thick in the isolated transmission for a long time – 10 or even 15 miles. After that, the lever will shift quickly and cleanly, and with considerable pleasure for the palm of the hand, although there is never the sort of pleasure that's there in the Ferraris with front-mounted transmissions. Such is the precision of the throttle and the fine, measured response of the engine that even when the roads are very slippery it is easy enough to mete out the power so that the rear tyres don't spin. The Daytona just gets on with it, efficiently. Push *too* hard on the throttle and the wheels *will* spin crazily, the tail snapping instantly and massively sideways: you will be between 45 and 90 degrees to the direction of travel at a stroke. Ah, but such is the Daytona's inherent balance and stability that releasing the power and snapping on a bite of opposite lock will bring it back perfectly into line. Knowledge of that sort of controllability makes it easy to come to grips with the power on hand, and to know that the power is there to be *used*.

And with knowledge of the communication from the chassis, coming through the seat of the pants, the palms of the hands and somehow even the soles of the feet, it is possible always to extract the optimum level of performance. You just bring on enough power until you sense that there will be loss of traction and readjust with your toes. What will surprise you, perhaps, is just how much of the performance you can use even on slippery surfaces.

On a dry road, unleashing full acceleration for the first time is electrifying. But the mind adjusts quickly and thereafter, while always thrilling, even stunning, it is temptingly usable. It is simply part of the Daytona. More than anything, more even than 0–60mph in 5.5sec and 0–100mph in 12.5sec, it is the *span* of the performance that is captivating. First gear runs to 59mph at 7700rpm, second to 86, third to 116, fourth to 146 and, yes, fifth *will* go to 174mph at

AND THE REVS KEEP RISING

just under 7400rpm. Going up through those gears, there is a long, sustained thrusting forwards. In the gears – for overtaking, for instance – that mighty torque gives you 70 to 90mph in just over 3.0sec in third, or 4.0sec in fourth and only 5.5sec in fifth. Push on the throttle in the Daytona, and you *go*. Even at 140mph in fifth there is solid push in the back, and you will be at 160mph within 15sec. All the while, the Daytona feels secure in your hands, never that it is fighting to get away. It has too much inner certainty of its own, this car, to be nasty or fussy.

It is set up to maintain a touch of understeer, just enough to be detected in the wheel angles in pictures and felt at the steering wheel by way of a steady tug in a bend taken hard. It can be neutralised with power, so the best way to corner the Daytona is to come into a bend fractionally below the ultimate entry speed, let it settle momentarily and then steadily squeeze on the power. You will feel the car balance out; you will feel it sweep around the bend on the line you have selected. Bring on more power if you wish to tip the balance the other way – when you are going sufficiently fast in a high gear or are in a low gear in a slow bend – and you will feel the tail start to go a little light and then edge into an oversteer attitude. More power and it will let go altogether, quickly, and you will have to get it back with the wheel or by lifting off. Never fear: it will come straight if you are as decisive as the car itself.

It is a positive, finely-controlled car to drive, yes; but it is not a light car. It requires real physical effort because the steering is not power assisted and although the brakes are powered they need a hefty shove to be made to work hard. Nor is the clutch for feeble legs. But the efforts all match, and if they make the Daytona hard work at town speeds, you are not aware of them intruding upon your pleasure when it's cracking on.

So you soon feel at one with this Ferrari, and you learn to revel in its performance and its possibilities; to *use* it. And it is perhaps the fact that you *can* find its limits and nudge them again and again that makes it special in a world where the cars that have taken over from it are mid-engined. Their limits, those of the Boxer and Countach, are higher in terms of pure cornering power but

FERRARI 365 GTB/4 DAYTONA

they are harder to find and even harder again to play with. You don't mess lightly with a Boxer; you can do it with a Daytona. The Boxer is more refined, more comfortable, more of an achievement because it combines those virtues with its performance. But is it any more exciting, any more rewarding? The answer is no, for one can't achieve quite the same one-ness with the BB that you can with the Daytona.

Some passengers may say the Daytona's ride is too firm at low speeds. Anyone who has savoured its performance to the full won't mind. In any case, in almost every other way it is hard to fault the Daytona (forget fine finish, or rust proofing or 12,000-mile servicing: you do not expect those things in this sort of Ferrari). Liken it, if you wish, to a shark for more than the obvious visual reasons. The shark, biologists will have it, stopped developing 20 million years ago because it could not be improved. It had reached a level of perfect efficiency. When the high-performance tide turned in favour of the mid-engined car it left the Daytona stranded on a patch of high ground. But, like the shark, it transcends time.

SIDEWAYS WITH SECURITY IN PORSCHE'S MASTERFUL DRIVING TOOL

PORSCHE 928S

1980

THEY ASKED ME ABOUT the Porsche 928S after I'd driven it 50 miles and I grimaced and said that it was so-so: that it seemed little faster than the standard 928 and, in the areas where that car was disappointing, a little more refined; that its abilities still somehow seemed tainted by the absence of a final element of development, and that I couldn't imagine liking it any more than I had most of the other Porsches.

But they asked me again after I'd driven the 928S for 500 miles and I grinned and said that it was superb: that it had taught me to understand, through the quality and the quantity of its abilities, the depth and subtlety of its development; that it was truly a masterful driving tool I would love to have, and that at £25,250 it seemed to be conspicuously good value.

I had been eagerly awaiting the arrival of the 928S, with my disappointment in the original and standard car countered only by faith in Porsche's developmental prowess and the knowledge of what it had done for the once-lowly 924 in the upgrade to the 924 Turbo. It wasn't a lack of belief in the path Porsche had followed in its switch from rear to front-engine cars: the Lancia Aurelia, Ferrari 275 GTB/4 and Daytona and (when properly set-up) Alfa Romeo Alfetta and Giulietta had shown the benefits of the front-engine rear transaxle layout Porsche adopted in pursuit of 50/50 weight distribution, tenacious roadholding and a sympathetic polar moment of inertia.

PORSCHE 928S

The 924 demonstrated that its balance and handling were outstanding, and when the 928 followed it onto the market it swiftly showed that it had notably better road holding and near perfect handling. You couldn't help but be impressed by the good-mannered performance of its chassis. It was easy, too, to admire the 928's detail design and the completeness of its equipment: here was a 143mph 4.5-litre V8-powered car with top-notch handling that also had the trappings of a limousine, the practicality of a hatchback, a six-year body rust warranty and once a year servicing. The 928, at a stroke, did a great deal to bridge the gap between the classic all-performance supercar and the well built, well equipped, fuss free luxury coupé.

Clearly, the 928 was a milestone. Some grumbled nonetheless that despite its large overall dimensions its seating arrangements were only two-plus-two. It was more concerning that the new alloy V8 wasn't entirely smooth, that there was a slight vibration in the drive train, that the 928 could be particularly sensitive to camber, causing the wrists to tire with the effort of holding it against the camber on long journeys on heavily-crowned roads. And that there was strong tram-lining under brakes on uneven surfaces and that in certain conditions the ride – normally so impressive for a car shod with 7in wide Pirelli P7s – could become uncomfortable.

These things stood as disappointments in the face of Porsche's overall achievement with the 928. Its all-new body enclosed a new chassis, new engine and new transmission, and it was the first big volume touring car to use Pirelli P7 tyres. But there was call for further painstaking development to give the 928 the sought-after blend of outstanding performance with genuine refinement. Given that, it seemed likely that the 928 could be magnificent.

Development of the 928 would have gone on anyway; that is a foregone conclusion with Porsche. But perhaps the pressure to speed up that development helped. There were the cries for more power, not only from hotshoes in Germany who had very clear ideas about what a Porsche should be, but from the likes of LJK Setright who, while viewing it as a sports tourer, said that the 928 should be faster because 'it costs a lot of money, because it does not have four proper seats and because something with 4.5 fuel-injection litres and a five-

AND THE REVS KEEP RISING

speed gearbox and those enormous brakes and a set of the world's best tyres jolly well has no business being anything else'.

More performance or not, Porsche *had* to spend more time under the 928's bonnet: it had developed a reputation, later confirmed by German government figures, which listed it among the cars that broke down most frequently. Unthinkable for a Porsche. And if there was to be a more powerful 928 that didn't swig too much fuel, there had to be aerodynamic development. That wasn't easy. Porsche, hooked on the 928's shape, had put it into production knowing it had aerodynamic drawbacks. The problem starts with the nose. The recesses in the front capping protect the auxiliary lights but dam up the air so that it is turbulent as it begins to flow up the bonnet. Then the proportioning of the bonnet to the cabin area is wrong, keeping the air turbulent until it reaches the roof. Over the roof, the flow sticks tidily to the metal. But it is badly upset by the steep step between the rear of the roof and the rear windows, so that it descends turbulently to the tail and swirls in the 928's wake. Nor does the air flow smoothly along the 928's flanks which, between the wheelbase, are too far inwards of the wheels and curl under too soon behind the front wheels. Those smooth front mudguards look fantastic but are aerodynamically inefficient.

Major panel modifications to make the 928 good through the air were out of the question but Porsche was able to improve matters a bit by adding spoilers at the chin and the tail, and changing to the flat 'moon' wheels. Together, they cut the drag to 0.39 – an unimpressive Cd by comparison not only with the aerodynamically impressive 924, which boasts a Cd of 0.35, but saloons like the Citroën GSA, Mercedes S-class and Renault Fuego which are all around 0.35 too.

Whatever Porsche has done to eliminate the problems that may have led to breakdowns is unknown. What it did do, for the 1980 928s, was to raise the standard engine's compression ratio from 8.5:1 to 10:1, switching to higher octane fuel and, while leaving its 240bhp unchanged, usefully increasing its torque from 267 to 280lb/ft at the same 3600rpm. This brought a significant performance improvement: 0–100mph in 17.2sec instead of 20sec. Fuel consumption improved by 15 per cent too.

PORSCHE 928S

The new 'superbenzin' engine formed the base of the 928S powerplant. But for the S, the capacity went up from the standard 4474cc to 4664cc by an increase in the bore from 95 to 97mm (with the stroke left at 78.9mm). Out of this came a full 300bhp at 5900rpm – against the standard 240bhp at 5250rpm – and a modest lift in torque to 284lb/ft at 4500rpm. Nothing else has changed. The rest is the well-known and impressive 928 story: 90 degrees between the banks of the V8, which is cast in alloy and has alloy pistons in linerless bores; a forged steel five main bearing crankshaft and precision-sintered con rods; one overhead camshaft per cylinder bank (driven by toothed belt) and self-adjusting hydraulic tappets striking inline valves; a wet sump, transistorised contactless ignition, Bosch K-Jetronic fuel injection and an electric cooling fan.

The transmission layout is the same as for the standard car's: engine-mounted, hydraulically-operated small diameter twin-plate clutch; driveshaft running in two bearings through a rigid steel tube connecting engine and gearbox; five-speed manual transmission with fifth direct, or three-speed Daimler-Benz-derived automatic, in unit at the rear with 2.75:1 differential. The two models' dimensions are the same: 98.4in wheelbase, 61 and 60in tracks, 72in width, 50.5in height and 175.1in length. According to Porsche, both weigh the same at 3197lb although that's going to be 3395lb with all the equipment standard on the S in Britain.

The suspension doesn't differ either: cast alloy upper and lower wishbones at the front, with the coil springs picking up on the top arm but the dampers that run within them extending downwards to act on the very wide-based lower arms. There is anti-dive and negative offset geometry. The steering is assisted rack and pinion. At the back, there is the 'Weissach axle' that Porsche developed specially for the 928 and named after its famous research and test centre near Stuttgart.

It's a clever piece of work that brings great benefits to the driver. In an essentially upper and lower wishbone arrangement, the upper link and the rear arm of the lower wishbone pivot on a cast alloy cross member that bolts to both the body and the transmission housing.

AND THE REVS KEEP RISING

The lower 'wishbones', which are extremely wide-based and made up of curiously dog-legged tubular steel, incorporate extra 'swinging links' at their forward extremities. These move within closely defined limits to compensate for wheel movements. By keeping the geometry constant, they stop the wheels toeing-out if you back off at speed in a bend, thus largely counteracting lift-off oversteer. There are cast alloy uprights, co-axial coil springs and dampers, an anti-roll bar and anti-squat geometry. For its greater performance, the 928S has thicker brake discs and hefty new callipers, along with those new, almost-flat wheels that are forged alloy 7J x 16in wearing 225/50VR16 P7 Pirellis. The standard 928 now uses 15in old-style wheels shod with 215/60VR 15 Pirelli P6s. They increase comfort at the cost of a five per cent loss in road holding.

The 928S may not look quite so pure as its standard stable mate but it's not changed much by its tweaks. If you don't like them, at least you can see that they are practical. The rubbing strip on the side will protect the flanks. The marketing men added it; the stylists tried to resist it. The flush-faced wheels will be easy to clean and the spoilers, it is to be presumed, will help speed, economy and stability.

Open the one-piece door and slip into the 928S and you will be impressed by Porsche's logic and attention to detail. Release the lever beneath the steering column, and when you move it to suit your reach the instrument binnacle moves with it, still a unique arrangement. Slip a hand underneath the right side of the binnacle and you can feel the button that blasts a stream of potent cleaning fluid onto the windscreen from a system separate from the main washer. Demist the rear window? The big control knob just inches from the wheel rim gives you three ways to do it. Drop a hand onto the armrest and you can adjust the mirrors electrically, and set the air vents there to your liking. Slide your hand down beside the front of the seat and you can adjust that electrically too. Reach out, and you grasp a new four-spoke leather covered steering wheel. It's all there, reminding you of the completeness of the 928, and the obvious quality comes from more than just the solid way the door thunks shut.

PORSCHE 928S

Turn the key – which has a tiny light in its body to help you find the hole at night – and the warning light system in the instruments will tell you if there is a fault in any of 12 important systems. Then the V8 fires and you're ready to go. First is over and back, opposite reverse in the presumption that you'll be using the fourth/fifth change rather more than first/second. Release the clutch; it's as nice as ever, thanks to those twin plates in the face of all that power. As you get under way, the shift seems rather better than before.

Initially, I didn't think the S was much more powerful than the last 928 I'd driven, and in the first few miles was disturbed by a slight vibration that made the V8 feel ever so slightly like a V6, and by the equally minor vibration in the drive train that could be felt when the hand was on the gearlever. But, after a first brief session with the car, those factors seemed to fade away and I began to appreciate that there is a marvellous elasticity to the bigger engine; that it feeds in its power tremendously progressively; that it has more than before with no penalty whatsoever. In heavy traffic, it felt more able and relaxed.

When I was out of the traffic, a decent shove on the throttle on the way out of a roundabout soon showed that the extra bite shifted the tail sideways to a degree unlikely in the standard 928. And – having come straight again in perfect answer to the helm – the way that the S then romped up through the gears to very high speed before I had to lift off confirmed the message: the 928S *is* a fast car, a deceptively fast and notably effortless car. On the open road, it builds superbly upon the attributes of the basic 928. It is especially easy to drive fast, effortless in *every* way. Porsche does not mention changes to the bushings or geometry, springs or damping but the old car's dogged following of the camber no longer seems to be there, and the front wheels' darting about under brakes is all but gone. Nor does the ride break up on poorer surfaces – or was it just that, despite 500 miles pounding around all sorts of British roads, I didn't encounter a type that the 928 can't tolerate?

What I do know is that – a desire for more lumbar support apart – I could not find worthwhile fault with this 928. Its road performance was flawless. Pushed into visually open bends with the power on

AND THE REVS KEEP RISING

in the higher gears, it maintained an ideal nudge of stabilising understeer. Pressed under brakes into blind bends that may have held hazards, it maintained absolute poise and impeccable direction, going where its steering commanded as cleanly as a whistle. If, coming out of bends where all 300bhp could be released the tail stepped out, it could be brought back without waggle simply by easing the power. Or the tail could be held wide out against steering lock. Such is the perfect response of the car, thanks primarily to that transaxle layout, to throttle and steering that it is entirely possible to push it sideways out of the first bend of an ess, bring it back in time for the closely-following second bend and then sweep sideways out of that one too. The balance of this car, the friendliness of its polar moment of inertia, is such that it is very easy to do with as you wish. And unless you are extraordinarily silly and push it beyond all reason, it only ever does as you wish. You can play with it, but what it really does is to give fantastically safe, precise, fast point-to-point motoring almost regardless of road surface and weather.

It is a driving tool: a beautifully considered, painstakingly honed tool that the driver takes and uses. It is a tool with 156mph capability that will reach 60mph from a standstill in 6.7sec and 100mph in 14.9 and that, when most of its capability *is* being employed, returns no worse than 14mpg and usually better than 18mpg. It is not the fastest car but there is little doubt that it is the kindest of the very fast cars, the easiest to drive fast, the easiest to trust. It doesn't attract you with great gobfuls of character; it entices you with its ability and holds you with the consistency of its manners. There will still be a sharp thump when a front wheel strikes a deep pothole in a city street. That is probably unavoidable with P7s so wide and a suspension set to provide such positive high-speed control. Now, however, that capability blends so much better with facility. Now, Porsche has gone closer to achieving its avowed goal for the 928: 'the perfect blending of a thoroughbred sports car with a deluxe coupé'. It isn't yet perfect, and it may never be quite that, but this is a tool worthy of the highest admiration, and hugely desirable because of it.

MOTORING, NOT DRIVING
ROLLS-ROYCE CORNICHE CONVERTIBLE
1980

I SAW A YOUNG man driving a Rolls-Royce Corniche convertible. He was dark, tanned, handsome, his shirt open deep at the neck and his sleeves rolled well back from the wrists. He was in a hurry, gunning the Rolls hard as he went past so that its nose lifted high and its radio telephone antenna whipped urgently. I looked down to watch him disappear in the mirror on the door of the Corniche I was driving, and wondered. What did he make of the Corniche? What had he expected when he began driving it?

It is, of course, a mistake to think that Rolls-Royces are the best cars in the world. If you're in touch with the broader standards of automotive engineering and have driven Silver Shadows, Corniches and Camargues you will know that they are not – although the new Silver Spirit recently announced may be a different kettle of fish. It is true that no other production car is as superbly detailed and beautifully finished as a Rolls-Royce; but if they are meant to be the best cars in the world then surely it's fair to expect that they are also the best engineered and thus set the standard for a combination of ride, roadholding and handling? A Rolls-Royce is seen by most people to be the pinnacle of motoring achievement. Pardon the dogma, but I think it really should be, especially if, as in the case of the Corniche convertible, it costs £66,366.

Even at that price, the Corniche convertible is not the most expensive Rolls-Royce. The Camargue costs a phenomenal £76,120. But the Corniche is considered to be the ultimate personal Rolls-Royce and is thus the most glamorous car in the range. With the Camargue, it is also the only model of the old

AND THE REVS KEEP RISING

Shadow-derived series that survives the arrival of the Spirit and its sisters, the long wheelbase Silver Spur limousine and the Bentley Mulsanne.

In its way, the Corniche convertible has been brought into line with its new brethren rather than being left as a relic of the previous generation. In 1979, Rolls-Royce quietly but significantly altered the Camargue and the Corniche convertible by replacing their Shadow-type rear suspension with that of the new Spirit, which is hydro-pneumatically damped, self-levelled and has less unsprung weight. This wasn't only to set up the Corniche (now in production for almost 10 years) and Camargue for their run into the '80s but is in accordance with the Rolls-Royce tradition of introducing major new mechanical components first into the two-door models. That way, Rolls is able to produce the new components in small numbers and have them in service before full-scale production begins. In this case, the installation of the new suspension was a very well kept secret.

'Having sorted out the front end,' says Rolls' chief engineer JH ('Mac') MacCraith-Fisher, 'we thought it was about time we did some work on the rear suspension. We'd had criticism from some of our customers and certain elements of the press, you know.' Over the phone, you can almost hear him grinning as he speaks. Rolls-Royce's targets for the new suspension were a better ride, better suppression of road noise, less body roll and keener handling.

The Corniche's 5200lb is carried by mini-block coil springs similar to the Opel Senator's. But the ride quality is delivered by new hydro-pneumatic struts that pick up from points 4in behind the wheels' centre line. Because these struts – which also provide the self-levelling facility – have very good rising rate capability, Rolls-Royce was able to set the suspension more softly over all and simultaneously achieve better load carrying ability while maintaining greater stability from lightly to fully laden. The effect is very much like that of the Citroën GS and CX suspension. Mac – in typically self-effacing Rolls-Royce style – doesn't mind admitting it. 'We're following in Citroën's footsteps,' he says.

As soon as you begin driving this revised Corniche you notice that it has gained a great deal from the new suspension, and from

ROLLS-ROYCE CORNICHE CONVERTIBLE

other refinement work. The steering, which used to be so awful before Rolls switched to rack and pinion with the introduction of Shadow II in 1977, is now beautiful. Initially, the rack wasn't all that impressive, but constant tuning, as Mac puts it, means it's now a pleasure to touch and turn the big, thin-rimmed wheel. The weighting is excellent and the smoothness of the motion quite delicious. And the response of the car to the steering is transformed. Then you notice that, at low speeds over knobbly city streets, the Corniche is riding very smoothly and quietly. The old traces of lumpiness and tyre patter have all but gone. Moreover, the car feels more stable and better controlled, making it even easier to wind through city streets. The Corniche has a surprisingly tight turning circle, is conveniently narrow for its length and high enough to give the driver very good vision.

While the ultimate performance is good rather than breathtaking (120mph top end and 0–100mph in around 30sec), the bagfuls of torque from the 220bhp 6.9-litre V8, passed along by the big GM automatic transmission, mean that there is real oomph away from standstill. So, in town the Corniche is a handy car, a marvellous car. It blends its manoeuvrability and response with quietness and real luxury so that driver and passengers are removed from the hubbub around them. It doesn't seem to matter whether the top is up or down. And the condition is real: it isn't just that you're riding behind that famous mascot.

While the Corniche benefits discernibly from its update, its body's lack of rigidity and the noise allowed in by the cloth roof mean that it obviously isn't the ultimate showpiece for the new rear suspension. It copes very well with poor surfaces, but too often bump-created tremors flow through the Corniche's vast, open body. You can feel them in the seat, at the wheel rim and see them at the scuttle. They're not severe, but they're there. Not even Rolls-Royce can overcome the difficulties of making a large open car that doesn't have the structural assistance of a rollover bar. So you learn to live with the tremors.

You must also learn how to live with the Corniche when it rains. It is a quick handling car in that, with power applied, it corners

AND THE REVS KEEP RISING

neutrally with an increasing tendency towards roll oversteer as speed interacts with the prodigious weight. In other words, be prepared for the tail to come around very quickly. In the wet, it lets go with little provocation. So you learn to use only a trace of power when you're cornering if you wish to avoid what many might regard as the unseemly sight of a Corniche going very sideways. All this happens at very modest speeds. Although there is more roadholding than before, the level in the dry still isn't very high either. There's just too much weight to contend with, and building in understeer would be no answer. On the open road, this means that you drive the Corniche as a stately open carriage, slipping along easily, tidily and very comfortably at 50mph where a Peugeot 505, 604, Opel Senator, Mercedes or Jaguar (to name but a few of the better saloons) would be just as effortless and comfortable at 70mph. If you press on harder, you encounter the roll oversteer too often to keep passengers' nerves intact. Here, the Corniche is an antiquated car with only the almost-as-heavy Bristol for behavioural company.

Driving within its limits is, however, a smooth and pleasant experience most of the time because the steering is so smooth and accurate and the body motion is (then) so well controlled. Occasionally, in crest-and-bend combinations, the steering goes uncomfortably light but the car as a whole retains commendable poise. In the back, so long as the driver doesn't go too fast and stays smooth and clean, you ride in an outstandingly peaceful manner. The ride is now magnificent and, top down, the car needs to exceed 70mph before wind buffeting becomes uncomfortable. In the front, the windshield provides admirable protection when the side windows are up. Beyond 70mph, wind noise grows from noticeable to the point where it spoils the stateliness. The problem in the cabin, front and rear, is that, despite the car's 17ft length, there isn't enough legroom. The front seats adjust electrically and multi-directionally (through finger pressure on small toggles on the respective doors) but even when they're right back there isn't enough legroom, or reach to the wheel, for anyone much over 6ft. In the back, unless the front seats are well forward (and that's out of the question unless the driver is short) legroom is Fiesta-class

ROLLS-ROYCE CORNICHE CONVERTIBLE

tight. The other things that are more than just disappointing are that, although the roof is raised and lowered electrically, it has to be manually and awkwardly clipped home, and covered by a separate tonneau when it's down. The seat belts are diabolical.

But what is so nice about the Corniche is the way things feel. The steering, the brakes, all the minor controls, the door locks, the action of the bonnet when you lift it. Rolls-Royce has made the quality of the movement of such things an art form, so beautiful to the touch that a Rolls-Royce is the most sensuous car there is – more sensuous to the fingers and the feet than any Ferrari or Lamborghini. That, of course, is the Rolls-Royce secret, the area where so much of its developmental time and money goes. From the moment you put the key in the lock you know you're in touch with the finest craftsmanship. That's a good feeling; a satisfying feeling.

You grow to like it very much. The difficulty, as I see it, is accepting that this element – along with the Corniche's visual elegance and (now) its excellent ride – is both its greatness and its weakness. Can you accept that, in your £66,366 convertible, four of you can travel in great style but can cruise above 80mph only if you don't mind a lot of wind noise? Or that you can't really hurry on any back road you may wish or need to take? Can you accept roadholding that, despite the new suspension, is still at a very modest level, and that at the first sign of rain you will need to be very, very circumspect? Can you accept that you may well be able to enjoy motoring in the Corniche, but not really driving? The car's mien, and still rather too much of its ability, is of another era altogether. Without an enormous reduction in weight it's hard to see it ever being any different. Enjoy it then for its presence and its image, not its prowess; its craftsmanship and tactility, not its dynamics. I wonder if that's how the young man in the Fulham Road relates to his Corniche?

STANDING TALL IN STUTTGART

PORSCHE 924 CARRERA GT
1980

IT IS A PLAIN, plain car. There is no ornamentation, no chrome. Everything is black. Even the word *Carerra* embossed on the right front wing isn't picked out in a different colour. The lettering on the tail is no more obvious. But the squat, fat wheel arches hunching over low, wide Pirellis P7s start to give the game away. So does the deep front air dam, not to mention the gaping air scoop on the bonnet and heavily dished rear spoiler.

And yet Germany knows this car is something special. Schoolboys run to the kerbside to ogle as it passes. Drivers who have clocked it in their mirrors on the *autobahn* dart out of its way. When it's held up in traffic, they press as close to it as possible, often to roll down a window, thrust forth a head and fire off questions. *Is it a turbo? How fast is it? What's it like? What does it cost?*

If you have a Porsche engineer in the car with you, he'll tell you that no Porsche has provoked such strong interest for years. Is it significant that its base is the lowliest of Porsches, the humble 924, and that it takes what began as a collection of Audi and Volkswagen parts to dizzy new heights? Is it seen to be the Porsche story re-enacted?

Although there is nothing written on the car to say so, the 924 Carrera GT is turbocharged. It is a direct development of, and next stop up from, the 924 Turbo. It has 40 horsepower more than the Turbo and it is *fast*. Its four-cylinder engine is still only 2.0-litres but it hits 60mph in around six seconds and tops out at 150mph. Yet it is remarkably frugal. At a constant 75mph it returns 33.1mpg

PORSCHE 924 CARRERA GT

against the Turbo's already impressive 26.8. It is refined. It is light and easy to drive, and even if you're not a Porsche race driver you're certain to admire its mighty road holding and its sensitive and beautifully balanced handling. You will, however, have to part with £19,000 to get one and you will probably have to place your order swiftly now that the lists are opening at your Porsche dealers. Porsche intends to make just 400 Carreras and only 75 will be right-hand drive for Britain.

That figure of 400 is a tell-tale. Like the previous Porsches that have carried the now-famous and emotive *Carrera* name, the 924 Carrera GT is a homologation base for the new generation of Porsche racers that will take over from the 911-based cars. The first of them ran at Le Mans this June, acknowledged by Porsche to have no hope of victory and not intended to be competitive in current Group Five racing but undertaking valuable endurance and developmental work ready for entry into the new Category B due in 1982.

Yet, by being beautifully built, trimmed and well equipped, the 924 Carrera GT, like the Audi quattro, clearly can't be dismissed as an homologation special. The racing car development is one thing; the development of the road car another, and Porsche has executed it very thoroughly. The equipment includes tinted glass, electric windows, electrically operated and heated outside mirror, electronic radio/cassette player and, of course, Porsche's six year anti-rust warranty and 12,000-mile service intervals.

But more than the fact that the Carrera is a complete car, it is also – again like the quattro – significant beyond the normal realm of the homologation car. The Audi is important for the relative cheapness, simplicity and undoubted effectiveness of its four-wheel-drive system; the Porsche bridges the gap, at an important time, between performance and economy. A 150mph car with an urban fuel consumption of 22.7mpg is now a reality.

Aerodynamics help a great deal. With a Cd of 0.36, the standard Porsche 924 has one of the cleanest of current car bodies. Despite much wider wheels and tyres, the Carrera attains 0.34. The key element is the very deep chin spoiler and the way it wraps right around to the outer edges of the front tyres, but the big new tail

AND THE REVS KEEP RISING

spoiler, the shaping of the wheel arch extensions and the fact that the Carrera is lower than the Turbo by 0.4in at the front and 0.6in at the rear all help, too.

The Porsche 928 is well known for its flexible nose and tail sections (with real impact bumpers hidden behind them). The 924 Carrera's chin spoiler is made of the same fibre-reinforced polyurethane. But the Carrera goes further and establishes a first in body construction: its front wings (and the rear arch extensions) are of that clever flexible material that looks so much like metal but can be bashed and dented only to spring back into shape without showing any sign of abuse. Apart from such low-speed anti-impact and stone chip properties, the polyurethane is lighter than even lightweight steel, so that the Carrera's front wings are 5lb lighter than if they were pressed from light steel.

The engine is a direct development of the 924 Turbo four. Even for the 320bhp Le Mans racer, the block, head and crankshaft go unaltered, although it gets a dry sump. But in a three-fold development, not only the power but the overall efficiency of the engine has been significantly increased. First, an intercooler (fed by the bonnet scoop) has been installed between the turbocharger and the inlet manifold to cut the temperature of the blown air being forced into the engine by 50 degrees C and at a stroke improve combustion by 15 per cent. Second, the compression ratio has been raised from the Turbo's 7.5:1 to 8.5:1, and the boost pressure increased from 0.7 to 0.8atm. Third, there is a new digital ignition system that provides exceptionally accurate spark control.

Together, these modifications lift the 1984cc all-alloy engine's power from the Turbo's 170bhp at 5500rpm (the standard 924 has 125bhp at 5800rpm) to a potent 210bhp at a still-modest 6000rpm. At 202lb/ft, the torque is up by 22lb/ft on the Turbo at the same 3500rpm (the standard 924 has 120lb/ft). These are impressive figures in impressive company: the Audi Quattro develops 200bhp at 5500rpm (and 210lb/ft of torque at 3500rpm) from 2.2 litres and the Lotus Esprit Turbo, again with 2.2 litres, delivers 210bhp at 6000rpm (and 200lb/ft at 4000rpm, although the Lotus does it without the aid of an intercooler).

PORSCHE 924 CARRERA GT

The Carrera's clutch is strengthened slightly to take the extra power, the gears in the five-speed transmission are tougher and the transaxle housing has been toughened. The drive shafts are also stronger. Porsche mentions no suspension alterations other than the modest lowering and the use of a heftier rear anti-roll bar although gas-filled dampers with firmer settings than the standard Carrera fluid units are optional. The standard Carrera wheels are 7J x 15 with 216/60-VR15 tyres. But 911 Turbo wheels (7J x 16 at the front, 8J x 16 at the rear) wearing 205/55 and 225/50 Pirelli P7s arc optional – and it was with the sports dampers and wide Pirellis that Porsche gave us our black Carrera. The brakes are as for the 924 Turbo but with special ducting to increase the front discs' cooling. An 18.5-gallon fuel tank gives the Carrera a range of 440 miles even when hard-driven. Air conditioning and a removable sunroof are options. Without them, the Carrera weighs 2600lb. Largely thanks to its transaxle layout, that weight is split 49/51 front to rear. Hallelujah.

If the 924 looks demure, the Carrera brings to its gentle shape a new dose of meanness and purpose. It bulges and hunches low over its wheels and the one unrelieved colour from nose to tail brings it more than a touch of menace. It is like a fighter plane compared with an airliner. Tumble into the cockpit and it's almost the same as the 924 Turbo. That means comfort, efficiency and beautifully fitted cloth and pvc trim. The Carrera, however, is deemed worthy enough to have not only the 911 Turbo's forged alloy wheels but also its chunky three-spoke steering wheel, and that brings a sense of business to the cabin.

As the first few miles slip behind the Carrera, you wonder whether the lesson learned in getting to know the 924 Turbo – that to get the best of its top-end biased performance and response you must stay in the lowest possible gear and keep the revs up – has made it seem as though there is less discrepancy between low and high rev response. But no; the Carrera has much better *all-round* performance. The response is swifter and the acceleration far more potent when you open the throttle at less than 3000rpm. The urge increases consistently as the revs then scoot beyond 3000

AND THE REVS KEEP RISING

and there isn't the peakiness – the on-off syndrome – of the 924 Turbo's engine. The higher 8.5:1 compression ratio means that the Carrera doesn't have the sagging response of what's really a low compression engine when the turbo isn't delivering decent boost. So the Carrera's isn't a wilder engine, with more top-end go. It's a more *driveable* engine with more performance across the board. It makes the Carrera easier to handle and get to grips with. Why not, you wonder, doesn't Porsche ditch the standard Turbo engine and use only the Carrera powerplant?

The gear ratios are the same as the Turbo's with, on paper, large gaps between first and second, second and third and fourth and fifth. At 6000rpm, first runs to 33mph, second to 60, third to 95, fourth to 115 and fifth to 150mph. But the Carrera's beefier torque curve does a lot to fill the gaps. At 2000rpm it has 130lb/ft of torque against the Turbo's 120, by 3000rpm it has 192lb/ft against 166 and from 2700 to 5700rpm there's more torque than the Turbo's peak figure.

Familiarity with the Turbo's gearshift will help you settle in quickly. The shift is essentially a fore-and-aft movement once you've left first, with very little lateral distance between the planes. Until you learn its subtleties, you tend to push too hard and get fourth when you want second, and fifth when you want third.

When you get some pace up, the Carrera doesn't feel dramatically fast. But it is certainly fluidly fast and, given a fairly clear *autobahn*, you'll soon find yourself clipping along at an effortless 130mph. If you increase throttle pressure then, you'll feel the car ease ahead obediently. It feels smooth and efficient; not brutish. It feels clean and positive through the air, and relaxed because of its terrific stability. The wheel rim jiggles slightly in the hands, in typical Porsche fashion, but the GT tracks straight and true and the effort at the rim is light enough. This is a refined homologation car, a very likeable car. The driver effort is modest enough and the sound level in the cabin low enough to permit easy conversation at such high speeds.

Take to back roads and the growing suspicion that Porsche has done terribly well with the Carrera's ride is steadily confirmed. The

PORSCHE 924 CARRERA GT

928S demonstrated that Porsche has learned at last how to work with P7s. The 924 Carrera shows just how well it's learned. The quality and the quietness of the GT's ride is extremely good while the suspension is as positive and communicative as you'd wish in a car so swift and so able.

The steering effort loads up considerably into tight bends at speed, but not too much. You can feel immediately that the grip is much stronger than that of the already good 924 Turbo. You know you can push really hard and not have to worry. The car hangs on like a leach. More tenaciously, you suspect, than even the 928S and somewhere close to that contemporary paragon, the Lotus Turbo Esprit. The greater grip and the feel of the wide tyres make the Carrera seem brawnier than the lesser 924s. Yet when you try hard in the right bend and do reach the limits, you learn that the delicately communicated handling feel and balance that has always been the 924's greatest asset is still present and correct. From neutral, on-rails cornering below its limit, the Carrera slips into the slightest nudge of understeer as the front P7s signal that you've pushed them as far as they'll go. You feel it in the skin of the fingers. Maintain your throttle pressure and the tail will edge out too; and then you can balance the car through the bend with the front sliding, the rear sliding, or both. In the wet – towards the end of our day with the Carrera, it rained and John Mason and I found plenty of nice long switchbacks – there is only slightly less grip, and the precision and the perfection of the handling even more satisfying.

The only flaw in the Carrera's behaviour is that, well as Porsche has applied the car to the P7s, their sheer width and flat-tread characteristics cause some tugging at the wheel rim on steep-crowned roads with bumpy edges. If you're hugging the edge of the road in a tight bend, for instance, the crown-and-bumps combination can have the wheels endeavouring mildly to turn off the road. It isn't the strong tramlining of cars like the early 928s and it isn't a problem; occasionally, you just have to increase your pressure at the wheel rim to maintain the precision of your course.

In a hard day's driving, you'll find there is nothing nasty about

AND THE REVS KEEP RISING

the Carrera. Its *raison d'être* may have been to make a new racing car legal but, through proper development as a road car, it's more refined and very much more desirable than the tamest 924. It is a fast car with near-supercar pace, grip in the highest of today's high echelons and handling that is among the very finest. It is comfortable as well as efficient in the cabin, so that its function there blends pleasingly with its ability on the road. There are elements of its feel – its greater beefiness over the 924 Turbo, generated mostly by the suspension – that may lead rear-engined Porsche fans to embrace it as coming closer to the appeal of the more potent 911s than they might have thought possible from a 924. Yet it fits perfectly as a stablemate to the imperious 928S too, for it imparts that same feel of unshakably impeccable behaviour. It demands less of the driver than the 924 Turbo yet it offers more. Add the Carrera's extraordinary fuel economy and you get a car that doesn't just stand very tall in Porsche's line-up but one that notches up another milestone in the reshaping of the supercar.

MANNERS MAKETH THE MASERATI

MASERATI KHAMSIN
1981

I SUSPECT I'M ALWAYS going to lust after the Maserati Khamsin. In a world where mid-engined supercars now rule, I know there will be days when I will still itch to unleash a big (14ft 5in), heavy (3520lb), large capacity (4.9-litre) front-engined grand tourer like the Khamsin.

Even among such strong front-engined GTs as the Aston Martin Vantage, Ferrari Daytona and Lamborghini Jarama – all of which can provide more raw excitement – the Khamsin stands out as something special. It combines the classic, brutal performance of the big, multi-cylinder GT with remarkable ease of operation thanks to an advanced and refined control system that is still unusual a decade after the Khamsin was conceived.

The Khamsin took over, late in 1973, from the sublimely beautiful but behaviourally corrupt Maserati Ghibli. Although fundamentally similar in concept to the Ghibli, and intended for a similar role, the Khamsin – like its mid-engined sister, the Bora – stemmed from very different thinking at Maserati. Citroën, which had bought Maserati from the Orsi family in 1969, was in charge and the impressive young engineer Giulio Alfieri was being given his head. He wanted his new models to lift the road cars of Modena in general and Maserati in particular to a new level of refinement and ability. The Bora came first, in 1971, relaunching Maserati into the true high-performance market with a finely-balanced, refined and outstandingly swift mid-engined sports car at a price well below its Ferrari and Lamborghini rivals'. The Khamsin, next up, was

AND THE REVS KEEP RISING

intended to please an equally cultivated if slightly less adventurous clientele, especially in America where the Ghibli's inability to meet safety legislation had crippled its sales.

Within the constraints of placing the engine in the nose and having it drive the rear wheels, Alfieri and his new French colleagues broke a lot of new ground with the Khamsin. Instead of the traditional and simple Maserati twin-tube frame they designed a complex structure of small-diameter square tubes and stressed sheetmetal box sections to give maximum flexibility to the bodywork's design. They put the engine hard back against the firewall, greatly helping weight distribution, allowing a low bonnet line and providing not only good crash crush space but enough room to house the spare wheel (in a well behind the bumper).

The Khamsin's suspension combines conventional upper and lower wishbones at the front with unconventional geometry. Alfieri's intention was to eliminate as far as possible all changes of wheel angle in the vertical plane on bump, rebound and while the wheels are turned, at the same time as having centre-point steering. At the rear, the fully independent suspension is formed by wide-based wishbones and twin coil spring/damper units (two per side), again with clever geometry to keep things as shipshape as possible, no matter what treatment is being meted out by the road and at no matter what speed.

Alfieri's keenness for such finely controlled suspension movements was so he could use the high-pressure hydraulics gifted to Maserati by Citroën, especially the ultra high-geared steering pioneered in the Maserati-engined Citroën SM. But with the Khamsin, Alfieri went further with the potent hydraulics than ever before. Apart from powering the brakes and the steering, raising the headlights and the driver's seat cushion, they power the clutch. Alfieri also gave the Khamsin a steering column adjustable for height and reach and used electricity to power other odds and ends – like the window lifts and radio antenna. He went as far as he could to make the driver's efforts minimal.

The Khamsin's body is another break with previous Maserati practice. Its immediate predecessors had been styled by Vignale

MASERATI KHAMSIN

or Ghia. Giorgetto Giugiaro designed the beautiful-looking Ghibli when he was styling chief at Ghia from late 1965 to April 1967. But by the time Maserati was looking for a design for the Khamsin, Ghia and Vignale had both been taken over by Ford. With Pininfarina locked in to Ferrari, that left only Bertone, or Giugiaro at Ital Design. Perhaps Giugiaro was just too busy working on the Bora and its Merak derivative. The upshot was that Maserati chose Bertone where Marcello Gandini – who'd succeeded Giugiaro as design chief and had drawn the Miura, Espada, Stratos and many other classics – promptly came up with the exceptionally wedgy Khamsin. Its small frontal area and clean shape gave it good penetration but initially the fit of its bodywork was so sloppy that wind noise was diabolical. Inside, too, the fit and finish were crude. That was sorted out a long time ago, and the Khamsin now is a car notable for the silence with which it slices through the air, and its cabin is as well trimmed as any hand-assembled model from Modena.

Although the Khamsin's lines look purposeful they're delicate enough to make it seem quite small when you're about to slip down into its cabin. There, you apply finger pressure to the rocker switch on the inside of the doorsill to choose the seat height you prefer. After finding plenty of legroom and adjusting the steering column to your height and reach, you enjoy better all-round vision than in any mid-engined exotic. Although you can't see the end of that sharply dipping nose, you can see the nearside edge well enough to make placement comfortable when you start to hammer along on tight roads.

And hammer the Khamsin certainly does. The all-alloy, dry-sump 4930cc 90-degree V8 has two camshafts per cylinder bank and four twin-choke downdraught Weber carburettors. It gives you 320bhp at 5500rpm and bagfuls – 354lb/ft – of torque at 4000rpm. With such oomph, this V8 shapes up pretty well against its V12 Ferrari and Lamborghini rivals. High gearing allies it to 26.6mph/1000rpm legs. At the 5500rpm redline in fifth – which the Khamsin attains so easily – that's just on 147mph. But at 6250rpm, which Maserati says is OK for short bursts, it's geared to cover the ground at 166mph. And it *will* do it – at least my well-run-in test car would.

AND THE REVS KEEP RISING

Where you get your real pleasure with a Khamsin, though, is from savouring the forceful mid-range performance in any and all of its five gears. They are particularly well spaced. At the redline, first runs to 44mph, second to 68, third to 98 and fourth to 130. Going hard up through them will have you at 60mph in 6.3sec and at 100mph in 14.4 – not the fastest times there are but good enough for a heavy car of the Khamsin's power. The best part is that the performance is effortless, and once you've settled down you revel not so much in wringing out those last few miles per hour or chopping off fractions of seconds but feeling the car respond instantly and satisfyingly in the 3000 to 4000rpm rev range. There, it surges forward – lazily if you care to tread lightly on the throttle or furiously if you plant your foot if, say, overtaking space is short. That rev range in third gear whips you from 53 to 72mph, in fourth from 70 to 95mph, and in fifth from 80 to 106mph. Choose your gear and play your tune.

What all this means is that the Khamsin isn't so much a lazy car to drive but a pleasantly effortless one. And its torquey performance blends happily with its light, smooth and super-fast steering, its soft, potent brakes, its dainty, short-throw clutch and its light though slightly notchy gearshift. At first, the steering might have seemed twitchy and difficult; hyper-sensitive. But you soon get used to it and the small, tidy movements that are all it needs. You start to *think* the car through bends, or lane changes, with just one hand on the wheel if you wish, and the other free to move the gearlever. Just as you need to get used to steering that is quicker than three turns lock-to-lock, and so very responsive, so you need to adjust to the brakes too. Don't leap onto them, or stamp on them. Squeeze with the toes and feel the swift, sure response, then work hard at perfecting your toe-and-heeling technique with a central pedal that needs only mild effort to bring such effective results. Light, considered, physical actions are all that you need in the Khamsin.

The good Alfieri has given you more than ease of operation too. His carefully calculated suspension geometry and the Khamsin's inherent overall balance mean that you need not fear pushing it to extremes. Its wheels stay impressively upright when you're

MASERATI KHAMSIN

door-handling through bends, and if it does push from its normally neutral cornering stance into oversteer it does so in a smooth, polished manner. It doesn't go far into oversteer either. It's as if the Khamsin has a natural loathing to let its rear wheels slide. But if you do force them out through excessive power or sheer cornering speed then the action is friendly and well controlled. Here, when you need it most, the communication of the chassis is telepathic. You feel the wheels slide and it seems the most natural thing in the world to flick on opposite lock and enjoy a moment's drift before the tail comes back just as smoothly as it edged out. In truth, it all happens swiftly but the messages are conveyed finely and the behaviour is so good that you have the impression of it all being – again – so effortless.

The Khamsin, of course, is not *all* sweetness and light. Its engine is mellifluous in the mid-range but beyond 5000rpm it grows harsh and lumpy and there's little joy in revving it hard. Those who love Ferrari and Lamborghini engines for the top-end magnificence may well condemn it as crude and boisterous. A dedicated Porsche man would find the detail and finish of the Khamsin's body at odds with his ideal although it is fine by Modena's standards. A Jaguar XJS owner may well disparage the lumpiness of the low-speed ride around streets like London's, although the motorway and open road ride is adequately comfortable.

But none of these things, for me at least, overcomes the fundamental and unique appeal of the Khamsin – the appeal that LJK Setright describes as something akin to seventh heaven. It's a car with he-man performance that can be driven as much with the mind as with the hands, arms, feet and legs. It's a car that, once you understand the alacrity of its responses, offers up its performance in such a civilised manner. Through the level of its performance it *can* be downright exciting to drive; through its finesse it is *always* sensuous and satisfying. And because of the allure of that mixture I, for one, expect to find it nagging at my mind for a long time to come.

STRIKE FORCE VECTOR: DREAM OR NIGHTMARE?

VECTOR W2

1981

THE AMERICAN DREAM? JERRY Wiegert knows it well. He's been wrestling with it for 10 years, it's cost him £500,000 and now he's almost dragged it into the daylight: a twin turbo 650bhp mid-engined projectile that he considers capable of delivering a devastating 237mph blow to the Ferrari BB 512, Lamborghini Countach and Porsche Turbo 3.3.

It's a militaristic dream. Wiegert calls his machine Vector W2, describes it not so much as a car but as a high-capability aircraft for the road and is fierce in his hope that it will plant the Stars and Stripes above the vaunted territory ruled for so long by Italy.

Wiegert has been militant about the execution of his dream. He's positioned himself carefully. He says he holds three automotive and industrial design degrees, and his studio-cum-workshop-cum-factory is in the quaintly decadent Los Angeles beach suburb of Venice. That centres him in a prime target area, the vast exotic car market of Southern California. And it gives him the supply lines he craves – the high technology and uncompromised componentry of the aerospace industry. Lockheed, Boeing, Northrop, McDonnell Douglas, NASA and Honeywell all have a presence here.

Aerospace and electronics links are fundamental to the Vector's construction and Jerry Wiegert's vision of its appeal, the nub of his answer to the question: *what is an exotic car?* In his blunt (but not entirely abrasive) way, he insists that there are no truly exotic cars other than the Countach and, at a pinch, Ferrari BB 512. The rest, he says sweepingly, are purely and blatantly built no

VECTOR W2

differently from Fiats or Volkswagens. 'It's my attitude,' he says, 'to put everything that's best into the car, regardless of cost. I've had stacks of so-called exotics – and really loved some of them – but none has been built with this sort of no-compromise attitude. Even Rolls-Royce don't do it: if they did, they'd use braided stainless steel hoses, special grade aircraft fittings and a lot of other truly high-quality components. My concept is to blend aerospace technology, materials and construction techniques with a futuristic design to prove that American creative, technical and business capabilities can challenge and surpass foreign competition in the automotive industry's most prestigious area.'

That's a daunting task, tackled – for the most part – impressively but sprinkled, by virtue of the nationalistic element, with traces of anomaly and even hypocrisy. Vector's final form has evolved from a series of outlines and models Jerry Wiegert began studying in the early '70s. Its shape is interlocked with its function and construction. It's a dramatic, exciting, brutal-looking little beast, not an object of immediate beauty. Wiegert reckons it conforms to the 'total form' philosophy, with its greenhouse area integrated with the lower bodyform. The windscreen, side and rear glasses mount flush with the glassfibre of the bodywork, and the plexiglass side lights curve at the crease lines to dip well down into doors. The wipers rest tidily in a flat area at the base of the windscreen.

Other than the mirror, nothing protrudes from the bodywork. The fuel filler is a flush-fitting and purposeful-looking device from an F-15 fighter. The underbody is perfectly smooth. For penetration, the car's nose tapers in plan as well as profile. The snout, like the lower, outer section at the rear, is deformable urethane that gives way then reforms when it's knocked. Hidden behind both are energy-absorbing struts for heavier impacts, then the progressively deformable main chassis structure. The doors swing upwards Countach-style but cut into the roof more than the Lamborghini's. Perhaps, overall, the shape is closest to that of Giugiaro's prototype Lotus Esprit, with its high, thin nose and its spoiler tucked back so far that it's just ahead of the front wheels. The bodywork is made of particularly resilient Kevlar, graphite and grp.

AND THE REVS KEEP RISING

If you look at the Vector's mechanical layout, you would say that it's inspired by that supercar pioneer, the Lamborghini Miura. The Urraco and Ferrari 308 GTB use the same format, with their engines mounted transversely behind the cabin. But that wouldn't be doing justice to the design clarity with which Wiegert has approached his car. In the curious tech-jargon common in California, he talks of its basis in 'the man-machine interface.' Getting maximum cabin space and comfort – width as well as length – in a car 14ft 4in long, 6ft 4in wide but only 3ft 6.5in high dictates a transverse engine. As a result, Wiegert gets the within-the-wheelbase (103in) weight balance he was seeking along with a cabin able to provide optional three-abreast seating as an alternative to the standard arrangement of two vast plush, electrically-controlled and fully-adjustable Recaros.

It's in the chassis's detail design and construction that Wiegert departs from familiar supercar practice. He steers a course somewhere between aircraft and racing car construction techniques. Vector has a race car-like semi-monocoque with large box section side members made of sheet aluminium, an aluminium honeycomb floor and bulkheads, and a structural steel roll cage, with the lot joined by aerospace epoxy and high-stress stainless steel rivets. The entire chassis weighs only 350lb but is uncommonly strong and rigid. The front suspension is familiar enough: unequal length upper and lower wishbones made from lightweight structural steel tubing, combined springs and Koni dampers and an anti-roll bar. There's a tight 5.5in of travel and to reduce harshness with such a taut system, Wiegert has used very high-density resilient bushes. He uses variable ratio rack and pinion steering, with or without power assistance according to the customer's preference.

It's the Vector's rear suspension that sets it apart. The only modern high-performance car with anything like it is the Aston Martin Bulldog. To minimise camber change and most consistently handle the *massive* power and torque of Vector, Wiegert – like the Aston engineers – reached the conclusion that a good old de Dion axle was best. The large diameter steel de Dion tube linking the rear wheels is located longitudinally by four *very* long trailing arms (matched pairs of equal length either side) and laterally by one

VECTOR W2

diagonal steel bar. Adjustable Konis hunch inside tightly-wound coil springs and there's an adjustable anti-roll bar acting on the de Dion tube. Vector runs handsome Center Line three-piece modular wheels that are light and strong, 9.5in x 15in at the front and 13 x 15 at the rear, carrying 225/50R-15 and 285/50R-15 tyres, initially P7s but latterly new low profile Firestones.

And what powers this mixture of old ideas and new construction techniques that end up weighing only 2500lb? Wiegert pronounces: 'The twin cams and multi carburettors of the Italian cars, and all the complexity and unreliability that goes with them, just aren't necessary now. I've been listening to people grumbling about the cost and difficulty of keeping their Italian exotics on the road for years. It's nonsense that guys should stand around at parties and mouth off about the megabucks it cost them to change the clutch in their Countach. What Americans really want is power with reliability and accessibility.'

All well and good, but to keep the very kernel of his dream American, and without being able to afford to develop and build an engine of his own, what else *could* Wiegert do but choose a Detroit V8? Having arrived at that impasse – he says he'd really have liked a turbine or a Wankel engine – it's what he's *done* with that Detroit V8 and how he's mounted it in his car that is really interesting and, it must be said, exotic.

The base of the Vector engine is GM's long-serving and much respected 'small-block' 5.7-litre Chevrolet V8. In its most powerful current production form (in the Chevrolet Corvette) it gives 193 SAE horsepower. Wiegert uses a Donovan aluminium block version of the engine, with the latest slant plug design heads also cast in alloy and fitted with very large stainless steel valves. The heads are ported, the internal components matched and the lot balanced and blue-printed. A five-stage pump scavenges the dry sump.

But it takes more than that to get the sort of power Wiegert wanted. On the flywheel end of the V8 lurk two Garrett AiResearch H3 turbochargers with smaller and lighter turbine blades than normal to quicken throttle response. They're some distance from the air intake ports but deliver their compressed air to critically

AND THE REVS KEEP RISING

designed and beautifully made aluminium plenum chambers and tuned-length manifolds. Bosch continuous injection, constantly monitoring the engine's demands, squirts fuel straight into the ram tube manifolds. Two Boost-guard wastegates, venting at between 10 to 15psi, release excessive boost pressure. It's possible to adjust the blow-off pressure from the dashboard, altering the engine's power. Wiegert claims the engine is giving 650bhp at 6000rpm. Despite its pushrod operated valves and hydraulic lifters he gives it a 7500rpm redline.

There is only one high-power American transaxle that could allow the Chevrolet V8 to sit transversely in the Vector's chassis: General Motors' own Turbo-Hydramatic 425, used in the front-wheel-drive Cadillac Eldorado, Oldsmobile Toronado and the 7.2-litre GMC motorhome. Perfect – a compact and natural partner for the V8, and automatic to boot, thus fulfilling Wiegert's objective of making the driver's handling of such vast power as easy as possible. But, as with the engine, he hasn't left the three-speed transmission alone. It's completely rebuilt and modified internally by drag racing experts B&M Automotive to cope with power far in excess of its normal dosage, and to change gear with lightning speed. Moreover, the transmission can be programmed from the cockpit to operate entirely automatically, in conventional fashion, or shift manually.

Wiegert has also devised a shift mechanism that brings motorcycle-type positive-stop gear changing to cars. There's a wide, flat lever that moves fore and aft within a recess in the left box member of the monocoque. Furthest forward, it selects – and is locked into – the transmission's Park mode. Lift it slightly to overcome the locking mechanism and tug it back an inch or so and you get Reverse. Tug it up and back another inch, then tap it downwards and you're in Neutral. After that, pull it back one-two-three times and you've come down to first gear, ready to move off.

Wiegert had to design a differential housing. It's made of cast aluminium and designed to allow fast in-car servicing or changes of its heavy-duty Gleasman helically cut gears. With the standard road differential of 2.42:1, the car gives 12.9mph/1000rpm in first, 21.8 in second and a whoppingly long-legged 31.6 in top. At

VECTOR W2

Jerry's 7500rpm redline that works out at an incredible 97mph in first, 164 in second and 237mph in third. Perhaps it is possible; but many others have failed trying to prove their cars were capable of considerably less. The brakes trying to cope with all this are 12.2 x 1.4in ventilated discs, inboard at the rear with their one-piece cast aluminium callipers mated to the differential housing.

When you swing up the engine cover to inspect Wiegert's handiwork in detail, you find a delightful sight. The bulkhead and rear chassis members gleam brightly. The rivets joining the sheet aluminium are in perfectly neat rows and all the edges are precisely cut. The braided stainless steel supply lines are like jewellery. Those glistening plenum chambers are like silver ingots. This might be a humble Chevrolet at heart but it's dressed up fit to kill. It's more than just the sight of the mechanical package and its support systems that is admirable. The turbochargers, waste gates, injection system, electronic ignition, the valve gear are all readily accessible. The engine can be removed without the transmission, or the transmission without the engine, the diff without either, or the whole drivetrain lifted out or dropped from the car. 'It's with this sort of mechanical and packaging interface that I feel the real intelligence of the car lies,' says Wiegert. 'It's this sort of considered ease of maintenance that's in demand among exotic car owners in America. People here understand this sort of approach. No-one knows why the Italians and the Germans and the British don't do it.'

The visual appeal of the Vector's cabin is much like that of the engine bay: metallic, mechanical, homogenous with the whole. The metal of the monocoque is exposed in considerable expanse as soon as you swing up one of the doors, giving you visual involvement with the chassis. Getting into the car is much like tumbling down into a Countach, though even more awkward because of the extreme width of the monocoque's siderails and the hefty side bolsters of the Recaros. Pull the door down into place and you're within a dramatically purposeful capsule, much like the cockpit of a sports prototype racer. A wider, roomier GT40 perhaps? Yet there's the feel and function of a fighter 'plane too: the F-15 five-point seat

AND THE REVS KEEP RISING

harnesses, the aircraft-type bargraph instruments, the illuminated push-push electric switches of the lesser systems, and, of course, the view forward.

From the outside, the Vector's glass looks dark, colour-matched to the bodywork and opaque. But looking out, there's just a trace of tint and no other visual restriction at all. As in the Countach, you see nothing of the nose. There's just the patch of windscreen and then the road in front of it, ready to reel beneath your feet as if you're sitting in the front row of a cinema watching a driving film. Vision to the sides is good, helped in tight corners by the dishing of the side glass. To the rear, the view is not quite as grim as in the Countach, and it's nice to be able to see the engine through the upper armour glass section of the bulkhead, as in the Miura.

The Posturpedic Recaro seats, electrically heated and adjustable, locate you perfectly. Winch up the belts and you can't move even if you wanted to. The steering column comes to you through adjustable reach and rake. The wheel arches cut well into the footwells but don't force the driver's legs more than a little towards the centre of the car. All told, it's a comfortable driving position.

Turn the ignition key and there's a loud, steady hum from the electronic ignition. A further turn, steady pressure on the throttle and a series of snuffles and mean snaps and pops erupt from the engine. A few moments later it fires and runs steadily, barking sharply. It may not be a quad cam V12 but it sounds savage. It idles evenly, and responds blisteringly to any prod upon the throttle, and without vibration reaching the cabin. The high-density elastomer bushes of the drivetrain's mounts work well.

If you've doubts about the unique gearshift, they're soon despatched. Up and back a notch brings it easily out of Park and into Reverse. Repeat the motion and you escape Reverse. A downward rap with the heel of the hand means that it's then locked into the Neutral and Drive modes and can't go forward again into Reverse or Park without being lifted. Three quick little tugs take you through third then second to first, and you're set to move. Nudge it forward an inch with the heel of the hand and you get second. Do it again and you select third. You have to lift it slightly to make the

VECTOR W2

next forward move into neutral. In fully automatic mode, you select third and leave it there.

The throttle linkage is accurate and progressive and moving off is readily controllable because of the cushioning and compensating effect of the torque converter. In the first few yards of the car's movement there's a clue to its high-performance worth and ability. There's a firm, positive quality to the feel of the suspension that experience tells you comes only from top line dampers working with carefully rated springs. It's an accurate tell-tale: the car feels right from the moment it moves. The pattern of the road comes through satisfyingly to the buttocks but there's real ride comfort as well. It's very much like the feel of a Countach S. The steering blends well with the behaviour of the chassis. Meaty in the hands, fairly informative, quick. The Vector is easy to manhandle in heavy Los Angeles traffic.

If you've been wondering about the prospect of 650 horsepower, a potential 0–60mph time of around 4.0sec and a standing quarter mile of 11.0sec at 130mph, then it all proves to be good tempered, and available in tiny doses because of the torque converter. When you're fully at ease with the gearshift and ready to unleash more than a few of the ponies, the car becomes a rocket that obliterates other traffic. You pick a spot ahead and *blast* into it. The torque converter masks whatever throttle lag there might be (and it seems to be well-nigh non-existent, as well it should), so the Vector pelts forward with the exhaust barking and your senses racing to keep up. The gearshift blends perfectly with this sort of performance. If you're in third, decide to go and want the most there is, you drop your left hand, tug twice and you're in first faster than any manual shift would let you drop one gear let alone two, and with instant response from the transmission itself. Subjectively at least, the Vector's response from relatively low speeds feels swifter – and the car more wieldy – than a Boxer or a Countach. It feels small and handy; a potent, precise, *little* speed tool.

Wiegert had given me a rev limit of 6000rpm because, he said, the V8 had just been reassembled after the latest round of developmental work. Changing up full throttle at that point brought

AND THE REVS KEEP RISING

changes that were amazingly quick and smooth. Down changes remain just as impressive at high speeds, too. Flick the handle back and the transmission answers immediately. There's the mildest jerk, the revs rise accordingly and you have either engine braking, or a lot more go.

When you hit the open road – today, wonderful Highway 1 north out of Los Angeles up the coast to San Francisco – the Vector flows along with silky and muscly long legs to whip past traffic that you can line-up from a long, long way back and simply gobble. Straights between bends disappear. It likes long, visually open bends where it can be set up on line and have the power brought on as it goes through. But of course it takes a long and *very* fast bend to permit a lot of power. You'll be flying by the time the exit looms. There is just enough response to throttle lift-off to adjust your line accurately, but rear end grip doesn't suggest it will break away. It has a feeling of security akin to that of the Lotus Turbo Esprit, a hefty compliment. However, I'd want to drive it on truly unrestricted roads and in tight, bumpy and demanding bends before I was sure about the real ability of its chassis. In the few tight bends I did find, the Vector bolted around without understeer and with practically no roll. On rails? Yes. Wet roads? Discretion. The drivetrain's response to the throttle could have you facing backwards in a flash.

Whatever the top speed of the Vector turns out to be, it feels directionally stable enough at the 160mph that was as much as I could manage on Highway One while watching out for the California Highway Patrol. There was no sign of breathlessness from the engine. The Vector felt as if it had more power and pace available than in a Boxer or Countach at upwards of 150 – as it should, with almost twice the power. Stability, though, wasn't Countach-sharp. In the Vector, you feel as if you want plenty of space around you when you're travelling fast.

It wasn't only room, traffic and the CHP that stopped me going faster. The Vector's brakes were terrible in high-speed applications, demanding two or three times the space you'd normally allow in a car of 160mph capability. Apart from the poor retardation, pushing the pedal really hard brought a lot of judder, and wicked tramlining

VECTOR W2

as the big Pirellis, pressed into the road, were tugged about by the tarmac's contours. I was thankful for the braking effect a down change would bring. Wiegert says he's ditching the Hurst-Airheart discs for a British Girling system, and there may be less tramlining with the Firestone Super Sport GP-125s he's trying. Even within the allowance one makes for a prototype, the braking problem was a discomfiting disruption to the otherwise satisfying experience of driving the Vector fast.

The cabin is comfortable and effective – the ride is firm but never too harsh. But the instrumentation is tedious; awful. In a car so fast, the flashing figures of the awkwardly sited digital readout left of the wheel are almost incomprehensible; frustrating, dangerous. The horizontal illuminated orange bar graphs for the minor functions might work acceptably, in that one out of line with the imaginary vertical constant that they should all touch, attracts your attention but they're hard to monitor individually. Wiegert says he's developing a head-up display, with the tachometer and speedometer readings projected onto the windscreen. He needs to do something.

Jerry Wiegert is taking orders for the Vector at $125,000 a pop – near enough £60,000 – and says production will start within 1981. But it isn't only to justify the price that he needs to proceed carefully and patiently to realise his dream. He's close – but he's under the impression that the final steps will be few, swift and painless. Is he naïve? Maybe. Then again, he could be demonstrating the sort of mammoth optimism displayed by most builders – and especially the Modenese – working towards the introduction of a new car. Watching his predecessors tells me that it'll take Jerry, champing at the bit though he is, longer than he thinks. He has to sort out the detail finish of the Vector's body and cabin, find effective instrumentation, perfect a wash-wipe system, make the headlight covers flutter-free and fit state of the art headlights if he's really being serious about all-round performance. He has to develop an anti-lock braking system that's up to the car's performance, he needs to eliminate tramlining under brakes and the bumpsteer that sometimes rears its head. That alone is no mean feat. If I were Jerry Wiegert, I'd be hot-footing it across the desert to Arizona to

AND THE REVS KEEP RISING

see Bob Wallace, now in Phoenix, who did more early Lamborghini development work than anyone. The Countach was his car. I'd be surprised if Bob wouldn't lend a hand.

Jerry also needs to put a *lot* more development miles behind the car than the 40,000 he's logged so far, however tough he thinks they might have been. I've no doubt, after my blast up Highway 1, that his drivetrain delivers massive performance. But will it turn out to have his much-vaunted reliability? Will there be parts of his clever chassis that don't quite make the grade long-term? Will it get into production? Is Vector's business case sound? Through intense drive and dedication, Jerry Wiegert's dream – and America's? – is at his fingertips. Mishandle it now and it could turn into a bitter, lingering, nightmare.

Postscript

The Vector W2 never made production. In 1990 Wiegert finally started selling a development of it called the W8. It did 218mph, with 0–60mph in 4.2sec and the standing quarter mile in 12.0sec, in a *Road & Track* test in March 1991. According to howstuffworks.com, its price rose from $283,750 in 1991 to $489,800 when production stopped in 1993. Just 17 cars were delivered. Wiegert was forced out in 1993 after Indonesian investors bought Vector. Ironically, the M12 the company then built between 1995 and 1999 was powered by a Lamborghini V12. Eighteen were built before things shut down again. Wiegert subsequently regained control of Vector. In 2012, Vector Motor Corporation's website said it was developing a new WX8 'hypercar' with 2000bhp that would be capable of 275mph.

REST AND BE THANKFUL
LOTUS TURBO ESPRIT
1981

MY FRIEND ROGER COOK was driving as we forged into Teesdale. 'What a road!' he said with delight as we cleared Middleton and saw the tarmac snaking for miles ahead along the dale's northern edge, picking its way between the moors rambling imperiously to our right and the valley tumbling moodily below. The trucks and most other cars had chosen easier, more obvious roads. We had to share the peace and pleasure of this one only with a handful of farmers shuffling along in Land Rovers, and a few nomadic sheep. The sun was dropping, making the sheep, the guideposts and the lines on the road show Persil-white against the moors' vivid colours – but it was off to our left and wouldn't be in our eyes. Perfect. I reached up and turned off the radio.

The 250 miles from London had given Roger time to settle into the Lotus; time to get an idea of its smooth power, crisp response and refined behaviour. He was now about to learn of its exceptional speed, its unerring precision, its tenacious grip, its immense stability and lovely cornering balance. He was about to discover the depth of the Turbo Esprit's ability and why, at a stroke, it has lifted Lotus to the highest plateau of sports car performance.

Earlier sessions with Turbo Esprits had given me that balmy knowledge and, as Roger began to wind this Turbo out in the gears, I nestled back into my snug leather lounge with a private smile, confident that the car would do nothing to alarm its driver and ready to enjoy the experience of watching him reach deep into its abilities.

The Lotus began to chew up the road. Most of the bends soon proved to be too slow for second, however tight they might have

AND THE REVS KEEP RISING

looked. Third was the right gear. Its flexibility, mid-range oomph and 91mph at 7000rpm gave it the right spectrum. It contained its own message too: the Turbo is very fast but is not *demandingly* fast. Its power is not peaky; it does not hide within a narrow rev range. You do not have to keep flicking away at the gear lever. The engine might be a 2.2-litre four but it delivers its performance more in the realm of a V8. So third is a fine gear for a series of bends strung close together. You could come out of a tight bend as slowly as 30mph and still have instantaneous acceleration, or charge through a faster bend and with revs in hand for a full-power exit.

Third is good until you've gained enough knowledge of the Turbo's balance, the entry speeds of which it is capable and its accelerative power to correctly choose second for slower bends and fourth for faster curves. You will want to do it correctly – to choose the right gear, select it at the right point on the road, use the right amount of power – not because the Turbo insists but because you've become aware of the smoothness and finesse with which it cruises, bends or not. You will wish to match its smoothness – as if you were an unerringly accurate guidance system – simply because it deserves to be driven like that.

Roger pressed on. He was starting to use the gearshift now. Occasionally, I tensed as we stormed towards yet another bend, particularly the right-handers where there was nothing ahead but the remnants of a skimpy fence and open air. Surely the car was going too fast? Yet Roger was accelerating, not braking. And before we'd get into the bend, I'd remind myself that it was my impression that was wrong, not his.

So my anxieties were fleeting, infrequent things, diminishing with each mile as I learned my own lessons. I switched to analysing my own environment. We were pushing hard through bends tight enough to generate a great deal of lateral force, yet I was still lounging comfortably in my red leather tub, bounded on one side by the soft padding of the door trim and on the other by the leather over the deep central tunnel, and held firmly by the seat's soft, deep side sections. I felt the lateral forces but was largely unaffected by them because the car corned so flatly.

Visiting the supercar makers in Modena is always a treat, not least wandering in among the cars being built. Countach, top, always a dramatic sight half-built or not. Lamborghini's Bravo prototype, centre, didn't make production. With the Miura's transverse V12, it would have been very fast. California's aircraft-inspired 650bhp Vector W2 was certainly potent but never went into production either. A later version did 218mph but only 17 were made.

The uprated 928S, above, at last revealed the real capability of the front-engined V8 Porsche. Optimum weight balance from its rear-mounted gearbox helped make its handling so impressive – a great car for all-purpose driving. Its 'little sister' 924 Carrera GT, left, was even sweeter and heralded the trend to smaller, powerful but more economical turbocharged engines. Lotus Turbo Esprit, below, also achieved great performance with a four-cylinder engine and cut the mustard with Italian rivals.

Maserati struggled to find its own identity at times. The Khamsin, above, with Maserati V8 power and Citroën hydraulic systems, was a curious though enticing mix of brawn and sophistication. Created after Citroën's involvement ended, the Quattroporte, below, was a simpler but effective and very luxurious big Jaguar and Mercedes rival, loved by the Mafia. Maserati had used high-tech systems from the revolutionary, characterful Citroën SM, bottom, a gracious tourer on fast, open roads. Bike and F1 racer 'Mike the Bike' Hailwood loved his.

Works Audi quattro blasts by Nichols' quattro, above, in a transport section of the '82 Monte Carlo Rally. Several days in the mountains convinced Nichols of the quattro's all-weather capabilities. Three years later the short, ugly but immensely effective quattro Sport, left, was a harbinger of supercars to come. In its ultimate rally form, the Sport quattro S1 had 500bhp. Heart-in-mouth, Nichols saw what that meant when Hannu Mikkola, below, pelted him through a Welsh forest.

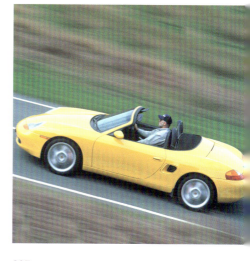

After a troubled gestation, BMW's Lamborghini-developed M1, top, was honed by race driver Hans Stuck into a deeply appealing car that embodied the best of its German-Italian heritage. Porsche's 959, a technical tour-de-force, above, introduced the era of the 200mph hypercars of immense all-round ability. All subsequent Porsches, especially 911s, have gained from its achievements. For years, the spirited but benign Boxster, right, set the standard for sports car handling.

United by elegant bodies and Italian verve, the Ferrari 400i, above, and Alfa Romeo 2000 GTV, below. The 400i was Ferrari's first automatic – reasonable, but you'd still choose a five-speed manual. The Alfa was Nichols' indulgence and evoked memories of many great drives in Alfas. One superb day out was in a friend's Ferrari 365 GTC/4 and BB 512, bottom. The GTC/4, sister to the more glamorous Daytona, was far better than many realised.

At home in Sydney: faithful MGA 1600, right, bought when Nichols was 19, served well until a diet of test cars, including potent Aussie muscle cars, took over. An English classic of superior style and quality, the Bentley Continental, below. Dentist Peter Frankel used it as his daily driver in London. The British sports car personified: the Jaguar C-type, bottom, that gave Duncan Hamilton and Tony Rolt victory in the 1953 Le Mans 24 Hours.

The first Ferrari Nichols drove was a 275 GTB, revisited later in faster, even more enticing 275 GTB/4 form, above. Gorgeous body, magnificent V12 engine, lovely handling but dreadful brakes. By hanging out at Ferrari for two days, Nichols was first to get into the 'performance above all' F40, below. Fast as the F40 was, the 627bhp and 243mph McLaren F1 lifted road car performance and capability to a gobsmacking level that's still amazing.

LOTUS TURBO ESPRIT

It was equally free of fore and aft pitch, maintaining its impressively even attitude whether braking or accelerating, rising over crests or dropping into dips. Bumps affected each wheel at a time, not the car as a whole, and then only very little. The suspension, while delivering all that directional and lateral stability, kept enough flexibility to absorb the bumps. Yet there was enough communication to be reassuring too. I marvelled. I was being transported as stably, levelly and comfortably as if we were still on an open main road. As a car for a passenger, the Turbo Esprit was displaying more than ample virtue.

Roger was driving masterfully but, at ease though I was, I could stand it no more by the time we'd covered the 22 miles to the township of Alston and there wasn't much left of the dale and its exquisite road: I had to have the pleasure of driving the Turbo there myself. As we entered Alston I was selfish enough to ask Roger if he'd mind swapping over.

Experience said *cool it*; settle in slowly. Establish an equilibrium. Play yourself into the car, and the car into the road. Don't make the mistake of going too fast too soon. Familiarity mercifully shortened the normally lengthy process of adapting to the Esprit's high steering wheel and scuttle, its intimidating 6ft 1in width and low driving position. So the car soon felt enticingly available. I wasn't as fussed about the height of the gear lever on the central tunnel as Roger had been. For me, that was countered by the short-throw delicacy of the shift mechanism itself. And if the narrowness of the footwell was annoying, there was the trade-off of short-action and well-balanced pedals, each engineered to match the weighting of the others – and the gearshift and steering – as closely as possible.

As we ambled through Alston, I mused that in the Turbo Esprit the 195/60VR15 Goodyear NCT radials on the front wheels pushed the steering's weight slightly beyond the usual impeccable Lotus balance. But that it had its own compensation too: there was the meaty feel of the small, thick-rimmed leather-covered wheel that blended well with the reassuring feel of the steering itself. Dribbling through Alston's narrow streets, I was pleased to have the Turbo's fine part-throttle response and its outstanding

AND THE REVS KEEP RISING

flexibility. Here was a docile car happy to be driven at walking speed in a congested street yet in a few minutes it would be travelling tremendously quickly.

On the open road again, what felt like 50mph was soon shown by the accurate speedo really to be more. The car felt unshakable. I concentrated on my gearshift points. At 7000rpm (with another 300rpm to go before hitting the ignition cut-out), first gave me 41mph, second 62, third its lofty 91 and fourth a towering 123. Fifth, I knew, would take the Turbo to a certain 152mph and, given a lot of room, maybe a little more. Fourth was more than enough, although such is the Turbo's torque – its peak of 220lb/ft spreads from 4000 to 4500rpm – that fifth would provide solid performance upwards of 60mph or so too. The choice of tempo was mine.

The bends were more open now and our speed higher. Again, the lack of flab in the steering, suspension and transition from one modest attitude to another, gave the impression that this car would never lose its unerring precision. Turn into a bend and it just followed the line precisely. Tighten to hug a bank in a blind corner and it did that perfectly too. Brake in hard and deep and neither end budged. Give it full power on the way out and the tail refused to move unless the bend was slow enough for first, or happened to contain a bump or two at the point where the full 210bhp was being unleashed. Even then a snip of opposite lock – a tiny flick of the wrists – or a split-second reduction in power had it back perfectly. So, with a feeling of unwavering trust in the Esprit I got on with the pure pleasure of making mincemeat of the road. 'What a car!' said Roger with admiration as we left Teeside behind and pressed along more open roads for Gretna and Scotland.

We were heading, ultimately, for the long, fast climb to the top of Rest And Be Thankful, in the hills above Loch Fyne. A few days earlier, when I'd told Roger where I was going, he'd soon found reason to leave his Radio 4 *Checkpoint* programme for three days 'research' in Scotland. We carved across the A74, which would have been the obvious route north to Glasgow, at Gretna and headed further west for Dumfries. There, as we closed on long rows of articulated lorries that were themselves being held up by doddering

LOTUS TURBO ESPRIT

cars, another aspect of the Turbo Esprit came into play: its raw acceleration. With oomph to the order of 0–60mph in 5.7sec and 0–100 in 15.5 we could hang back, spot a gap 'way up ahead and then steam past with room to spare. It didn't seem to matter how short the straight. If we were down to 40mph, full throttle in second had us at 60mph in just over two seconds. That sort of overtaking prowess brings a combination of confidence, safety and exhilaration that creates a feeling of relentlessness.

We knew we had enough performance to deal with anything we encountered on the final stage of our run towards Glasgow. Soon, though, we encountered little more than the odd truck and a few cars, all despatched as if they were motoring in a different time period. Darkness closed in. The Turbo's lights were up to the job and we cruised even faster than I had anticipated. It was in long bends that the Esprit was perhaps most impressive of all. Once it had been settled with a little throttle lift-off, turned in and then stabilised with the faintest reapplication of throttle so that it felt as if it were being restrained by a gigantic soft-gloved hand, it followed the curves perfectly, kissing the verge in the left-handers and gluing itself to the road's white line in the right-handers.

That state of control and stability when you're in a long and blind bend, and you must hang in equilibrium between a trailing throttle and power application, is crucial – perhaps the ultimate pointer to a sports car's quality. The Lotus was better than flawless, capping its in-bend balancing act with its vigorous thrust out of the bends when their exits were in sight and the throttle could be floored. Superb, too, was the way it could bolt out of a demanding right-hander to be faced just a few yards later with a left. More often than not there was no need to brake before turning in. When it *was* necessary, the Lotus slunk into the road while the brake pedal delivered feel by the millimetre and millisecond. Again the nose resisted any tendency to run wide or to twitch in too far and force the tail out. You could play, to see if any latent fault lurked, by really standing on the brakes. Still the chassis remained imperturbable.

So the effort needed to cover the ground so swiftly was satisfyingly low. Happily, there was great comfort with it all too. The

AND THE REVS KEEP RISING

Turbo's suspension works as quietly as it does competently. Roger, I noted, was asleep long before we neared Kilmarnock and swung properly north onto the A77 for Glasgow. I've had some fine drives to Glasgow, but this one had been the best and I was as fresh as I was happy as we pulled up for the night. 'Is it as good as it looks?', asked a man at our destination, and all Roger and I could do was look at each other and grin like a pair of Cheshire cats.

It was raining next morning as we worked our way along Loch Lomond side round the top of Loch Long heading for the soaring hills and great swooping glens to the lochs of the south-western Highlands. Not even the Turbo's prowess could take us beyond the mimsers huddling nose-to-tail. We kept our distance and relaxed with the warm feeling of comfort and security that the Lotus imparted.

But we broke loose on the long, open, glorious run on the Old Military Road up to Rest And Be Thankful above Loch Fyne. The Lotus dashed up the four-mile climb like a racehorse turned loose on gallops. I'd dreamed of attacking this soul-stirring road with a properly fast car; the Lotus delivered.

We spent the rest of the day exploring the lochs and working with Ian Dawson, with whom we'd linked up to take pictures. Even pottering about had its use: it threw up the exceptional flexibility of the Turbo's engine, the way it would pick up so smoothly and unhesitatingly from as little as 1500rpm in second, third or even fourth. In fifth, it was responsive enough to provide notable pace from around 2000rpm. Serious acceleration started from around 2500rpm and beyond that it was dynamite. Yet there was no peakiness, often a characteristic of turbocharged engines. Only the curious twitter of the waste gate dumping excess pressure when the throttle was released at high revs reminded us that the engine was turbocharged.

The only difficulty in handling the car on narrow roads – or in the city – stemmed from its vision. Most mid-engined cars' rear and side vision is poor. The Esprit, with its striking styling, is among the worst and the Turbo further handicapped by the louvers over the engine. Turning in tight areas or parking required careful checking of the electrically adjustable mirrors and a lot of neck-craning.

LOTUS TURBO ESPRIT

On the way back to Glasgow, to avoid the congestion along Loch Lomond side we took the alternative road from Arrochar to Helensburgh, and found that the Lotus handled its endless stream of dips and crests with the aplomb we'd come to expect. It crested the sharp rises flatly and never bottomed in the dips. On a road that would have had many cars with a lot of road clearance and long suspension travel trundling sedately, we travelled unabated.

Heading south again, we took the A74 towards the borders but swung off again at Gretna to retrace our steps; we weren't about to bypass that marvellous road through Alston. There, we changed drivers once more so that we each drove the sections we'd missed on the way up. Again there was very little traffic and we pushed the Turbo really hard. There were enough bumps in some of the bends to make my wrists ache as I pressed the car in as fast as visibility allowed. Still the Lotus refused to run wide, or to be deflected by bumpsteer. It just went where I directed it, with the wheel jiggling solidly in my hands as the wheels rode over the irregularities.

I used all the road and ran hard in each gear, braking as late as I could. It was glorious, and brought with it another special moment. I came over one crest to find the road spearing down to a visually open right-hander that ran through 90 degrees to a short straight and then a 90 degrees left. I kept the throttle flat, swung really hard into the bend and entrusted everything to the roadholding. The tyres loaded to the limit – 1.1g, Lotus claim – but the Esprit went around with just a trace of understeer, felt as a slight lightening at the wheel, and then a nudge towards something approaching, but not quite, oversteer as the tail was pushed hard down by the full power of maximum revs in third. The g-force was high but there was still time for the mind to note the car's flatness. The following left-hander was of smaller radius and I had to brake hard for it and take second gear. Then it was back on the power again to feel the car balance out as it left the bend behind and romped onwards. I'd never been around a couple of tight corners quite so quickly and nor had Roger. We grinned at each other and pressed on for London, content now just to cruise sedately.

When we filled the car we found that we'd returned 20.8mpg after

AND THE REVS KEEP RISING

all our hard-charging, little less than the 21.3 we'd obtained on the way north. Even with all of our stopping and starting in Scotland we'd bettered 20mpg. Later, when I filled the car in London after covering the final part of the return trip on the A1M and M1 at a brisk cruise, the figure was 26.1 mpg. Set against the Turbo's performance and cross-country pace, the figures were incredibly good.

When we'd been driving the Turbo swiftly and using all the gears and the performance, we hadn't noticed noise. On the motorway, we were conscious of a fairly high but not objectionable level of sound from the tyres and wind noise that increased significantly with speed. If you were to be travelling beyond 120mph across Europe you wouldn't have much chance to listen to the radio, though the Turbo still stands as commendably refined overall. The ceiling console installation of the stereo system was too fiddly for practical use. We wished for more luggage space too. Two small bags will fill the boot. Another can be squashed around the spare wheel in the Esprit's nose. It would also have been nice to have had aesthetic temptation beneath the engine cover. Its securing lugs, the oil filler cap and the plumbing looked cheap and messy thereby failing the car's real engineering which is of the highest design and developmental quality. I had been happy to tell people about the Turbo; I didn't want to show them its innards.

But our long and happy excursion had left neither Roger, the perfectionist, nor me, the sceptic, in any doubt about the Turbo Esprit's road-going brilliance. It transported us and inspired us; it confirmed my view of its desirability, judged against any criteria, and more than satisfied my whim for a stirring drive into the Highlands.

Postscript

After 12 years on Radio 4 with *Checkpoint*, Roger Cook moved to ITV where his programme *The Cook Report* screened for another 12 years, cementing Roger's reputation as Britain's most fearless and effective investigative journalist. His book *More Dangerous Ground* (Book Guild) tells how he tackled terrorists, organised criminals, drug-runners, government incompetence and injustice.

ROME FOR DINNER? NO PROBLEM

MASERATI QUATTROPORTE
1981

WE WERE UP TO our ears in decadence, and loving every minute of it. There we were, the four of us, lounging in sumptuous leather and being whisked down the *Autostrada del Sole* towards Rome at a steady 135mph. Steve Cropley, in the front, had been lazily fiddling with the radio. In the back, it wasn't quite loud enough but I wondered whether I could be bothered asking him to turn up the sound, or whether I could be bothered to listen at all. It was easier, dreamier, to nestle further into the rich leather and enjoy the sound from somewhere down below of the big Michelins zizzing on the roadway, the swishing from somewhere off to the right that came with every car we passed and, from somewhere up ahead, the faint high hum of the big alloy V8 and all its cams and carburettors. Occasionally there was the shrill of airhorns as Ermanno, at the wheel, gave notice of our progress to someone running slower. But the horns didn't break the idyll: they were helping to maintain it, welcome guardians of our addictive reverie.

We whistled south, and a drifting mind, atop a relaxed body, began to play idle games. *How pleasant Vienna had been this morning. What should we do after dinner in Rome this evening? Where should we stop for lunch? Perhaps Ermanno knows somewhere off the* autostrada *near Bologna?*

We were indeed drawing close to Bologna. But we hadn't come from Vienna and we weren't going to Rome. We were turning off the *autostrada*, soon to head up into the hills and explore the car's handling, braking and acceleration; to play with it instead of simply

AND THE REVS KEEP RISING

letting it get on with its job. But in those few swift miles down from Modena the Maserati Quattroporte had shown how well it can get on with the job of sweeping four big people along at better than two miles a minute. We had seen its luxuriousness as we opened its doors, smelt the richness of its leather as we got in and felt the comfort of the seats even before we began to move. Then, as we left the Maserati factory in Viale Ciro Menotti behind, we could feel the familiar husky power of the 4.9-litre V8 hauling the car seamlessly up through the long gears of the ZF gearbox.

Plainly, the car wasn't brutally fast – no car weighing 4190lb and possessing only 280bhp could be – but it was clearly a long, easy strider and we had a good idea of its capability well before we reached the famous motorway. As the good Ermanno Cozze, that Maserati stalwart, eased us along, rounding up the Piaggios and Lambrettas, Bambinos and 127s, Giulias and Alfettas, and posting 80mph or so on every short stretch around the outskirts of Modena, we learned about the Quattroporte's refined briskness and balance, eager but elegant ability. Then we reached the *autostrada*, surged along the entrance road and, with Ermanno running out to 6000rpm in third and fourth, were swiftly heading for that effortless fifth gear cruise of 135mph. We three passengers, not long from our drive from London to Modena, were swiftly in no doubt that, should our driver suggest going on to Rome, we'd be ready with a resounding *Yes; of course*.

But then grand touring cars are Maserati's domain. Even when it was earning kudos with such evocative sports racers as the Tipo 61 Birdcage, its road cars were aimed more at grand touring than outright sportiness. On bendy or bumpy roads, its chassis generally were not impressive but given a motorway they'd happily eat miles as if they were minnows before a barracuda. The idea was to point the car in the right direction and then let the engine drag you along at an average well beyond two miles per minute – Modena to Paris then dinner and a show, as former Maserati engineer Giulio Alfieri reminded us recently. Thus, by giving its road cars this nature, Maserati placed itself in a slightly different position from other fast car makers and sold steadily to customers who were generally older and wanted more than two seats. In the '60s, Maserati emphasised

MASERATI QUATTROPORTE

this role by making a saloon called the Quattroporte. Its appeal was undeniable: a car with the performance and character of a Maserati but possessed of normal saloon attributes, too.

Maserati no doubt hoped for sales to government officials and heavyweight industrialists, but the attraction of the Quattroporte wasn't lost on the Mafia either. Between 1964 and 1968, Maserati made 800 Quattroportes, occupying territory untouched by the other Modenese and only really cut across by Mercedes-Benz and Jaguar. The concept remained popular at Maserati after the first Quattroporte went out of production and, under Citroën's ownership in the early '70s, a new model with high-pressure hydraulic systems was under development as a sister for the Bora, Merak and Khamsin.

You'll still find two Citroën Quattroporte prototypes in a corner of the factory, bonnets up and bits and pieces missing. Their obviously French styling and hydro-pneumatic suspension didn't gel with Alessandro de Tomaso when he took over Maserati in 1975 after Citroën bailed out. His engineering director Aurelio Bertocchi, who replaced Alfieri, along with most of Maserati's remaining engineers were happy to ditch the project. But the *concept* was in friendly hands. Bertocchi had been at Maserati in the days of the first Quattroporte and, as soon as he had the Kyalami (based heavily on the De Tomaso Longchamp) underway to plug the 2+2 gap in Maserati's range, he forged ahead with a fresh Quattroporte. This time Giorgetto Giugiaro did the styling and Bertocchi followed the simple but effective chassis design used in the De Tomaso Deauville four-door, Longchamp 2+2 and the Kyalami. After being unveiled at the Turin Show in 1976 and a very thorough years' development, the new Quattroporte went into production late in 1979. Within a year, Maserati sold 120 in Italy. As they'd known at the Viale Ciro Menotti all along, the market for exotic saloons is quite healthy.

The Citroën Quattroporte had been soft, slightly quaint-looking. For the new one De Tomaso and Bertocchi wanted strong, forceful lines that immediately gave the car a muscle-bound image. But they wanted conservatism and elegance too. Giugiaro combined the elements quite well. He eschewed a low, sleek nose and went for a high, flat bonnet line behind a bluff nose that carries a deep,

AND THE REVS KEEP RISING

chrome Maserati grille – no token outline here! With the bonnet line so high, Giugiaro kept unacceptable depth out of the front wings by raising the bumper and using a small half-spoiler to mask the front of the chassis. The deep channels along the flanks form a line for the rising waist to work against, creating a wedginess that establishes an air of performance and authority. It's a tough, chunky, business-like car, a solid-looking express that says it will remove its occupants from the melee on the roads around them. The rising profile also means that the boot is large and deep enough for four occupants' baggage on a journey crossing several countries.

The Quattroporte's body is all pressed steel, and unitary with the chassis. That, of course, means a different construction process from the other Maseratis, with the exception of the new 'little Quattroporte' 2.0-litre V6 saloon due out soon. The mechanicals are familiar. Beneath the bonnet goes the elderly but still impressive all-alloy Maserati V8 used in the Khamsin and Kyalami. Maserati has employed the engine in 4.2-, 4.7- and 4.9-litre capacities. The Quattroporte, like the Khamsin and top Kyalami, uses the big gun 4.9, a mildly oversquare unit with two chain-driven cams per cylinder bank, a low 8.5:1 compression ratio and fed by four twin-choke Weber carburettors. In the Khamsin the 90-degree V8 gives 320bhp at 5500rpm; in the Quattroporte, its tune is a little softer to deliver 280bhp at 5600rpm. It supports that with 289lb/ft of torque at 3000rpm, the high point of a torque curve flat enough to make the Quattroporte flow so effortlessly to high speed, and admirably flexible if you want to leave it in a high gear to amble in heavy traffic. The manual gearbox, with its slow and wide-gated ZF shift, is thus no handicap, and the three-speed automatic transmission that most Quattroporte buyers choose is never left short of oomph.

The suspension holds no surprises. It's well tried and appropriate, familiar in Modena and close to – if not patterned on? – that of Jaguars of the past two decades. At the front there are lower wishbones, coil springs, telescopic dampers and an anti-roll bar. At the rear, the driveshafts act as upper links and work with lower links whose ends are sandwiched between twin coil spring and damper units. Their location is assured by trailing arms. The steering

MASERATI QUATTROPORTE

is servo-assisted rack and pinion; the brakes heavily ventilated discs, inboard at the rear, with no anti-lock system even if they do have potent but delicately balanced servo assistance.

This sort of design thoroughness you take for granted, knowing current Maseratis. It's inside the cabin that you direct your real attention. Here, the Quattroporte delivers in an equally straightforward, thorough and welcoming Italian manner. The Quattroporte is big but not huge. At 16ft 4in long and 53in high on an 110in wheelbase, it's somewhat tidier than a Mercedes SEL. But it's roomy inside, and plush, plush, plush. Given good designed-in room, the aim has been to furnish the car in obviously hand-finished fashion. There is a mass of that beautifully fine, light-coloured Italian leather, with its hand stitching showing on the seats, armrests and console. There's wood veneer in the dashboard edge, console and upper part of the doors. Otherwise, everything from the waist down other than the deep pile carpet is that lovely rich leather. It looks soft, expensive, exclusive and inviting.

And, feeling privileged, you find that it's as good as it looks. The smell helps create the atmosphere, but the seats really are good. Big, deep electrically adjustable armchairs in the front, with big armrests on the doors and between them, and a great big lounge of a back seat. A fat bolster that can be pulled down separates you from your travelling companion if you wish – and you will; this car makes you feel that its luxury is quite personal. It's all in extremely good taste, like a pair of conservative but exquisitely lasted Italian shoes. It fits; it feels good; as if it's made just for you, and for hours-long occupancy. With ducts, fan and temperature controls in the rear, all four occupants can select, within reason, the climate they desire.

So you select your climate, snuggle down into the leather and let the driver, the engine and the suspension carry you hither. The ride isn't as soft or quite as refined as a Jaguar XJ's but it's cossetting enough and there's a certain comfort from the positiveness of its communication. It suggests that there will be plenty of stability and control when you're cruising quickly. Indeed, the combination of the suspension's communication and the engine's note and feel give the Quattroporte a character beyond that of just another

AND THE REVS KEEP RISING

limousine. The feel and sound, however subdued, leave you in no doubt that this car is precisely as conceived – a luxury grand tourer for four, made by Maserati.

When you drive it – and the chances are that you'll need to drag yourself away from that marvellous rear seat to do so – the seat adjusts precisely as you'd wish, the wheel and pedals are as well balanced as only Maserati, among the Italian makers, seems able to effect and your station within the car gives you a fine visual command. The alternative automatic transmission may seem more appropriate, but the clutch isn't strictly for he-men and the ZF gearshift moves well enough if you take it slowly. So you let the Quattroporte flow out in the gears with the torque doing the work and the speed rising surprisingly swiftly. You won't disturb your passengers, but the rate of progress, the feel and sound is enough to give you, the driver, adequate satisfaction. The steering has little feel but it's accurate – or at least the car answers cleanly when you move the wheel. The fairly firm springing and damping helps. There's no lurch of the body, no wallowing. Thus, although it's a big car and you're aware of the other three people lounging around you, you come to terms with the driver's role quickly.

You find yourself clipping easily along at a steady 70mph on winding roads you know the Ferrari test drivers use to evaluate ride and handling. The Maserati feels big and solid but not a barge. You clear a crest and find the road going left and needn't worry about the Quattroporte being thrown off balance. It rises slightly on the suspension, settles, and turns precisely as you direct it. You can trust it: you can motor swiftly and surely and your passengers can enjoy your efforts if they care to take note, or merely lounge and daydream, listen to the radio, or sleep. If they know cars they may tell you that an XJ12 travels more quietly (and more quickly), that a Mercedes SEL has a little more legroom, that a Lagonda's ride is a little softer. But they'll find it hard to criticise the Quattroporte's own particular balance, and, surely, they won't be able to deny that it has its own particular character as Modena's only saloon. That character, in the end, is the essence of its appeal. Even for those who know that it does nothing better than a Jaguar V12 or a big Benz, that's likely to be enough.

CHASING THE MONTE IN THE ALPES-MARITIMES

AUDI QUATTRO
1982

GO, THEY SAID, AND cover the Monte Carlo Rally. And if the prospect of a week's hard driving in the ranges of southern France suggested a use for the chains I'd just bought for the office Vauxhall Cavalier, then I also knew that there was a car infinitely better suited to the job: an Audi quattro.

I'd been among those who'd gushed about the quattro after Audi let the first of us clamouring journalists take a couple to the mountains for an afternoon during the car's launch at the 1980 Geneva Show. Audi had been careful to develop and present the car as more than just a hot-shot four-wheel drive homologation special tasked with carrying Audi's name into top-line rallying with unprecedented impact. Ingolstadt's engineers were too thorough and conscientious for that. As the project developed, their belief in the quattro's abilities grew too strong to let its potential as a grand touring car be wasted.

As I pressed the quattro through the Swiss mountains that afternoon, it wasn't so much the fact that its traction was so strong or that the 2.2-litre inline five had the performance of a 3.0-litre V6 that bowled me over. It was the fact that, concurrent with its unusual ability, the quattro was so composed and refined. So damned *nice.*

It was enlightening to discover how much of its 200bhp could be put down on snow. Other things were equally admirable. Coming back onto a motorway, I ran it to 130mph with two wheels on the tarmac and the other two on the grass verge. It didn't mind. I pushed it hard enough through a demanding bend to reach its

AND THE REVS KEEP RISING

grip's limit. Its nose only pushed a little out of line. A small, swift, reduction in power called it back. In faster, more open bends, if I fed the power in progressively it would be the tail that edged out eventually. It could be held with just an ounce of opposite lock and drifted in a lovely, subtle sweep out to the bend's exit.

I marvelled, too, at the ride's quietness and quality, the steering's efficiency, the engine's smoothness, the 4 x 4 drivetrain's refinement, and the cabin's room and comfort. I stepped out of the car liking it enormously, and grateful to Jörg Bensinger and his fellow engineers for what they'd created. Back in the office, I grabbed my typewriter and wrote that the quattro was a marvel that rewrote the motoring rulebook.

Later, I wondered if I'd been over enthusiastic. Then colleagues Ronald Barker, Ian Fraser and Steve Cropley drove quattros in Germany and Britain and I spent a lot of time in a UK quattro too. We concurred: the quattro's sheer ability and the loveliness of its feel and character made it exceptional.

Others disagreed. Critics moaned it wasn't as good as we reckoned. They said it has nasty brakes and tricky handling at the limit that caused crashes. But were they blaming the car for its drivers' indiscretions? Of eight quattros advertised in a Bavarian newspaper one weekend, five had been badly crashed. The owners said they had grown used to the quattro's cornering power, particularly on wet roads, but forgotten they still only had conventional braking ability. The sense of invincibility the quattro can create had run away with them. All wanted anti-lock brakes and greater stopping power, full stop.

We learned, thanks to *Autocar*, that it's not easy for Audi to set the quattro's suspension correctly in production and that it only handles properly if it's spot-on. *Autocar*'s ill-handing long-term test quattro was transformed after its geometry was reset. Chasing the Monte, spending a week all but living in a quattro, driving it a long way in all sorts of conditions, was a chance to find out once and for all whether I was right or wrong about Audi's coupé. Fact is though, when I weighed it up, I could not think of a better car for the task in hand anyway.

AUDI QUATTRO

I picked it up a few days before our departure for France and it swiftly began to re-impress me. The engine stood out for its smoothness and responsiveness. The power steering felt similarly smooth and clean. On London's rough streets its ride was comfortable and refined. It took a few minutes to adjust to driving from the left-hand side because, with the quattro's high tail and waistline the cabin seemed rather claustrophobic and the rear vision slightly awkward. The clutch immediately felt good and the gearshift pleasant, although I had to remember to change gears with an easy, dreamy sort of motion if I'd run up a lot of revs because of the heavy-flywheel effect typical of this engine.

I'd been pleased when Audi told me that the quattro was on Michelin TRX Mud and Snow tyres. On wet London roads they instantly demonstrated tenacious grip and surprising comfort and quietness. Within minutes that seductive feeling of invincibility began to develop. Temper it, I told myself. Don't fling the quattro into roundabouts and push the upper reaches of its road holding. Enter modestly and then power out, capitalising on the car's ability to put its power onto the ground. *That's* its advantage. The more slippery the surface, the greater its edge. In a way, *slow in/fast out* applies more to the quattro than other cars. Just remember that, and reject the 'invincible' notion.

It also became clear, in day-to-day use around London, that the white quattro attracted an extraordinary amount of attention. A surprising number of the people who turned or stopped to admire it knew what it was. You saw them clearly mouthing the word: *quattro!* The reaction was the same in France. At immigration and the toll booths, uncommonly cheery officials wanted to know all about it, and whether we were off to the Monte. As it happened, they were admiring two British-registered quattros. Ray Hutton, *Autocar*'s editor, had decided that the Monte was a perfect excuse for him to spend a hard-charging week with his newly-sorted quattro. We met by chance on the ferry early on Sunday morning then ran together, cutting a high-speed swathe through the melted slush on the *autoroute* until, north of Paris, I stopped for fuel.

With cold weather gear for three plus cameras and kit, we'd

AND THE REVS KEEP RISING

bemoaned the quattro's awkwardly small boot when we loaded up. Smaller, handier items ended up on the spare seat in the rear. Otherwise, the Audi's ability and comfort as a high-speed long-range tourer became increasingly obvious. It was little affected by often-deep water on the road. Wind gusts didn't disturb it either. While the M&S tyres were slightly noisier than the standard tyres would have been, the noise level was still low enough to allow effortless conversation or use of the cassette deck at an even 100mph. At 90mph the quattro felt good. It was even better at 100 and no less happy at 110mph. Beyond that, the noise increased slightly but at an even 130mph it was still relaxed enough. Without gendarmes, we would have chosen to run at that pace. The ride was excellent, although both front occupants would have preferred slightly more lumbar support from the heavily bolstered seats. The only flaw of any importance was the way water from the road or washers swirled around the bottom of the screen, needing over-long use of the wipers to clear it.

With mist descending as we neared Lyon, we swung off the road well pleased with the rate and quality of our progress. Next day, swinging east, we burst into clear sunshine. It was a hint of what was to come: the warmest, sunniest January week in the Monte's 50-year history. For all but a couple of occasions in the higher peaks, we weren't going to need our snow tyres. But they were proving to be no handicap on the dry roads and we stormed through Grenoble and began the zig-zag to Monte Carlo. The quattro came into its own as we began to climb, using its power to slip effortlessly past slower cars and trucks and keep flowing swiftly up through the bends. It was now obvious that patches of water across the road were of little consequence so long as that slow in/fast out rule remained dominant – although 'slow in' in this case is beyond most cars' ultimate cornering speed.

Before long we nipped off the N75 onto a mountain road that, the next night, would form one of the Monte's special stages. It was narrow, bumpy and tortuous as it went up and over the mountain. No sooner had we started into it seriously than two points about the quattro became clear. First, that first and second gear are too low and widely spaced. Since the engine needs to be above 3000rpm to stay in boost and respond rapidly, you need to come down to second quite early, and, to bridge the long step from third, blip the throttle heartily on the way. It's the same going back to first, which, on a road packed with hairpins, you'll be doing a lot. So the quattro requires a considered approach if the driver is to maintain swift and smooth progress. To stay above 3000rpm, he has to gauge exactly which gear he'll need for each bend.

However, it's here that the second point emerged. Despite the tightness of the bends and the road's bumpiness, the quattro showed why it's so attractive as a rally car – its ability to put power down. Full-on in first or second, it surged out of the bends, wasting neither time nor horses with wheelspin that would have been there in a front-drive car, or the tail-wagging likely in a 200bhp rear-driven car. The travel and suppleness of the suspension travel was a perfect companion for the spread of power to the four tyres. Here, too, the fluid action and accuracy of the steering – and ergonomics of the driving position – came into play. Beyond judicious concentration, there was no strain in sweeping the quattro along a difficult road at a pace that brought comments of surprise – *ie*, that it was possible – from the passengers.

When we rejoined the main highway, having noted a fine spot to watch the rally stage the next night, the Audi readjusted its gait to a swift, sure cruise. Along many miles of short straights and visually open bends, we could hold a steady and relaxed pace of between 90 and 110mph. The trade-off – if you could call it that – was a fairly high level of body roll when we were cornering really hard. In the longer bends, loading the tyres to maximum with full power in fourth – which runs to 123mph – made it heel until it seemed as though there was no travel left. The five or six crews running virtually standard quattros in the rally would no doubt find the suspension settings too soft. We struck rain about 70 miles out of Monaco but that, as we well knew by then, was no handicap. We finished a long, hard day's drive with happiness and even greater satisfaction than the day before.

The rally left Monte Carlo early the next morning and we were

AND THE REVS KEEP RISING

out promptly to get ahead of the cars to our vantage points in the stages before the gendarmes closed the roads. The low limits of first gear (33mph) and second (56) was frustrating at times up some of the tighter climbs, where at times we needed to work our way past gaggles of cars, but the totality of the performance was fair compensation. Through that long day's driving it became obvious that the Audi could be driven often right up to the limit of its performance. That means seriously fast point-to-point times. In the driving seat, what I liked so much was the consistency of the chassis, the engine's smoothness and its willingness above 3000rpm, the accuracy and the action of the steering and my physical location behind the wheel. The gearshift, clutch and instruments too. I had a tool with which to travel quickly, but I also had a *car.*

As for the brakes, they weren't awful but there was something that made them feel spongy and not entirely trustworthy. Only once, going hard down a pass, did I get some serious fade but there was always a feeling of insecurity lurking between the pedal and the discs. Until I learned that I could overlook it, it led to earlier and longer braking than in a car with reassuringly sure brakes. In the dry, you don't think much about anti-lock brakes. But in the wet and on ice you can't get them out of your mind. It's so obvious that the quattro can go so much faster than is normal in these conditions yet you are only too aware that it can stop no better than most.

In the evening, as we went back to the stage we'd driven the day before, we could go further up the mountain than the rest of rally fans because, with our four-wheel drive, we could move off the narrow road to park. We smirked.

We let the rally go on through the night, dashing hundreds of miles across south-eastern France, and picked the cars and drivers up again the next morning. On the way back up into the Alpes-Maritimes we struck a long, fast, open but challenging bend. The quattro took it flat in second. At the limit, I found as often before that the front pushed a little wide, with enough time and warning for action if necessary. As with understeer in a normal car, that action was to ease the throttle. What happened then, though, is peculiar to the quattro. It hangs a second in limbo and you feel

AUDI QUATTRO

much as if you're in a roller coaster going over the top of its arc: sort of weightless; suspended. For a fraction of a second, it can be scary, and I don't know what happens if you take no action. What you *do* is go back on the throttle immediately. The Audi sweeps out towards the exit, perhaps with just the slightest trace of oversteer for which you may need a touch of opposite lock. The ultimate step is a final oversteer semi-drift that is gorgeous – but the split second in which you hang in between is not a pleasant time. That, I suspect, is what has led to the criticism of the quattro's on-limit handling. That, and a reluctance to correct its line with power.

Feeling now well in tune with the car, I drove *hard* for the rest of the day. Hard enough to derive whopping satisfaction from trying to get every yard of every mile *right*. When I thought I had the quattro really flying, I found that it generally had more pace up its sleeve. I began to brake it really hard and deep into the bends and found that, while weaving very slightly, it tightened its nose down and into the apex as only the good cars do. And as fast as we thought we were going, we enjoyed the buzz of being overtaken by eventual winner Walter Röhl in his Opel Ascona 400 and, particularly, runner-up Hannu Mikkola in the works quattro as they blasted in, out and past the traffic on the transport stages. Finally, after an hour-long spurt on a constantly twisting road we drew up at the end of a section and there was Ray Hutton and crew. The others hurried off to pore over the rally cars. Ray and I leaned against my Audi for a few minutes and chuckled as we told each other that we'd just had the best day's driving for a very long time. Ray had locked the diffs on his Audi for the last couple of hours to see if he could sharpen the handling. There wasn't much difference.

And after another day's driving in the mountains and then the calm 110mph lope of our journey back home (in a day, *autoroute* all the way) our admiration for the quattro was deep. But there was more than that. All three of us – photographer Martyn Goddard and navigator Peter Horsfall, who'd both come with no preconceptions about the quattro – loved it, too. It was always smooth and effortless, quiet and comfortable. It was easy to drive quickly and it was easy to drive *fast*. Several cars could have bettered it in specific

AND THE REVS KEEP RISING

areas but I doubt any contemporary could match its all-round ability so completely. It's this *completeness* that's so appealing. In its own way the burbling five-cylinder engine is captivating. Perhaps it would be better if it were not a turbo engine so that it had more power and response low-down. It would be better if the gear ratios were better spaced. It would be better if the brakes had more bite and very much better with ABS. It would be better if water didn't swirl around the edges of the wiper blades after you've washed the screen. It would be better with a bigger boot. It would be better with more penetrating headlights. But, given the performance – we timed a surprising 140mph top speed – and given the load, what's not to like about fuel consumption of 18.7mpg when using all the power in the mountains, and 19.8mpg overall for 2439 miles? As an all-rounder at ease in a greater variety of conditions than any rival high performance car, the quattro stands higher in my estimation than ever. I scorn its critics and doff my cap to its engineers.

QUEST FOR PERFECTION
FERRARI 400i
1983

I SMILED AND LET the boy in the Renault 18 Turbo go. I hadn't noticed him at the intersection. I was miles away, listening contentedly to the V12 purring beneath the Ferrari's bonnet. When the lights changed, I pressed gently on the throttle, heard the purr change to a thrum and felt a majestic swell of power start to waft the car forward. Then the cream Renault 18 Turbo shot past on the inside. Its exhaust's puff of smoke and its tail's quick dip signalled its driver's purpose: keep the throttle flat, snatch full-bore changes… and beat this Ferrari off the lights.

There was a time when I'd have mashed the throttle to the floor to show that a tinbox with a quick serving of turbo power doesn't get away with that. But while – keeping in mind behaviour appropriate to this classically elegant Ferrari – I wasn't particularly keen to get involved, I was curious, too. I was intrigued by the Renault's speed. I might have been easing quietly away from the lights by Ferrari standards. But by other standards and with the pressure in my back as evidence, I was not in a snail's race. How much of the Ferrari's muscle would I need to flex to keep in touch with this Renault?

To begin, I tried just a little more pressure on the throttle. The beat of the thrum quickened, the swell of power turned from majestic to forceful, the nose lifted another inch or two and the extra pressure in my back was an instantaneous indication of what my toes had triggered. It wasn't quite enough though. More. The reaction was the same but the response was greater.

The tachometer needle swung towards the redline, the automatic transmission shifted with just enough of a jerk to show that it

AND THE REVS KEEP RISING

was beginning to work, and the Renault's tail began to fill the windscreen. Another puff of smoke; another quick dip of its tail: it was still being wrung out. But with plenty of throttle travel and horsepower left, the Ferrari was on its heels. Merely maintaining the same throttle opening would have sent it surging past. I smiled again and eased off and let the Renault storm on. The 400i, even in automatic form, still has enough iron within its velvet glove.

I'd been wondering about that. Just before I'd picked the 400i up from Britain's Ferrari agents, Maranello Concessionaires, I'd been musing that it was 10 years since I'd first seen that svelte two-plus-two body and slipped into it to dash into the hills on a test run with Ferrari's senior driver. It was new then and called the 365 GT/4, which meant that it had the long-serving 4.4-litre V12 with six twin-choke Weber carburettors instead of today's 4.8-litre version with Bosch K-Jetronic injection. The gearbox was, of course, a five-speed manual; an automatic Ferrari was still a dealer's dream.

I saw that day the driving finesse that explains so much about the purpose and spirit of the cars from the Modena. I also learned while my driver was punting the 365 GT through one series of mountain curves after another, often on cobbled or broken surfaces, that the grand tourer in his charge had aplomb and refinement to match its speed and beauty. Only the Lamborghini Espada, then, had a range of qualities that could match it.

The Espada, alas, is gone and the Ferrari lives on, losing none of its beauty but improved and adapted to keep abreast of the times. Whenever one looms into view, my wife reminds me that it is the car she'd love to have. But, 10 years on, is the Ferrari 400i *the* grand tourer? Might your £41,498.70 (with an extra £772.42 for rear air conditioning) be better spent? It is, after all, more than twice the price of an XJS, its only V12-powered rival.

For sheer, elegant beauty – fundamental to a grand touring 2+2 – I don't think the 400i is rivalled, and certainly not by the ungainly XJS. Rolling your eye or, better still, your hand, up one of the Ferrari's A-pillars shows how sensuously Pininfarina has made them flow into the roof, and the roof into the C-pillars. Such exquisite multi-directional curvature is just part of a masterpiece of

FERRARI 400i

line and proportion that hints at its age through a mix of curves and hard edges. It is nevertheless still splendid at a time when depressingly few cars, even expensive ones, are beautiful.

Rightly, Pininfarina has changed little about the body through a decade of production. Most alterations were made in 1976 in the switch from 365 to 400 when the chin spoiler was enlarged and reshaped, six round taillights gave way to four, and five bolts replaced the knock ons securing the road wheels. The main element in the making of the 400 was not visual at all. Changing emissions rules demanded a softer state of tune while buyers simultaneously wanted equal performance, so Ferrari lifted the V12's capacity to 4.8-litres and power to 340bhp at 6500rpm. The new characteristics mated well with the three-speed General Motors transmission, the first automatic offered in a Ferrari.

Emission and fuel consumption pressures balanced against driveability meant replacing the carburettors with Bosch injection in 1979, dropping the power to 310bhp at 6400rpm. Then, too, came the welcome switch to Michelin's superb TRX tyres rather than the XWXs that had served faithfully for so long on this and other Ferraris. In the latest round of modifications, the camshafts and exhaust manifolds were altered to provide stronger low-end torque and power and the final gearing reduced slightly, all aimed at faster acceleration. The rear suspension gained a hydraulic self-levelling system. Changes inside brought new switches and a different console with bigger air conditioning vents. The seats and leather of the door cappings were redesigned to look softer and more tasteful. Outside, as the body went into its 11th year, the changes were minute. Truly beautiful cars, in their second decade, do not need to change.

It was this beauty that made me pause and once again admire the 400i's body before I took the keys, opened the door and slipped in among all the leather. Style and good taste abound. The pronounced rake of the all-black leather-bound wheel says immediately that you're in a Ferrari cockpit. You have an instant impression of the purpose of the car you're in. But the curvature and the glove-soft leather of the seats and the door coverings pronounce in their subtle way that you're in a *gentleman's* conveyance.

AND THE REVS KEEP RISING

When you turn the delicate key in the tiny ignition lock in a moment you'll hear that high, wavering, spine-tingling wail that emanates only from the starter motor of a Ferrari. It goes on for a few seconds until the engine fires and then you have the fine, multi-part harmony that is a large four-cam V12 coming to life and settling immediately into a steady beat. Press the throttle and hear the gentle zizz of the cams quicken to a flurry and the quavering, just audible whine of the electronic ignition system drop to a slightly lower tone. Feel the body shrug slightly with the heave of power, but notice the absence of vibration or harshness.

So you drop your left hand to the big chrome T-lever looming from the central console, squeeze to release the detent and pull it back. Steady pressure on the throttle makes the distant sounds rise and blend and somehow even in the very first moments of movements everything seems so harmonious and controlled. Ah, a Ferrari!

It glides out into the traffic and you play it cool and keep it steady, letting the quality of the sound and the feel sink in, letting the car lead your tempo and actions. Its demeanour suggests relaxed, accurate, economical movements. You want to strive to strike a gracious relationship with the 315 horsepower pulling you along so effortlessly, and the chassis that will allow it to take you to 146mph.

If, when you've settled comfortably, and the readings on the temperature gauges – water straight ahead, between the big tachometer and speedo; oil on the console, with the clock and fuel gauge – are satisfactory, you may like to press the throttle right through its long travel to see how rapidly the V12 can shift 4000lb. Then you'll hear a deep melodious throb from the exhausts join the rising but still gentle flurry from beneath the bonnet. It's now a vibrant accompaniment to the visual pleasure of seeing the nose lift and the road edges begin to flick past.

The transmission will let the V12 hang on until it reaches its power peak at 6400rpm, with another 100rpm in hand before the tachometer face turns red. The shift from first to second will come fast but with a little jerk at 58mph. And if you're not stirred by the acceleration – to the order of 0 to 60mph in 7.5sec – you will know

FERRARI 400i

that you're moving very briskly. From the relentless feel and sound of the engine and the implacability conveyed in a multitude of other ways, you know it's going to go on for a long time, too.

You will know that the Ferrari has the resource and character to demand nothing more of you than a light touch on the wheel and a firm foot on the throttle while it deals with a hard-wrung Renault 18 as if it's just another fly annoying a grazing thoroughbred. If the road's there and you keep the throttle down, the second gearshift comes at 98mph, a tiny jerk in a sustained stream of acceleration that won't tail off until the 400i is spearing along beyond 130mph. It's only the last few mph that will come up slowly. The aplomb, security and impression of indefatigability will still be there, just as it was when you were dawdling. You will know that this behaviour fits perfectly with the beauty of the 400i's body and the elegance of its interior to make it a consummate grand touring car, ripe for long, fast, relaxed and rewarding journeys.

We went west. We took the motorway and cruised gently, mostly just wafting along a little faster than the other traffic and enjoying the economy of effort, mental and physical, of simply having to press just the throttle a tad more to break away from bunch ups with a swift sprint. We relaxed in our leather cocoon, able to make such effective time but feeling as if we were travelling slowly. I would have liked a whisker more lumbar support though.

I fell to thinking, of course, that for all its style and taste, for all its grand touring aplomb, the Ferrari was no better than an XJS and in certain ways its inferior. The Jaguar is a full second quicker to 60mph, for instance, appreciably faster at the top end, quieter and has an even more comfortable ride. But such considerations soon began to fade and I went back to my contentment with the Ferrari's flair and character, arriving at our destination with enough satisfaction to linger a few moments before switching the V12 off.

We were now in rolling country with a mixture of tempting B-roads and lanes. I knew, and the next day confirmed, that the 400i would be a handicap in the lanes. It's fast and its steering is sharp and its brakes are magnificent but trying to use much of its pace in lanes barely wide enough for a Mini invites damage to

AND THE REVS KEEP RISING

precious bodywork. So just motor gently and let the V12 purr lazily. It will not object.

Seek out the B-roads with width enough to allow for an oncoming dairy tanker mid-bend. There you can lock the gearlever in second and use lots of throttle to lift the 400i to the upper edge of its performance envelope, hearing the V12 forsake its purr for a snarl and bolting down the straights or through the kinks to the real bends.

At last you can get the chassis' proper measure. You know from the miles in town and on the motorway that the suspension has refinement. It's firm but there's no harshness and nothing more than a just-audible rumble from the tyres. But now it shows that it maintains perfect stability as the car howls over crests. It does not let the exhausts graunch in a shower of sparks as it whips into hollows. It soaks up bumps without moving off-line, to please the driver; and without jarring, to please the passengers.

Now, the 400i goes fast and clean and you turn the wheel with purpose but not effort and see the nose clip the banks tight at the apexes, precisely where your mind had determined that it should be. Now, the Ferrari is balanced tautly on the throttle. Easing the pedal on the way into bends brings a minute, tasty tightening of line. A full stroke on the way out brings potent acceleration and attitude that finally edges – beautifully – into the tiniest twinge of power oversteer as the inside wheel begins to lift and the outside loads to the point where its Michelin slides. Don't lift off. A flick will keep it straight.

What is this? A svelte £42,000 grand touring car, 11 years old and with four people nestling into its leather buckets hustling along byroads with its driver fit to bust with pleasure? Yes; and then you haul in the XR3i on the next little straight and you sail past and brake hard and smoothly into the next bend. Your passengers, aware now of the car's capability, carry on talking.

But from the driver's seat not all is perfect. You've long since discovered that the power is perfectly matched to the brake and chassis' reserves and you know that when the road's visually open you can use all those horses. So on the way into the bend you want

FERRARI 400i

second gear for the stabilising effect of its engine braking, and on the way out for its response. But there's a jerk when you tug the lever back that jiggles your passengers' heads, and there's another when the transmission changes up again. When the bends come thick and fast you find, too, that first gear won't engage unless you're going very slowly. And such is the quality of the handling that second, at low revs, doesn't offer enough acceleration. There might be more than 300bhp there, but you want more.

The answer, if you wish to apply those prancing horses to perfection on a winding country road like this, is the manual transmission, available without extra cost as alternative to the standard automatic. With that gearbox, you can choose from five ratios rather than three to get the right power and, by balancing clutch, throttle and brakes, change down smoothly. Your passengers will be more comfortable, you will reap more reward and the car will be faster and better balanced. In town, though, you'll have to live with a clutch that is positive but not light and forsake some of the painless pleasure the 400i automatic brings in snarls.

The question for me is not whether the 400i delivers what one expects of a classic front-engined 2+2 grand tourer. It's which *transmission* to have. In city tangles and on the motorway, the automatic took away effort and allowed me to enjoy the Ferrari's more sensuous pleasures. But when I drove back from those country roads knowing again what the combination of this V12 engine, this Maranello chassis and this Pininfarina body could offer, I forgot the motorway and, though time was precious, planned a route on small roads that was longer but would let the 400i's promise through.

It sailed along, working so effortlessly at a satisfying pace that the other traffic just came and went. See a line of cars, brake, look, spot an opportunity, press the throttle and go – all with such a feeling of indomitability that the journey brought pleasure and not fatigue. Yet it could have been smoother and it could have approached perfection more closely. With the manual transmission I could have matched my revs and power more neatly to the bends and overtaking manoeuvres. It comes down to that in a grand tourer with the finesse of this Ferrari. It creates a standard that

AND THE REVS KEEP RISING

prompts you to seek perfection. To that end, I'd order mine with the manual transmission and wait for it to come up from Modena. I'd live with the dipping of the clutch in the city and delight in the rewards of the five-speed transmission on the open road. That way, given that the Ferrari 400i is, among today's grand touring coupés, an unrivalled statement in style, I could strive to extract *all* that it has to offer.

WHITHER THE LIMIT?
AUDI SPORT QUATTRO
1985

So put me on a highway
Show me a sign
And take it to the limit one more time.

THE SIGN SAID NUREMBERG and the speedo read 163mph. But the limit? The limit was nowhere in sight. I wondered if I would even near it. This car seemed to have so much. I'd already learned that it flew from zero to 60mph and back to zero in less than eight seconds. Its acceleration was enough to mash me hard back into the seat. It put its power down in corners like no other car I'd driven. Its braking force made my eyes feel as if they'd shoot from their sockets. And it was so stable at 150mph and more that it was an effortless matter to reach out and slip *The Eagles* into the cassette deck.

Take it to the limit? That had been my desire; my idea of a perfect antidote to too many days in the office, in London. The Sport quattro had seemed the perfect car – a car built for Group C rally homologation with no road-going function other than allowing its driver to escape into the solitude of driving hard and fast, balancing time and motion against each other until finally, if only for an instant, the balance is perfect and the car is at its limit.

But with this Audi perhaps it was an old-fashioned notion, an idea that belonged to a time when cars had less grip and the edges of the envelope were closer. Even in a Ferrari Testarossa or 288 GTO there was the likelihood that sooner or later the tail would flick out as the power overcame the grip.

In the first 10 minutes, this Audi suggested that the new era for supercars promised five years ago by a handful of engineers

AND THE REVS KEEP RISING

from Ingolstadt had come to pass; that within this chopped-down Ugly Duckling Kevlar body lurked the ultimate automotive technology of the moment: a turbocharged and intercooled four-valves-per-cylinder engine with the most sophisticated electronic management; permanent four-wheel drive; competition suspension components; powered rack and pinion steering controlling alloy wheels carrying Michelin racers; and nothing less than Porsche 917 brakes with second generation anti-lock circuitry. It suggested that it had such high reserves of roadholding and braking, coupled with such speed that, without Hannu Mikkola or Michele Mouton in the driving seat, reaching its limits on the road could be beyond sane likelihood.

All this began to dawn when Peter Hagemeister, not long switched from flying Phantoms and Starfighters for the Luftwaffe to demonstrating cars for Audi, took me out for the most articulate introduction to a car I've ever experienced. We were running along one of those thin ribbons of road that weave between Bavaria's forests – at a notably effortless 110 to 120mph. At first, despite his relaxed mode, I thought Herr Hagemeister was exaggerating when he remarked that we were travelling at perhaps 80 per cent of the Sport's potential. I was tense, ready for a bend or an obstacle to catch him unaware. And there were times when I was certain we were flying towards bends at a pace that *would* be too much for even the Sport's 1.2*g* cornering power and his cool reactions. But had I known then, as I was to discover later, how little Peter was asking of the brakes as he slowed to corner without any drama at all, I needn't have given our progress a moment's concern.

As he kept devouring the little forest roads with such great speed and such little fuss, despite patches of damp and frequent strips of badly broken tarmac, I began to realise that the Sport quattro was rather different, rather more significant and very much better than I'd imagined. I'd known it would be fast. With 306bhp, even in a car weighing 2860lb, it had to be. Audi's figures said 0–60mph in 5.1sec and a top speed somewhere upwards of 156mph. For my escapade, that was what mattered.

Beyond that, the Sport had seemed a lost, unfortunate car – a

AUDI SPORT QUATTRO

homologation special conceived so Audi Sport could counter the Lancia Rally 037, only for the attempt to be eclipsed before it began by Peugeot's 205/16. Devoid of the prestige of the Porsche 959 and the visual appeal of its Ford RS200 counterpart, the Sport seemed to hang in limbo, an ugly Audi seeking 200 buyers at around £55,000 a time. The word was that only 20 had been sold.

The reality is a bit different. First, after going out with Herr Hagemeister, 40 German and Swiss drivers have put down £55,000 and replaced cars like Porsche 928s and AMG-worked Mercs with a Sport quattro. With Audi keeping 50 Sports for rallying and other internal use and 20 coming to Britain, there are 90 still available from the factory. Second, even when you're a passenger, the Sport swiftly emerges as much more than a rorty homologation special. Moreover, and this is the really good news, rather than being lost in limbo it has profound significance for Audi's development of very fast four-wheel drive road cars.

The difference in the way the road-going Sport behaves from the raucous steed it might have been is in Audi's perception of its relevance to its four-wheel drive programme and its customers. The original quattro was a road car that, with engine and other relatively modest development, won rallies by dint of superior mechanical layout. It could put more power down more of the time. The Sport starts from the other end. First and foremost, it's the basis for the current Audi team rally cars and available to private rally entrants as a potential winner. Yet, trimmed for the road, it is a fine grand tourer, refined and well equipped. However, despite their different roles, the two Sport quattros are remarkably similar mechanically, a testimony to the validity and versatility, the ruggedness as well as the refinement of the Audi four-wheel drive concept.

The Sport engine is Audi's first purpose-designed competition unit of modern times. Audi says boldly: 'Everything possible has been done to the ancillaries to make an engine which, in power, weight, economy and size, is far ahead of any previous high performance engines.' What that means is that the Sport's undersquare 2133cc five cylinder block is 50lb lighter than the old engine's and isn't just Audi's first all-alloy block – it brings new technology to alloy engine

AND THE REVS KEEP RISING

construction by having its alloy cast directly around thin-walled cast iron liners.

The twin-cam all-alloy head is also new for Audi. It's the first cross-flow head for the five-cylinder engine. Its combustion chambers are fashionably compact, with the four valves set at just 25 degrees. And for the first time in a four-valve head, the valves are located asymmetrically. Smaller valve angle apart, this has the advantage of allowing the combustion chamber volume to be concentrated below the exhaust valves (they are parallel with the block's centre line; the inlets are angled outwards at 25 degrees).

The plugs are positioned exactly in the centre of the four valves and, since the distance between the two banks of stems is so small, the camshafts are so close the intake cam is driven directly from the exhaust cam by a pair of helical gears. The double-flow induction system ensures that the same quantities of air and fuel reach each cylinder, and with the throttle valve well forward there's the shortest possible distance to the exceptionally big intercooler that cuts air heated to 140 degrees C at maximum boost down to a mere 60 degrees C. That's one of the main contributors to the power.

The massive exhaust manifold's five branches only merge immediately before entering the turbocharger housing and, with the wastegate also at this point, Audi makes best use of the exhaust gases' energy. Overall, the arrangement of the components is planned to facilitate further development of the engine, so there are very few external differences between the road and rally engines.

The all-electronic LH injection system is a turbo engine first, using a heated wire to measure the air mass and correct for boost pressure, water and air temperature to provide the most efficient mixture at all operating points on the data map. The electronic data programmed ignition system is the one Audi pioneered with the original quattro. The overall engine efficiency and control is so good the compression ratio is 8.0:1 and, together, the mechanical and electronic components result in power levels that would have been considered impossible for road-going engines until very recently. With almost 150bhp per litre, an output previously only matched by racing engines, the road-going Sport powerplant delivers 306bhp at

AUDI SPORT QUATTRO

6800rpm. The rally engine, in its wilder state of tune, lifts the output to 450bhp, and drives through a six-speed transmission.

The drive system is the familiar Audi four-wheel drive layout, with centre and rear differential locks, but strengthened in accordance with rally experience. The suspension – virtually identical at both ends, with lower wishbones, struts, radius rods and very thick anti-roll bars – is also rally-developed, and so are the brakes. Essentially, they're the four-piston, fixed calliper type made by AP Lockheed and used on Porsche racers. The anti-lock system is specially developed for four-wheel drive and, apart from the manual override that rally drivers want, is switched out automatically when the central diff lock is engaged. Otherwise, there can be stability problems.

The Sport is cut down from the four-seat quattro by having 12.6in sliced from its wheelbase and 10.6in from its overall length. This helps make the competition car 600lb lighter than its predecessor but by the time the road-going Sport gets sound deadening and the gamut of cabin niceties that runs to just about everything except, curiously, electric windows, the weight is 2860lb. Except for the doors, the bodywork is either Kevlar or fibreglass reinforced polyester.

In Herr Hagemeister's hands, I gained an initial idea of how well all this came together on the road. The performance was an obvious assumption; the Sport's refinement wasn't. But it shone through the moment the car slipped, docile as a lamb, away from the factory. It could have been anybody's ordinary Audi 80, impressive for a firm but particularly comfortable ride, for the subdued tone of the engine and refinement of the drivetrain, for a lack of fuss that's extraordinary for a car of its Jekyll and Hyde nature.

But when the car was mine, when I dropped Herr Hagemeister back at the works, picked up photographer Ian Dawson and headed north for Nuremberg, the totality of what the Sport really offers on the road began fully to unfold. Your starting point is the delightful discovery that the car is marvellously easy to drive. The engine is entirely fuss-free. It starts promptly, idles evenly, pulls cleanly and is as flexible as it is free-revving. If you stroked the throttle gently, you

AND THE REVS KEEP RISING

might never know it harnesses 300 horses. To go with this docility, the clutch is barely heavier than standard, the gearshift strictly cooking Audi, the steering light and quick and the ergonomics all that are expected from current Audis, with everything within reach. Indeed, the only giveaway in the cabin to the car's ultimate ability is a speedo reading to 300km/h, a tachometer redlined at 7600rpm and the whopping bolsters on the sides of the Recaro seats.

With the engine warm, I tapped up full power in second as we curved around the tight loop taking us out of Ingolstadt and on to the *autobahn*. Just extra loading at the wheel, a trace of Audi's designed-in understeer... and extraordinary cornering speed. In a front-drive car, the nose would have been running wildly wide; in a rear-driven car, even a mid-engined one, the betting would have to be that the tail would have been pushing out. This car just put its power down and raced around the bend. By way of education, I backed off hard. There was just the easiest, gentlest tightening of the nose with the Sport maintaining such poise – though its attitude had changed – that the flick of opposite lock I applied instinctively was entirely unnecessary. Going back on the power, the transition was as gentle and stable the other way. To lose traction altogether, to make the thing slide... how hard would you need to go?

As the *autobahn* speared out ahead of us, I ran it out to the rev limit in second – 84mph – then on through the gears, and grinned as Dawson uttered 'My God! – this is a 2.0-litre engine?' and was pressed back in his seat. Third gave us 122, fourth 144 and, with the road clear enough, the Sport went storming on to well above 150 before I let it settle. What was so pleasing about the delivery of the power was that it came in so smoothly. Rather than going from very little oomph, as in many turbo engines, to an awful lot, all of a sudden, the Sport engine went from smooth flexible torque to great power in a lovely progression. It built smoothly and more powerfully than I'd expected, to around 3900rpm, then started to go harder until, by 4500rpm, it was going very hard indeed, the tachometer needle zinging around to the redline and a watchful eye needed to stop it running hard into the rev limiter.

What was most impressive about the way the car ran at 150-odd was its manifest stability. I can't recall a car more relaxed at this sort of speed. It asked for nothing from me. I took my hands off the wheel and it never deviated from its line. A few minutes later, hands still off again, I pressed hard on the brakes. It was unbelievable. The car sank into the road as if a giant had grabbed its rear bumper. The speedo plummeted, we were pressed against our belts, and Dawson said, accurately, that his eyes felt as if they were being crushed from behind. The speed was lost more rapidly than in any road car I've driven and yet the Sport, braking so hard, just stayed straight and stable. What's more, the pressure needed on the brake pedal was hardly more than steady pressure from the tip of my shoe, and the feel coming back spoke volumes. Finally, down around 60mph or so, there were a couple of pings, like little springs letting go, as the anti-lock released and re-gripped.

It was a revelation. I accelerated hard again and this time kept it going. Seven thousand rpm in fifth: 153mph. Seven two: 157mph. Seven three: 159. Seven four: 161, as easy, as steady, as smooth as you like, with little wind noise and lovely engine thrum. With such stability, and knowledge of the braking power just a toe movement away, it was a snack to cruise so very swiftly. There always seemed more than enough time and distance to clear any Mercedes or Porsche that swung out to pass something slower.

But we soon saw the exit from the *autobahn* that we knew led to a network of lovely little roads running through the Altmühl Valley. A few gearshifts later, the Audi was running along them, eating the miles at an effortless 120 to 130mph. As it had been when full out on the *autobahn*, here, too, it seemed to have such exceptional stability. It allowed me that mental state possible in truly great cars: plenty of time to look and judge and act; to drive cleanly and accurately, fast but not flustered.

When the bends became tighter and closer, the power to sprint between them was one thing; the combination of the stability and the brakes were another – a combination that allowed loads of the power to be used often. Moreover, the quality of the ride meant both comfort and such absorbency that bumps didn't upset the Audi enough to budge it offline. Nor, despite the squat 235/45 VR15

AND THE REVS KEEP RISING

Michelins, did it tramline under brakes. All I had to watch for was deep water, where the wide tyres were liable to aquaplane.

As all this went on, thoughts of the Audi's rather ridiculous stunted body had long since been left behind. Here was a captivating machine that was both sports car and GT, more approachable for a vehicle of its capability than any other. If I wished to nit-pick I might have said that the steering seemed to have rather too strong a pull to the straight ahead in steady-state driving through long bends, making the wrists tired for the first half hour or so. I might also have said that there was no sensuousness to the clutch or the shift; but that would be petty. The shift was too efficient for that.

I found sensuousness in the feel and delicacy of the brakes, quite apart from revelling in their addictive performance. They always seemed to have more to give, and the knowledge that I couldn't lock them and go sliding straight on through a bend was a pleasure in itself. I found sensuousness in the flow of power of the engine, in its sound and its snap in the top third of its rev band. But most of all I found sensuousness in the feel of the chassis. After three hours driving, constantly learning about the Sport quattro and increasingly delighted rather than just surprised by its abilities, I found a tiny, empty road snaking off through a series of forested hills. It wound upwards from the river flats for 10 miles or so, and where the sun hadn't reached beneath the trees it still glistened with damp.

In its approachability and consistency, the Audi had made me feel completely at ease. And now I ran it flat between the bends, and braked into some so hard that the pings duly came from the anti-lock system, then steered for the apex and poured on the power and felt it all go down to the road. It was then, heading for the exits, that the tastiest moments came. The Audi balanced out, the steering going light and delicate and asking for little more than the caress of finger and thumb on the leather rim. Power on, the car swung through its barely detectable understeer to neutrality, with the message conveyed through the seat and the wheel that it was pushing evenly against the outer edges of its front and rear tyres.

The fact was, I was doing very little except obey the golden rule of *slow in, fast out*, but the car was giving me profound pleasure. And

AUDI SPORT QUATTRO

if it wasn't at its limits, it was at what prudence told me should be mine. I knew that Hannu or Michele or Walter Röhl would have switched off the ABS and twitched the car sideways before the bends and gone through in an oversteering swoop, cursing all the while for more power and better engine response. I didn't mind. What I liked was the elegance of the Audi's feel as I braked and cornered and accelerated and wrung great reward from it at a level that suited me. I drove fast, I felt safe and I began to think that if I lived in Switzerland or Austria and wanted to drive swiftly in all weathers, this would probably be the car to have. And when I thought of the body and glanced over my shoulder at the token rear seats, I thought of what Ferdinand Piëch, Audi's R&D chief, had told me a few hours before. Now that Audi has seen – and, I suspect, been seduced by – the level of performance demonstrated by the Sport quattro, it intends to keep a car with at least its capability in the model line-up. But it won't just be a homologation car, and it won't have an exotic two-seater body. It will be what Piëch calls a proper Audi: a full five-seater with room for baggage; a car shaped by the Audi philosophy where form follows function. He says his engineers have found that the four-wheel drive system will easily cope with *twice* the Sport's 300bhp.

I forsook the *autobahn* for the run back to Ingolstadt, driving two hours through the valleys and the forests, and leaving it dangerously late to go on to Munich to catch the plane home to London. I reflected that the promise held out by the original quattro – and I will never forget the week I spent chasing the Monte Carlo Rally in one – now seemed to be greater than ever, and that the friendly character that made the first one so pleasant to drive fast was still present in this, the swiftest four-wheel drive road car yet available. This car, with its technology and its ability, had let me play with it and given me ample reward. And if it all meant what a grinning Piëch hinted it would, there'd be another car on another plateau and the pleasure of driving would go on anew. *The Eagles* cassette went back into the deck, and as the miles slipped beneath our Michelins, I played it over and over again. *So put me on a highway. And show me a sign. And take it to the limit one more time.*

SUMMER'S COMING. TIME TO GO DRIVING
ALFA ROMEO 2000 GT VELOCE
1986

THE SUN CAME OUT the other day, and I walked across the common to the garage where I keep the Alfa. The doors creaked open and there she was: blue, pristine, voluptuous; as lovely as the day she was made. I dabbed the throttle a few times, and the twin-cam fired and settled at once into its perfect idle. I backed her out and left her running while I ran my eyes around her. *What a testimonial to Giorgetto Giugiaro's ability.* This was the 13th car he designed. Extraordinary the way he got the proportions so right, sketched the pillars so delicately, made the tall dip and the lines flow so seductively, created such a classic.

A few years ago, it seemed to me that too many Alfa Romeo GTVs were rusting away and I really should have one to take out when the roads are right. It wasn't just the shape – though I must confess that the idea of having one of the finer fruits from Giugiaro's extraordinarily productive six years at Bertone was bait indeed. The bigger lure was that I kept remembering a series of wonderful drives in GTVs. Every time I tested one – or simply wheedled one from Alfa Romeo on the flimsiest of excuses; they always understood – it became a time of motoring inspiration.

The 1750 and 2000 GTVs seemed to have a sensuality and drivability that transcended performance. In the '70s, their technology was already old and their roadholding on unfashionably narrow tyres was modest, but they seemed to have a measure of the spirit and character to be found in Maseratis, Lamborghinis and Ferraris that's intrinsically Italian.

ALFA ROMEO 2000 GT VELOCE

By taking 27.7sec to reach 100mph, the 2000 GTV was hardly a slouch for a 2.0-litre, though that sort of time looked tame compared with the acceleration of the Italian supercars and the big bore American pony cars. Nevertheless, I'd grown to love the flexibility and the sparkle – the *class* – of Alfa's twin-cam four, to revel in using a gear lever located as if it were an extension of your arm, to delight in the feel of such taut and communicative steering, and to relish the bite and the progressiveness of the twin-booster disc brakes and the way they could be used to tighten the GTV's line into bends. I'd grown to love the way the Alfa sort of jiggled at the rear as it felt its way over the road's surface, a legacy of its well-controlled coil-sprung live axle. I loved the impression of quality as well as character in every aspect of its engineering, and the way that that made the car seem such a partner for the driver in the pursuit of pleasure on the road; the built-in inference that motoring is about something other than covering the ground between two points.

All this reached a climax, I recall, in a long series of bends as I charged home through the mountains of New South Wales to Sydney after a 1000-mile weekend trip in a 2000 GTV. Between the bends, the GTV would nip up through the gears to 100mph or so (77mph in third, 104 in fourth at 6000rpm). It seemed, as a matter of course, just to cock itself perfectly into the comers. Pushing really hard coming in fast under brakes, the nose would hunch down onto the road and press so tightly into the bend that almost no steering lock was necessary. Occasionally, too much braking force, with too much weight on the nose, broke the rear wheels' grip, and the tail would flick out. But mostly, it was merely a matter of balancing the GTV deliciously on the knife-edge between optimal braking force, optimal cornering attitude, and breakaway. Swift pedal work and the location and motion of that peerless gearshift allowed, all the while, a flurry of heel-and-toe downshifts so that the moment the GTV reached the bends' apexes it was in the right gear, ready once more for full throttle.

It seemed to me that this was what driving a sports coupé was all about. It also seemed to me that this ability of the GTV to be

AND THE REVS KEEP RISING

balanced so finely and driven so consistently and sensuously at the very limit of its roadholding, and in a way that brought all the elements of its performance into total harmony, was the nub of the character that made the GTV special.

Contemporaries like the BMW 2002tii were faster from 0–60mph in 8.2sec versus 8.9sec – and had a bit more grip, but the GTV's dynamic qualities were somehow aesthetic. It was urgent, lively, and alive, talking to you every minute of the way through the wheel, the gear lever, the pedals, and, most of all, the seat. I marked it down as having the sort of thoroughbred qualities that are ordinarily much higher-priced; the blend of character and dynamics that is usually the preserve of Ferraris, Lamborghinis, Maseratis, certain Lancias, Lotuses and the Porsche 911.

In the spring of 1981, the GTV seemed to me to have lost none of its grace, and near London I found an immaculate 2000 and bought it: a '72 model, dark metallic blue, 39,000 miles, two owners, properly maintained, apparently carefully driven and garaged most of its life. Here was that old feel again: a car with a charming engine that idled perfectly then revved lustily; steering that, though with a trace of wear, was full of life; brakes that, though slightly down on power, had a lovely feel; a gearshift that, though with a little wear on second's synchromesh, was pure pleasure. My memory had served me correctly.

Now, the roadholding feels dated, but the handling is sufficiently sharp so that when pressed correctly into bends and taken through in a way made possible by its razor-edged balance, it can still dent the pride of hot hatch drivers. On the open road, it's still interesting and satisfying, and, even by today's standards, remarkably stable. But what's so good about the GTV is that it has enough character to put real enjoyment into driving in city traffic. For that reason alone, it's prompted me to drive it in London far more than I had anticipated. Every minute spent in it is a reminder of the spirit and the skill that spawned it.

I wish the steering wasn't quite so heavy, and it's vital to remember to allow far more stopping room than my wife's Saab Turbo needs, for instance. Travelling swiftly is harder work, and

ALFA ROMEO 2000 GT VELOCE

less obviously safe, than covering long distances in the Saab, too. The GTV is best taken out just by its driver. Alone and unhindered, within the GTV's own special time warp, he or she can savour the sensuousness that the car embodies; the flourish that epitomises all that is great about the Italian vision of creating cars. So these next few weekends, now that summer is signalling its coming, I'll be drifting across to the garage, tinkering and polishing and getting the Alfa ready. The roads will soon be right.

RIDING SHOTGUN WITH HANNU MIKKOLA

AUDI SPORT QUATTRO S1

1986

HANNU MIKKOLA DOESN'T SMILE. He just says '*Ready?*' then nods, whacks his foot onto the throttle, and pops the clutch. The Sport quattro S1 erupts like a bronc from a rodeo chute. Its wheels rip into the gravel. In seconds – about *seven!* – it's topping 100mph. It bounds over a crest and, roaring like a hungry lion, charges down the track weaving into the Welsh forest.

The speed is unbelievable. The rate at which we're catapulting through the trees scrambles my senses. The thrust mashes me into my seat as if I'm trapped, helpless, in a runaway rocket blasting inches above the ground. Through the blur, all I can see are the pine trunks crowding the track and, where they thin, the steepness of the bank dropping away. Blind fear takes over. My panicked brain screams that it's impossible to drive so fast down a forest trail. Don't let this be the day the quattro breaks or Mikkola makes a mistake.

Him? He's just sitting there, tight in his harness, tweaking the wheel this way and that in precise little movements; snaking a hand out to snap the lever up or down the six-speed gearbox; dancing his left foot over the clutch and brake pedals; dabbing the throttle with his right. His face is impassive, a mask of concentration, his eyes reading every inch of the road.

Driving against the clock, he's looking always to unleash the quattro's potential. Every instant, every yard where there's a chance, he gives the 500 horsepower its head. The response is phenomenal: blasting from 4000 to the maximum 8500revs in each gear takes barely a second. In moments, on the shortest straights,

AUDI SPORT QUATTRO S1

we're shooting up to the 120mph maximum that the Audi is set to run in these conditions.

For many of the corners, he slows earlier than you might expect – then tweaks the car sideways. He does it by upsetting the stability with a quick flick of the wheel while simultaneously braking with his left foot and keeping the throttle on with his right. With the car 'cocked' for the bend, he balances the drift – often at well upwards of 100mph – with the throttle and steering, constantly adjusting both, within milliseconds, as he controls the slide. By mid-bend he's applying full power, exploiting the four-wheel-drive advantage. Lord, this thing is so fast through the bends and so bullet-like out of them.

For one tight blind bend, Mikkola treads hard on the brakes as he whips down through the gearbox. The deceleration is as ferocious as the acceleration, flinging me forward until the belts cut into my shoulders and my eyes feel as if they'll pop out of their sockets. The instant he's slow enough, Hannu is back on the power, the engine snarling in a new burst, and we're sliding again, the nose tucked in so tight it's almost scraping the bank on the inside, while the tail's out under the branches and over the drop on the outside. A mistake with steering or power and we're dead.

My senses are still reeling as we charge full-tilt along a semi-straightaway cut across the mountain face. Just before a kink where Mikkola will get sideways again, the trunk of a fallen tree juts up above the track. Its tip is level with my head. The trunk seems to hang in slow motion, waiting to smash through the windscreen. I feel the blood drain from my face. Mikkola doesn't let up. An instant before disaster, he tweaks the Audi into a 100mph slide and pokes its nose under the trunk. The tree passes six inches above the bonnet and clears the windscreen by three or four.

Ahead, the track is breaking up into a jagged mass of loose slate. It *must* rip the tyres to shreds. We charge on. The car doesn't waver as it tears across the busted slate. Here, as on some of the other rough sections we've blasted through, the Audi's ride comfort is remarkable. There is none of the dreadful crashing you might expect; just a jiggling that conveys tautness. It feels like a car that

AND THE REVS KEEP RISING

will do precisely as its driver asks, within fractions of a second, without jarring.

But the noise! The engine's snarl, rising and falling as Hannu constantly goes on and off the power, up and down the gears, is wicked. Stones blast the underbody. Frequently, branches smash against the nose and flanks as he tucks the car beneath the pines. The accuracy with which he places the car, time after time, makes you want to gasp. At the end of the longest straight, we're full chat, and he flicks the S1 sideways and takes it, still flat, across a kink where the track ducks into a pleat in the mountainside. The outer front wheel is over the precipice; it rejoins the track precisely where he wants it for the next manoeuvre, and all at 120mph. This is to witness, from inches away, a top sportsman walking the tightrope.

As suddenly as it does everything else, the track dives sharp right between stacks of freshly cut timber. The gap seems barely wide enough. Hannu brakes hard, weaving a little, puts the car sideways precisely the right amount, and sweeps through hard on the power. At 60mph there are inches to spare. Now it's full tilt through the gears again, in a charge up the short hill to the tape indicating the end of the section.

'It is over,' he says matter-of-factly on the headset. I look at my stopwatch. Just under six minutes for just on seven miles of this slippery, treacherous forest track. We have averaged 70mph.

But back at the encampment, where the mechanics' van and a smattering of quattro saloons are arrayed around a clearing, Mikkola isn't entirely satisfied. At 500bhp, the engine response is too much for the loose surface. Even with four-wheel drive in its latest, leading-edge form, he's getting slippage and having to lift off, he tells development engineer Dieter Basche. I hadn't noticed. Willy, the chief mechanic, goes to the van to get a smaller turbocharger.

For a week, Hannu, Dieter, Willy, and three more mechanics have been in Dyfi Forest developing the quattro S1 as part of the programme for the 1986 rally season. They've worked through a selection of suspension options, trying first one spring and damper combination, then another. Finally, Mikkola and Dieter, who rides with him on each test circuit of the course, are happy with the way

AUDI SPORT QUATTRO S1

the car is sitting on the road. They work as a team, Hannu relaying his views of the car's performance and Dieter co-ordinating it with his engineer's knowledge, as well as with what his backside tells him.

They've sorted out a new ultra-high-performance braking system made by the English company Alcon. The temperature tags on the brakes have been reading 650 degrees Centigrade: red-hot. In days, the brake maker's engineers have come up with pads that give Mikkola the feel and braking power he wants. 'Getting pads that can withstand constant left-foot braking while you've got 500 horsepower charging hard is a hell of a challenge,' says one of the young engineers. 'But we've done it now.' Hannu nods. 'Yes, the brakes are terrific,' he says.

They've spent days on one of the most difficult tasks of all – evaluating new centre and rear differentials, which split the torque to the front and rear wheels in various ways and lock up with different degrees of progression. At the level of sophistication that four-wheel-drive rally cars have reached, the split and progression are crucial to handling balance, not just grip. Working painstakingly, logging and comparing the results through Dieter's little computer, they decide first on the centre diff and then, after another two days' work, the rear diff. The mechanics are so adept that they get the diffs in and out and send Mikkola off on another blistering circuit within 29 minutes. At last, Hannu is happy with the handling. As we finish our circuit and trundle back to base he says: 'The balance is very good now. I can start to go very fast.'

Now there's just the engine to finalise, to bring into line with the drivetrain and the suspension settings for these sorts of loose surfaces. To cut the power and temper the five-cylinder engine's response, Dieter tells his mechanics to mount a smaller turbocharger and a different Motronic engine management system. Mikkola wants power – now it will be around 460bhp instead of 500 – but doesn't want it developing so fast that it sets the wheels spinning mid-bend, forcing him to lift off, wasting time.

While Willy and the boys work, Mikkola takes a 90 quattro and drives the circuit, slowly, checking the surface. His lines in the S1 are etched into the track's dirt and gravel as if a huge vacuum cleaner

AND THE REVS KEEP RISING

has sucked off the top few inches along two perfectly flowing tracks, clean and neat as a railway line. Before the bends the tracks swerve out and then in, where he's tweaked the car sideways.

'Rally driving is a bit like downhill ski racing,' he says. 'We have to take similar lines through the bends, turning before the corner so we can accelerate into the next bend earlier. Skiers use their bodies; we use the wheel and the throttle.

'To win in rallying, you have to be very single-minded. Most of all you need the will to win, often against great pressures when things aren't going right. You need the gift, obviously, but you need very fast reactions, and you must have balance; to be able to feel what the car is doing. When I'm driving fast, and it all goes the way I like it, that's a wonderful feeling.'

But spending weeks testing in some remote forest, trying something and failing, then waiting while the mechanics pull the car apart – the drudgery behind the scenes – seems almost excruciatingly tedious. In 1985, Mikkola spent almost 40 days out testing. His colleague Walter Röhrl stayed similarly long in the forests too.

'Sure, I'd rather be with my family in Finland or Florida. But if you want to win, you have to do it; you have to get the edge on the other cars and the other teams. It becomes enjoyable when you see that you can make the car better and faster, so that it's not just the driver who makes the difference.

'Because the layout of the S1 is so similar to that of the road Audis, I also like to know that the work we're doing is valuable to customers. This is a very quick way to develop new systems and components. If we can use them in the production cars, it justifies the money we're spending. One of the new differentials we've been developing is likely to go into other quattros.

'And although this new S1 is a long way on from the original quattros we rallied – the big wings give terrific stability, the response from the new turbo engines is now incredibly quick, and the handling is in a different league – there's a long way we can still go.

'While the 500bhp we've achieved now can be too much for really

AUDI SPORT QUATTRO S1

slippery surfaces, I think we'll get to 600bhp before we reach four-wheel drive's limits. That's going to be very interesting. With our current performance, the cars are very challenging to drive. They're so fast, you have to concentrate really hard every inch of the way.'

Dieter Basche, who has to ride with Hannu as he pushes the quattro day in, day out, during testing, shows visible signs of stress near the end of the session. 'Sometimes,' Dieter says, 'when I reflect on how fast we're going and what could happen if something broke or Hannu made a mistake, I have to force myself into the car. The speeds are so high now that even some of the seasoned navigators are admitting to being scared.

'But we're determined to keep on winning rallies, and I have a job to do. So I get in and, like Hannu, just concentrate on how the particular component we're evaluating is performing. In the end, it's worth it.'

Willy signals that the car is ready again. Hannu and Dieter don their headsets, Dieter sets his computer, and they strap themselves into the flimsy-bodied beast. The engine snaps into life and idles with a sound as guttural as a World War I fighter plane. Mikkola runs an eye around the cabin while the engine warms. He has gauges that cover everything from fuel, oil and turbo boost pressure to engine, gearbox, and differential temperature. There's a speedometer, of course, so that the drivers can keep an eye on speeds on public roads between stages.

But the main instrument, easiest to see, is the tachometer, reading all the way to 9000rpm. Across the centre of the dash are a mass of fuses, and ahead of the passenger – in rallies, the navigator, of course – the radio equipment and the computer for plotting times, speeds, and distances.

Hannu decides that all is well. In a few moments, the S1 is belting around the mountain in the evening light, its roar rolling through the valleys like thunder. You can *hear* the eagerness of the engine. This time, though, those curious fluttery whistles of the wastegate dumping the excess boost are less frequent; Mikkola isn't backing off as much. Six minutes later, Hannu and Dieter climb out grinning. 'It's perfect now,' says Hannu. 'I can *drive* it now. Let's go home.'

LEARNING TO LOVE THE 911
PORSCHE 911 CARRERA
1986

FROM THE UPSTAIRS WINDOW I could see the sun coming pale over the downs, stripping back the mist. I finished feeding the baby. She gurgled happily in her cot while I tugged on some jeans, reached for my old Eddie Bauer goosedown, and tiptoed past my sleeping wife.

The Porsche was in the barn. I should have left it there and gone back to bed, but the day and the place and the opportunity were too inviting. We were on a friend's farm in Wiltshire, the beginning of the West Country, my favourite part of England, where the roads wind over the downs and, on the lowlands, dash between the cream stone towns.

So I heaved up the great roller barn door and felt a tingle as I saw the 911, rampant red between the combine harvester and the farm's Peugeot estate car. The key turned *thunk* in the door lock; the engine churned just three or four times before it snapped into life and settled into its distinctive, thrilling rumble. The messages were clear: quality, power, character.

Down the long gravel drive and onto the highway, as I savoured the ritual of changing gears slowly and running the revs carefully and watching the oil temperature gauge begin to climb, I began to think about the way my attitude toward the standard Porsche 911 had changed. Seven years ago I had said stridently that I wouldn't care to own one. It was mostly to do with wariness of the handling at the limit. With the tail hunched down under the power, the grip was inspiring. But I didn't like feeling that I had to keep a constant guard against misreading a bend, coming in too fast, and having to back off abruptly. On Porsche's Weissach skid pad, I'd learned

PORSCHE 911 CARRERA

how swiftly the 911 of the late '70s snapped into a spin when you did that. There was also the worry of entering a wet downhill bend and, with alarmingly little provocation or warning, having the front brakes lock up so that you slid straight on. And I didn't much like the 911's nervousness at speed. It seemed to suggest an inherent instability that, no matter how well the engineers had overcome the flaws of the rear-engined layout, revealed that it was a rather tortuously balanced compromise. All this induced in me a touch of paranoia: if I drove a 911 often enough, would it get me in the end?

Now, here I was, warming up this 1986 Carrera, itching to get going and, after a splendid week at the wheel, trying to find a reason not to buy one; weighing it against the 928S I'd been trying a few weeks earlier and deciding in favour of the 911… the sports car rather than the high-performance tool.

What shifted my position so radically? Well, my views and priorities have changed. So has the 911. I've watched intrigued as Porsche's engineers have gone on honing the 911 ever brighter, with its deficiencies decreasing in direct proportion to its desirability. It's less nervous in a straight line, the grip is more tenacious, the handling is more consistent; even the heater works reasonably well, at last. Moreover, where I once placed more value on the greater roadability of the Ferrari 308, the Lamborghini Urraco, the Maserati Merak, and the Lotus Esprit Turbo, I now need the greater utility and versatility of the Porsche for every day life in a city like London. This one had even passed the test of taking man, wife, baby, and necessary paraphernalia, away for the weekend.

Now the engine was warm, and on roads I knew well, I let the car go. Open up a car that tosses off 14-second standing quarter miles and is doing 120mph in 21sec and you *move*. With 3.2 litres of Porsche flat six you also get stirring response in every gear. A cruise at 90 to 100mph in fourth, with the revs smack on the torque peak, is quick enough to be interesting, slow enough to leave plenty of safety in hand. In fast bends, the engineered-in understeer called for real effort at the wheel until, at the apex, I could crank on the power, pressing the tail down and neutralising the handling to

AND THE REVS KEEP RISING

zing out fast. This was classic, glorious 911 motoring. For the tight bends, the meaty brakes needed a hefty push but bit hard and fast, and the shift worked neatly if not really pleasantly to get me down from fourth to second and ready for the same potent blast out into the clear. Slow in, fast out

On a couple of the longer straights, that 231bhp showed what it could do, the car feeling lively but not nervous, as 911s did in the past. All the while, there was that lovely hewn-from-the-solid feel that *is* the 911. The feeling that your involvement with the car is very physical. That it's small but nuggety. That you have to push it and watch it because in character it's a sports car of the old-fashioned kind. And of course I had the noise, which is like nothing any other car possesses: the whine of the air-cooling fan, then the basso profundo from the exhaust.

So I dashed through Wiltshire as the day came up. I ran into a patch of rain as I came down from the hills, but so long as I didn't try to use all the roadholding on the way into the bends, the 911 still romped along as swiftly as it had in the dry. Even in the wet, I had difficulty making the tail break away with power. When it did, it went quickly but nicely, caught readily enough by a swift wrap of opposite lock.

By the time a few West Country men had started to dribble out onto the roads, I'd had a wonderful time: the classic Sunday morning in one of the world's best sports cars. But then, as I stopped concentrating, I learned that the 911 still had something in store for me. I wafted too fast toward a corner and, on a still-wet road, pushed the brakes too hard too fast. They locked and I slid and had to get off them to get my steering back. The way out was to overshoot the ideal line and run embarrassingly wide. I drove on, amazed at how easily I'd been lulled into thinking I was going slowly and then been caught. Why hasn't Porsche given the 911 anti-lock brakes?

I concentrated anew and drove the last 20 miles hard, then sat down to breakfast a satisfied man. I'd had a glorious balance of challenge and reward, with the Carrera never making any bones about what it was or how I should handle it. And it wasn't my

PORSCHE 911 CARRERA

moment, when I locked the brakes and slid, that made me decide, two weeks later, to look beyond a 911 for my next car. The decision was swung by the need for more space, more refinement and a feeling I'd been harbouring for some time that my next car really should have four-wheel drive and anti-lock brakes. So my Audi quattro arrives soon – but every time I see a 911 I'll praise its owner and long a little bit.

A GATHERING OF HORSES
FERRARI BB 512 AND 365 GTC/4
1986

WE MET AT THE manor house in Oxfordshire at eight, quaffed a quick cup of tea, and then strode across to the garage and took out the Ferraris. The Boxer fired with that guttural thunder that always sends a chill down your spine. The GTC sang into life just as willingly, but with a lighter, more melodic tone – the classic sound of a 4.4-litre V12 Ferrari against that of the 5.0-litre flat-12, but both quite magnificent; both soul-stirring appetisers for the day ahead.

For me, it was to be a welcome return to two of my favourite Ferraris. For my friend David McLaren it was to be a day out with the cars that hold pride of place in his garage. For both of us – skipping work like naughty schoolboys – it was an occasion. We were taking David's BB 512 and 365 GTC/4 to the annual Ferrari day at Hampshire's Thruxton racing circuit, an unmissable event for a lot of people.

Both of us knew, too, that while lapping the fast and interesting Thruxton would be entertaining, the highlight would be the 100-mile thrash there and back, swapping mounts and enjoying the different challenges and pleasures of a front-engined Ferrari V12 of the old school and a mid-engined flat-12 of later days. We could have used motorways but, while David leaned over the Boxer fixing a sticky slow-running jet, I pored over maps on the kitchen table, planning a route that linked one interesting back road to another.

David chose the Boxer first, and I wasn't surprised. It's his toy, a Sunday morning car that won't accommodate the kids; a no holds barred two-seater that spells *excitement*. However, as I climbed happily into the two-plus-two 365 GTC/4, I knew it wouldn't be long before David stopped to change over. This 1973 GTC with 66,000 on

FERRARI BB 512 AND 365 GTC/4

the clock occupies a special niche in his affections. It served him faithfully for several years, dealing daily with a London commute and then making unadulterated pleasure of Friday night dashes to the country. Now retired, resprayed, re-braked, re-bushed, and resplendent, it's a gracious older lady – a fine example of a Ferrari that was overshadowed in its heyday by its mechanically similar but more glamorous two-seater sister, the Daytona, although it's being increasingly recognised as one of the finest two-plus-two GTs to emerge from Maranello. Many see it as a more rounded, more usable car than the Daytona.

As David got the Boxer cracking along roads he knew well, the GTC swiftly began to make its point. It wasn't going to be left behind. The fact is, with its V12 tuned only slightly softer than the 174mph Daytona's, it has the same 340bhp as the Boxer. With 61, 90, 110 and 130mph coming up in the gears at 7500rpm and a top end in fifth of 155mph, the GTC is still a very quick old dear indeed.

Easy to drive, too, I was soon reminded; rather like a Daytona in balance, but softer, tamer, less urgent. I remembered the impressive ride quality, the light and reassuring power-assisted steering (now with just a little wear-induced slackness around the straight ahead), the unhindered vision. I also enjoyed again the crispness of the GTCs traditionally mounted gearbox, working so perfectly with the V12. And that engine! Here was all the legendary flexibility and smoothness as well as enticing performance. From anywhere above an idle, it delivered a clean surge of power, pulling strong and fast and yowling high into the rev band so eagerly I had to keep a close watch on the tachometer for fear of sailing beyond the 7500rpm warning zone.

The combination of that refined drivetrain, the fluid steering, the glorious brakes, and the suppleness of the suspension made this 3900lb coupé seem anything but heavy – an agile, easy-to-manage car. I had no qualms about trying to stick to the flying Boxer's tail. When we really began to press on, using all the power out of the bends, the GTC tightened up as only a good front-engine, rear-drive car can do, swinging delectably into oversteer that could be balanced by the throttle and a tweak of opposite lock. With its roadholding

AND THE REVS KEEP RISING

limits lower than the Boxer – lower than many fast modern cars – the GTC was running on its handling. Me? I was having to *drive*.

But as quick as the GTC felt, the Boxer, when we swapped, seemed to be from another performance league altogether. There was a harder, beefier, more potent edge to the engine's response and character, reminding me that, even in comparison with a great V12, Ferrari's flat-12 is truly remarkable. It delivers such a whack of power down low and then, around 4000rpm, leaps onto the cams and pelts you back into your seat. The BB felt much more immediate overall, more intimidating – perhaps because you're aware of that stupendous engine so close behind you and because you see little more than the road in front. It was so different in the bends too, pushing into quite strong understeer that called for more of a slow-in, fast-out approach, then hunkering down over the rear wheels and neutralising when the power came on.

Like this, even with all the power on, it seemed nigh impossible to unstick the Boxer's tail on a dry road. As always though, I remembered that if I did, I'd better catch it damned quick or the vast rearward weight of the engine and transmission would have me in a spin without further ado. It didn't arise. I just stormed on, more invigorated in the BB than in the now sedate-seeming GTC, and gloried in the gutsy way the Boxer goes about things. This harder-sprung, more purposeful car came into its own at very high speed. Where the GTC might begin to move about on an undulating stretch as speeds increased, the Boxer felt fit to storm on, with much in hand, to something well upwards of the 160 I'd experienced in them many times before. Where the GTC engendered affection, the Boxer engendered respect.

We arrived at the track glowing with the pleasure of our oh-so-fast 100 miles on those lovely weaving roads. After that, I wasn't too fussed about putting in too many laps on the circuit, and, while David pushed on enjoying his cars at the limit, I wandered amid hundreds of equally pristine Ferraris, chatted here and there, and pondered the delights of the drive home.

BOLD, REGAL, ELEGANT, GRACEFUL – AND RAPID

BENTLEY 'R' TYPE CONTINENTAL
1987

WE HAD JUST PARKED the car in a square in Kensington, London, when a moustachioed American walked up, ran his hand along the mudguard's sultry curve, and said: 'I've got a couple of nice cars back home. Jaguars. What's this? It's *pretty.*' He was told it was a 1955 Bentley 'R' Type Continental with bodywork by HJ Mulliner, good for 119mph, and the fastest and most expensive production four-seater of its day; and, in answer to his next question, that it was worth $65,000 at today's exchange rates

What its owner, 46-year-old Peter Frankel, didn't mention was that he drives his Bentley Continental, one of 208 made between June 1952 and May 1955, every day. It takes him through central London to be parked outside his dental surgery, and on weekends down the motorway to Wiltshire. With 236,000 miles on the clock, it cruises comfortably at 90mph and will still show 120. 'I see no reason to have a new car,' Peter said, in his quiet way, when we adjourned to the pub for a couple of Sunday lunchtime pints. 'I had a Flying Spur, which was awful above 90mph. But in the six years I've had this Bentley, it has made my motoring particularly pleasing. For all its luxury, this car has given me back a sports car experience and I don't think I shall ever sell it.'

He isn't alone in his attachment. Briggs Cunningham is among four owners who still have Continentals they bought new. According to Stanley Sedgwick's booklet (published by the Bentley Drivers Club), other buyers drawn to the Continental included A Onassis, S Niarchos, the emperor of Bao-Dai, the Princess of Berar, Comte de

AND THE REVS KEEP RISING

Villapadierna, Lord Carnegie, Donald Campbell, Prince Frederick of Prussia, Marquis du Vivier, and the Shah of Iran.

The Continental's attraction is understandable. HIF Evernden, who led the project and designed the Continental with Rolls-Royce's stylist JP Blatchley, says in Sedgwick's book that the car 'was evolved not only to look beautiful, but to exhibit those characteristics that appeal to the connoisseur of motoring: a high maximum road speed coupled with a correspondingly high rate of acceleration, together with excellent handling and "roadability".'

Tyres to carry a two-ton car at 120mph didn't exist in 1950, so the weight had to be kept below 3800lb to allow sustained speeds around 115mph. Bentley asked the London coachbuilder HJ Mulliner to make the body entirely in light alloy. Even the front seat frames were alloy; handily, so was the engine – 4566cc for the first 126 Continentals, and 4887cc for the last 82.

Superior aerodynamics were an important partner for the reduced weight. A scale model spent a long time in the Rolls-Royce aero division's wind tunnel. 'Tests were made,' says Mr Evernden, 'not only to establish the air drag, but also to study the effects of yawing and side winds. In this latter respect, a form of fin on the rear wings can add a useful restoring force.'

So the immensely beautiful bodywork flows back from the stately radiator and swoops between the finned rear wings that Evernden's engineers developed in the wind tunnel. It looks *fast:* bold and regal, elegant and graceful. Many times, when I've been passing Peter Frankel's dental surgery in Knightsbridge, I've stopped to admire his Continental. At least once a week, someone leaves a note asking if he'll sell. Other messages say how wonderful it is to see the car being kept on the road.

I wondered how hard it might be to drive this 32-year-old mass of alloy –more than 17ft long and almost 6ft high – in London's traffic, day in and day out. Luckily, the Continental is narrow and, because you sit up high, you can sight clearly down the long bonnet, with the crisp edges of the wings showing you where the sides are. What took me the longest to become used to was the weight of the cam-and-roller steering: you need to take a good grip on the big three-

BENTLEY 'R' TYPE CONTINENTAL

spoke wheel and heft it around. Well before the bend, too, because the Continental is slow to answer the helm by today's standards, and initially it understeers strongly.

Once we were out on the open roads of Berkshire and I was in tune with the car's character, I found it easy to cruise at 60 or 70mph on wet roads. I soon took the steering effort for granted. Given early turn-in, the Bentley sailed securely through the bends. From the passenger's seat, it had felt as if it might sway into roll oversteer. But it clung well, and, although I was always aware of its old-fashioned height, I quickly felt relaxed and confident, without having to move the lever on the steering wheel to adjust the rear shock damping from soft to hard. The nicest thing I discovered was the lightness, the responsiveness, and the power of the drum brakes.

Peter's car has a four-speed automatic transmission instead of the standard four-speed manual. It worked briskly and smoothly, and its manual downshift from top to third was ideal for maintaining pace through the bends and up the hills. In a 1952 road test, *The Autocar* magazine quoted a 0–60mph time of 13.5sec and a standing quarter-mile in 19.5sec. That's not stunning today. But what's impressive about the Continental is the torque. There's a rasp from the big in-line six then it winds the car forward and keeps the momentum going. This car doesn't feel particularly fast; it just feels relentless.

On the motorway, I saw what Peter meant about the car's touring prowess. It surged smoothly into the traffic and took its place among the quicker cars, settling happily into a cruise at around 90mph, with a remarkable lack of engine noise and not much road or wind noise. Sitting behind classic instruments set into a finely worked wooden dashboard and being ensconced in a cabin trimmed beautifully in grey hide completed the impression of motoring in an altogether superior manner. The car's quality transcended its age, and by the time we stopped, I understood why Peter Frankel hefts it through the traffic every day – and why Stanley Sedgwick says the Continental is the most worthwhile car to come from Crewe in the post-war years.

AS DIFFERENT AS THEY COME
CITROËN SM
1987

WHILE I WAS TESTING a group of high performance cars with different drivetrain layouts – front engined, front engined with rear transaxle, mid-engined – it occurred to me that there wasn't a front-wheel-drive exotic I could have included. I started thinking wistfully of a front-drive coupé that, for a few years in the '70s, had stood tall among the swiftest and most desirable cars.

It was the Citroën SM – quirky, complicated, unique, and effective. If you came to grips with it, chances are it left an indelible mark on you. I called Martyn Goddard, my photographer friend, who has had an SM for seven years. He picked me up at six the next morning, and we went driving.

The SM emerged in 1970 as the expression of Citroën's long-held desire to build a true grand touring car that would carry the honour of France. The Citroën engineers had a clear vision – yet the SM really only happened because Citroën, who'd rather rashly bought Maserati in 1968, needed to show off the benefits of the deal. The Parisians asked Maserati for an engine, quickly. In just *three weeks*, Ingegnere Giulio Alfieri gave them an all-alloy V6. It was derived from the 4.1-litre V8, and it delivered 200bhp.

The SM was unveiled two years later. In production, the new 2673cc Maserati V6 was tuned for 170bhp at 5500rpm. The transaxle was mounted ahead of it, putting the engine well behind the front wheel line. The necessarily-long nose also housed a vast array of hydraulics running the suspension, brakes, and remarkable new Varipower steering. Across the long nose, glass fairings

CITROËN SM

shielded the swivelling and self-levelling headlights, making a powerful contribution to the aerodynamics. In plan view, the SM was like a teardrop, with the rear track narrower than the front. The only semblance of a spoiler was a kicked-up lip on the trailing edge of the boot lid. Wind tunnel tests on scale models gave a Cd of 0.25. The production cars read 0.32, still outstanding at the time. Apart from springing and damping, hydro-pneumatic spheres took care of self-levelling and ride height adjustment. The system had been well proven in the great Citroën DS. The steering was more revolutionary: fully powered with an artificial feel system loaded according to car speed and front wheel angle, and so fast there were only two turns lock to lock.

The car was a sensation, of course. The incredibly quick steering, push-button brakes, and massively complicated engineering terrified some people as much as delighting others. With 170bhp pulling 3200lb, the 16ft Citroën was no roadburner. Nought to 60mph took 8.9sec. But its aerodynamics let it run to 135mph in effortless and relaxed style. Rightly, the SM was hailed as a superlative grand tourer, happy to cruise all day at 120mph.

But it was doomed. Citroën had high hopes for success in the US but the company lacked the necessary service backup. Sales initially flourished in Europe then slowed and collapsed with the 1973 fuel crisis. Peugeot took over bankrupt Citroën at the end of 1974, and its profit-focussed accountants soon killed the SM. Fewer than 20,000 SMs had been built; 2037 had gone to America

Just getting back into an SM made me smile. The steering wheel is small and elliptical, the instruments are oval, and the facia swoops across the car like an eccentric sculpture. Getting comfortable was never difficult in the SM: the wheel adjusted for height and reach, and the seats were superbly shaped. The engine was a bit of a surprise: rougher and more agricultural than I remembered, although, as a 90-degree V6, it was never all that smooth. Still, it made a nice sound as we accelerated out of London, and it never turned rougher as the SM started nibbling the motorway. Its qualities were clear – unerring stability, magic carpet ride, and great refinement. This 15-year-old car was whisking us west in a manner still relatively rare.

AND THE REVS KEEP RISING

When we swung off the M4 and sallied forth into the Marlborough Downs in Wiltshire, the car's limitations joined its virtues. It hadn't taken long to readjust to the extraordinarily quick steering – first time, you usually run off one side of the road, correct, and then go off the other – and to enjoy merely having to nudge the wheel a quarter of an inch, or maybe half, to flow through most bends. There was that old feeling of simply 'thinking' the car along. While the bends stayed open, the SM stayed superb. But when they tightened, and were still wet from the melting frost, the nose slid wide if the car came in only a little too fast. Too much power too soon brought instant loss of traction, and if the bend was really tight, the inside wheel lifted and spun. Here was the downside of front-wheel drive, even from such masters as Citroën. These are the things that limit its use in high-performance cars. Ess-bends showed up the SM's own worst foibles, such as the way it lurched from rolling hard one way to rolling hard the other as the body tried to keep up with the steering. In the wet, the hugely powerful brakes, activated merely by toe pressure on a mushroom-like pad on the floor, needed caution to avoid lockup.

So, rather than try to push hard along narrow roads, I took it comparatively slowly until we were back on more open highways, and then let the car spear along in the refined way it liked best. Then it was magnificent, the front-wheel drive working beautifully with the aerodynamics to maintain exceptional stability.

It made me feel I could go on driving all day and all night. 'I love it most when I go to Scotland and back,' said Martyn, 'or through France to Germany.'

In time, the SM's rivals became faster and faster. We can only wonder what might have been if Citroën had continued the SM's development. Could it have given the car more power and still transmitted it to the road effectively? Even so, with the SM's qualities as a grand tourer still impressive today, Citroën made the point it set out to make.

GERMAN GROOM, ITALIAN BRIDE, TALENTED OFFSPRING

BMW M1

1987

IT WASN'T THE RIGHT sort of weather for a 160mph supercar. Worse, we were pressing along England's busiest motorway, the M1, with four hours to go before we could peel off into the loneliness of the North Yorkshire Moors. But the gales and the traffic, the constant hazards of a teeming motorway blighted by road works, weren't flustering the car at all. This squat two-seater, BMW's classic mid-engined M1, was flowing effortlessly through the rain, wind and road works. It purred silkily, letting us chatter and listen to the radio's warnings of even nastier weather ahead.

Soon after I had started driving it – after I'd adjusted to the restricted vision usual in mid-engined cars – the M1 had started suggesting that it would be as sweet as I knew it was fast. On this streaming-wet Monday morning, it was remarkably easy to handle, given its layout and, especially, that it was conceived as a race car. Logic said it would be unwise to brake hard on the glistening roads, where the BMW was likely to share the mid-engined cars' familiar Achilles' heel of locking up the front wheels. Otherwise, it let me settle into a well-laid-out cabin with clear instruments and easily reached controls. It let me work with a light clutch, an undemanding gearshift, and a fuss-free engine.

In and out of slippery roundabouts, the chassis soon relayed the glad news that it was free from delinquent tendencies. Its nose gripped staunchly, it turned in cleanly, and its tail clung on

AND THE REVS KEEP RISING

doggedly whenever I could let the 3.5-litre engine run well up into its rev band.

The point was made all too clearly at a Porsche 911 Turbo's expense. Out of one junction, I prodded the 277bhp six heftily to exploit a gap in the traffic. Hard on the BMW's tail, the Porsche driver did the same. Perhaps he was intent on powering past to show where German supercar prowess lay. It seemed a neat enough match, too: 300bhp and 0–60mph in 5.3sec for the Porsche, 277bhp and 5.6sec for the BMW. But, as the M1 stormed out of the turn and its tail slid out neatly, it asked for just a dab of opposite lock and a little moderation of the throttle. In the mirror, I saw the Porsche's tail come lunging right around – and the startled look on its driver's face. The 911 flicked back the other way, then fishtailed. Chastened, its driver slowed, dropped back and stayed there. The BMW flowed on.

By the time our M1 had wound through the outer London traffic to the M1 motorway, photographer Colin Curwood and I were at ease in a race-inspired exotic that felt remarkably unintimidating, despite weather more suited to a Range Rover. As the Pirelli P7s sliced northward through the water, we had the satisfying feeling that we could drive on and on if we wished – beyond Yorkshire, beyond England, right to the roof of Scotland.

When we had put 120 miles or so behind us, the traffic thinned and we loped and enjoyed the BMW's comforting stability in the crosswinds as well as its quietness and ride comfort. Occasionally, I pressed the throttle through more of its long travel, felt the lusty six's muscles flex, heard its wail deepen and let the speed run up. The steadiness remained, and the quietness too.

There are clear reasons why, despite having been conceived as a race car, the BMW M1 ended up as one of the most civilised mid-engined road cars. They are the same reasons that nearly killed it before it was ready to be raced or sold. First, the fact that the M1's body was designed to BMW Motorsport's brief by Giorgetto Giugiaro. Second, Lamborghini engineered its chassis. And third, its final development was done unexpectedly back home in Munich because Lamborghini had gone broke and couldn't see the project through.

BMW M1

When BMW started the M1 project in the mid-1970s it wanted a purpose-designed race car that could take up the battle its front-engined CSL had lost, after a strong initial showing, to the Porsche 935 in the Group 5 'Silhouette' formula. With more than 800bhp from the twin-turbo version of the 3.5-litre twin-cam six, BMW had proved the engine. What it needed was a mid-engined chassis that could deploy it to best advantage. In tamer tune, the purpose-built racing car could also run in Group 4. The homologation rules called for a minimum of 400 cars to be built over two years. If the race car had an in-line six mounted amidships, then all the rest had to have the same layout and body shape. The boss of the then-new BMW Motorsport division, Jochen Neerpasch, formulated a plan.

He didn't have small-volume design or construction facilities in Munich so he went to Italy. Giugiaro's Ital Design team gave him an aerodynamically clever body, linked visually with the pretty Turbo show car BMW had experimented with early in the '70s. Lamborghini's job was to engineer the chassis, do all the development, then build and deliver the 400-odd road cars. Gian Paolo Dallara, the suspension wizard responsible for the Miura and Countach and, later, innumerable racing cars, was among the Lamborghini engineers working with BMW's team on the chassis design. He was back at Sant'Agata Bolognese as a consultant. Dallara had developed some clever theories for getting the best from the Pirelli P7 tyre and was starting to develop the fine suspension of the Countach S. The M1 joined the programme, and the two suspensions were developed in parallel.

BMW decided that the M1's base specification should be the 470bhp Group 4 format, with the ultimate turbocharged 850bhp Group 5 racer soaring off in one direction and the road car in the other. The chassis – complex, but simpler than the Countach's – was fabricated from steel tubing and sheet. The suspension, engineered around 205/55 and 225/50VR-16 Pirelli P7s on aerodynamic Campagnolo wheels, was typical of both race car and Modenese road car practice: alloy hub carriers located by unequal length wishbones, adjustable coil springs encircling adjustable Bilstein dampers, with lots of anti-dive and anti-squat geometry.

AND THE REVS KEEP RISING

The unstressed fibreglass body panels were riveted and glued to the frame.

The engine – the origin of the 24-valve powerplant that would do such impressive service in the BMW M5 saloon and M635CSi coupé – was based on the 3.5-litre six from the 635CSi, but developed to a point where the two had little in common. The 93.4mm bore and 84.0mm stroke gave a capacity of 3453cc. High-performance components included a forged alloy crankshaft, longer connecting rods, redesigned pistons, and – most important – the 24-valve cylinder head with two chain-driven camshafts. Kugelfischer-Bosch mechanical injection squirted in the fuel, and the ignition was fully electronic, with a 6900rpm cut-out. Seven hours of bench testing ensured each engine duly delivered the specified 277bhp at 6500rpm and 239lb/ft of torque at 5000rpm. In the 2876lb road cars, this meant performance of 161mph and 0–60 mph in 5.6sec. The canny Neerpasch ran the Group 4 racers in the high-publicity Procar series at Grand Prix meetings while he fought to keep the M1 project alive after The Troubles in Italy began. These cars were reckoned to dispatch 0–60 in around 4.0 seconds. The full-house twin-turbo Group 5 models were something else again.

The M1's initial development went well. The Bavarians were impressed by Lamborghini's efforts. But when production was due to start early in 1978, Lamborghini was on the verge of bankruptcy and couldn't go ahead. Hastily, BMW – with the help of finance director Pier Luigi Capellini and engineer Marco Raimondi, who had both left Lamborghini – sorted out alternative arrangements that ultimately worked well. Noted metal workers Marchesi of Modena fabricated the chassis. The beautifully smooth body panels were moulded by Trasformazione Italiana Resine, then fixed to the chassis by Ital Design, which had been persuaded to step into the breech. The bodies then went north to Stuttgart, where the coachbuilders at Baur did the fitting out and installed the drivetrain BMW supplied. Finally, BMW did the testing and ensured the quality control. The first cars went on sale, a year late, in February 1979. It's amazing the delay was so short.

BMW M1

BMW's engineers had taken over the final development programme, too. I remember Martin Braungart, who was in charge of the project at BMW Motorsport, saying: 'Lamborghini had taken the car to a very impressive level. Our work went hand in glove with theirs, and you can't pinpoint a stage where their influence faded and our own ideas prevailed. We didn't have to make any drastic changes – all our work with suspension settings, for instance, was simply evolutionary.'

Racing driver Hans Stuck conducted much of the testing on a special 250-mile route BMW mapped out around Bavaria. 'It even included some rally stages, and we really thrashed the cars around it,' Stuck said. 'As we progressed toward the ideal blend of roadholding, handling and comfort, we reached increasingly higher average speeds, and drove faster and faster. This kind of month-in, month-out testing really sorts out a car. I have no hesitation in saying that the M1 is a very, very well developed car. I can't think of another supercar that has the same degree of refinement and durability.'

Eight years later, that message was coming through loud and clear as Colin and I finally swung off the M1 for the moors. The BMW had felt stable, composed, quiet and comfortable on the motorway. It retained those virtues on the narrow highways it was now covering equally effortlessly. The demisting system was working tirelessly, the long single wiper clearing the screen well, and the airflow, whether by Giugiaro's design or convenient accident, kept the side windows clean. Maintaining a surprisingly high cruising speed required nothing more than smoothness and a keen lookout for standing water that could make the front wheels lift and shy offline. To tiny inputs at the wheel, the nose moved in quickly and neatly. Only in a bend where a tiny crest preceded the apex did it break and slide. Lifting off stopped it from going too far. Even a lot of the lovely engine's power could be used judiciously through and out of the bends, too. All the while, there was the supple, controlled ride and almost uncanny poise.

But the weather beat us in the end. By mid afternoon, it still wasn't possible to take a camera out of the bag. We phoned from a storm-ravaged village, and the weather bureau said there'd be no break for days. We drove the 250 miles back to London, locked

AND THE REVS KEEP RISING

the M1 away for a week, and went back to Yorkshire when the late summer weather was as it should have been. This time, the heather crowning the moors glowed deep purple in the sunlight, and we could see the roads running clear before us. Those laid down by the Romans ran straight and fast across the moor tops. Others wriggled down from them into the dales.

This time, we could open the six right out and enjoy its top-end oomph as well as its low-end docility. Yet, as I knew well by now, it didn't have to be revved hard to give its best. The depth and spread of its torque were much greater than a peak point of 5000rpm suggest. The race-bred six was anything but a beast wanting to work only at the top end. From 2000rpm, it had more than enough to give, an important factor in making the M1 so easy and relaxing to drive. It soon turned out that the gearing was equally good, too: 46, 69, 98, and 131mph in the first four gears at the 6500 redline, with a little in hand before the cut-out clamped down.

With nothing to hold it back, the M1 romped along the fast open roads, turning in eagerly, going around smoothly, rolling little, and feeling good. One tight bend, taken hard high up in third, showed what happened when the roadholding ran out. Grip was still good but, with the relatively narrow tyres, decidedly dated. The tail edged out with the speed and power, telegraphing its intentions quickly and clearly, and calling for just a twitch of opposite lock. Do it once and you could do it a dozen times. The M1 had that sort of vice-less consistency and, crucially, that sort of availability to the driver. *It's so effortless* I kept thinking. Fluid and precise, lovely in the hands and through the seat of the pants. It asked its driver for little more than guidance; and swift response if he overdid it.

Stability stayed part of the mix at higher speeds on the straighter sections. So did the ride quality. Our progress remained as comfortable and encouraging as it was rapid. A whisper of wind noise grew at the upper end, but didn't become annoying. The six's sound was a pleasing reminder of its power and proximity, but it never grew intrusive.

Plunging from the moor tops into the lanes tumbling down the hill sides to find a pub for lunch, the M1 revealed another forte:

BMW M1

with the roads dry, the braking was smooth, progressive, and potent. I could sprint hard down little straights, brake late and feel the car squirming onto the road without deviating from the line I wanted into the corners. There was, too, always the right gear for the right throttle control as the car pivoted around the bends.

Storming back up the dale sides was even better. The rear Pirellis took all the power, and the plentiful mid-bend bumps couldn't move the tail off line. When it did go, it was simply through excessive power and by then I knew how easy and pleasing it was to indulge in that sort of oversteer. So it pelted up the hills like a lithe and powerful fell runner, not as quickly as later, similarly powerful cars with wider tyres, but as adroitly and enjoyably as you'd wish. Thank you, Hans.

We roamed the lovely roads – tight and tiny and big and open – of the North York Moors until the sun dipped low and turned the heather almost scarlet. What a contrast to the crushing greyness and lashing rain that had driven us away just a week earlier. This time we left feeling fulfilled, knowing that, while the BMW had been admirable in the wet, it was inspiring in the dry.

When we rejoined the motorway and began rolling away the miles home, we had time to reflect on the sombre efficiency of the cabin, a legacy of the M1's input from Munich rather than Modena. Black cloth and leather. Six clear and orange-lit instruments set simply in a black crackle-finish panel. Minor controls easy to see and use. Decidedly un-Italian, but not fault-free. The bulkhead stopped the seatbacks from reclining far enough, and pedals' offset meant clutch leg discomfort. It needed more cabin space. We were happy enough with the luggage space in the tail, which had taken a good mix of personal items without their becoming too heated by the engine just inches ahead.

Back in London, the M1 proved as easy to drive in traffic as it had been out on the road. It is a pleasing, docile, and liveable car that reveals many of the best qualities of two admirable motoring worlds, the German and the Italian. Its parentage might have been mixed and its adolescence turbulent but in road car form, at least, it blossomed into splendid adulthood to be one of the most refined yet charismatic, fleet yet approachable supercars. The shame is that

AND THE REVS KEEP RISING

it lived for only two years and only 457 M1s emerged from that complex production arrangement.

Clearly, because it is still such a capable, enjoyable, and desirable car, even by much later standards, the M1 could have been developed to stellar heights. It served its purpose for BMW and died. Happily, a good measure of its spirit and prowess live on in the M-power saloons and coupés that have come in its wake.

197MPH IN THE ORIGINAL HYPERCAR

PORSCHE 959

1987

WE CAME OUT OF the bend at around 125mph in fifth and on to a straight that ran clear for a mile or more across rural Germany. With its throttle going down hard, the Porsche 959 lunged on in an instant from 5800rpm through to 6500 where all 450 horses were unbridled, and then on again to 7500 and 160mph, where I needed to tug the little gearlever through to sixth. In top, the thrust of that volcanic power band – as both turbochargers blew hard – went on again and the scenery pelted at us crazily. By the time I needed to brake hard for a tight right-hander we'd hit 190mph.

I grinned as I braked, all the way down to 30mph, because stopping was just as effortless; all part of the efficiency and ease and control; all part of the stupendous performance of the Porsche 959.

I'd started the task of tackling Porsche's fastest-ever road car with a measure of trepidation. Responsibility, I kept telling myself, had to be the order of the day: don't feel compelled to try to run flat-out; don't attempt to push this four-wheel-drive paragon of automotive technology near its cornering limits – just take it as it comes and go as far as you feel able, nothing more.

But in 12 hours the 959 had taught me to relax; to know that I could use all of the 2.8-litre flat-six's 450bhp even in the wet. It taught me that I could open it up on any half-decent stretch of road and travel at speeds that would have been unbelievable if they weren't so uneventful. It taught me that I could push beyond the edge of its staggering roadholding and not fear the consequences. It

AND THE REVS KEEP RISING

taught me that all I had to do was to calculate speed and distance as never before and not run out of road.

But most of all, as my spirits soared with the increasing realisation that I was driving a car that rewrites the supercar rules, the 959 demonstrated that Porsche has achieved the fantastic goal it set in 1980: creation of a car that nudges the performance envelope of contemporary racing cars yet can be handled confidently by a normal driver. Here is a car that accelerates from 0–60mph in 3.7secs, to 100mph in 8.5secs, to 150mph in 21.5 and runs on to 197mph but can be driven by you, me and our wives or sisters in comfort and in any weather, anywhere, anytime.

On the flight into Stuttgart, I had harboured a certain amount of apprehension as I reread the description of the 959's revolutionary features such as the twin turbocharger system, the electronically variable four-wheel-drive system and adjustable suspension, the race-like anti-lock brakes, and the anti-lift aerodynamics. My friend Kevin Smith from *Automobile* magazine, who'd driven a 959 shortly before at the Nürburgring, had wondered whether, on the road, the car would prove to be blindingly quick but so competent that it was almost boring. I ran into Kevin again as I checked into my hotel in Stuttgart. He was just returning from a long day's drive in the 959 on the *autobahns* and ordinary roads, and the miles had opened his eyes.

'The car is *gorgeous*,' he enthused. 'It tootles along in the traffic then you strike a stretch of open road and you're up to 180 or 190mph. You don't *mean* to go that fast but it just seems so natural that you're there in no time. And it demands nothing of you. It's stable, it's relaxed, it's wonderful.' I slept a little easier.

All that chimed in with the aims set down by Porsche's development chief, Professor Dr Ing Helmuth Bott. He'd told me over a quiet drink after the tech briefing: 'We wanted more performance than any road car had ever had – but we wanted a car that any driver, man or woman, with an average amount of experience, could master within the range of his or her normal abilities and within a short learning period. They should not have re-orientation problems when switching from other cars.'

PORSCHE 959

So this ultimate road and rally Porsche (it's homologated for Group B rallying, hence a production run of 200) is based on the 911 to keep the Porsche virtues of small size, uncompromised cabin, easy vision and reasonable luggage space. Then Prof Bott's team crammed it with technology that, while allowing mere mortals to access the performance, also created a test bed for advanced systems 'which may become interesting for our normal production cars'. 'We decided,' said a proud Prof Bott, 'to fill this car with more technical systems than anyone has done before.'

Early the next morning I ran my eyes over Kevlar and aluminium bodywork that integrates the best of the Porsche 911's visual character with aerodynamic addenda and inlets that are as beautiful as they are functional. In the low dawn light, the rear fenders that flow like extruded toffee into that lovely rear wing looked the most sensuous elements. But I knew from the Porsche engineers' papers how, along with the smooth undercladding and a host of other detail shaping and tuning, they contribute to the 959's achievement of zero lift and similar loading on the wheels at low and high speed. This breakthrough is one of the keys to the 959's exceptional high-speed stability and safety. With that preoccupying the Weissach engineers, they were happy with a drag coefficient of 0.31, given that the car has a small frontal area and, at 2970lb for the sports version, is relatively light.

As you unlock the door and slip into the cockpit you find there are other benefits from Porsche's decision to base its technological tour de force on the 911. The doors don't open very wide but you sit up nicely in the familiar 911-esque cabin behind the upright windscreen, with nice big windows at the sides and the sort of clear rear vision unknown in the pacesetting supercars that have gone before. So, as you start to ease the 959 out of the car park, there is none of the initial intimidation that afflicts a novice Countach driver, or the bulk that makes a Testarossa awkward.

But then Porsche thought hard about all of this. The 959's ends are shaped and proportioned to allow for ramps, the computer cuts off drive to the front wheels at parking speeds, and in the 'Comfort' version the height adjustment system makes parking against high

AND THE REVS KEEP RISING

kerbs painless. Other features in the Comfort model are folding rear kids' seats, air conditioning and a second driving mirror. The trade-off is an extra 110lb for a power-to-weight ratio of 317bhp/ton against the Sport's 339.

Slipping into Stuttgart's sparse early morning traffic in our Sport and heading north couldn't have been easier. The flat-six engine had fired immediately and idled perfectly. The clutch was light and quick. With power assistance, the steering was even lighter than a 911's although slightly more anaesthetised, and the ride was taut but comfortable. There was nothing to suggest the phenomenal performance potential: no quirkiness and appreciably more refinement than a 911. The magnitude and appeal of the 959 was starting to show.

On the *autobahn*, I soon saw what Kevin Smith had meant. In the first mode of performance (using just the first, full-time turbo) the acceleration hardly felt lacking by any normal standard. But once the tachometer neared 4000rpm and the second, part-time turbo kicked in too, the 959 simply took off, thrusting us back into our seats with a potency well beyond even a 455bhp Countach (power-to-weight ratio 311bhp/ton). It was then a matter of changing gears thick and fast and recalibrating the eyes and the brain to deal with scenery that someone had just dialled up to *fast*.

The vast difference between the two modes of performance is salvaged by the fact that the first is strong enough not to be disappointing. And the second is contained by the ability of the drive system, the chassis and the aerodynamics, so that it feels nothing other than downright exhilarating. It isn't like having the smooth and consistent flow of a big flat-12, but it certainly is as effective: 100mph feels like 50. The road clears, even for a short way, and without worrying much whether you're in fourth, fifth or sixth, you floor the throttle and the car shoots down the road. In moments you're at an equally relaxed-feeling 160mph. Then another aspect of the 959's balanced make-up comes into play: the brakes. It takes merely a squeeze of your big toe on the pedal to bring the speed back down again. Press the throttle once more and you're back in the stratosphere.

PORSCHE 959

After a few miles of this, when the 959's effortlessness and stability make you realise you really are driving something that heralds a new era, you run hard into sixth. If the road is clear, you're soon at 180mph and that's fine. The engine keeps growling and with remarkable ease you're beyond 190. It's not entirely arrow-like: there is some impression of the front working around over ripples that at this speed have become bumps, and there is loud jolting over the bigger irregularities.

But on the whole you soon learn that you can run this car to its 197mph maximum without fearing anything other than someone else getting in your way. Yet it's as well to remember that, magnificent as the brakes are, it will still take around three-quarters of a mile to stop from maximum speed. Later, on another *autobahn* and suddenly striking miles of dense traffic, came another kind of respect for the 959. From travelling at up to 190 a few minutes before we were suddenly down to a stop-and-start trickle, but there was no temperament from the engine or any other part of the drivetrain. The 959 is as unfussy in these conditions as it is at the other end of the scale.

And on two-lane roads, among the trucks and tractors of rural Germany, often as not you glance at the speedo and see that you're slipping along at 100mph and you're surprised because you're doing nothing other than easing along at what seems like 60. Then there's a tractor and you drop down to 1000rpm in fourth, and that's no bother either.

It was on one narrow road like this that we hit rain and a streaming wet surface. Touching a switch on the steering column stalk changed the four-wheel drive system's traction program from dry to wet, and we stormed on, unaffected. Apart from subtle differences in the way the torque is apportioned to the wheels for wet or dry surfaces, there is a third instantly available program for snow and ice, and another for ultimate traction in deep snow or mud. So, if the traction of this 450bhp car had been impressive in the dry, with never a trace of wheelspin, the benefits of its complex four-wheel-drive system came out now in the wet. On those sodden roads, I was able to peep past the trucks then plant my foot and

AND THE REVS KEEP RISING

go, deploying that sensational acceleration in every gear, including first. Within a few miles it was clear that the 959 really was now hunting in a territory of its own. No way could this sort of power be put down in a two-wheel-drive car.

The wet roads revealed other things: that aquaplaning was the only real danger. Deep water called for lower speed. When the roadholding was broken in bends, the 959 simply slid mildly at the front, in line with Porsche's deliberate programming that understeer should increase with speed or lost traction. The best thing wasn't so much the stability as the clear and instant communication of what was happening. All I had to do was lift the throttle a fraction and the nose drift would stop. It was subtle stuff, and the message now was that the 959, for all its computerised administration, was still a fingers and toes handler of a car. My soul rejoiced.

Back on dry roads, I now felt more than happy to run the car *very* hard. In a wonderful series of switchbacks I found that I could push right to the limits of the 959's superb grip – better than 1*g*, Porsche says – and beyond and have it do nothing nasty. Brought in hard in third to a 70mph hairpin, it demonstrated all the benefits of its technology. With its ABS, I *couldn't* lock the brakes as I strove for the last degree of retardation. The 959 just followed the wheel and went around the bend until the power and speed began to create that carefully calculated understeer. Because the bend opened out beyond the apex, I could keep my foot hard down and sweep out to the exit, with the car's attitude going to neutrality as the engine's full power approached. Finally, there was the tiniest shrug of oversteer.

At different times after that I lifted off when near maximum power and all the car did was tighten its line neatly. There was no way that tail – so strident in these circumstances in a contemporary 911 – was going to come around. So here, when cornering at a speed I suspect would have been unmatched, was the 959's supreme message: supreme safety.

I kept driving hard, on tight roads and fast open roads. I pushed brutishly on deliberately crude lines into some tight-ish bends at 90mph and got strong understeer that said 'back off', and when I did the car just stuck again and tracked around. I ran around other

PORSCHE 959

bends in gears too high and with revs too low. It made no difference other than that the performance felt flat compared with the verve of being at the right revs in the right gear. I pressed through long open bends at 130mph in fifth, feeling the car holding firmly to its line and asking for nothing other than guidance.

I went on driving late into the night, able to enjoy much more of the Porsche's performance than I had envisaged before I started, running it flat wherever possible just to go on experiencing the thrill of its acceleration. Through it all, the 959 remained supremely safe and easy to drive. It was effortless and untiring. It was comfortable and convenient although there were times during the heat of the day when the air conditioning of the Comfort model would have been welcome. I would want the fold-down seats too, mostly as a luggage platform to counter the 959's only obvious drawback: almost non-existent space in the front boot.

For days after it was all over I couldn't stop thinking of the Porsche 959 and its exemplary behaviour. The great Italian supercars feel and sound more sensuous, and are more challenging and perhaps more rewarding to master. But no car, to date, has impressed me so deeply as this one. Its performance alone makes it more thrilling than anything else I've driven – but I love it most because it gives so much and asks for so little.

That is Porsche's achievement. It has built a racing car for road drivers, with it mattering little whether the road is wet or dry. And magnificent as that achievement is, the good news is that it is the tip of an iceberg. Other Porsches will gain the 959's technology and, steadily, degrees of its prowess. Other manufacturers have been set the challenge of keeping up.

YOUNG MAN'S FANCY
1960 MGA 1600
1987

I WOULD LIKE TO drive an MGA again. But perhaps I shouldn't. Perhaps I should heed the advice: *never* go *back*. To drive an MGA again might sour too many memories of raw and carefree youth, of being a country kid with his own sports car making it as a newspaper reporter in the big city.

The day I bought the MGA was the most thrilling of all. I was 19. It was seven years old, and British Racing Green. I'd spotted it shining from among the family sedans in a dealer's yard when I was coming back from a job out of town. Every afternoon for the next week I left the office early to go and rub my hands over its flowing panels, sit behind its wire-spoked steering wheel, gaze beneath its bonnet, and even, when the dealer realised I was probably a Sure Thing, take it out in the beating sun for a delirious couple of miles.

And then it was mine, exchanged for the tired but reliable General Motors Holden EJ that had brought me in from the country, together with another $A900 raked up from my savings and a tame finance company. I signed the papers at 3.55 on a blistering summer's afternoon and drove off into the Valhalla of the miles ahead without even paying the old Holden the respect of a farewell glance.

In my heart of hearts, I knew that the rust inside the MG's left front mudguard was worse than I wanted to admit, and the noise whirring from first gear was ominous. These things were minor flaws, I blithely told Jenny, the matronly secretary who was the only person still left at the newspaper office who could be persuaded to accept a ride home. She only lived half a mile away.

I dropped her off and raced down to the television station to wait for one of my friends to finish his reporting shift. Previously,

1960 MGA 1600

the glamour in our circle of friends had been all his. Arrogantly, I boasted, the MGA would run the legs off his TR3A. It did, too: a little later we raced up the longest hill out of the city, the sprightlier MG steadily drawing ahead of the slow-revving but hard-slogging TR3 to turn my bravado into pride. The reason, I discovered later, was a warm camshaft and a ported and polished cylinder head the dealer hadn't known about or didn't bother to mention.

Together, that night, we parked outside the house of some girls who were throwing a party, the blue TR3A sitting close behind the green MGA. I felt 10ft tall as we walked in. Ken smiled. He was used to the feeling. I lasted until about midnight before suggesting to the most vivacious girl I'd ever met, a tempestuous Hungarian blonde called Maria, that a stroll outside might be pleasant.

In the moonlight, she noticed the cars. My heart pounded as she asked if I knew who owned them. In minutes we were off into the night, with Maria kneeling in the seat, holding the top of the windscreen, lifting her face to be caressed by the wind and throwing her head back so that her long hair streamed in a golden flurry. 'Faster,' she said *'Faster!'*

I remember not the mechanics of the driving, not the gearshifting or the feel of the wheel in my hands or the sweep of the needles around the dials. I remember the exhilaration of flying through the moonlight and the smell of the eucalyptus trees and the Godiva-like vision beside me, in *my* MG, as we raced along the road to a remote beach. I remember the feeling of joy and freedom, the shared elation of two souls rushing toward the pounding Pacific surf and the stars of the southern sky on a balmy evening. If someone mentions the appeal of an open sports car, that is the moment to which I return.

With as much exuberance as innocence, we ran hand in hand through the foam, then sat in the sand and picked out the constellations and watched the luminous plankton dancing in the breakers and waited for the dawn. Then, with a subdued, almost dreamlike sense of happiness, we wandered back to the MG, and Maria curled up and snuggled, sleeping, into my shoulder as we drove home through the long shadows and the crisp air. Enough heat rose from the footwells to make the cockpit snug. The exhaust

AND THE REVS KEEP RISING

note burbled pleasingly behind us. Now I noted and enjoyed the light and crisp feel of the quick little gearshift, the fluid motion of the steering – so direct, with its rack-and-pinion, after the old Holden – and the steady beat of the doughty little 1600cc engine. It felt good, my MG. It felt like a friend.

It went on to serve me well. It spent most of its life with the roof stowed and only the tonneau clipped over the cockpit at night. It took me across town to work. It took me to weekend beach parties. It was tough and durable. It took me on flat-out 1000-mile trips in blistering Australian heat and never faltered. When Maria's flaring temperament proved to be too much, it took me on to other girls. At a time when young men in sprawling Sydney dubbed some girls 'GI' – Geographically Impossible – I never minded how far away they lived.

But after four years the rust in the wing couldn't be ignored, and the noise from the chipped first gear was like a lion roaring through a mouthful of marbles. I spent a winter stripping the MG down and rebuilding it, working late into the night at a friend's repair shop. I replaced the gearbox with a works close-ratio transmission picked up for a few dollars from an MG competition department sale. I replaced the carburettors, fitted free-flow Abarth exhaust headers, and made the brakes, suspension and body perfect.

As a 10-year-old car, it was much admired. And I enjoyed several more rewarding journeys in it, especially a lengthy dice where, thanks to the engine tweaks, it saw off a new MGB. But the trouble was, I'd started writing about cars. Each week I had the latest and the greatest. Some were V8 muscle cars capable of up to 140mph and standing quarter-mile times of less than 15secs. Some were Ferraris, Lamborghinis, and Porsches. The MGA, flat out somewhere short of 110mph and barely able to nudge 18sec over the standing quarter, faded in my affections. I sold it, too cheaply, to a kid I hoped would get as much from it as I once had.

There are times, though, when I wish it were still mine. But I wonder what I'd make of the MGA now, decades after driving it for the first time. I could borrow a friend's and find out but it will be better to resist, I think, and just hold on to those untrammelled memories.

WEST, WITH A FINE SALOON

JAGUAR XJ6

1988

BY THE TIME WE reached Somerset, two hours into the journey, I knew I'd chosen the right car. The rain was becoming heavier, the bends and dips and crests were more frequent, and, at mid-morning, there was a good deal more traffic. It didn't really matter to the Jaguar. Its accuracy through the bends and stability over the crests were flawless. The response of the twin-cam 3.6-litre six with four-speed automatic was swift enough for quick-fire overtaking. The rear suspension and the specially designed Dunlops handled the power without wheelspin. At the same time, the XJ6 provided quite exceptional comfort and refinement. Its pace was accompanied by near-perfect gentility.

It was a combination that allowed me to drive fast enough to satisfy my desires, without any concessions to the fact that my passenger was my 69-year-old mother. Once, when we were sailing through the long curves of a stretch of two-lane traversing a wide valley, she asked how fast we were going. 'Ninety,' I said, half expecting her to start in fright. 'Is it worrying you?' 'No,' she said. 'I'm comfortable.' It was a telling reaction: a keen judgment of the new Jaguar's prowess and of the achievement of its engineers in creating a suspension that impressively combines grip, handling, ride, and quietness.

There were many ways in which the Jaguar demonstrated its quality. Over crests, when the road suddenly dived left, ran down a little way, and then flicked right, it was at its best. It would simply drop and turn to follow the banks with no lost motion. As the big wheels rose and fell, the body stayed flat and tidy and we were never less than cushioned. All I had to do was rest in my deep

AND THE REVS KEEP RISING

leather bucket and guide the Jaguar with tiny movements of that big leather wheel, delighting in the precision and the sweetness of its obedience.

There were times, on the streaming roads, when I expected understeer. It did not come. There were other times, booting hard out of tight bends or roundabouts, when I thought I'd get oversteer. That happened only once, after I had told Mum to hang on and had floored the thing in second. Even then, the slide was more of a shrug, instantly and easily corrected.

In a way, it was a voyage of discovery – and not merely because I was taking my mother, in England from Australia, to find some long-lost relatives in Cornwall. I hadn't driven the new XJ6 since its release well over a year earlier, and I had been disappointed to see that, as the car began to appear on the streets, its styling looked dowdy alongside that of the smart BMW 7-series. Would the Jaguar, judged after I'd come to know the admirable BMW well, seem as impressive this time?

Some aspects of the XJ6, apart from styling, certainly do come off second best. Its cabin is lower, dropped down over the side rails, so getting in and out is more difficult. The interior – leather and walnut notwithstanding – seems more awkward and fiddly than the ergonomic-looking BMW's. The Jaguar's instruments and controls look almost amateurish, and the stupidly placed hand brake jabs your thigh. At idle, the six from Coventry seems rougher than its Bavarian counterpart. Moving off, the ride seems a touch soft after the BMW's. The driver begins to fear that this car will wallow, barge-like. But it takes only a few miles – the first few corners, really – to discover that within the suppleness of the Jaguar's suspension lays tremendous control.

You begin the process of learning that, in addition to the wondrously quiet comfort it delivers, the XJ6 can be driven every bit as enthusiastically as the BMW. In due course, you will also learn that, where the edges of the road are rough and broken, the Jaguar's stability under both power and brakes is markedly superior. And, at high speed, you will find the XJ's steering is the more informative and pleasurable of the two. The brakes, too, are magnificent: your

JAGUAR XJ6

foot seems to sink into a progressive, firm sponge that delivers as little or as much stopping power as you want.

You also discover that the engine, if never quite as silken as the BMW's, is smooth and lively enough, working with a pleasing thrum when it's rising hard through the rev band. Despite their seemingly haphazard design, the minor controls work very well indeed. And the J-shaped shift pattern for the automatic transmission is a paragon of logic and efficiency, in contrast with the tediously complex BMW arrangement. With the electrically adjustable seat correctly set, the Jaguar's driving position has a comfort and a character all its own. You seem to sit low, almost lounging, but you can see perfectly, steer easily and relax and just guide the car. It is as good on a long and fast journey as it is in slow city traffic.

A few times during our trip west there were clonks from the rear suspension. Also, some owners have complained that the low speed ride isn't as satisfactory as the old XJ's. Jaguar says minor damping changes should provide the answer, at the cost of a slight deterioration in handling at very high speed. But I found little else to cause a ripple of dissatisfaction. Once we were across the river Tamar and into Cornwall, we pottered, found the long-lost relatives, and then wafted on to our little hotel as the rain cleared above that ancient smugglers' coast. We stayed at the Criterion Hotel. It stands perched over the water in the village of Cawsand, which has been virtually unchanged for 300 years. As we left the Jaguar in the communal car park on the edge of the village and walked through the tiny, weaving streets to the cosy hotel, I was well pleased with the day's journey. We ate well that night, and then popped in for a drink at one after another of Cawsand's six pubs, enjoying the rolling accents of the Cornishmen swapping tales on a damp winter's night.

The next day, as we drifted under scudding white clouds along the coast and then swung back over bleak Bodmin Moor and began the 300-mile run home, there was nothing to diminish the Jaguar's stature or the pleasure it provided for both its occupants. Home in London, I handed it back to its regular custodian with great reluctance.

'NOTHING BUT SHEER PERFORMANCE'

FERRARI F40

1988

HOW EASY IT IS! After all the anticipation, all the trepidation, all the wariness about driving the fastest Ferrari ever built for the road, it turns out to be an effortlessly stirring experience. Wariness? Well, the twin turbo V8 just behind the F40's seats punches out 478 horsepower at 7000rpm. Its torque is a staggering 425lb/ft at 4000rpm and all of this is in a two-seater weighing just a couple of hundred pounds more than a Golf GTI.

From the passenger seat, I'd gained a clear idea of what that means in neck-snapping acceleration. It wasn't just the brute force of the propulsion. Above the snarl of the engine I'd heard the intermittent chirping of the rear race-bred Pirellis as they were pushed, despite being 13ins wide, to the verge of wheelspin all the way through first and second and into third. And, just before it was my turn to squeeze into the driving bucket and cinch up the racing harness, Ferrari test driver Doriano Borsari happened to mention that he'd recently clocked the F40 at a two-way average of 202.5mph.

Named to commemorate 1987's 40th anniversary of Ferrari, the F40 began as an idea in 1986, took to the test track in Spring 1987 and, in less than two years, hit production. In the final few months of its development, its test programme has included 15,000 miles run at a steady 150mph, with 48-hour periods at an average of 187mph when Ferrari's test drivers have had the vast, high-speed Nardo circuit in Southern Italy to themselves. From that has come different spark plugs, better oil cooling and, from Pirelli, a few tweaks to the P-Zero radials. Production cars have a lip on

FERRARI F40

their front spoiler that fine-tunes the airflow and increases stability above 180mph.

The approach Ferrari has taken to the F40's creation – and, indeed, its very motives in making the car – is not without detractors. By comparison with that technological tour de force, the four-wheel-drive computer-controlled Porsche 959, the F40 is a simple car. It is essentially a fairly light mid-engined two-seater packing a great deal of power, with little out of the ordinary in its layout or build apart from its composite materials construction. Some observers have condemned this approach and Ferrari's intentions as a cynical money-making exercise hatched after Maranello's marketing men saw how much buyers were paying for the limited edition Ferrari 288 GTO second-hand – and how hot was demand for the Porsche 959 at £150,000.

An outraged Ferrari dismisses these suggestions as ludicrous. Giovanni Perfetti, from the marketing department, says the F40 harks back to Ferrari's roots. 'We wanted it to be very fast, sporting in the extreme and spartan,' he says. 'Customers had been saying our cars were becoming too plush and comfortable. The F40 is for the most enthusiastic of our owners who want nothing but sheer performance. It isn't a laboratory for the future, as the 959 is. It is not *Star Wars*. And it wasn't created because Porsche built the 959. It would have happened anyway.'

Whichever way you look at it, the performance potential and desirability of a late-'80s Ferrari packing almost 500bhp in a composite materials body designed by Pininfarina to have particularly good aero characteristics, wasn't lost on a host of prospective buyers. Ferrari announced that it planned to make 400 F40s and well over 3000 people, proffering fat deposits, promptly began haranguing dealers. Although Ferrari soon lifted the run to 950, to be completed before October 1989, only faithful and long-standing Ferrari customers will get F40s. 'Despite our best efforts, some speculation will be inevitable,' says Dr Emilio Anchisi, head of Ferrari North America. 'A few owners may find the car too much for them and decide to sell, knowing that they can get twice what they paid.' In the UK, the delivery price is £163,000. Only 60 of the 300 Britons eager to pay will be lucky.

AND THE REVS KEEP RISING

What are they getting? A car whose dramatic looks begin with a needle-like nose and flow on over a 328-like centre section peppered with NACA ducts to culminate in a vast rear wing; a car that finally steals the Countach's visual thunder. It's mean, but there's beauty in its balance, proportion and detailing.

Using materials and techniques adopted from Ferrari's Formula 1 cars, the F40 is built by cladding a particularly strong and rigid tubular steel platform chassis and cabin section – a kind of cage that enshrouds the occupants and provides the suspension and engine mounts. The panels, moulded from light but immensely tough Kevlar, are bonded to the frame with advanced adhesives. The materials and methodology meet Ferrari's objective of cutting weight by 20 per cent while increasing torsional rigidity threefold over an equivalent all-steel construction.

Just as the car's shape, if not its construction, is inspired by the Ferrari 328 and the GTO Evoluzione that flowed from it, so the engine's roots rest there. The 90-degree all-alloy V8's bore has been enlarged, taking its capacity from the GTO's 2855cc to 2936cc, and its two water cooled IHI turbochargers deliver boost to 1.1 bar rather than 0.8. Its new crankshaft is ducted for better lubrication. The con rod bushes are silver/cadmium. The pistons have a pronounced squish effect and are cooled by oil jets directed inside their crowns. The 32 valves have hollow stems and heads. And the inlet manifold's eight butterflies operate as one.

The complex Weber-Marelli injection and ignition system has sequential injection, twin injectors per cylinder and many features used in F1 engines. Basing its calculations on butterfly angle and engine revs, the system also measures the supercharging pressure before allocating the precise measure of fuel. It also governs the ignition for individual cylinders through a static high-tension system with four coils that have dual outputs. Further, the boost pressure is controlled in co-ordination with the fuel supply and ignition regulation. The system's computers also keep an eye on anything irregular but Ferrari says its main advantage is the way it minimises turbocharger lag.

This engine work lifts the V8's power by almost 20 per cent over

FERRARI F40

the GTO to give the F40 478bhp at 7000rpm and 425.3lb/ft of torque at 4000rpm. For owners who want to go racing – and some have indicated that they will – Ferrari is offering larger turbochargers and wilder cams that take the power up to 680bhp. The standard transmission, complete with oil cooler, is the five-speed derived from the GTO. The racing version is a dog clutch unit.

The F40's suspension follows the proven and rarely bettered path of wide-based and unequal length upper and lower wishbones. There are anti-roll bars at both ends and the suspension components are fabricated like works of art. At the rear, the coil spring and damper units rise from the top of the alloy uprights. At the front, they sit between the upper and lower wishbones. The steering is, of course, rack and pinion and the massive vented and drilled Group C disc brakes have alloy centres bolted to their cast iron braking surfaces to reduce unsprung weight. As a measure of its straightforward, track-like approach in today's automotive world, the F40 does not have an anti-lock system. It does not even have servo assistance.

Everywhere, the precision and beauty of the F40's engineering is breathtaking: the suspension; the plumbing and wonderful engine manifolding; the wheels; the front underpan when the bonnet is raised. Inside – in a cabin that is deliberately stark but lacking nothing that really matters – the racing car impression is emphasised by the drilled alloy pedals. Nothing covers the raw honeycomb pattern of the carbon fibre on the inside of the doors, in the footwells and on the buttresses running down each side of the cockpit. You tug cords to open the doors. If the outside styling hasn't told you this car means business, the cabin certainly does.

Getting in there is not easy. You must crouch, swing your right leg in, edge your backside into the tightly moulded bucket (owners will be fitted for one of the three sizes available) and then settle down. It takes a few moments more to plug the straps of the five-point harness into the centre buckle. When you're ready to fire up, you discover that the F40 is blessed with an uncommonly un-Italian driving position. The pedals are offset only slightly to the centre, the distance to them is good and the wheel is neither raked too much towards the horizontal nor too far away. You feel well set-up to begin.

AND THE REVS KEEP RISING

The key operates only the fuel and electrical systems. The starter responds to a small, squishy rubber button on the dash just to the right of the wheel. Press it once and the V8 snaps immediately into life and idles smoothly. When you feed the clutch out, you find that it takes up evenly and easily: you're not going to stall. The shift, as you go up through the gears gingerly for the first time, feeling things out, reacquainting yourself with the wicked curves of Ferrari's Fiorano test track, has the familiar notchiness of the 328's but it's not difficult. There's nothing hard or nasty about the drivetrain either. And there's a pleasing naturalness about the steering. It's direct, smooth and not too heavy.

Turn it and the car responds flatly and without a trace of lost motion. Everything feels right – *perfect* – there. In a surprisingly short time you feel ready to start pressing on. And when you do that, slowing back to a trickle, re-engaging first then flooring that tall, drilled metal throttle pedal, the F40 runs through a short period of tameness and then, coming up to 3000rpm, begins to take off. It builds speed rapidly until the tachometer needle nudges 3800 and there's a frantic rush as the car lunges forward, pinning you hard into the seat. It's smooth but, dear me, it's potent and you need to keep your eyes darting between the road and the tachometer, watching the needle thrash towards the 7750 redline.

The take-up into the next gear is flawless and, with the turbos cranking hard, the blast of acceleration just goes on again and you seem to be in a blur of time conquering distance, gearshifts and noise. Not that the noise is overwhelming, but if you switch your attention to it for a moment you're well aware of the level of the growl and then the turbochargers' whirr and the whole hollow wail. It has the tonal quality of an F1 engine, if not the sheer ferocity. From outside, if you stand and listen, you hear the frantic whoosh as the turbos start to drive oh-so-hard.

But, to be honest, when you're behind the wheel there's too much else to consider, at least when you're on an open and challenging track. It takes only the first couple of bends to demonstrate the precision and response of the steering and the sheer grip that's lurking beneath you. You start coming into successive bends harder

FERRARI F40

and find that the F40 edges into a nice, modest, deliberate-feeling understeer. The feel is such – through the wheel, and somehow through the whole car – that you know instantly what's happening. And you can choose whether you lift off or power on.

If you lift, the nose tightens instantly and obediently but without a trace of viciousness. Even if you come off deliberately abruptly, having had a lot of power on, the tail moves but does not snap out. The F40 has poise, balance and manners, not to mention gluey roadholding, and all with such a satisfyingly meaty feeling. If you choose to power on, the car pushes swiftly through its understeer and tightens progressively through to full power oversteer. The wonderful thing is that you can feel it, degree by degree, and balance the attitude as finely as you like. The communication comes through the seat as beautifully as it does through the wheel and the precision of the throttle is as keen as that of the steering.

What matters, though, is how many revs you have. If you've stayed in a gear that's too high for a tight bend and the revs drop much below 3000, the engine feels flat and you wait, in the understeer attitude, until it climbs back to around 3500 before you have the power you want. From anywhere upwards of 3800, the response is electric and you're *driving*. Given that you're in the midst of the power band and, given that fantastic communication of the chassis within the overall level of grip, the F40 is then a delightfully precise and easy car to drive, as well as being downright exciting.

As you ladle on the power and feel the rear edging round obediently, you simply adjust minutely with the throttle or counter by winding off lock and sweeping right out to the edge of the road. It's magical and you delight in the fact that this stunningly potent car is so accessible. Within just a few laps, the wariness has long been dispatched in favour of respect. Opening right up out of the bends means the most ferocious blast down the straights – Ferrari gives the 0–200km/h (125mph) time as 12sec – and you need to be watching and reading the distances accurately because the raw acceleration means that it can be so very easy to just go too fast.

At first, the unassisted brakes seem hard and unyielding. You learn to *push*, to get your foot right into them, and you discover then

AND THE REVS KEEP RISING

that they haul you down from speeds well beyond 150mph with tremendous security and without a trace of their power abating. In the dry, at least, it seems hard to get them near to locking up. And when it's braking hard, the Ferrari maintains faultless stability. You need only to concentrate on the line you want into the bend, not on keeping the car on course. This car gives; it does not fight. It's impeccably stable at speed too – at least up to the 160mph or so it's possible to do at Fiorano.

I don't yet know whether the F40 is intractable in traffic, fearsome in the wet, uncomfortably harsh on bumpy roads or too noisy on long journeys. It has no luggage space and getting in and out is awkward. But I do know this: on a smooth road it is a scintillatingly fast car that is approachable and even charming in its nature; a car that is demanding but not difficult to drive, blessed as it is with massive grip and, even more importantly, superb balance and manners. You can use its performance – the closest to race car levels yet available in a production car – and revel in it. Rich boy's toy it might be. *Sports car* it most certainly is.

STUFF OF LEGENDS
JAGUAR C-TYPE
1993

DUNCAN HAMILTON TELLS A vivid tale in his wonderful book *Touch Wood!* about his 1953 Le Mans win in a C-type Jaguar. Thinking about it made me chuckle as I drove down to his son Adrian's exotica-packed showroom in Hampshire for an appointment with that famous, self-same C-type.

On the eve of the '53 24-hour race, Hamilton and his co-driver Tony Rolt were disqualified after a practice car mix-up. Officials said they'd hear an appeal next morning but Duncan and Tony were convinced they'd be out. They set off to drown their disappointment in an all-night binge. But next morning the race committee settled on a 25,000 Franc fine. Small problem: where were Duncan and Tony? What *state* were they in? Jaguar owner William Lyons whistled around Le Mans' bars in his MkVII saloon and finally spotted them, sleepless and worse for wear, lolling over cups of coffee in Gruber's restaurant. It was 10am. The race was six hours away. Hamilton and Rolt, berated by their wives, tried frantically to sober up with cups of coffee and steaming baths. Two hours before the off, Hamilton said he felt so bad there was no way he could drive. Then he tried a hair of the dog. Rolt promptly called for a double brandy too. By start time at four o'clock they felt good enough to race.

Twenty-one laps later Rolt was in the lead. He and Duncan duly pulled off Jaguar's second Le Mans victory at a record average of 105.85mph, winning *The Motor* trophy for being first to average more than 100mph at Le Mans. Duncan and Tony's spirited drive notwithstanding, the 3.4-litre 1953 Jaguar C-types were clearly something special. They were first, second and fourth, trouncing the 4.5-litre Ferraris of Ascari/Villoresi and Hawthorn/Farina. Beyond

AND THE REVS KEEP RISING

the reliable performance that had given them victory in 1951, they had something else. They were the only cars with disc brakes.

But technical prowess is one thing. The C-type is also beautiful, a car so smooth from the front it looks as if it's moulded from liquid. But there's purpose among the beauty; a trace of meanness in its flanks. My heart beat a little faster when I turned into Duncan Hamilton Ltd's courtyard and saw Duncan's car, chassis number XKC 051, gleaming in the sun, waiting for me. It's immaculate; like new, no battle scars. After four years' persuasion, Adrian Hamilton bought it back from Briggs Cunningham, the American racer and collector, in 1984. Its body was off. The original was one of the lightweight skins for the '53 Le Mans. Adrian thought it was too fatigued, dented and twisted to be refitted. He had the car restored, with a new body in standard-thickness aluminium, by DK Engineering's David Cottingham.

Purists might mutter about lack of originality but there's no denying its beauty. Tilt the one-piece nose section forward to expose the suspension and engine and you can feast your eyes. The much-triangulated tubular steel chassis, which gave the C-type lightness and rigidity, is readily visible. It's intriguing to see the upper and lower wishbones of the front suspension working with torsion bar springing. Torsion bars provide the rear springing too, with the live axle located by low-slung trailing arms. A triangular torque reaction link from the top right side of the axle to the chassis behind the driver's seat stops the axle lifting on one side under hard acceleration, cutting wheel spin.

Apart from their 100lb lighter bodies, Dunlop disc brakes and triple-plate clutches, the '53 Le Mans C-types ran three twin-choke Weber carburettors instead of twin SUs. They boosted the 3442cc twin cam's mid-range torque and response and lifted power to 220bhp against the standard C's 204bhp at 5800rpm. What does 220bhp do in a 40-year-old, 13ft 1in car weighing around 2000lb? After you've eased past the dainty little door, stretched over the wide side rails and wiggled down into the bucket, you get a pretty good idea immediately you turn the key. That legendary XK six snaps into loud, crackling life. A couple of blips make it clear there's bite behind the bark.

JAGUAR C-TYPE

The engine has enough flexibility to make moving off and low-speed manoeuvring trauma-free. Delight: the clutch is light and works with plenty of feel through a very short throw. Same goes for the servo-assisted brakes. No need for a he-man shove here. The steering's part of the same team – much lighter than I'd expected.

So you're soon off down the kind of English lane you'd seek for such a classic English sports car on an early summer's day. The view down the bonnet over the louvers and curves is sexy; not as sultry as in a D-type, but enough to get the juices flowing. And the noise from those two big pipes kicking out from beneath the left flank is soul-stirring. It starts as a bass drone backing the crackle. But open the Webers and it changes instantly to a savage bark that turns every head within earshot and sends horses dashing to the ends of their paddocks.

The engine pulls hard and fast, getting potent from just upwards of 3000rpm. With its eagerness to rev and a redline at just 5700 you need to watch the tachometer. The gearshifts are easy enough on the way up and the ratios match the engine well, so the performance feels uninterrupted. I'd guess at 6–7sec 0–60mph, 18sec 0–100; enough performance to live with many of today's fast road cars. It's the in-gear performance at higher speeds that's most impressive. Push the C's short-travel throttle and that engine snarls and *goes*. The oh-so-clear character of the car is that it just wants to pelt on down the road. To race. To do its job.

The quality of the brakes – special, even after all these years – adds to that. This is a fast old racer you're confident you can stop. So swift is the brakes' response that I soon learned to watch the cars behind me on the way into A-road roundabouts because many couldn't stop as quickly as the Jaguar. While the rack and pinion steering is light, it has lost motion at the centre. So it's here and in the suspension behaviour that the C-type feels old, agricultural even; definitely an earlier generation than the D-type. When the road is smooth, and certainly at higher speeds, it runs nice and true, feeling aerodynamically stable. But over bumps the tail cocks this way or that, depending on the directional loading, so you're constantly correcting across the steering's centre. It becomes second nature after a while.

AND THE REVS KEEP RISING

In bends, you turn straight through the lost motion onto lock and the response is excellent. No understeer. The nose points in well and you can get onto the power. The car then hunches onto the outside rear wheel and, with the back axle so close to your bottom, you can feel exactly what's happening. Keep the throttle down and the tail will then slide tidily, responding well to a swift flick of opposite lock. In the right bend, this is a car to drift in the old-fashioned way.

Unless you're on surfaces with lots of frequent, lateral bumps is it not uncomfortable. Then, it thumps you hard in the kidneys. Above 110mph, the wind blasts around the aeroscreen fiercely enough to make you want goggles. Without them, vision becomes the limitation; the car wants to charge on. Top speed in a standard C-type was 146mph. The lightweights topped 150mph at Le Mans.

I might have groaned and dashed for cover when the heavens opened during my day in the C-type. But it was a chance to get closer to the experience of running an endurance race in one. The Dunlops' grip was surprisingly good so applying the power was no problem. But below 80mph the water drops clung to the aeroscreen so I had to drive with my head out in the airstream and winced as the raindrops peppered my face. Water poured over the side of the cockpit onto my legs and seeped up through the floor. I imagined what it was like trying to see at 150mph in the fog at dawn down the Mulsanne straight. I remembered, too, that Duncan was going that fast when a bird smashed through his aeroscreen and broke his nose. He carried on regardless.

When the sun returned, I drove hard on a long, clear leg back to Adrian Hamilton's, opening up the six hard whenever I could to enjoy the lunging power and its savage aural expression. I'd learned to allow time for double-shuffle downchanges because whatever synchromesh there was had long since departed. I took advantage of the brakes to have the car ship-shape before the bends. I got on the power early, feeding the steering back against the tail's action. I knew now that driving the C was a matter of anticipating its bump or corner-induced action against the centre play in the steering, constantly working the wheel against the chassis' motion, and enjoying the instant responses of the steering, brakes and engine. Compared to a D-type, the C was cruder and wilder than I'd expected, less comfortable and in many ways more demanding. Some would say more rewarding. Real sports car stuff, and a treat; oh yes, a treat.

Footnote

Duncan Hamilton's enthralling autobiography *Touch Wood!* has been republished by his son Adrian. Copies are available from www.duncanhamilton.com/touchwood/

1000 MILES IN ITALY IN A MILLE MIGLIA SWEETIE

FIAT 1100 S MM

1993

I HAVE A SOFT spot for Fiat coupés. When I landed in Sicily in 1973 for the final Targa Florio a Fiat 124 Sport Coupé bravely took me on my first excursion on the right-hand side of the road, through rush hour Palermo. Burnie, Tasmania, was never like this. Not even Sydney. Somehow my companion Pete Smith, the Fiat and I emerged unscathed on the road east and duly arrived at the mediaeval town of Cefalu, our home for the next couple of weeks. The 124 Sport served us faithfully, taking us the length of Italy, in and out of Modena, Bologna, Milano and across to Monaco for the Grand Prix. Fiat insisted we should go to Rome in a 124 Spider, so in Turin we swapped the coupé for its open sister and went back down to the Eternal City in that.

Twenty years on, I went back to Italy in another Fiat coupé. This time it was an 1100 S MM, built in 1948. It was made for the Mille Miglia, a race even more famous than the Targa, run over 1000 miles out and back from Brescia in northern Italy. I'd been enthralled, like so many, by Denis Jenkinson's account of riding to victory in 1955 with Stirling Moss in the Mercedes 300SLR. 'The boy' despatched the 1000 miles in 10hrs 7mins 48sec, an average of 97.98mph, to set an all-time record. In 1991 colleague Peter Robinson and I ran the retrospective Mille Miglia in a 300SL as part of the Mercedes team, whooping with joy every time our team-mate Stirling tore past us in that glorious SLR. Hearing him blast past us and seeing him flicking that legendary silver car through bends in front of us is a sight we'll never forget.

FIAT 1100 S MM

The quaint 1100 S MM calls on its smooth bob-tailed body to extract surprising pace from its 1.1-litre/52bhp engine and four-speed gearbox. First time out in 1947 an 1100 S MM finished fifth with another sixth. In 1948, MMs passed much more powerful cars to take second, third and eighth. Our little Fiat had a fine pedigree, well-known to the crowds that packed Brescia for the retro Mille Miglia's start.

We accelerated away from the famous starting ramp at 9.20.50pm through thousands of waving, cheering people with the efficient police pointing the right way and egging us on. All the way on the three-hour night leg to Ferrara, the Fiat's surprisingly good lights picked up gaggles of mums, dads, kids, grandpas and grandmas. We pulled into the square in Ferrara and headed for our beds imbued with the Mille spirit.

Next morning, as we jiggled forward in the exotic throng to await our starting time, we enjoyed the sight of John Surtees settling into his BMW 507, Stirling and Suzy Moss snuggling into their Mercedes 300SL, and Jochen Mass warming up the 300SL Carrera Panamericana among scores of other magnificent cars. The older cars – not necessarily slower – run ahead, starting at 30sec intervals; the later and generally much quicker cars come further back. At 159th, we were around the middle of the 330-car field. A control car runs every 50 entrants. If you pass one, you're out. The real Mille Miglia was stopped in 1957 after the Marquis de Portago's Ferrari 335S killed him, his co-driver and nine spectators. Even so, the pace is enough to allow plenty of enjoyment.

Our Fiat's engine had been rebuilt just before the event. On the long straights down to the coast at Rimini we could feel it loosening and singing ever more sweetly. No question about the aerodynamics. Once we built up speed, the Fiat slipped along on the merest sniff of throttle. Our problem was the four-speed gearbox. Even double declutching up and down, every change was a challenge. Third to second was a nightmare. For Fiat, Italy and Australia's honour, we avoided changing down near spectators. Our honour soon took a battering in the time trials. Scoring in the retrospective Mille Miglia means hitting electronic time controls to the 100th of a second. We

AND THE REVS KEEP RISING

were more concerned with simply enjoying the driving, vistas and atmosphere and could but giggle at how far out we usually were.

The real driving began as we started to wind through the valleys in the Appenines. Peter made the most of the swift curves, driving in third and fourth, keeping the lines clean and winding off lock as he snipped past the apexes. It was a pleasure to witness and to feel. We were beginning to discover how well our little Fiat could cover the ground. Towards Monti Sibillini we topped a long climb at Castelluccio to see a spectacular vista open out before us, with the road snaking down to a vast, flat valley and then spearing across its bottom. The peaks on all sides disappeared into the cloud. We vowed to come back in a Ferrari one day.

As in so many other towns, a mayoral party flagged us down in Leonessa and pretty girls in regional costume handed us local biscuits and fruit juice, fortifying us for the long climb to Fonte Nuova ahead. The altitude affected the Fiat's performance and we were down to a crawl in first. But it didn't overheat and to frequent exhortations, first hopeful and then cheerful, of 'come on little girl, come on' she just kept plugging away to the mountain top for a view back over the best series of hairpins I've ever seen. Into the rain down the other side we learned that no understeer and strong, fade-free brakes were among the Fiat's virtues. We were beginning to understand why the 1100 S MMs did so well in 1948.

On the run to Rome in the dark, our headlights died. We were on a straight stretch but there was nowhere to pull off. Peter grabbed our torch to flash at oncoming cars, then behind as a 300SL came up quickly. Its quick-thinking driver realised we were driving blind, slowed and lit our way until we could stop in a village to reattach a loose wire. We collapsed into bed around at 11.30pm. It had been a long day.

The next was just as wonderful. Viterbo, the morning's first big town, was bathed in sun and the streets packed. Viterbo must have a substantial ladies' college: for 100 solid metres, the roadside was packed with gorgeous girls, all shouting Peter's name from the programme: *'Robeenson!, Robeenson!'*

Lovely towns and the same joyous scenes came thick and fast.

FIAT 1100 S MM

Schoolchildren leaned from classrooms windows or were lined up outside by nuns and teachers to wave and shout. In Montefiascone, a black-frocked priest leaped in the air and blew a whistle, inciting his kids to do the same. And emerging from tight streets into the crowded Piazzo del Campo in Sienna, site of the famous palio horse race, is something never to be forgotten.

Nor is the drive up the Futa pass, between Florence and Bologna. One bend after another, mostly climbing, it's a great test of handling, balance and brakes. Not for nothing is it familiar territory for Ferrari, Lamborghini and Maserati test drivers who whip down from Modena. The Fiat shone. With quite quick, accurate steering that never got heavy, it turned in and held firmly to its line, never understeering. It maintained more grip than we'd expected then, at the limit, told us when the outside wheel was starting to slide and answered the helm well. Add the ever-reliable brakes and a surprisingly comfortable ride and you get a car capable of swift point to point times even though its power is so modest. We were now very fond of our stout-hearted little Fiat.

The Mille Miglia spirit was particularly good to us on the Roman-built two-lane Via Emilia from Bologna to Modena. Police motorcyclist Vincenzo Patti came past, blue light flashing and siren nee-nawing, leading a 10-strong collection of Mille Miglia cars. We joined in and watched with delight as Officer Patti, like a 75mph mother duck, parted the traffic. He swung his right foot out at the cars we were overtaking and waved the oncoming steam aside with stylish sweeps of his left hand. He waited at the Modena control while we talked to Ferrari president Luca di Montezemolo then led us on again all the way to Parma. What a cop!

We buzzed on through the languid dusk across the flat Oglio valley, the Fiat never missing a beat, to the final time control at Montichiari, near Brescia. There was sad news: the 1927 Bugatti Type 40 GS we'd seen crashed beside the road had rolled after its steering broke, killing driver Robertus Van Slype and injuring his wife Anna.

The crowds were teeming as we wound back into Brescia to the official finish. Two hundred metres from the end we saw our families waving. We stopped and tugged my seven-year-old daughter Georgia in with us. She looked around the Fiat's low, narrow cabin. 'It's very small,' she said quietly. Outside, the chorus of bravos changed to 'Ciao bambina'. After we parked the Fiat proudly in the main Brescia Fiat dealer's showroom, Robinson stepped up, patted its bonnet and said with feeling: 'Thanks old girl — you're a bloody good little car'.

Next day we learned we'd come 193rd in the time trials and were indeed the winning Australian team. We'd have slunk away if we hadn't been. There *was* only one other Australian crew. I couldn't have thought of a better way to celebrate 20 years of motoring in Europe. On the road, in Italy, in a red Italian coupé.

'OKAY MATE, THAT'S PROBABLY ENOUGH.'

McLAREN F1

1994

I WOKE SEVERAL TIMES in the night. And in those still moments I realised that this was the first time the emotion I'd felt before driving a fast car was more fear than excitement. Before breakfast, I was going to be behind the mid-mounted wheel of a car in a league – several leagues – beyond the performance capability of any road car I'd driven before. As the first light began seeping through the curtains, I ran through some of them in my mind. Miura, Daytona, Boxer, Countach, 250 GTO, Vector, Aston Martin Vantage, Porsche 959, F40, Viper, Diablo, Ferrari 456, 512 TR. No Jaguar XJ220, I realised, but it didn't matter much. I knew the McLaren F1 waiting outside was far quicker than even the Jaguar.

In the bar the evening before, with the McLaren F1 fresh from recording its first set of acceleration figures, its designer, former Formula 1 designer Gordon Murray, smiled shyly and confessed that it was quicker even than he had expected. There was more. Jonathan Palmer, the former Formula 1 driver who helped develop the F1, sidled up and told how Gordon had run its acceleration traces against a McLaren MP4/8's. Upwards of 130mph the F1 was faster than the grand prix car. I remembered too the first words my colleague Andrew Frankel, who'd just run the performance figures on the McLaren, had uttered when we rendezvoused. 'It is faster,' he said with awed deliberation, 'from 180 to 200mph in sixth than a Ferrari 512 TR is from 50 to 70 in fifth.'

He drew the silver Correvit tape from his breast pocket and reeled off more stupefying data: 0–60mph in 3.2sec; 0–100mph in 6.3;

AND THE REVS KEEP RISING

0–200mph in 28 seconds dead. Quicker to 150mph than a Porsche 911 from 0–100. We pored over the in-gear acceleration times and my jaw dropped further. In second, the Macca shot from 60–80mph in 1.2sec. In third, it needed just 1.7sec to whip from 90–110mph. And in fourth it despatched every 20mph increment between 30mph and 130 within a 10th of 2.2sec.

Neither Andrew, *Autocar*'s road test editor, nor I had ever seen anything like this. 'When you drive it,' he said with a slow shake of his head, 'you will be gobsmacked.' Over dinner, Gordon Murray, the man driven to make the car that would put his fiendish quest for low weight into practice, said as an aside: 'You know, this car wouldn't make a bad little racer. But for the GT class, I'd have to detune it by 100 horsepower and add a lot of weight.'

So, in those deep night hours, I contemplated all this and, just short of a cold sweat, wondered what 627bhp in a six-speed car weighing 2500lb was going to feel like on roads with bumps and crests and twists and turns and broken surfaces. Could I handle it? How much of its power could I apply? How often? How much of its potential could be unleashed. What speeds would we see?

For sure, I reckoned, I wasn't going to get the thing flat in fifth, which tops out at 180mph. Sixth, which would propel the Macca at least to 230mph and probably more, looked like it'd be for nothing other than a deserted *autobahn*. How wrong I was. When I walked outside, before many souls were stirring, the deep metallic green McLaren was parked next to a Mercedes 300CE. I'd never thought the F1 beautiful but, when you know what it does, the purposefulness of its styling, where every aspect is dictated by function dedicated to performance and, just as importantly, usability, is breathtaking.

I was fascinated to note that its wheelbase was almost exactly the same as the Mercedes coupé's. But so short are its overhangs and so low its roof that it looked diminutive next to the Mercedes. Critically for using it anything like properly on winding roads, the F1 is not only shorter than all previous supercars, it's narrower too, even compared with the relatively petite Ferrari F40. Yet it seats three people and doesn't mind if they're amply proportioned and well over six feet tall.

McLAREN F1

As I looked down into its cabin, I remembered Gordon's and body designer Peter Stevens's desire to achieve not just the lowest possible weight but a level of room, comfort and practicality alien to very fast mid-engined cars. Long before Murray and Steve Nichols designed the all-conquering McLaren MP4/4 that gave the team an incredible 15 victories in 16 races in 1988, he'd dreamed of making a performance car like this – 'a super sports car to end all supercars, a unique and advanced vehicle that would be usable, fast and safe but, above all, a pure driver's car'.

His starting point was to put the driver in the centre to obtain the two important goals of having the feet unobstructed by wheel arches and a seating position so far forward it would allow remarkably good vision. Passengers would go either side of, and just behind, the driver. Peter Stevens would say later: 'We wanted to give something close to the Formula 1 driving experience. It's not an F1 car for the road but it uses the same uncompromising approach to design and construction. So you end up sitting in the middle with everything equidistant from the wheel. You can see the corners and judge distance so much more easily than in a conventional supercar.' Murray also wanted a large capacity normally aspirated engine giving a minimum of 450bhp with the instant response and flexibility not possible with turbochargers. It would drive through a transverse gearbox to keep the masses within the wheelbase.

When Stevens joined McLaren in March 1990, hot from designing the Lotus Elan M100 and Jaguar XJR-15, he worked for months without making any styling sketches. He shared Murray's vision and wanted to have the packaging worked out before he took up his pencil. 'I didn't want any preconceptions of how it was going to look,' he says. 'In the past I would have begun drawing but then you compromise and force the design. Sometimes you fall in love with a design too soon and try to force it to fit an inappropriate package.'

When they knew the all-critical package would work – the driver would be able to get in and out; the passengers wouldn't feel they were 'outside' the car – Murray asked Stevens for certain other themes and details. 'I wanted the air intake on the roof for clean air and easy water separation,' Gordon says. 'That meant we

AND THE REVS KEEP RISING

were committed to a spine. There were other details defined by the package. The twin radiators meant a high nose and I wanted a lobster-claw look like the early Brabhams *[which Murray did]*. I also told Peter I wanted the car to look more mechanical the further back you looked, with grilles, vents and stacks.

'That's why, when you look at the car from the back, you can see the engine, although not as much as I would have liked because of the size of the silencer. I'd also wanted something that was '60s, all soft curves, but it couldn't look retro. Neither of us wanted a fashionable shape that would date. The way I see it, Peter's skill was inventing the look of the F1 in spite of everything I imposed.'

When you peer down through Peter's engine cover, past the two great carbon fibre tubes that funnel the air from that rooftop intake, the heart you see is the extraordinary S70/2 6064cc V12 made expressly for McLaren by BMW. Murray reckoned only three companies could make the big, high-revving non-turbo engine delivering at least 100bhp per litre that he wanted: Ferrari, Honda or BMW. Honda, providers of McLaren's race engines, made most sense. But, after discussing V10 versus V12 and good initial progress, Murray says Honda seemed to get nervous about green issues and, after Jaguar and Bugatti came along with 550bhp engines and it was clear the McLaren would need around 5.3 litres from a V12, the programme 'just sorted of drifted into oblivion'.

So Gordon talked to BMW Motorsport's boss Paul Rosche who had created the 1100bhp BMW engine in the Murray-designed Brabham BT52 that won Nelson Piquet the World Championship in 1983. 'We'll do the engine for you,' Rosche said, and duly created an all-new, all-aluminium 60-degree 48-valve V12 with variable valve timing that met Gordon's weight and length limits. During development, Paul kept phoning Gordon to announce ever-higher power figures. In the end, they settled for 103bhp per litre for an output of 627bhp at 7400rpm and a staggering 479lb/ft of torque from 4000 to 7000rpm. At just 1500rpm, this fabulous piece of Bavarian engine making delivers more torque than a 4.0-litre Jaguar's maximum. With the McLaren weighing just 2508lb, Murray and Rosche achieved a power-to-weight ratio of 4lb/bhp –

McLAREN F1

550bhp/tonne. Add in a Cd of 0.32, with all the right kinds of trim and stability factors, and this is a car set to fly.

And oh how it flies! I'd thought, with the fears of the night still riding on my shoulder, that I'd be circumspect in the beginning. But, without the intimidation of a compromised driving position or awkward vision, you find yourself using a great deal of the F1's potential much sooner than you'd expect. The central driving position – far easier to wriggle into than you might imagine – is the first godsend. It gives anybody up to 6ft 4in good head and legroom, and locates them perfectly. The pedals, spared the encroachment of a wheel arch, are straight ahead and uncramped. The rake of the steering wheel and its relationship to the gear lever are just as stellar.

So is the vision. The sultry tops of the wheel arches bob into view left and right to give you location reference but never obstruction. What you see, thanks to that short, scalloped-out nose and deep windscreen, is a great panorama of road. The main instruments are so well located that you need drop your eyes only a few degrees to check the rev-counter and speedo. So great is the feeling of rightness about this environment that you feel swiftly at ease about driving from the centre. Indeed, all of us lucky enough to drive the Macca found we adapted quite naturally. Within a couple of miles we'd forgotten about it. It never seems difficult to place the left or right of the car in narrow spaces.

Nor are you in for aggravation from the drivetrain. The engine starts instantly and a few exploratory blips acquaint you with the lightning response of an engine with an ultra lightweight flywheel. Press and the revs rise instantly. Lift off and the revs die just as fast, like a racing engine. The clutch is light – a friendly thing that does its job flawlessly. So the F1 can be dribbled in tight town traffic with ease. Its manners are impeccable. The engine murmurs quietly behind you, letting you trickle in the higher gears without complaint. This is a *complete* engine.

But get onto clear roads and decide you're ready to run to the redline and you get a breathtaking response and forward propulsion new even to those familiar with the world's quickest cars. The

AND THE REVS KEEP RISING

driver's task becomes one of adjusting sight and data processing to cope with the speed at which the road ahead – the horizon itself – is arriving, and snapping through gearshifts. When your foot's flat, you're in each gear for such a short time. It's literally *wraaap,* shift; *wraaap,* shift; *wraaap*, shift. The engine seems unimpeded by the car around it.

The tachometer needle whips around so fast that, after the first second or so of acceleration, you must flick a glance every few milliseconds to catch it before it strikes the little black marker at 7500rpm. First is done at 65mph and 3.5 seconds; second in only another 2.4 seconds at 95mph; third takes a tad longer at 3.9 seconds before it puts 125mph on the unerringly accurate speedo; and you're in fourth for a staggering three seconds before you're looking at 150mph.

That's a total time from standstill of a blurr-filled 12.8 seconds. Even in fifth, you've only got 7.5 seconds before you're reaching for top at 180mph. And if you keep your foot down, let me assure you that the lunge to and beyond 200mph continues with similar potency. We had test track space for only 211mph. Jonathan Palmer logged 235mph at the Nardo test centre in Italy. With higher gearing, Gordon Murray's view is that the Macca may do even more. *[He was proved right: with the rev limiter disabled, an F1 driven by Andy Wallace ran to 242.95mph at 8100rpm at VW's Ehra-Lessien test track on March 31 1998. ^]*

Any difficulty applying this performance doesn't stem from the F1 itself. Its traction is fantastic, its stability is flawless, its accuracy on the road is impeccable. Your problem as the driver is to deal with the speed. The acceleration is so intense that on ordinary roads – let alone anything like a four-lane – you will blast often into the 170–180 zone where you might have hit 120–130 in a normally quick car. Think what that means for mixing it with other traffic. You'll be passing them so rapidly, closing on them so quickly, they may be so shocked they pull over and park. It's been known.

So ably does the F1's chassis apply the V12's 627bhp and so firmly do its aerodynamics glue it to the road, so balanced and effortless does it feel, that it's hard for the driver to know the speed

McLAREN F1

envelope without seeing the speedo. You may well encounter a scenario like this –

The passengers, tucked back either side of the driver, are sitting comfortably. The driver, settled in and feeling at ease, is going for it now. The car exits a long bend at 120mph in third. The driver snaps into fourth and presses on through fifth then rapidly into sixth along the straight that follows – though it's not very long. He won't have time now to glance at the speedo. The passengers, who do have that luxury, are aware of just how fast the car is going but are amazed to see how rapidly the needle is sweeping past 200mph and heading for 210. They start looking at the uphill kink at the end of the straight. Even in the McLaren, it doesn't look like a 200mph bend. They're wondering if, even with the McLaren's brakes, there's going to be space to fling off enough speed; or, if not, whether they are bold enough to travel through it at the pace the increasingly confident driver will contemplate. One of them will say what the other is thinking. 'Okay mate, that's probably enough.' He'll back off, and they'll tell him later that he'd have hit 220mph before he reached the corner. He will be amazed. Such is the realm of the McLaren F1.

Apart from the F1's speed over the ground, what the driver will also have discovered is the blistering speed of its gearshift. Gordon Murray worked to a shift time target of two milliseconds. So the gearshift zings from slot to slot as quickly as you can snap your hand and dip the clutch. Because everything marries up so well, the shifts are smooth as well as lighting fast. So there's pleasure in that even if there isn't much in the feel of the shift itself. What you can do, because of the response of the engine, is to vary shifts and go as fast or slow as you like, playing tunes, straight-shifting or double declutching.

You will want to do that because of the V12's sound. It's tame at low revs but when you hit the throttle it snarls like nothing except a big unblown sports car race engine from the '70s. It's a spine-tingling deep gurgle that builds to a loud, quickfire rolling crackle. As Andrew Frankel said: 'For its flexibility, throttle response and

AND THE REVS KEEP RISING

power alone, this V12 would probably wrest the title of world's best engine from the Ferrari 512TR. But the sounds it makes puts the issue beyond doubt. It's smooth, subtle and above all quiet when you want it to be but it gives you everything you have ever wanted from an engine note when the throttle is opened wide.'

Because the engine's air intake runs down between their heads, the passengers hear even more than the driver of this orchestra from hell. On long trips, they will eventually find it tiring. Otherwise, it's unbridled joy; an aural interpretation of every fraction of an inch that the driver moves the throttle.

At town speeds, the steering loads up heavily with lock. But on an open road it is quick, clean, accurate, transparent and free of the kick-back that – seeing the 235/45ZR17 tyres – you might have feared. Sitting in the middle, with this information system in your hands, you know you can put this car exactly where you want, and be aware of every grain beneath its tread rubber at every moment. In slow bends, if you can see the exit, you can push in until you feel a trace of understeer then unleash the V12 and press through neutrality to a full-blooded tail-slide. It's not a fearful thing to do. In the dry, the F1's compact size is a bonus. You feel you can play with it; that you won't be overwhelmed by width or mass. The immediacy and consistency of the throttle response from such a big unblown engine adds to your confidence. Your right foot elicits a crisp, linear answer that harmonises with the chassis' behaviour. In the wet, though, the tail comes around to meet you quickly. If you're judicious, and as long as your reactions are up to it, the McLaren will answer your correction faithfully. But it's best to keep your Caution Hat on in inclement weather.

It's in high-speed bends that the F1's chassis shows its extreme prowess. It knuckles down and grips, whipping you around the corner at speeds you will not have experienced before and will scarcely believe. Neither end moves, even when the rear tyres are being seriously bullied by the V12's power. Adverse camber doesn't worry it and bumps don't move it off-line. It is, as it needs to be, unfailingly accurate.

Passengers noting all this will be aware – perhaps, as with the

McLAREN F1

speed, more than the driver – that the F1 backs its g-generation with an exceptionally good ride. It is firm and delivers the right feeling of control and stability on typical country roads, but it never jars. The F1 has pace with class. The only flaw emerges on concrete and coarse-surfaced motorways where a slight jitteriness becomes annoying on long trips.

It is an extraordinary achievement, this car. When the three of us who'd shared an astounding foray into the new playground of the 200mph car climbed out and settled down with a drink to reflect, I felt silly for entertaining those night fears. *Mighty* is the word that kept coming to mind; mighty in *every* way. The F1's performance will forever thrill a driver well used to the upper reaches of power and speed. Its chassis will allow even those with less experience to drive it and do OK, and even to feel comfortable with it. All they will need to do is be mindful – *constantly* – of how extraordinarily quickly they can reach and maintain speeds that call for unwavering vigilance, and be ever-aware of the gap that exists between their speed and the rest of the traffic's. Gordon and Peter's clever design will allow drivers to take two passengers and to consume distances in shorter times and greater comfort and security than has ever been possible. Some may climb out at the end of a blast and wonder if the F1 is in fact too fast. The brave will relish the challenge and the rewards of a car that redefines ultimate performance. No need for cold sweats. No need at all.

* *Autocar*'s video of Andy Wallace driving the F1 at 243mph is here – http://www.autocar.co.uk/car-news/motoring/mclaren-f1-20-years Just listen to that engine!

DANCING WITH THE TEMPTRESS

FERRARI 275 GTB/4

1997

SO NOW I'M ALONE in this Ferrari, 275 GTB/4. Twenty years since I last drove one. Special, not just because it's stood so high in my esteem all that time; it also happens to be the first Ferrari I ever drove, a few years further back again. Hell of an introduction: instantly condemned all those who'd said Ferraris were fast trucks. Whet my appetite for the Old Man's cars big-time.

Question now is whether this visual temptress will match the golden image in my mind. Two decades on, after all the other cars from Maranello I've been lucky enough to pedal – *racing berlinettas, the mid-engined cars, the latest barnstormers; the sixes, eights, turbos, flat-12s and old and new V12s* – will this relatively simple old dear from 1967 hold onto its place as one of Ferraris' greatest road cars? For many, it's the quintessential Ferrari: front-mounted carburettor-fed V12 driving the rear wheels; voluptuous two-seat body with no luxury trappings; and the last model built directly under Enzo Ferrari's eye before Fiat 's involvement.

There are various reasons why the 275 GTB garnered such respect, and they're voluminous enough to outweigh the flaws that are also part of its make-up. First, the behaviour of a well-balanced and carefully sorted front-engined/rear-driven car has an appeal that, for many, betters the snappier feel of a mid-engined model. It's usually a more relaxed feel; a more open and approachable nature that lets you come closer to the limits more quickly, more often and less worryingly. When you're there, communication through your hands and the seat of your trousers may well be more

FERRARI 275 GTB/4

intense. Within the tiny time frames of mid-bend behaviour, front-engined cars will usually extend the experience's duration because their polar moment of inertia is longer than that of mid-engined cars, which are designed so they'll change direction quicker.

In the early '60s, Enzo Ferrari's front-engined dual-purpose road and race Gran Turismo berlinettas – *hail* the 250 GT Short-wheelbase – had reached a level of chassis ability that blended impressive roadholding with clean and consistent handling. They epitomised the wonderful feel of a classic front-engined sports car. Its ultimate expression came in the 250 GTO of 1962–64, last of the breed before the gulf between road and race cars widened to a chasm with the move to the mid-engined layout and more single-minded purpose of the 250 LM.

It would be another decade before Ferrari switched to mid-engines for the road with the 365 GT Berlinetta Boxer. For the mid-1960s, Enzo's most serious road car was going to remain firmly front-engined. But it would turn out to be a landmark because pressure from marques like Jaguar and Lamborghini was making it clear that live rear axles, however well they performed in the SWB and GTO, were no longer good enough on specification sheets; that five gears were de rigueur; and (ultimately) that four overhead cams were a lot sexier than two. So the incoming 275 Grand Turismo Berlinetta, revealed at the Paris Motor Show in October 1964, was set to boast a new level of sophistication and performance.

The main change was in the suspension. In a transference of knowledge from the 250 LM, in came an independent rear suspension with admirable upper and lower wishbones, anti-roll bar, and coil springs around telescopic dampers. But Ferrari's first irs for the road wasn't the GTB's only technical departure. The new rear end made it possible to indulge in a quest for optimum weight distribution by shifting the all-new, all-synchro gearbox – the first five-speeder properly designed for road use in a Ferrari – to a transaxle between the rear axles. It was fed from the engine and clutch by a surprisingly slender open drive shaft steadied halfway along by a chassis-mounted bearing. Vibration, bearing wear and high repair costs led, two years into the GTB's life, to a heftier shaft

AND THE REVS KEEP RISING

enclosed in a torque tube. But the main thing was that the GTB gained 49/51 weight distribution

The engine moved on too. In yet another development of the classic 60-degree V12 designed by Gioacchino Colombo, the bores went out another 4mm, lifting the capacity to 3285cc against the 250's 2953cc. With a single cam per bank, 9.2:1 compression ratio and three twin-choke Weber carburettors it was rated at 280bhp at 7600rpm, with enough torque, smoothness and response to make your soul sing. A six-Weber option delivered another 40bhp for racing.

Two years later, as a riposte to Lamborghini whose V12 boasted four cams, Ferrari went the whole hog. From the competition department, with remarkably little modification, came twin cam heads. The six Webers became standard, along with a race-style dry sump. Power went up to an even 300bhp at 8000rpm and the extra camminess and top-end response made the two-cam cars, however impressive, feel tame by comparison. So here, in the 275 GTB/4, was a classic front-engined Ferrari with the fundamental appeal of its predecessors, a more-wicked-than-ever V12, an up-to-date suspension, five-speed gearbox and better balance thanks to the transaxle.

Shame about the brakes. The discs' diameters were retarded by the unfashionably small 14-inch road wheels. Their callipers were big but flexed under pressure. And the servo unit couldn't store enough at low revs to pull the car up after several applications. Several unfortunate owners would discover that, after they'd slowed from very high speed without too much trouble, there was nothing left to bring them to a final halt at the next intersection. In the make-up of the GTB, the braking system was, and remains, an embarrassment.

Not so its GTO-inspired body. Perhaps there's the *hint* of a customiser's feel about the way the tiny cabin squashes down so low onto the shark of a body, but this is a car dripping with voluptuousness. It evokes the vision of how a Ferrari should look for people of all ages, not just those for whom it was their dream car in its heyday.

There was one other aspect that helped make the GTB special —

FERRARI 275 GTB/4

the man who wove its ingredients together: Mike Parkes, the gifted English chassis engineer and race driver. Ferrari, noting his track success in GTOs, recruited him to develop its road and race cars between works drives that culminated in an F1 seat. Mike knew how to make a car handle.

The result of his efforts was a car lauded during its four-year life – especially after the four-cam's arrival – for the way the sheer guts of its performance was backed by a ride and handling combination that struck a new standard for the world's fastest road cars. It was still quick enough to be raced with success (and could be ordered with an aluminium instead of a steel body, among other tweaks) but had a layer of road-going sophistication beyond its predecessors offering anything like similar performance – 52mph, 75, 101 and 127 in the gears and better than 160mph, with 0–60mph in a bit over six seconds and 0–100 in 14.5sec: still pretty strong stuff.

For all this, the 275 GTB was overshadowed and, for a long time, overlooked, when its own successor, the 365 GTB/4 Daytona elbowed it aside in 1968. The Daytona was heavier but, with another 52bhp, was quicker again while delivering more creature comforts like air conditioning and electric windows. It was *The Governor*. But if today's prices are anything to go by, the 275 is now viewed as the more desirable: a 275 will generally cost double or triple what's needed for a Daytona in similar condition.

How does it cut the mustard on the road now? For a start, it's a comfortable old thing because that little bucket seat, while devoid of backrest adjustment, is surprisingly correct for a wide variety of people. That makes the driving position good and the vision, apart from the rear three-quarter angle, is terrific. Clutch is strongly sprung but not wickedly heavy. Gearshift standard stuff with first left and back – opposite reverse – in the open gate and the top four in the main H. Engine starts easily after the usual single prod to prime the Webers and that long, slow whirr before the 12 cylinders start their steady rumble. Sigh of relief, once you're rolling, that the steering is light and even; at park speeds the wheels feel as if they're super-glued to the road.

AND THE REVS KEEP RISING

Nothing intimidating about the learning process then. Indeed, what had me marvelling and rapidly rediscovering affection and respect for the 275 was its openness and friendliness. In just a few miles of interesting Hampshire roads it swiftly began communicating the depths of its virtues. It still felt quick enough to play in Porsche 928 territory, for instance – in other words, it has serious go both through and in the gears – but had enough grip to keep the power down despite a drizzle-sheened surface. The steering might not be rack and pinion but Mike Parkes got it to the point where it guides the car adroitly with very little lost motion. So you can point it accurately into the bends with both confidence and surprisingly little lock.

Then real delights begin. Feed in the power and the nose tightens into the bend, allowing you to start winding off lock. All the while, the messages flowing from the rear wheels fairly zing across the inches to your backside. You can feel exactly what's happening with your outside wheel and, perhaps even more importantly, what's *about* to happen. It loads up and comes round to the point of neutrality, and you know that's precisely where it is. You've brought the steering back to mid-ships by now and you do the rest with the throttle, playing it against the chassis like the fine instrument it is. Want the rear wheels round a bit more because the bend is tightening? Just add a smidgeon of pressure to the throttle. Need them to hold station and have the front come out a touch? Ease back a gnat's. So sensitive is the throttle and so instantaneous the response from the V12 – both in gaining and losing power – that at times you feel as if you're doing nothing more than flexing the sole of your foot. Such pleasures are not the stuff of everyday cars.

Nor is such a taut link between engine behaviour and chassis action. The two, in the 275 GTB/4, are soulmates; inseparable, the one interwoven with the other. Driving this car is a complete hands, feet and seat-of-your pants experience. Aural too, because all the while comes the wonderful, unmistakable, inimitable sound of a carburettor-fed four-cam Ferrari V12: the ever-changing bellow of the exhausts with the constant zizz of the cams laid across the top.

In a very short time, then, you feel that you can get close to

FERRARI 275 GTB/4

this Ferrari's edge, and that you can trust it as much as you can enjoy it. It feels balanced – that neither front nor rear will bite you – and because of that it feels nimble. Moreover, where its modern counterparts, shod with far wider wheels and tyres, require more road room because they tram-line under brakes on uneven surfaces, this one runs straight and true and ever-clean. There's a sense of security in that.

If you can, find a road with some bends tight enough to need second with, between them, straights that'll let you run out all the way in second and hard into third. Head into the first bend and blip (gloriously) down through the box, taking care not to rush the very deliberate action, and set your revs around 3000. Then bring on the power, hear and feel the V12 get back onto its cams and feel all that communication and adjustability and revel in this wondrous through-the-bend behaviour. Coming out, with the tail held just short of needing opposite lock, let that engine rip through its cacophony of sounds and feel its thrust as it snarls towards its 7600rpm redline. Notice how rapidly the next bend approaches. Brake, leaving three times the distance you'd need in a modern car of this performance, and do it all again. And hope you can go on doing it all until you're out of fuel because it's here that the performance, finesse and soul of the 275 GTB/4 will talk to you long and loud and make you want to woop with joy.

Apart from the brakes, other foibles include dreadful ventilation and hopeless heating, and wipers that are only just tolerable. But the boot is reasonable for a couple of people for a weekend and the car's motorway cruise is unwavering and relentless, with acceptable road noise, remarkably little wind noise but an ever-present level of exhaust bark that, while rendering a radio useless, isn't tiring. Everywhere, the ride quality is endearing.

This remains a great car that stands proud as a provider of the classic, magical feel of a great front-engined V12 Ferrari. Since I first drove a GTB I have loved the optimum balance and benign polar moment of inertia endowed by its front-engined/ rear transaxle layout, since employed to such good effect in the Daytona and 365 GTC/4, the 924, 944, 968 and 928 Porsches and,

AND THE REVS KEEP RISING

hurrah, now returned in Ferrari's own 456 and 550 Maranello. I have special memories of shatteringly quick journeys in the gutsier, harder-edged Daytona but ask me to pick between these two great Ferrari GTBs and I'll plump for the 275 GTB/4. There's something about its lighter, daintier, more nimble feel and the sweetness of its overall balance that makes it irresistible. The Temptress still possesses her powers.

CONVERSATIONS WITH A BOXER

PORSCHE BOXSTER S
2001

AT LAST THE ROAD cleared and I could let the Boxster S go; let it run; let it flow. Gone was the traffic, and the last village. The road snaked gently into the distance, fast and open, with enough straight for the flat-six to punch through to its 7200rpm redline in second gear and maybe third before I'd need to ease off. I knew by now how eagerly, smoothly and swiftly the water-cooled 3.2 would respond. It'd push the yellow nose forward without a moment's delay and rush into the red with an enthralling urgency and evenness, a deeply satisfying combination of power, long flat torque curve and serious refinement. And all with a sound evocative of a 911 yet somehow distinctive, too – a deep bass throb that builds to a wail with, layered over it, the shrill whine unique to a horizontally opposed Porsche engine.

With full power – 252bhp at 6250rpm, enough for 0–60mph in 6.0sec and 100mph in 14.2 – and the rapidly gathering pace came the blend of abilities that characterise the Boxster S. Sharp, fluid steering. The chassis's responsiveness and poise. Its ability to keep the car flat on the road while effortlessly absorbing ripples or bumps. The harmony of the powertrain. It felt like a thoroughbred horse revelling in being given its head yet ready to deal, unruffled, with all eventualities.

So I began to press on, soon noting that the swiftness and accuracy of the steering could be tempered further by minor adjustments to the throttle. If, in tighter bends, the nose nudged into a little friendly understeer, a tiny easing of the pedal brought it

AND THE REVS KEEP RISING

back immediately. Or, if I took the opposite route and pressed harder, the extra power of the S – 32bhp upon the 220 of the standard Boxster – edged the tail around enough too. Either way, the Boxster cocked itself into a perfect attitude, then relied on roadholding strong enough to keep the tail glued down even with full power in the lower gears. It wasn't going to be deflected by bumps either. All that came, eventually, was a lovely hint of oversteer. The tail felt as if it had kicked slightly out beyond the front and the Boxster swept through the bends in something bordering on a drift, its roadholding matched to its power, and the driver balancing the lot with throttle and steering.

The communication was the key. When the front tyres squidged into understeer, my fingers felt it at once. When one of the rear tyres was pressed hard over and coping with bumps, all that information came through the seat. Yet the messages were gently delivered, never with harshness. Perhaps, among all its abilities, this is where the Boxster is most special.

I was on these revealing roads because I'd come to see friends deep in the West Country. I'd come in the Boxster S because it seemed ideal, a car that would gobble a couple of hundred motorway miles with refinement then, on back roads, offer unbridled driving pleasure. I wanted to see, too, why Jaguar is using the Boxster S as the benchmark for the upcoming F-type. Nick Barter, Jaguar's director of product development, had told me: 'The F-type will be beautiful, but we're also determined that it will be as good dynamically and as practical to use every day as a Boxster S.' That tells you a lot.

And what do you find when you begin a relationship with the Porsche? First, that it's comfortable. The small leather wheel is nicely upright. The pedals are perfectly placed, and ideal for toe-and-heeling. The seat adjusts just as you'd like and is perfectly shaped. Within moments you can establish a faultless driving position. Hours later, you will be just as happy. Other things contribute to your wellbeing. Forward vision is unhindered and the door mirrors provide an uncommonly good rear view. The instruments could hardly be clearer, and all the minor controls are equally easy to see and use.

PORSCHE BOXSTER S

When the Boxster starts to roll, it delivers more good news. The short-throw clutch is clean and light, taking up mid-stroke with lovely feel. It coheres exceptionally with the electronic throttle pedal, ensuring effortlessly smooth starts and relaxed creeping in traffic. So good is the engine management that, apart from perfect response anywhere in the rev band, the drivetrain will tolerate being placed in sixth gear at less than 1000rpm.

Add an exemplary gearshift with short throws and a precise action and you have a drivetrain calculated to delight, never tax you. Finding out how well the gear ratios match the engine – first, second and third run to 42, 71 and 102mph, fourth goes to 127, fifth to 153 and sixth tops out at 161, the engine's power peak is another joyful exercise.

The steering, quick enough at three turns lock-to-lock and commanding a convenient turning circle, always tells you what surface is passing beneath the asymmetric Pirelli P-Zeroes. The ride on the optional 18-inch wheels is firmer than on the standard 17-inchers but the quality of the damping makes it comfortable, always. Then, of course, there are the brakes, big cross-drilled discs purloined from the 911 Carrera. Responding to a light, progressive pedal, the discs haul the S down efficiently time and again. My fear, with the big tyres, had been tramlining. But there's none. The stiffness of the body helps the dynamic behaviour, providing a stable platform that allows the chassis to work so capably, and ridding the Boxster of the scuttle shake that afflicts too many open cars.

On the way back to London I ran contentedly into the night on the motorway with the top down and the climate control at a pleasant 25C. The wind deflector between the roll hoops kept turbulence down to a lick around the back of my neck. The noise at a decent cruising pace was modest enough, but just too loud for the radio. I didn't care. Roof up – push a button, then click home the central locking lever – the Boxster was civilised enough to make the end of the long drive seem untiring, though the road noise was prominent on some surfaces.

At the end of it all, over the last few miles, it was the word 'uncompromised' that kept suggesting itself. The Boxster S covers so

AND THE REVS KEEP RISING

many bases so very well. Its cabin comfort is outstanding. Its body is decently rigid. Its gem of an engine is powerful while modest in its thirst. The gearbox is delightful. The chassis talks to you. The handling is inspiring and safe. The grip is all you would wish it to be. The brakes are remarkable. Best of all, these elements blend into the whole with rare harmony. The Boxster is spirited but gentle and easy, too: easy to enjoy, easy to live with; easy to love. Jaguar's engineers have their sights on the right goals.

SOURCES

The primary magazines and dates where the stories in this book were originally published –

Holden Monaro GTS 350, *Classic & Sports Car*, October 2011
Ford Falcon GT-HO Phase III, *Sports Car World*, October 1975
Corvette Stingray, *Automobile*, April 1988
Lamborghini Countach LP400, *Sports Car World*, August 1973
'Mr Ferrari is waiting to see you', May, *CAR* 1974
Porsche 911 Turbo, *CAR*, December 1974
BMW 3.0 CSL, *CAR*, March 1975
Maserati Bora, *CAR*, April 1975
Lamborghini Urraco 3000, *CAR*, November 1975
Ferrari 308 GTB, *CAR*, July 1976
Maserati Merak, *CAR*, August 1976
Lamborghini Espada, *Classic & Sports Car*, October 2011
Ferrari BB 512, *CAR*, January 1977
Lamborghini Countach, Urraco and Silhouette,
    CAR, February 1977;
    Car and Driver, September 1977
Porsche 911 Kremer, *CAR*, March 1977
Mercedes-Benz 450SEL 6.9, *CAR*, June 1977
TVR Taimar Turbo, *CAR*, October 1977
Jaguar XKD 516, *CAR*, November 1977
Lamborghini Countach S, *CAR*, January 1978
Lamborghini Silhouette, *CAR*, August 1978
Ferrari 250 GTO, *CAR*, January 1979
Among the Modenese, *CAR*, April 1979
Aston Martin Volante, *CAR*, September 1979
Ferrari 365 GTB/4 Daytona, *CAR*, March 1980

Porsche 928S, *CAR*, April 1980

Porsche 924 Carrera GT, *CAR*, August 1980

Rolls-Royce Corniche Convertible, *CAR*, October 1980

Maserati Khamsin, *CAR*, May 1981

Vector W2, *CAR*, June 1981

Lotus Turbo Esprit, *CAR*, November 1981

Maserati Quattroporte, *CAR*, September 1981

Audi quattro, *CAR*, April 1982

Ferrari 400i, *CAR*, July 1983

Audi Sport quattro, *CAR*, August 1985

Alfa Romeo 2000 GTV, *Automobile*, May 1986

Audi Sport quattro S1, *Audibilis*, spring 1986

Porsche 911 Carrera, *Automobile*, August 1986

Ferrari BB 512 and 365 GTC/4, *Automobile*, September 1986

Citroën SM, *Automobile*, February 1987

Bentley 'R' Type Continental, *Automobile*, March 1987

BMW M1, *Automobile*, April 1987

MGA 1600, *Automobile*, April 1987

Porsche 959, *Autocar*, 4 November 1987

Jaguar XJ6, *Automobile*, May 1988

Ferrari F40, *Autocar*, 18 May 1988

Jaguar C-type, *Autocar*, 16 June 1993

Fiat 1100 S MM, *Autocar*, 7 July 1993

McLaren F1, previously unpublished

Ferrari 275 GTB/4, *Classic & Sports Car*, April 1997

Porsche Boxster S, *Autocar*, 30 May 2001

Lyrics from The Eagles' *Take It To The Limit* reproduced by kind permission of Warner Bros Music Ltd. Words and Music by Randy Meisner/Don Henley. Original publisher Benchmark Music/Kicking Bear Music. British Publisher Warner Bros Music Ltd.

PHOTO CREDITS

Page 129: *Holden Monaro GTS 350,* Wheels; *Ford Falcon GT-HO Phase III* Wheels/*Uwe Kuessner.*

Page 130: *Targa Florio scene, Peter Smith; Corvette Stingray, Pete Lyons.*

Page 131: *Lamborghini Countach, Mel Nichols; Enzo Ferrari, LAT.*

Page 132: *Maserati Bora, Phil Sayer; Lamborghini Urraco and Ferrari 308 GTB, Richard Cooke.*

Page 133: *Maserati Merak SS and Lamborghini Espada, Richard Cooke; Ferrari BB 512,* CAR/*Richard Davies.*

Page 134: *BMW 3.0 CSL, Mervyn Franklyn; Porsche 911 Turbo, Mel Nichols; Porsche 911 Kremer,* CAR/*Richard Davies.*

Page 135: *Three Lamborghinis, Mel Nichols; Lamborghini Countach S, John Perkins; Lamborghini Silhouette, Alex von Koettlitz.*

Page 136: *Jaguar D-type, Ian Dawson; Ferrari 250 GTO,* CAR/*Richard Davies; Ferrari 365 GTB/4 Daytona, Colin Curwood.*

Page 281: *Lamborghini factory and Lamborghini Bravo,* CAR/*Richard Davies; Vector W2, Wendy Harrop.*

Page 282: *Porsche 928S, Martyn Goddard; Porsche 924 Carrera GT, John Mason; Lotus Turbo Esprit, Ian Dawson.*

Page 283: *Maserati Khamsin, Richard Davies; Maserati Quattroporte,* CAR/*Colin Curwood; Citroën SM, Martyn Goddard.*

Page 284: *Audi quattro on the Monte Carlo Rally, Martyn Goddard; Audi quattro Sport, Ian Dawson; Audi quattro S1, Colin Curwood.*

Page 285: *BMW M1,* Automobile/*Colin Curwood; Porsche 959,* Autocar/*Dougie Firth; Porsche Boxster,* Autocar/*Stan Papior.*

Page 286: *Ferrari 400i,* CAR/*Dougie Firth; Alfa Romeo 2000 GTV, Ian Dawson; Ferrari 365 GTC/4 with Ferrari BB 512,* CAR/*Ian Dawson.*

Page 287: *MGA 1600, Mel Nichols; Bentley 'R' Type Continental, Martyn Goddard; Jaguar C-type,* Autocar/*Stan Papior.*

Page 288: *Ferrari 275 GTB/4, Ian Dawson; Ferrari F40,* Autocar/*John Mason; McLaren F1,* Autocar/*Ian Dawson.*

INDEX

2CV (Citroën) 123
18 Turbo (Renault) 309
30 (Renault) 205
124 (Fiat) 382
180B (Datsun) 157
250 GTO (Ferrari) 11, 207-19
275 GTB/4 (Ferrari) 12, 396-402
308 GTB (Ferrari) 95-101
365 GT (Ferrari) 51-3
365 GT4 BB (Ferrari) 222-3
365 GTB/4 Daytona (Ferrari) 235-43
365 GTC /4 (Ferrari) 340-2
400i (Ferrari) 309-16
450SEL (Mercedes-Benz) 20, 145-67
911 Carrera (Porsche) 336-9
911 Carrera 3 (Porsche) 140-1
911 Kremer (Porsche) 128, 137-44
911 Turbo (Porsche) 64-70, 176-7, 259, 350
924 Carrera GT (Porsche) 256-62
928S (Porsche) 244-50
959 (Porsche) 21, 357-63, 371
1100 S MM (Fiat) 382-6
2000 GT Veloce (Alfa Romeo) 326-9

A Man and a Woman (film) 116

acceleration
250 GTO (Ferrari) 211, 216
275 GTB/4 (Ferrari) 399
308 GTB (Ferrari) 97-8
365 GTB/4 Daytona (Ferrari) 236, 238, 241-2
400i (Ferrari) 312
911 Carrera (Porsche) 337
911 Carrera 3 (Porsche) 140
911 Kremer (Porsche) 139
911 Turbo (Porsche) 64, 67-9
928S (Porsche) 246, 250
959 (Porsche) 358, 360
2000 GT Veloce (Alfa Romeo) 327
BB 512 (Ferrari) 110, 113-14
Bora (Maserati) 82
Boxster S (Porsche) 404
C-type (Jaguar) 379
Carrera GT (Porsche) 256, 259
Corniche Convertible (Rolls-Royce) 253

Countach LP400 (Lamborghini) 43
CSL (BMW) 74
Espada (Lamborghini) 107
F1 (McLaren) 387-8, 392-3
F40 (Ferrari) 374-5
Falcon GT-HO (Ford) 26, 27, 30-1
Khamsin (Maserati) 266
M1 (BMW) 350, 352
Monaro GTS 350 (Holden) 24
'R' Type Continental (Bentley) 345
Silhouette (Lamborghini) 206
SM (Citroën) 347
Sport Quattro (Audi) 317-18
Taimar Turbo (TVR) 173
Turbo Esprit (Lotus) 280, 291-2
Urraco 3000 (Lamborghini) 89
Volante (Aston Martin) 233
W2 (Vector) 275
XKD 516 (Jaguar) 184

Advocate (newspaper) 13
Albuquerque (new Mexico) 158
Alfieri, Giulio 263-4, 266, 296, 347
Alston (Cumbria) 289-90, 293
Anchisi, Dr Emilio 371
Autocar (magazine) 16, 20-2, 223, 302, 345, 388, 395
Autosprint (magazine) 61-2

Baraldini, Franco 117-18, 188, 198
Barker, Ronald 302
Barter, Nick 404
Basche, Dieter 332-3, 335
Bazzi, Luigi 56
BB 512 (Ferrari) 109-15, 222-3, 340-2
Bellei, Angelo 222-3
Bensinger, Jörg 302
Bertocchi, Aurelio 297
Bertocchi, Guerino 228-9
Bertone (design house) 265, 326
Billing, Martin 202
Blackpool 168-9
Blain, Douglas 12-13, 15-6
Bora (Maserati) 78-87, 105, 263-4
Borsari, Doriano 370

INDEX

Bott, Helmuth 358-9
Bottrill, Les 178
Bourke (Australia) 23-4
Boxer (Ferrari) 21, 50-1
  see also BB 512 (Ferrari)
Boxster S (Porsche) 403-6

braking systems
250 GTO (Ferrari) 211, 214-15
275 GTB/4 (Ferrari) 398
365 GTB/4 Daytona (Ferrari) 238
911 Carrera (Porsche) 338-9
911 Turbo (Porsche) 65, 69
959 (Porsche) 361-2
Bora (Maserati) 87
Boxster S (Porsche) 405
C-type (Jaguar) 379
Countach LP400 (Lamborghini) 39, 44
Countach S (Lamborghini) 191
F40 (Ferrari) 373, 375-6
Merak SS (Maserati) 106
Monaro GTS 350 (Holden) 24
Quattro (Audi) 306, 308
'R' Type Continental (Bentley) 345
Silhouette (Lamborghini) 202
SM (Citroën) 348
Sport Quattro (Audi) 318, 321, 323-4
Sport Quattro S1 (Audi) 333
W2 (Vector) 273, 277
XJ6 (Jaguar) 368-9
XKD 516 (Jaguar) 180, 184, 185-6

Braungart, Martin 353
Bravo (Lamborghini) 226
Brazier, Steve 117, 121-3, 125
Brewer, Warren 13
Broad, Ralph 170-1

Capellini, Pier Luigi 195, 197-9, 352
Capri RS3100 (Ford) 72
CAR (magazine) 8-9, 12-13, 15, 18-20
Car and Driver (magazine) 12-13, 16, 19, 166
Cavallino Restaurant (Modena) 223-4
Cawsand (Cornwall) 369
CB radio 148-9, 154-62
Checkpoint (radio programme) 290
Cheetah (Lamborghini) 198-200
Choularton, Charles 201, 206
Cincinnati (Ohio) 165
Clarkson, Jeremy 18-19
Clovis (New Mexico) 160
Colombo, Gioacchino 56, 398
Cook, Roger 279-80, 289-90, 292-4
Cooke, Richard 88, 90-4, 105
Corniche Convertible (Rolls-Royce) 251-5
Corvette Stingray (Chevrolet) 32-5
Cottingham, David 378
Countach (Lamborghini) 14-15, 116-28
Countach LP400 (Lamborghini) 36-46
Countach S (Lamborghini) 187-94

Cozze, Ermanno 227-8, 295-6
Cropley, Steve 8-9, 12, 15-16, 20, 295, 302
CSL (BMW) 71-7
C-type (Jaguar) 377-81
Cumberland Lake (Kentucky) 164
Curtis, Alan 231
Curwood, Colin 236, 350, 353

Daily Mirror (newspaper) 8-9, 13
Dallara, Gian Paolo 117, 188-9
Davies, Richard 221, 226
Davis, Jr., David E. 12-13, 16, 19-20, 145-7, 151, 153-60, 163-6
Davis, Jr., Jeannie 146, 147-8, 150, 153, 160, 165-6
Dawson, Ian 183, 292, 321-3
Daytona (Ferrari) 21, 50, 142
  see also 365 GTB/4 Daytona (Ferrari)
De Angelis, Giuliano 222-3
de Portago, Marquis 383
de Tomaso, Alessandro 102, 197, 227, 297
di Montezemolo, Luca 385
Dino 246 GT (Ferrari) 33
Dino 308 GT4 (Ferrari) 89

Edwards, Derrick 179, 181-2
Elstein, Jonathan 19

engine capacity
250 GTO (Ferrari) 210
275 GTB/4 (Ferrari) 398
308 GTB (Ferrari) 96-7
365 GT4 BB (Ferrari) 222-3
365 GTB/4 Daytona (Ferrari) 239
365 GTC/4 (Ferrari) 341
400i (Ferrari) 311
911 Carrera (Porsche) 338
911 Kremer (Porsche) 137-8
911 Turbo (Porsche) 65-6
928S (Porsche) 246-7
959 (Porsche) 357, 360
BB 512 (Ferrari) 109-10, 222-3, 341
Bora (Maserati) 81-2
Boxster S (Porsche) 403-4
C-type (Jaguar) 378
Carrera GT (Porsche) 256, 258
Corvette Stingray (Chevrolet) 33
Countach (Lamborghini) 119
Countach LP400 (Lamborghini) 38, 45
Countach S (Lamborghini) 188, 193
CSL (BMW) 72
Espada (Lamborghini) 107
F1 (McLaren) 388-91
F40 (Ferrari) 370-3
Falcon GT-HO (Ford) 27
Khamsin (Maserati) 265
M1 (BMW) 350-2
Merak SS (Maserati) 106
Monaro GTS 350 (Holden) 23
Quattro (Audi) 301

411

AND THE REVS KEEP RISING

Quattroporte (Maserati) 296, 298
'R' Type Continental (Bentley) 344
Silhouette (Lamborghini) 206
SM (Citroën) 346-7
Sport Quattro (Audi) 318, 319-21
Sport Quattro S1 (Audi) 332-3, 334-5
Taimar Turbo (TVR) 170-1
Turbo Esprit (Lotus) 290
Urraco 3000 (Lamborghini) 89
Volante (Aston Martin) 232
W2 (Vector) 268, 271-2
XKD 516 (Jaguar) 177, 180

Espada (Lamborghini) 107-8
Evernden, H. I. F. 344
exhaust caps 138, 141

F1 (McLaren) 387-95
F12 (Ferrari) 21-2
F40 (Ferrari) 17-18, 21, 370-6
Falcon GT-HO (Ford) 24, 25-31
Fantuzzi, Gian Franco 17-18
Faure, Nick 66-70
Ferrari, Alfredo ('Dino') 62
Ferrari, Enzo
    and 250 GTO (Ferrari) 208-9
    and 275 GTB/4 (Ferrari) 396-7
    and 365 GTB/4 Daytona (Ferrari) 237
    appearance of 47
    and Fiorano test circuit 54
    and Maranello factory 47-9, 51, 57-8
    meetings with 11, 15, 57-62
    and *My Terrible Joys* 48, 49, 51-2, 53-4, 56-7, 59-63
    and T4 (Ferrari) 222, 224-5
Ferrari Motor Company 48-50, 53-7, 202, 222-3
Fini Restaurant (Modena) 220-1
Fiorano (Ferrari test circuit) 54, 99-100, 374, 376
Fiorini, Fiorenzo 191, 193
Flagstaff (Arizona) 149-50, 154
Flying (magazine) 166
Focus (Ford) 21
Forghieri, Mauro 224
Fort Apache (Arizona) 155-6
Frankel, Andrew 387, 393-4
Frankel, Peter 343-5
Franklyn, Mervyn 76
Fraser, Ian 15, 302

fuel consumption
400i (Ferrari) 311
450SEL 6.9 (Mercedes-Benz) 155, 158-9
911 Kremer (Porsche) 141
911 Turbo (Porsche) 64, 70
928S (Porsche) 246, 250
Bora (Maserati) 82-3
Carrera GT (Porsche) 256-7
Corvette Stingray (Chevrolet) 34

CSL (BMW) 73-4, 77
Falcon GT-HO (Ford) 29
Quattro (Audi) 308
Turbo Esprit (Lotus) 293-4
Urraco 3000 (Lamborghini) 93

Gandini, Marcello 265
gearing *see* transmission
Geneva Motor Show 40, 301
Ghibli (Maserati) 263-4
Giugiaro, Giorgetto 265, 297-8, 326, 350-1, 353
Goddard, Martyn 307, 346, 348
Goodwood (racing circuit) 211, 214
Gozzi, Franco 17, 48-51, 53-4, 57-9, 61, 202, 221-5
Grand Canyon (USA) 150
grip *see* roadholding
GSX2 (Citroën) 124
GTV 2000 (Alfa Romeo) 21
Gurney, Dan 146

H.J. Mulliner & Co. (coachbuilder) 343-4
Hagemeister, Peter 318-19, 321
Halstead, Stewart 169-70
Hamilton, Adrian 377-8, 380-1
Hamilton, Duncan 377-8, 380-1
Hardie Ferodo 500 (Australian race) 23
Harrop, Wendy 9
Haston, John 84
Hoel, Don 152-3
Horsfall, Peter 307
Hotel de Paris (Monte Carlo) 36-7
Hutton, Ray 303, 307
hydraulic systems 80-1, 264

Ickx, Jacky 33, 50

Jarrett, Keith 128, 143
Jenkinson, Denis 382
Johl, Armin 200, 206
Joliffe, David 117, 123

Khamsin (Maserati) 263-7
King, Pete 144
Kirkcudbright (Scotland) 78, 85
Kremer, Erwin 137, 142
Kremer, Manfred 137, 142
Kuessner, Uwe 26-31
Kyalami (Maserati) 227-8

Lamborghini, Ferruccio 197
Lamborghini Motor Company
    and availability of test cars 18, 36-7, 117
    finances of 18, 195-201, 352
    and M1 (BMW) development 189, 191, 198-9, 206, 350-3
    Sant'Agata factory 117-19, 191, 195-201
Le Mans 24 Hour (1953) 377, 380
Leimer, Rene 117, 119, 195, 196-8, 200
Lelouch, Claude 116

INDEX

Leonard, Elmore 12
Lilley, Martin 169
Lyons, Pete 18, 32-5
Lyons, William 179, 377

M1 (BMW) 198-9, 206, 349-56
MacCraith-Fisher, J H ('Mac') 252-3
Mallet, Don 19
Maranello Concessionaires 310
Maranello Plant (Italy) 48-50, 53-7, 202, 222-3
Marko, Helmut 14
Mason, John 17, 195-6, 201, 203-5, 261
Mason, Nick
    and 250 GTO (Ferrari) 11, 207-8, 209, 213, 215, 218
    and 365 GTB/4 Daytona (Ferrari) 236
    and XKD 516 (Jaguar) 176, 178-9, 181-2, 186
Mass, Jochen 383
McLaren, David 340-2
Memphis (Tennessee) 162
Merak SS (Maserati) 102-6
MGA 1600 (MG) 21, 364-6
Mikkola, Hannu 307, 330-5
Mille Miglia race 382-6
Minden, George 231
Mississippi River (USA) 162
Miura (Lamborghini) 21
Modena (Italy) 15-17, 36-7, 45-6, 48-9, 56-7, 116-19, 220-9
Monaro GTS 350 (Holden) 23-4
Mont Blanc 107-8, 122
Montagnani, Giorgio 228
Monte Carlo Rally (1982) 301, 303-7
Morntane Engineering 179, 182
Moss, Stirling 37, 382-3
Motor (magazine) 16, 20
MP4-12C (McLaren) 22
Murdoch, Rupert 8
Murray, Gordon 387-90, 392-3
My Terrible Joys (book) 48, 49, 51-2, 53-4, 56-7, 59-63

Nagari (Bolwell) 25-8
Nardo (racing circuit) 370, 392
Nashville (Tennessee) 162-3
Neerpasch, Jochen 351-2
Nichols, Steve 389

Palmer, Jonathan 387, 392
Pantera (de Tomaso) 228-9
Paris Motor Show (1964) 397
Parkes, Mike 339-400
Parry-Jones, Richard 20
Patti, Vincenzo 385
Perfetti, Giovanni 371
performance levels, increase in 21-2
Perkins, John 191, 193
Phillips, Roger 18, 117, 119, 121, 124-6, 201-2
Piccolo Madonie (racing circuit) 33-4

Piëch, Ferdinand 325
Pininfarina (design house) 53, 111, 225, 237-8, 310-11
Pink Floyd 11, 208
Piper, David 214
Piquet, Nelson 390
Pourret, Jess 208, 213

pricing
275 GTB/4 (Ferrari) 399
400i (Ferrari) 310, 314
911 Kremer (Porsche) 137
928S (Porsche) 244
BB 512 (Ferrari) 109, 115
Bora (Maserati) 79, 86
Carrera GT (Porsche) 257
Corniche Convertible (Rolls-Royce) 251, 255
F40 (Ferrari) 371
'R' Type Continental (Bentley) 343
Sport Quattro (Audi) 319
Taimar Turbo (TVR) 172
W2 (Vector) 277
XKD 516 (Jaguar) 176, 180

Quattro (Audi) 301-8
Quattroporte (Maserati) 295-300

'R' Type Continental (Bentley) 343-5
Raimondi, Marco 188, 199, 201, 352
Redman, Brian 33

roadholding
250 GTO (Ferrari) 218
275 GTB/4 (Ferrari) 399-401
308 GTB (Ferrari) 98, 100
365 GTB/4 Daytona (Ferrari) 236, 241-2
365 GTC /4 (Ferrari) 341-2
400i (Ferrari) 314
450SEL 6.9 (Mercedes-Benz) 157
911 Carrera (Porsche) 338-9
911 Kremer (Porsche) 139-40, 142-3
928S (Porsche) 248, 250
959 (Porsche) 361-3
2000 GT Veloce (Alfa Romeo) 327-8
BB 512 (Ferrari) 112-13, 342
Bora (Maserati) 83-4, 86
Boxster S (Porsche) 404
C-type (Jaguar) 380
Carrera GT (Porsche) 261
Corniche Convertible (Rolls-Royce) 254-5
Countach LP400 (Lamborghini) 41, 45-6
Countach S (Lamborghini) 187, 189-90, 192-3
CSL (BMW) 76
F1 (McLaren) 392, 394
F40 (Ferrari) 374-5
Falcon GT-HO (Ford) 27, 28-9
Khamsin (Maserati) 266-7
M1 (BMW) 349-50, 353-4
Merak SS (Maserati) 103-4
Quattro (Audi) 301-2, 303-4

AND THE REVS KEEP RISING

'R' Type Continental (Bentley) 345
Silhouette (Lamborghini) 122, 123-4, 202-3, 205, 206
SM (Citroën) 348
Sport Quattro (Audi) 322-4
Taimar Turbo (TVR) 174
Turbo Esprit (Lotus) 291, 293
Urraco 3000 (Lamborghini) 90, 92-3
Volante (Aston Martin) 234
W2 (Vector) 276
XJ6 (Jaguar) 367-8
XKD 516 (Jaguar) 185

Robinson, Peter 8, 24, 31, 382, 384, 386
Röhl, Walter 307
Rolt, Tony 377
Ronnie Scott's (jazz club) 144
Rosche, Paul 390
Rossetti, Georges-Henri 197-8, 200
Route 66 (USA) 147

Sanderson, Ninian 84
Sant'Agata Plant (Italy) 117-19, 191, 195-201
Sayer, Malcolm 179
Sayer, Phil 79, 85-6
Scheckter, Jody 60, 224
Sedona (Arizona) 150-1
Setright, Leonard 16, 178, 219, 245-6, 267
Sgarzi, Ubaldo 18, 107, 117, 195, 225-6
Silhouette (Lamborghini) 19, 116-27, 195-206
SM (Citroën) 346-8
Smith, Kevin 358, 360
Smith, Madison 163
Smith, Martin 20
Smith, Peter 14, 382
Sport Quattro (Audi) 317-26
Sport Quattro S1 (Audi) 330-5
Sprague, Peter 231
Stanzani, Paolo 197
Sterzel, Stanislao 187, 191-2
Stevens, Peter 389-90
Stewart, Jackie 146
Stuck, Hans 353
Sunday Mirror (newspaper) 13
Surtees, John 383

suspension
250 GTO (Ferrari) 211
275 GTB/4 (Ferrari) 397-8
365 GTB/4 Daytona (Ferrari) 238
365 GTC /4 (Ferrari) 341
400i (Ferrari) 314
450SEL 6.9 (Mercedes-Benz) 166
911 Kremer (Porsche) 137, 140-1, 143
911 Turbo (Porsche) 65
928S (Porsche) 247-8
BB 512 (Ferrari) 111-12
C-type (Jaguar) 378, 379
Carrera GT (Porsche) 259
Corniche Convertible (Rolls-Royce) 252-3, 255

Countach (Lamborghini) 121
Countach LP400 (Lamborghini) 39, 44
Countach S (Lamborghini) 187, 189-90
CSL (BMW) 72-3
F40 (Ferrari) 374
Khamsin (Maserati) 264, 266
M1 (BMW) 352
Monaro GTS 350 (Holden) 23-4
Quattro (Audi) 305
Quattroporte (Maserati) 298-9
Silhouette (Lamborghini) 121, 203
Sport Quattro (Audi) 318, 321
Taimar Turbo (TVR) 170-1, 174
Turbo Esprit (Lotus) 289, 292
Urraco (Lamborghini) 121
Urraco 3000 (Lamborghini) 93
Volante (Aston Martin) 232-3, 234
W2 (Vector) 270-1
XJ6 (Jaguar) 367-8, 369
XKD 516 (Jaguar) 178, 179

T4 (Ferrari) 222, 224-5
Taimar Turbo (TVR) 168-75
'Take it Easy' (song) 154
'Take It To The Limit' (song) 317, 326
Targa Florio race (1973) 14, 32-4, 50, 61-2, 382
Taylor, Simon 20
The Complete Book of Lamborghini (book) 18
The Dark Side of The Moon (album) 11
The Eagles 154, 317, 325
The Ferrari Legend (book) 208
The Köln Concert (album) 128, 144
The Rolling Stones 147
Thruxton (racing circuit) 340, 342

top speed
250 GTO (Ferrari) 209-11
308 GTB (Ferrari) 98
365 GT4 BB (Ferrari) 223
365 GTB/4 Daytona (Ferrari) 238
911 Kremer (Porsche) 139
911 Turbo (Porsche) 64, 67-8
928S (Porsche) 250
959 (Porsche) 357-8, 361
BB 512 (Ferrari) 110, 223
Bora (Maserati) 86
C-type (Jaguar) 380
Carrera GT (Porsche) 256-7
Corniche Convertible (Rolls-Royce) 253
Corvette Stingray (Chevrolet) 34
Countach (Lamborghini) 125-6
Countach LP400 (Lamborghini) 36, 42, 43
Countach S (Lamborghini) 188, 192-3
CSL (BMW) 75
F1 (McLaren) 393
Falcon GT-HO (Ford) 27, 30-1
Khamsin (Maserati) 265
Monaro GTS 350 (Holden) 24
Quattro (Audi) 308
'R' Type Continental (Bentley) 343-4

INDEX

Sport Quattro (Audi) 318
Taimar Turbo (TVR) 170
Volante (Aston Martin) 230
W2 (Vector) 268, 276
XKD 516 (Jaguar) 180

Touch Wood! (book) 377, 381
traction *see* roadholding

transmission
250 GTO (Ferrari) 211-12
275 GTB/4 (Ferrari) 397-8
308 GTB (Ferrari) 97-8
365 GTB/4 Daytona (Ferrari) 238, 241-2
365 GTC /4 (Ferrari) 341
400i (Ferrari) 312, 315-16
450SEL 6.9 (Mercedes-Benz) 166
911 Turbo (Porsche) 64, 66, 68
928S (Porsche) 247-8
1100 S MM (Fiat) 383
BB 512 (Ferrari) 109-10, 111, 114
Bora (Maserati) 81
Boxster S (Porsche) 405
Carrera GT (Porsche) 259-60
Corvette Stingray (Chevrolet) 33
Countach LP400 (Lamborghini) 39, 41, 42-3, 45
CSL (BMW) 72
F1 (McLaren) 393
Khamsin (Maserati) 266
Monaro GTS 350 (Holden) 23-4
Quattro (Audi) 303-4
Quattroporte (Maserati) 298, 300
'R' Type Continental (Bentley) 345
Taimar Turbo (TVR) 172-3
Urraco 3000 (Lamborghini) 91
Volante (Aston Martin) 232
W2 (Vector) 272-3, 274-5
XKD 516 (Jaguar) 178, 180-1, 184

Tuckey, Bill 8, 12
Turbo Esprit (Lotus) 279-80, 289-94
Turin Grand Prix (1947) 56
TVR Motor Company 168-70

Urraco (Lamborghini) 116-27
Urraco 3000 (Lamborghini) 88-94

Van Slype, Robertus 385
Vantage (Aston Martin) 231
Verdon-Roe, Eric 20
Volante (Aston Martin) 230-4

W2 (Vector) 268-78
Wallace, Andy 388, 395
Wallace, Bob 14, 18, 32, 36-46, 119, 278

weight
250 GTO (Ferrari) 210
308 GTB (Ferrari) 97-8
400i (Ferrari) 312
911 Turbo (Porsche) 65
959 (Porsche) 359
BB 512 (Ferrari) 110
C-type (Jaguar) 378
Carrera GT (Porsche) 259
Corniche Convertible (Rolls-Royce) 252
Countach LP400 (Lamborghini) 39
CSL (BMW) 73
F1 (McLaren) 388
F40 (Ferrari) 372
Khamsin (Maserati) 263
Merak SS (Maserati) 103
Quattroporte (Maserati) 296
'R' Type Continental (Bentley) 344
Sport Quattro (Audi) 321
Volante (Aston Martin) 232, 234
W2 (Vector) 270-1
XKD 516 (Jaguar) 180

Wheels (magazine) 12, 24, 31
Wiegert, Jerry 268-73, 275, 277-8
Wolf, Walter 188, 198-9

XJ6 (Jaguar) 367-9
XJS (Jaguar) 125-6, 310, 313
XKD 516 (Jaguar) 176-86